And Die
in the West

AND DIE
IN THE WEST

The Story of the O.K. Corral Gunfight

Paula Mitchell Marks

University of Oklahoma Press
Norman

To Alan,
who has always been there for me

Library of Congress Cataloging-in-Publication Data

Marks, Paula Mitchell, 1951–
   And die in the west : the story of O.K. Corral gunfight / Paula
Mitchell Marks.
    p. cm.
  Originally published: New York : Morrow, c1989.
  Includes bibliographical references (p.   ) and index.
  ISBN 0-8061-2888-7 (alk. paper)
   1. Tombstone (Ariz.)—History. 2. Frontier and pioneer life—
Arizona—Tombstone. 3. Violence—Arizona—Tombstone—History—19th
century. 4. Earp, Morgan, 1851–1882. 5. Earp, Wyatt, 1848–1929.
6. Holliday, John Henry, 1851–1887. I. Title.
[F819.T6M37 1996]
979.1'53—dc20

96-18367
CIP

The paper in this book meets the guidelines for permanence and
durability of the Committee on Production Guidelines for Book Lon-
gevity of the Council on Library Resources, Inc. ♾

Oklahoma Paperbacks edition published 1996 by the University of
Oklahoma Press, Norman, Publishing Division of the University, by
special arrangement with William Morrow and Company, Inc., 1350
Avenue of the Americas, New York, N.Y. 10019, and Wallace Literary
Agency, Inc., 177 E. 70 Street, New York, N.Y. 10021. Manufactured
in the U.S.A. First printing of the University of Oklahoma Press edition, 1996.

3   4   5   6   7   8   9   10

Acknowledgments

Over the years, the story of the "gunfight at the O.K. Corral" and of the men who made it happen has stimulated a host of heavily dramatized fictional accounts, many of them masquerading as fact and varying wildly in the "facts" presented. The abundance of distorted narratives stems in part from our love affair with the mythical American West. The Tombstone gunfight story—with its stagecoach robberies, love triangles, shoot-outs, and vengeance killings—contains many of the elements of western myth and thus lends itself to treatments in which the characters in the real, complex Tombstone drama turn into extreme frontier stereotypes—the venomous, completely asocial bad guy, the noble law bringer, the prostitute with the heart of gold. In part, too, the distorted narratives and caricatures stem from the fact that nobody at the time of the confusing fight could agree on who the good guys and bad guys were.

Thus, a researcher delving into the gunfight story quickly encounters contradictory accounts of the characters and actions of the participants, as well as widely diverging interpretations of what was really going on in Tombstone during the Earps' stay there. Fortunately, a handful of diligent researchers collecting the stories of old-timers and combing old records over the years have greatly enhanced the chances of presenting a reasonably accurate narrative of the Tombstone drama and of the people, neither all good nor all bad, who participated in it.

In the 1920's, Walter Noble Burns and Stuart Lake, although guilty of mixing fiction with fact and perpetuating the myths, nonetheless performed factual research which helped future generations of researchers. Frank Waters in the 1930's interviewed Virgil Earp's wife, Allie, and in 1960 produced a decidedly dark, but well-researched, look at the Earp brothers and their part in Tombstone's troubles. Ed Bartholomew followed with his own extensive research on the less-than-savory aspects of the Earps' career.

At the time this volume was published, Glenn G. Boyer and the late Alford Turner had published significant works of "Earpana" and were considered the chief authorities. However, between the first publication of this volume and this reprint, much of Boyer's work has been discredited by subsequent researchers and by Boyer's own admissions that he fictionalized voices and events. At the time I wrote, others who had provided valuable research on Tombstone, on the gunfight, and on the participants included Jack Burrows, Odie Faulk, John Gilchriese, Pat Jahns, Douglas Martin, John M. Myers, Bob Palmquist, Gary L. Roberts, C. L. Sonnichsen, and Ben T. Traywick.

Thanks are due to all of these people and to the many whose names appear in my bibliography. The works of my predecessors in mining this field both provided useful information and pointed me toward valuable primary resources. I should note, however, that any mistakes that have crept into the narrative are mine and mine alone.

In addition to the indirect help of previous researchers, a number of people directly assisted in the conceiving and writing of this book. First, my agent, Robert Gottlieb, set me on the track of this story and provided encouragement along the way. My editor, Harvey Ginsberg, was a warm and helpful presence throughout. Tombstone resident and fellow writer Ben T. Traywick shared his own research collection with me, proved a generous and ready source of information, and took me on a most enjoyable outing to the Chandler Ranch, where the Clanton and McLaury brothers shared their last breakfast together. Ben's openness to a newcomer to "Earpana" and his keen understanding of the fact that better information and better insights may always be just around the corner made my task more pleasant.

The curators of a number of historical collections assisted me in gathering materials for this book. In particular, I would like to acknowledge Peter Blodgett of the Huntington Library, Lori Davisson and Deborah Shelton of the Arizona Historical Society, Carol Downey of the State of Arizona Department of Library, Archives and Public Records, and Elaine Gilleran of the Wells Fargo Bank History Department, San Francisco.

Thanks are also due to Jeanell Buida Bolton, whose comments on my early chapters helped me strengthen and focus the work; to Glen Wilkerson, who brought his legal expertise to bear on the Spicer hearing and the judge's decision; and especially to Anna Beth Mitchell, an indefatigable researcher whose good humor is matched only by her good sense.

Finally, I acknowledge with gratitude the continuing patience of my husband, Alan, and my daughter, Carrie, who have for the past two years shared my attentions with the inhabitants of a nineteenth-century boomtown named Tombstone.

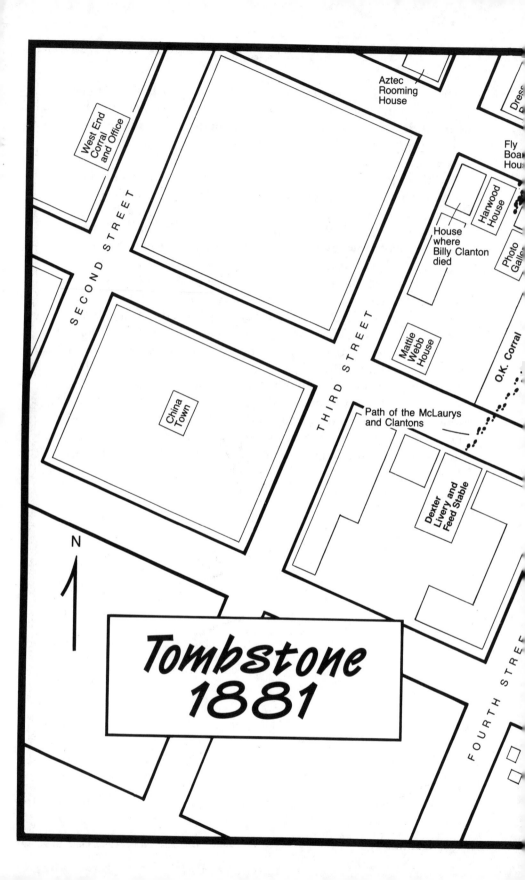

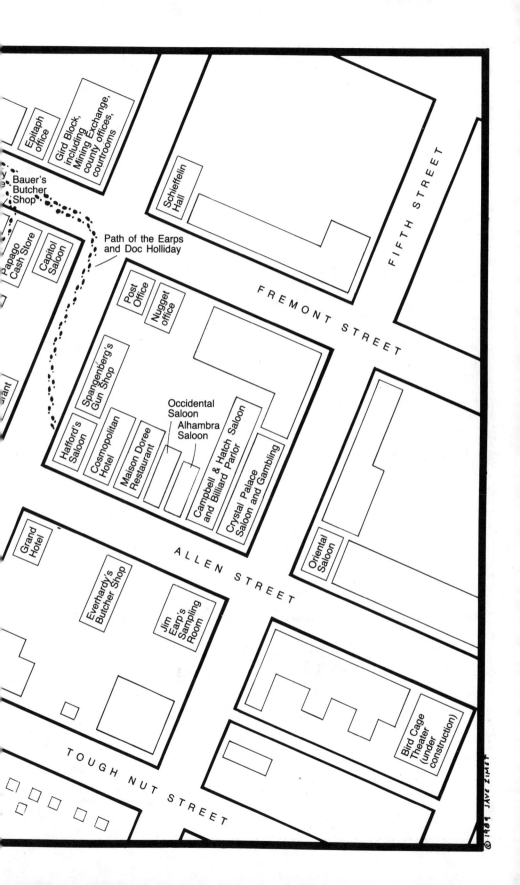

Note on Documentation and Sources

In using quotations, many from nineteenth-century sources, I have occasionally corrected spelling and altered punctuation for clarity's sake. In particular, I have taken the liberty of standardizing the spelling of names. For example, the McLaury brothers were frequently referred to by contemporaries as the "McLowrys" or "McLowerys"; I have generally changed the spelling to "McLaurys" except in rare cases where the form differs significantly ("McLearry").

Readers will find all quotations endnoted, with the exception of a few very brief ones, a few that clearly relate to endnoted quotations nearby, and a number from contemporary newspapers and from George Parsons's journal. Newspaper quotations which I drew from secondary sources are endnoted, but those which I gleaned directly from the newspapers, if clearly dated in the text, are not. Parsons's journal entries are endnoted only when the specific day of the entry is not included in the text.

Because the original court documents relating to the gunfight are no longer available, I used two alternate sources in preparing the chapters on the gunfight and subsequent hearing. In the 1930's, a Works Projects Administration writer named Pat Hayhurst produced from the original inquest and hearing records a slightly edited version, part verbatim transcript and part summary. Various copies of this Hayhurst document exist; I studied the copy in the Arizona State Department of Library, Archives and Public Records and supplemented it by reviewing the verbatim inquest and hearing testimonies provided in the pages of the Tombstone *Daily Nugget* during the 1881 legal proceedings. Of the two sources, the *Nugget*'s pages provide a clearer and fuller picture of the course of the trial, but the Hayhurst transcript/summary, which was published with Alford Turner as editor in 1981 under the title *The O.K. Corral Inquest*, is more accessible to anyone wishing to study the gunfight further and provides a generally accurate record.

Contents

Contents

Then enter, boys; cheerly, boys, enter and rest;
You know how we live, boys, and die in the west;
Oho, boys!—oho, boys!—oho!

—GEORGE POPE MORRIS

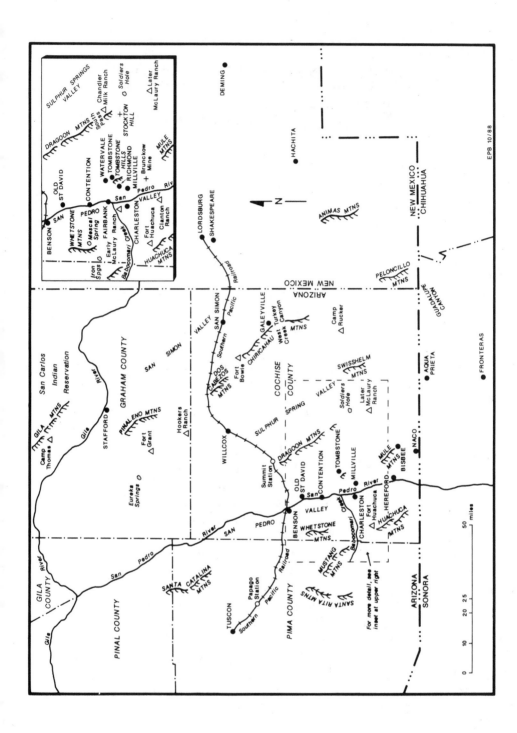

CHAPTER 1
Trails to Tombstone

The funeral was to be a grand one, in true western boom-town tradition. Residents of Tombstone, Arizona Territory, gathered in the chill air of a gray October afternoon in 1881 to view the bodies of Billy Clanton, Frank McLaury, and brother Tom McLaury lying in state in the window of the local funeral parlor. The three were decked out in the finest clothes and most ornate caskets the mining town could supply. Each wore a stiff white shirt, black suit, and black cravat; each occupied a gleaming black coffin embellished in silver. Only twenty-four hours earlier, the faces of the three men had radiated pride, anger, fear, and despair as they had fought for their lives on a Tombstone street. Now their features shared the bland relaxation of death.

In midafternoon, the bodies were loaded into hearses for the journey to the cemetery about half a mile north of town. The corpse of tall, stocky Billy Clanton occupied the first vehicle, an elegant glass-sided carriage valued at eight thousand dollars. The bodies of handsome, open-faced Tom McLaury and the shorter, shrewd-featured Frank were loaded into a second elaborate hearse as the Tombstone brass band gathered to lead the procession. About 4:00 P.M., the musicians began playing a ponderous dirge for the dead and led the way along Allen Street, Tombstone's main thoroughfare.

The rough wooden sidewalks bordering the first three or four blocks of the route were packed with spectators—mining men and merchants, dance hall girls and gamblers, carpenters and saloonkeepers. The two hearses, which would have looked appropriate gliding along the most elegant boulevards of New York or Boston, rattled instead over the dirt street of the remote silver mining settlement, past a jumble of saloons and corrals, general merchandise stores and barns. Immediately behind the hearses came the carriages of family and friends, followed by about three hundred pedestrians, twenty-two carriages and buggies, a four-horse stagecoach, and a number of horsemen.

Slowly, the procession made its way to the cemetery, a straggling collection of graves on a rocky, mesquite-studded hillside with a spectacular view of the rugged Dragoon Mountains across the valley floor to the east. Here Billy Clanton was lowered into the ground as members of his ranching and rustling family from their spread on the San Pedro River looked on. Only two months earlier, Billy's father had been buried on a knoll in the Animas Mountains of New Mexico; now brothers Phin and Ike led the mourning clan.

The McLaurys were placed in one grave. A Western Union telegram was on its way to an emissary in Fort Worth, Texas, where the McLaurys' closest relative, brother Will, lived: "Inform McLearry [*sic*] that his brother[s] Frank & Thomas were killed here yesterday they have over three thousand dollars."

So no family was present to mourn the McLaurys, but Tombstone was giving them a noble send-off. Now, with the smoothing of the dirt over the graves, the tempo of a frontier boomtown funeral usually shifted. The band would soon swing into a raucous number, and a good many of the participants and onlookers would return to town ready to dull their own sense of mortality in an alcoholic haze at the saloon of their choice. "There's a lot of fun in a first-class funeral," the local *Daily Nugget* would observe some months later.

This had been a first-class funeral, all right, but the spectacle and music could not obscure the fierce tensions dividing the populace of Tombstone. Clanton and the McLaurys had fallen in the gun battle which was to become popularly known as the gunfight at the O.K. Corral, and opinion was sharply divided as to why it happened, who was to blame, and what would or should happen next.

The coroner's jury report certainly didn't help clarify matters. It merely stated facts already obvious to Tombstone residents, many of whom had witnessed the gunfight: that the three men had met their deaths through "the effects of pistol and gunshot wounds inflicted by Virgil Earp, Morgan Earp, Wyatt Earp and one Holliday, commonly called Doc Holliday." The *Daily Nugget* commented dryly, "The verdict reassures us. We might have thought they had been struck by lightning or stung to death by hornets."

At issue, of course, were the actions of the three Earp brothers and Holliday. Wyatt Earp and Doc Holliday are legends today; in Tombstone, they were real men embroiled in intense controversy. To their Tombstone supporters, the three "fighting Earps" and Holliday had struck a blow for western law and order in dispatching Clanton and the McLaurys. In this interpretation of the fight, distilled into legend by subsequent generations of Western enthusiasts, the four had served as efficient, even heroic law enforcers in ridding the Tombstone area of members of a troublesome rustling element. But the Earps and Holliday had many detractors as well, people who claimed the gunfight proved them the worst of frontier opportunists, using the law for their own nefarious ends and killing three harmless ranchers in the process. The latter view was expressed in a sign which hung above the bodies in the funeral parlor window: MURDERED IN THE STREETS OF TOMBSTONE.

A third perspective was provided by George Parsons, a San Francisco bank clerk who had moved to Tombstone to seek his fortune in the mines. He returned from a Huachuca Mountain mining camp the day of the funeral to find citizens "apprehensive and scary." An Earp partisan, Parsons nonetheless identified all the gunfight participants as "desperate men" in a "desperate encounter," noting in his journal that "bad blood had been brewing some time" and "the worst is not yet over some think."

Indeed, the outbreak of violence that would come to be known as the gunfight at the O.K. Corral was just one particularly bloody thread in a tangled skein of frontier animosities and intrigues that lent credence to the already burgeoning myth of the Wild West. In legend, then and now, the frontier West was a place of frequent, sudden, random violence, with noble law bringers battling desperadoes bent on creating or maintaining chaos. However, seldom can events in the real frontier West be accurately interpreted in such easy terms.

Significantly, early westerners themselves could seldom agree on who the good guys and bad guys were in the headlong rush of settlement across the trans-Mississippi American landscape. Different political and economic factions quickly sprang up with different views regarding who had right to what and how the community or region should develop.

As a result, the line between law and lawlessness was hard to define with any unanimity and could be extremely fine in "the expansive, transient, pluralistic society that was America in the nineteenth century." Such a society made it easy for a fellow to play dual, often dangerously inconsistent roles—rancher and rustler, law enforcer and outlaw. Cautionary was the revelation of the double life of Henry Plummer, elected sheriff of a Washington Territory gold camp in 1863. Plummer soon turned out to be leader of a large band of robbers and murderers. Furious vigilantes summarily hanged him in January 1864, but they could not banish the natural suspicion that extended across the West in each new encounter with a stranger. Was he who he appeared or stated himself to be? Could he be trusted? Could he perhaps be trusted in some matters and not in others? Men often made faulty judgments based on limited information and ingrained prejudices, uneasily aligning themselves according to political affiliations, economic interests, and geographic origins.

The problem of identity was particularly acute in the transitory mining towns. Their citizens were a highly mobile, heterogeneous lot trying to "get rich quick" and viewing each other as rivals and potential threats anyway. Shortly after his arrival in Tombstone, observing the "considerable trickery" involved in establishing mining claims, George Parsons had vowed, "One must rely entirely upon himself and trust *no one* else."

In such an environment, suspicions and rivalries grew and festered. The story of the Clantons and McLaurys, of the Earps and Holliday—the story of all the hopefuls who flocked to the Tombstone area as it began to boom—is one of a confused and complex scramble for money and power.

Prospector Ed Schieffelin started the whole greedy rush. Ironically, for decades American emigrants had ignored southeastern Arizona with its seemingly endless stretches of desert, stunted vegetation, bare brown hills, and craggy precipices. An adventurer penetrating this hostile environment had to watch for Apaches, ration his water as he searched for scattered hidden water holes, dig mesquite roots with a pick in order to build a fire, and share his bedroll with scorpions and tarantulas. He could expect to ride for days without meeting another person or stumbling across any sign of human habitation.

None of this deterred Schieffelin from poking about southeastern Arizona's San Pedro Valley in search of a bonanza. "He was about the queerest specimen of humanity ever seen," recalled one Arizona pioneer, remembering the prospector's "black curly hair that hung several inches below his shoulders," his long, matted beard, and his worn clothing "covered with patches of deerskins, corduroy, and flannel."

Schieffelin was a classic member of that perennially hopeful fraternity of men traversing the western landscape in pursuit of the biggest and richest vein of gold and/or silver the continent had yet produced. Born in 1847, he had barely reached puberty before he was panning for gold in Oregon's Rogue River country. He moved on to California, Nevada, Idaho, and Utah, his all-consuming and unsuccessful quest shakily financed by a string of temporary jobs, such as woodchopping.

Finally, he turned to Arizona Territory, a region carved out of New Mexico Territory in 1863 on the strength of its mineral wealth. Ever since the first Spanish explorers and priests had laid claim to its arid expanses, men had recognized Arizona's mineral potential. In 1736, between five and ten thousand Spaniards had converged on the Nogales area southwest of the San Pedro Valley at news of a *planchas de plata,* or "sheets of silver" strike, quickly removing this surface treasure. Further Arizona mining would require heavy machinery, but the area's remoteness and the Apaches' fierce resistance to any encroachment, particularly in the southeastern section, effectively blocked both mining and settlement. Americans managed to set up a few promising mining operations in the 1850's, but the Indians killed off enough workers to send the others packing.

Despite such obstacles, many territorial leaders saw mining as the best potential economic basis for Arizona settlement; Governor Richard McCormick in the late 1860's promoted laissez-faire policies, such as no tax on gross products of mines, in order to encourage mineral development. But the dormant state of mining affairs only began to change decisively with an 1876 silver strike at Globe, giving birth to the Silver King mine. Here, as they did across the West, hardrock miners drilled and blasted in deep, dank tunnels, hauling the broken ore to the surface in one-ton ore carts for processing at nearby mills and smelters.

Then solitary Ed Schieffelin, exploring the most dangerous and out-of-the-way corner of the territory, began moving toward the Southwest's largest silver discovery.

He arrived at the newly established Fort Huachuca, a rugged outpost on the western edge of the San Pedro River valley at the foot of the Huachuca Mountains, about April 1, 1877. From this base he began exploring, despite cynical predictions from the fort's soldiers that, with the Apaches active in the area, all he would find would be his tombstone.

Others had found theirs. A lone mine had been established in the isolated valley almost twenty years earlier by German mining engineer Frederick Brunckow, who believed the area contained great mineral riches. In 1857 he had begun to test this belief at the mine site, soon enlisting the aid of two partners, brothers James and William Williams. The three employed former St. Louis high school chemistry teacher J. C. Moss, a German cook, and a number of Mexican laborers. In the summer of 1860, William Williams traveled to the army's Fort Buchanan to get supplies and returned to discover the buildings which housed the men in ominous darkness.

He entered one, groping for matches, and found instead a body lying in a pool of blood. Stumbling across a second body, he decided to go to the fort for aid. The detachment of soldiers that returned with him found James Williams, Moss, and Brunckow murdered, the last at the bottom of a mining shaft with a rock drill through his body. The Mexican laborers had killed the men, packed up everything of value they could find, and headed for the border with the unwilling German cook in tow.

In 1874, the mine caused further bloodshed when two rival claimants, Joseph Holmes and Milton Duffield, clashed. The combative Duffield, a former United States marshal, attempted to evict Holmes from the mine buildings; Holmes responded by shooting him in the head, and the former law officer joined Brunckow in a burial site on the San Pedro.

When Schieffelin arrived in 1877, two men employed by yet another owner were doing the annual assessment necessary to hold on to the unworked claim. They hired Schieffelin as a guard, and he used his time wisely. As Schieffelin himself later remembered, "While standing guard I could see the [then unnamed] Tombstone hills very plainly with my field glasses and I took a fancy to them, noticing that there was quite a number of ledges . . . all running in the same direction, about northwest and southeast." Soon he moved up the valley to do his own prospecting.

That August, Schieffelin traveled the approximately seventy miles northwestward to Tucson and filed claims for himself and one of the two assessment workers, William Griffith. Remembering the comments of Fort Huachuca's soldiers, he filed the locations under the names Tombstone and Graveyard. Then he returned to the San Pedro Valley, despite the fact that the few ranchers who had pushed into the area were abandoning it in face of the continuing Apache threat. That fall, he collected samples from various promising locations and got down to thirty cents cash before heading to the Signal mine in northwestern Arizona, where his brother Al Schieffelin was working. Ed hoped to convince Al to accompany him to the Tombstone area and help him look for the big strikes which he sensed he had been close to locating.

Al Schieffelin was unconvinced, but he took three of Ed's ore samples from the San Pedro Valley to Signal Mine assayer Dick Gird. After evaluating two of the three, Gird turned to

Al and commented, "The best thing you can do is to find out where that ore came from, and take me with you and start for the place." The third sample, from Ed's Tombstone location, assessed even richer than the others, at two thousand dollars to the ton.

The Schieffelins and Gird made secret plans to depart for the San Pedro Valley, but other Signal miners sensed something was up, particularly when Gird turned down the superintendency of the mine. By the time the three started out in mid-February 1878, another group of hopefuls had preceded them southeastward; Ed and his confederates managed to pass this band, but by the time they reached the valley, they found yet another contingent of prospectors scouring the area.

The three partners swiftly established themselves in an old adobe near the Brunckow mine, and Ed hurried to locate his biggest bonanza. He soon found a silver vein so rich he could press a coin into it and leave an exact imprint. Gird assayed Ed's sample from this location at fifteen thousand dollars to the ton, exclaiming, "Ed, you lucky cuss—you have hit it," and the Lucky Cuss claim was born. Soon afterward, Ed located the Tough Nut, as in "tough nut to crack."

Meanwhile, a gloomy prospector named Hank Williams had received some encouragement from the Schieffelins and Gird, with the understanding that he would share anything he found with them. In locating the Grand Central, he at first failed to honor the bargain. But after much discussion with the three partners, he finally sliced off for them a portion which they dubbed the Contention. The Lucky Cuss, despite its surface richness, would prove to be a small vein, but the Tough Nut, Grand Central, and Contention locations would become the biggest and the best properties in the area, with the last destined to become Arizona's most productive mine.

Suddenly southeastern Arizona's problems—its remoteness, Apaches, scorpions, lack of sufficient wood and water— seemed minor. Only a few years earlier, General William Tecumseh Sherman, faced with the task of deploying troops along the arid frontier, had advised Congress to "get Mexico to take . . . back" all of Arizona Territory. He would reverse his position in the midst of Tombstone's boom, judging the Southwest "a permanent mine of silver to the United States."

So the silver seekers came, as did a variety of other opportunists. Since the California gold rush of 1849, one mining excitement after another had electrified the West, from the mad scramble after gold in the Colorado Rockies in 1858 and 1859 to the Black Hills rush of 1876 in Dakota Territory. Many had learned that a surer route to riches, or at least a comfortable income, lay in providing for the wants and needs of the dreamers. Have the whiskey flowing when a hot, dirty prospector hit town; cater to his gambling urge with a session at the faro tables; offer him sex and female companionship for a price; sell him mining supplies; provide him with much needed water and lumber; be on hand to represent him in the inevitable litigation that ensued when he did manage to locate something worthwhile.

The community of Tombstone, fittingly named after Schieffelin's early strike, evolved out of all these needs and desires. At first, it was just a collection of canvas shanties and bear grass shacks clustered near Ed's Lucky Cuss claim and close to a spring that provided water. Dubbed Watervale or Waterville, the site was located about five miles east of the San Pedro and about seven miles northeast of the old Brunckow mine. But as the Tombstone mining district coalesced into an area eight miles wide and five miles long, the community shifted about two miles to the southeast to occupy Goose Flats, an elevated slice of open desert under which the Tough Nut mine ran. The site, surrounded by dry gulches and bordered on the south and southwest by the bare, rounded Tombstone Hills, commanded a panoramic view of the desert floor. Mountain ranges undulated in the distance to the northwest, southwest, and southeast, while the harsh Dragoons jutted upward only eight miles to the east. For a brief and heady time, as one old-timer later remembered, "all roads led to Tombstone."

Among the first to feel the pull of the flourishing mining camp were men such as the Clantons and McLaurys, isolated ranchers and cattle punchers who inhabited the few southeastern Arizona cattle spreads. Their lives consisted of hard physical labor and extended, monotonous movement across the wild expanses. "You soon got into the habit of squinting your eyes, a habit so noticeable in oldtimers in looking at the landscape," wrote one early rancher, "and, too, you acquire a patience you never knew before—a patience to look calmly at some spot on the horizon, maybe fifty or more miles away— the spot you hope to arrive at sometime in the future—and you resign yourself to the slow shuffle of your cow-pony mount who will tire out if you push him faster."

Now suddenly, miraculously, out there in the middle of an endless expanse of desert, the ranchmen found a bustling camp of prospectors, burros, and miners, where a fellow could market his meat-on-the-hoof, whet his considerable thirst in a canvas tent saloon, and sober up with hot coffee, fried bacon, and sourdough bread.

Billy Clanton's brother Ike bought into the action in 1878, that first year of Watervale's existence, establishing his Star Restaurant. It wasn't fancy—nothing in the community was at that point, and Ike's enterprise was probably simply a short-lived food stand.

The Clantons could claim to be old Arizona settlers. Like many western families, they had ranged from Missouri to Texas, Texas to California, California to Arizona. About 1868 or 1869, Newman "Old Man" Clanton established his brood, including five sons and three daughters, on the Gila River in southwestern Arizona and claimed a desert water hole on the trail between Yuma and Phoenix. The site is known as Clanton Well to this day; a nearby wash and hill also bear the Clanton name. By 1873, Clanton had moved eastward along the Gila, which bisects southern Arizona, and was ranching and farm-ing near the United States Army's Camp Thomas, about 140 miles north of the future site of Tombstone and just south of the Gila Mountains.

Old Man Clanton has been portrayed as everything from a hardworking farmer to a free-ranging desert crime boss. He was neither as honorable as some would have him nor as crim-inally powerful as others would make him. Like most early settlers in the territory, he was flexible—ranching, farming, freighting goods, operating an inn at Camp Thomas in the mid-1870's. He didn't stop at legal activities, however; just about every source agrees that he and his sons rustled and bought rustled stock, participating in the free and easy raiding conducted both by Arizona bands and by Mexican bands criss-crossing the Mexican border.

Eldest son John Wesley, born in 1841, apparently disassociated himself from the family's activities. That left Phineas Fay, born in 1845; Joseph Isaac, or Ike, two years his junior; Peter Alonzo, born in 1858; and William Harrison, or Billy, the baby of the family with an 1862 birthdate.

A photo of Old Man Clanton from his Arizona years shows a stocky, balding patriarch with a luxuriant white beard. Son Ike was lean and curly-haired, favoring a mustache and dandified goatee. He and brother Phineas would be described by a Tucson newspaper as "wiry, determined-looking men, without a pound of surplus flesh." Peter Alonzo would die before Tombstone boomed, while Billy would grow to a more substantial size than either Phin or Ike.

A short distance south of the Clantons' holdings near Camp Thomas lay Fort Grant, and beyond that the Sulphur Spring Valley, where pioneer rancher Henry Clay Hooker was already developing his famous Sierra Bonita spread, home of a variety of cattle breeds, saddle and carriage horses, dairy cows, poultry, Poland China hogs, and even greyhounds. This valley, as well as the Dragoon Mountains to the west and the Chiricahua Mountains and San Simon Valley to the east, had been reserved in treaty with Cochise for the Chiricahua Apaches, a fact only the Chiricahuas apparently appreciated. In 1876, another man who would figure in the Tombstone drama, the young, self-confident Indian agent John Clum, would move them under orders from Washington to the San Carlos Indian Reservation on the north side of the Gila Mountains, with a few of his more resistant charges escaping southward through the Dragoons and down the San Pedro Valley to Mexico.

Through the early and mid-1870's, ranchers continued to covet the San Pedro Valley for their herds almost as much as Ed Schieffelin would want it for his bonanza, but the few tentative attempts at ranching in the valley sputtered and died as a result of the same problems which lone miners faced.

Nonetheless, cattle ranching—and rustling—began to grow in southeastern Arizona in response to the supply needs of the military posts and Indian reservations. By 1881, the San Carlos Reservation alone would require three and a half million pounds of beef annually. Drovers from Texas, restless, solitary young men, came to Arizona with the herds of such

Texas cattle barons as John Chisum and John Slaughter and
wound up establishing their own small ranches or rustling
holding pens.

Frank and Tom McLaury probably rode into Arizona this
way, trailing Slaughter's herds. The inscription on their coffins would give their place of birth as Mississippi, but the two
actually were born in New York State. Their family then emigrated to Iowa, where their father practiced law and farmed.
Of the eleven children born to Robert Houston McLaury and
Margaret Rowland McLaury, argumentative Robert Findley,
or Frank, born in 1848, was the eighth, and quiet Thomas
Clark, born five years later, was the tenth. The dark-haired
young men had visited older brother Will in Fort Worth before turning westward. They arrived in eastern Arizona in
1877, lighting in the Camp Thomas area about the time Old
Man Clanton moved his own ranch again, twenty-four miles
south to a location near Fort Grant.

The adolescent Billy Clanton continued to hang around
the old home place, bought by a family named Jones, while
brothers Phin and Ike freighted goods to Globe. About January 1878, when the Schieffelins and Gird were at the Signal
mine anxiously planning their trip to the San Pedro Valley,
Frank McLaury appeared at the Jones ranch looking for work.
He helped build corral fences, temporarily batching with
Melvin Jones and with Billy Clanton, then took a job procuring beef with the butcher at Camp Thomas.

Melvin Jones would later recall an episode in which Frank
assisted him in pursuing three discharged Camp Thomas soldiers who had stolen several sets of harnesses. When Jones
received authorization to follow the three, he remembered, "I
was to take one good man with me, and Frank McLaury was
the good man that I took." When the two caught up with the
soldiers, Jones reported, Frank heatedly rejected a bribe offered by the thieves and joined him in delivering them to the
justice of the peace. Jones considered the McLaurys honest
ranchers, a view that would be echoed by others, but the two
"ceased to be seen very often around Camp Thomas after the
Tombstone mines began to boom."

In fact, both the Clantons and the McLaurys would relo-
cate closer to that ready cattle market, that oasis of comfort

and conviviality mushrooming in the San Pedro Valley. Old Man Clanton moved about fourteen miles southwest of Tombstone, to a knolled site on the west side of the San Pedro River, where he built a thick-walled adobe fortress of a ranch that commanded a view in every direction. At about the same time, Dick Gird was supervising construction of a mill for the newly formed Tombstone Mining and Milling Company on the river about four miles north of Clanton's new location. Gird himself would live in richly furnished quarters at the mill, throwing elegant parties, while across the river a town grew to accompany the new operation. Called Charleston, it quickly acquired a rough reputation and attracted a mixture of Mexican laborers, Fort Huachuca soldiers, foreign mill-workers, cowhands, and rustlers. A few miles to the north, among the luxurious grasses and cottonwoods along the Babocomari River, the McLaurys established a ranch. An 1878 Arizona guidebook, in reporting the region's excellent ranching potential with information gleaned from a Prescott *Miner* correspondent, would note in an apparent reference to Frank and Tom, "The McGarey [*sic*] brothers have a ranch on the [Babocomari] creek . . . being principally engaged in sheep and cattle raising." Nearby, where the Babocomari met the San Pedro, another satellite of Tombstone, Fairbank, would flourish briefly.

But Tombstone was the main draw for the migrants pouring into southeastern Arizona. From the northeast, they trailed through New Mexico, passed through the green grandeur of the Chiricahua Mountains on New Mexico's eastern border, crossed the plain of Sulphur Spring Valley, increasingly arid as one moved southward, and entered the San Pedro Valley through the South Pass of the Dragoon Mountains, where Cochise had maintained his stronghold only a few years earlier. From the northwest, travelers journeyed southeastward from Tucson across a high, cactus-studded plain along a poor excuse for a wagon road. The 1878 Arizona guidebook described the first stage of the journey as "decidedly uninteresting and dreary."

The landscape, though on a huge scale, has a marked similarity. The peaks of the Santa Rita [Mountains] are purple in the glowing southern distance. The rugged, bare San Catalinas are gray and bald in the hazy west. The wondrous tones of the haze that rest on the far outlines form a deep contrast to the gray alkali plain, whose dust flies around the craunching wheels of the stage, and the burning sky above, if the journey be made in summertime.

Tombstone-bound travelers veered to the south, skirting the Whetstone Mountains, crossing the San Pedro River, and traversing gulches and low hills until the town spread out before them.

On December 1, 1879, three of the five sons of Nicholas Porter Earp and Virginia Cooksey Earp reached the end of this Tucson-to-Tombstone thoroughfare and viewed the jumble of shacks, adobes, and hastily constructed board structures that constituted the mining community.*

At thirty-eight, James Cooksey Earp was the eldest and smallest of the three, an itinerant gambler, bartender, and hack driver whose affable nature and shoulder wound incurred in an early Civil War battle kept him safely removed from the troubled milieu his younger brothers would inhabit.

Thirty-six-year-old Virgil, former stage driver, night watchman, and Prescott, Arizona, constable, carried a deputy United States marshal commission with him to Tombstone. Virgil was the most solidly respectable of the brothers, but he had a temper. By one account, the strapping six-footer with russet-blond hair had already flattened a stage driver who had carelessly raked one of Virgil's horses while passing on the wagon road.

The third brother, thirty-one-year-old Wyatt Berry Stapp Earp, arrived from a stint as assistant marshal of that "Queen of the Cowtowns," Dodge City, Kansas. Wyatt had run through a dizzying variety of frontier occupations, from buffalo hunter to lawman and part-time gambler. He usually—but not always—appeared on the right side of the law, and he, more than Jim and Virgil, more than younger brothers Morgan and Warren, who would come later, throve on the pos-

---

*Although most accounts have the three brothers arriving together, some researchers contend that Virgil was already in Tombstone when James and Wyatt appeared. The Prescott *Weekly Miner* of November 14, 1879, reported Virgil "about to pull out for Tombstone."

sibilities for money and power which Tombstone afforded. He and Virgil resembled each other so much in size and appearance that people would occasionally confuse the two.

The Earp brothers did not come galloping alone over the dusty landscape to Tombstone, in movie matinee style. Prosaically, as befitted future upstanding citizens of this newest and fastest-growing frontier community, they arrived with their wives and wagons loaded with household items. Not a marriage license has been found for the lot, but two of the liaisons were to prove long-lasting. With Jim came Nellie Bartlett Ketcham, also known as Bessie, a widow whom he claimed to have married in 1873, and her teenaged daughter, Hattie. Virgil, who had already legally married twice, brought tiny, feisty Alvira Packingham Sullivan, Allie for short, whom he had found waitressing in a Council Bluffs, Iowa, restaurant during his stage-driving days in 1874. Wyatt, a widower from a brief early marriage, had with him Celia Ann Blaylock, nicknamed Mattie, a Fairfax, Iowa, native with whom he had apparently taken up residence in Dodge City.

The Earps were a clannish family. Early in her relationship with Virgil, Allie Sullivan Earp attempted to read the future with cards.* Five black spades appeared, leading Virgil to comment, "Five brothers, all dark and handsome like me! That's what you got married into, Allie! A spade flush!" Allie protested uneasily that she had cast her lot only with him, but the cards did not lie. Somehow two or more of the brothers wound up together again and again, their fortunes intertwined, despite their individual peregrinations.

They did so under the patriarchal influence of father Nicholas, who stressed family loyalty and fostered an "us-against-them" mentality in his offspring. Glenn Boyer, in his controversial *I Married Wyatt Earp,* has Josie Marcus relating that Nicholas

---

*I have made cautious use of actions and statements attributed to Allie Earp in Frank Waters's *The Earp Brothers of Tombstone: The Story of Mrs. Virgil Earp* (Lincoln: University of Nebraska Press, 1976 ed.). Allie shared her memories with Waters in the 1930's but rejected the resulting manuscript, and Waters did not publish the account—unflattering to the Earps and particularly to Wyatt—until after Allie's death. I believe that many of the statements reflect Allie's perceptions of events better than she was willing to acknowledge, but on particularly controversial points, I have referred in the text to the Waters narrative rather than simply to Allie herself.

"knew only two kinds of people—friends and enemies. His friends could do no wrong and his enemies could do no right."

Nicholas and his wife also had set a roving example. Jim and Virgil had been born in Kentucky, as had an older half brother, Newton. Wyatt's place of birth was Monmouth, Illinois, while Morgan and Warren Baxter had entered the world in Pella, Iowa. There were three sisters, too, although only the youngest, Adelia Douglas, would survive to maturity.

Like Old Man Clanton, Nicholas Earp has been portrayed in widely divergent ways, depending on the attitude of the portrayer toward the Earp brothers. Thus, Nicholas was either a respected member of any community to which he attached himself or a peripatetic low-class saloonkeeper. Actually, the historical record shows that Nicholas was the former, a responsible farmer and cooper, or repairer of barrels and casks, who was elected or appointed to positions of trust within various communities. During the Civil War, he served as a deputy United States provost marshal for the Pella, Iowa, congressional district. But he got the urge to go to California, and in 1864 he organized and headed a wagon train bound for that shimmering land.

This move outside the agricultural Midwest opened up a variety of frontier experiences to the Earp boys. Discharged Union soldier Jim went along, turning off for the boomtown of Austin, Nevada. Sixteen-year-old Wyatt traveled with his parents to San Bernardino, California, and soon began teamstering between Wilmington, California, and Prescott, Arizona. Virgil, after serving in the Union Army, made his way to San Bernardino at war's end and began teamstering with Wyatt. When the family decided to return to the Midwest in 1868, Virgil and Wyatt worked on the Union Pacific grading crews along the route the family followed eastward, back to Monmouth, then to Lamar, Missouri, to settle near Earp relatives.

From Lamar, the Earp brothers ranged westward again— Jim to Montana, the Kansas cow towns, and Texas; Virgil to Iowa, Kansas, and Prescott, Arizona; Wyatt to the Kansas cow towns, Texas, and South Dakota; Morgan to Kansas and Montana. Their parents, too, pulled up stakes again, returning to California in 1876.

So as Tombstone began to boom, the Earp family was scattered across the West. Then, in 1879, Wyatt started rounding up his brothers for the move to Tombstone.

Purportedly, he hoped to run a stage line between the town and the railroad extending horizontally across the territory to the north, but his previous and subsequent activities give no indication that he was interested in so mundane a career. He had a dominant, aggressive personality that brought him to the forefront among the brothers, and he was a true gambler, a player of the odds, with a tough, unyielding streak, a man who excited both admiration and disdain. To Indian Agent Clum, who became editor of the Tombstone *Epitaph*, he would be "quite my ideal of the strong, manly, serious and capable peace officer." To Tombstone resident James Baker, later an Arizona house representative, Wyatt and his brothers would offer "*absolutely nothing . . .* for a decent man to admire in any way."

Wyatt was, in fact, a perfect example of the western peripheral man, treading the thin line between law and lawlessness, respectability and notoriety. Born in 1848 and named after his father's commander in the Mexican War, he had won his first law enforcement job in Missouri in 1870, beating half brother Newton in a four-man race for constable of Lamar Township. If Newton had any hard feelings, he didn't show it. He quietly moved to a homestead in Kansas and named his first son after the victor.

Wyatt, however, didn't last long in the position. He had married Urilla (or Rilla or Willa) Sutherland in January; she died less than a year later, possibly of a fever or in childbirth. A murky rumor has survived that Wyatt had some kind of trouble with her brothers and cleared out. Whatever the situation, four months after the November constable election, a "Wyatt S. Earp" was arraigned in Fort Smith, Arkansas, along with John Shown and Edward Kennedy for stealing two horses worth one hundred dollars each from a man in Indian Territory. Shown's wife charged that Wyatt and Kennedy had plied her husband with liquor to get him to participate in the theft. Wyatt was taken into custody in April in the Cherokee Nation. Codefendant Kennedy eventually won acquittal on the horse-stealing charge, but Wyatt apparently posted his five-hundred-dollar bail and disappeared.

He resurfaced in the buffalo hunters' camps on the Kansas plains during the 1871–1872 hunting season. Here he made a lifelong friend of fellow hunter Bat Masterson, who would later recall that Wyatt at the time of their initial acquaintance weighed "in the neighborhood of one hundred and sixty pounds, all of it muscle." He was six feet tall, "with light blue eyes and a complexion bordering on the blond." As for his character, the western frontier would know "no braver nor more desperate man than Wyatt Earp."

When the Kansas cow towns began to boom in the early seventies, Wyatt began frequenting them, along with Jim and Morgan. The year 1874 found Wyatt and Jim in Wichita. The latter began bartending at Pryor's Saloon; one Wichita old-timer later recalled that Jim fell asleep at the whiskey tap one morning "after being up all night with a gang of money spenders." The "liquid treasure" ran all over the floor, but Jim's boss forgave him when he saw the full money till.

Wyatt meanwhile was back on the right side of the law, performing a handy piece of private investigative work with a Wichita police officer by tracking the thieving "Higgenbottom outfit" and forcing them to pay for a stolen wagon. The local *City Eagle* concluded of the two detectives, "These boys fear nothing and fear nobody."

Wyatt and Jim were not the only Earps living in Wichita. A number of women whose names show up regularly in city records on prostitution charges went by the Earp name. Included among the number were Bessie and Sallie Earp, charged not only with prostitution but with illegally running a bawdy house. Censuses do not show Jim and Wyatt living with Bessie and Sallie, but researchers hostile to the Earps point to the fact that Jim's wife, Nellie, was also called Bessie and that Sallie might be Wyatt's Celia.

In April 1875, Wyatt gained an appointment to Wichita's police force as one of two policemen working under a marshal and an assistant marshal. Wichita pioneer David Leahy later remembered that the mayor "offered some objection on account of Wyatt's size for he had an idea that small men would be harder to hit with a bullet than big ones." Nonetheless, the new officer did not prove to be an easy target and served about a year. Then, on April 5, 1876, the Wichita *Beacon* reported a "difficulty" between Wyatt and a city marshal candidate. "Erp [*sic*] was arrested for violation of the peace . . . and was relieved from the police force," the paper reported, citing as the cause of the altercation Wyatt's frustrated desire to bring his brothers into Wichita law enforcement. The confrontation ended his Wichita career, for in May 1876, the month after his dismissal, the city commission recommended vagrancy laws be enforced against the "two Earps," identified variously as Wyatt and Jim and as Wyatt and Morgan. Morgan had been arrested and fined for an unnamed offense in Wichita in September; in Dodge City, however, he had worked for Ford County Sheriff Charlie Bassett.

Dodge proved hospitable to Wyatt, too, as he picked up a city policeman appointment there within a month of his forced exit from Wichita. From 1875 to 1879 he called the cow town home, alternating between work as assistant city marshal and extended gambling stints in South Dakota and Texas.

In Texas, he met Doc Holliday, a loner who nonetheless attached himself to the cow town lawman and gambler with a fervor. "Damon did not more for Pythias than Holliday did for Wyatt Earp," Bat Masterson would later write. The statement was ironic, either intentionally or unintentionally, for Doc would also be the catalyst for many of Wyatt's troubles.

John Henry Holliday's life reverberated with incongruities. Born in August 1851 in Georgia, only son of a small-town civic leader and a religious mother, Doc was to garner a reputation as one of the touchiest drunks in the West. An 1872 graduate of the Pennsylvania College of Dental Surgery, he preferred gambling to prying in people's mouths. Close friends with a cousin who became a nun with a saintly reputation, he lived with a virago of a prostitute and dance hall girl from Hungary named Big Nose Kate Elder. A reed-thin, tubercular weakling, he nonetheless incited fear in his opponents.

There were hints of trouble in his youth. His mother died when Doc was fourteen, "deeply anxious about the faith of her only child" and having prepared a written statement of her own faith "so her boy might know what his mother believed." Three months after the funeral, father Henry B. Holliday married a twenty-three-year-old neighbor, a situation easily unsettling to an adolescent boy. The youth remained at home in Valdosta, Georgia, for at least four years, then departed for dental school, reportedly on the heels of an incident in which he shot at black bathers at his favorite swimming hole. (Masterson would later allege that Doc had actually dispatched two of the swimmers with his gun, thus giving birth to his reputation as a dangerous gunman.)

By 1875, Doc's tuberculosis had been diagnosed and he was practicing dentistry and gambling in Dallas, Texas. He opened the new year by getting into a violent argument with a local saloonkeeper, leading the Dallas *Weekly Herald* to report that the two had "relieved the monotony of the noise of firecrackers by taking a couple of shots at each other." Masterson placed Doc in the summer of 1876 in Denver, where he "carved up the face and neck" of a "quiet and gentlemanly looking sport."

The gambling dentist probably met up with both the impetuous Kate and with Wyatt Earp in Fort Griffin, Texas, in fall 1877. By June 1878, he was advertising as a dentist in Dodge—"Where satisfaction is not given money will be refunded." He supposedly had trouble drawing customers because of his coughing fits, but the diminutive Allie Earp would recall asking him to pull a loose tooth and receiving an ill-tempered reply: "Keep your baby teeth in your mouth where they belong. I've got no use for them."

Like the Earp brothers with whom he aligned himself, the blue-eyed, ash blond Holliday was to excite widely varying reactions among those who met him. The main thing that made him stick in people's minds was his attitude toward his own mortality. He was dying, anyway; Bat Masterson said that he not only looked the part of an unhealthy man but "incessantly coughed it as well." Whether he expired in a coughing spasm or a whiskey bottle or a hail of lead seemed to make no difference to Holliday. Records show him with only one confirmed killing before his move to Tombstone, the shooting of a drunken ex-army scout in Las Vegas, New Mexico, in 1879. But increasingly, he courted trouble.

In this respect, he was matched only by John Ringo, a

second alcoholic with suicidal tendencies and one who would become the champion of the McLaurys and Clantons. If Holliday's fourteenth year had proven traumatic, it couldn't match that of Ringo, the eldest son of a family traveling by wagon train from their home in Missouri to California in the same year Nicholas Porter Earp led his train westward. As Ringo's father stepped from the wagon with a shotgun on the trail in Wyoming, apparently looking for Indians, the gun fired accidentally. A witness related to the Liberty, Missouri, *Tribune* that the load entered the elder Ringo's right eye and passed through the top of his head. "At the report of his gun I saw his hat blown up 20 feet in the air and his brains were scattered in all directions," the witness explained, adding, "I never saw a more heartrending sight, and to see the distress and agony of his wife and children was painful in the extreme."

Mother and children proceeded westward, eventually settling in San Jose, California. At nineteen, the hard-drinking John left home, surfacing in Texas as a member of the Scott Cooley gang during the bloody and confused Mason County Range Wars. Ringo apparently participated in two revenge killings. In one, the victim, a gambler named Cheyney who had lured a member of the Cooley faction to his death, invited the killers onto the porch and was killed while drying his face with a towel.

Ringo was named in the grand jury indictment in the Cheyney murder and was recognized in Texas newspapers as a leading faction member. He and Cooley were arrested in Burnet, Texas, in December 1875; transferred to Lampasas, they were sprung from jail by friends in May 1876. Ringo enjoyed a few months of freedom before being recaptured. During late 1876 and most of 1877, he saw the inside of a few Texas jails, including, in 1877, the Travis County lockup, which then housed the deadliest gunman of the era, John Wesley Hardin. However, the Cheyney killing case was eventually dismissed, and in late 1878 Ringo was elected as a constable in Loyal Valley, Mason County. In 1879, he wandered westward into Arizona, where he quickly became a leading rustler.

A photo of Ringo taken about the time of the Tombstone gunfight shows not a rakish outlaw but a bland, properly dressed man with a disappearing hairline, his face saved from anonymity only by a bushy mustache. But, then, he probably had the picture made to impress his genteel sisters in California, who had rejected their frontier sibling when he decided to drop in on them after a number of years.*

If his sisters didn't like him, many Arizona contemporaries did, despite his illegal activities and an apparent cruel streak while under the influence. He cut a mysterious and romantic figure, living in a picturesque Chiricahua Mountains retreat near Galeyville, headquarters for southeastern Arizona rustlers. He even owned and read a small collection of books and received letters from California written in an elegant feminine hand, leading to romantic speculation that he was a highly educated man and a tragic lover. Women found him gentlemanly and courteous. But about the time the Earps rattled into Tombstone, Ringo fired a pistol ball into the left ear and neck of an unfortunate bar patron in Safford, Arizona, when the man turned down his offer of whiskey in favor of beer.

Much was happening that December of 1879 that would set the stage for events to come. The first week of the month, a *Pinafore on Wheels* troupe hit town, playing to capacity audiences. Among the cast members was an eighteen-year-old dark-haired Jewish beauty from California, Josephine Sarah Marcus, who would return and contribute to the troubles in Tombstone. Twenty-eight-year-old Morgan Earp, too, reportedly made his first appearance in Tombstone at the end of that week, although recent research has shown he probably arrived some months later. Tall, lithe Morgan, favoring Virgil and particularly Wyatt in looks, would only add to the confusion some Tombstonians expressed as to which Earp brother was which. However, Morgan didn't have Wyatt's drive or Virgil's solidity. He had served briefly as a peace officer in Dodge; otherwise, his work experience before he reached Tombstone is sketchy. Generally affable and likable, he nonetheless possessed a temper like Virgil's and Doc Holliday's—too easily triggered.

---

*Biographer Jack Burrows offers this conjecture in *John Ringo: The Gunfighter Who Never Was* (Tucson: University of Arizona Press, 1987).

That month also saw the arrival of future Earp champion John Clum. Cocksure of himself, class-conscious, and inclined to dramatics, he, too, stirred up a wake of admirers and detractors.

Clum, a New England farm boy, had briefly studied theology before lack of funds led to a job with the army Signal Service as a weather observer in New Mexico. When he was nominated by his Presbyterian denomination for the Indian agent position, the prematurely balding New Englander became "Boss with the white forehead" to thousands of Apaches at the San Carlos Reservation. His policies, such as Apache self-government, showed a real concern for his charges, but he felt hamstrung by the bureaucratic inefficiency and graft of the government Indian Service, as well as by army officers who wanted to extend their control onto reservations.

Thus, he resigned in disgust in 1877 and moved to Tucson, where he obtained a law license and began a career as a journalist. Clum was publishing the *Arizona Citizen* in Tucson when news of Tombstone's development brought him across the San Pedro River for an appraisal of his chances as a newspaper publisher and editor there.

Just after Christmas, another character in the growing Tombstone cast wandered down from Phoenix. William "Billy" Breakenridge had rambled through the West, leaving his Wisconsin home as a teenager and participating as a youthful volunteer in Colorado's 1864 Sand Creek Massacre. Breck, as he was often called, didn't have the stomach for scalping but traded a buffalo robe for two such trophies and sent them to his sister when she requested a lock of his hair. His mother, as she made clear in a blistering missive, was not amused.

Breakenridge eventually began working as a field engineer in Colorado, then guided an emigrant party to Arizona, where he became a Phoenix surveyor and deputy sheriff. Word of the rich Tombstone claims lured him to quit Phoenix and begin prospecting the San Pedro Valley as 1880 began.

As with other personalities on the Tombstone stage, Breakenridge excited widely divergent reactions among his contemporaries. They did agree that he was a mild-mannered, amiable man, a bit dull, actually, looking and acting more like a Sunday school superintendent than the deputy sheriff he would become. An 1880 photo shows a portly, pleasant-faced gentleman, the type of kindly uncle who would always carry candy in his pockets.

However, the faction that would develop around the Earps would have no use for kindly candy-toting uncles. They would consider the affable Breakenridge too thick with the "cowboys," a term which came to mean all those living outside Tombstone who rustled or were friendly with rustlers. To the Earp faction, Breck would be perceived as weak and concilatory; one Earp supporter would later deride him as "a nice young girl." To others, however, he would be seen as the right man for a difficult job, "the mainstay of the sheriff's office."

Breakenridge, Clum, and the Earps all converged on Tombstone just as it metamorphosed from a raw mining camp into a village, incorporated on December 9, 1879, with a justice of the peace court to be set up, ordinances to be passed, and a town marshal to be appointed. Over this local structure arched a county government, a territorial government, and the United States government itself. Arizona had passed from Mexican and New Mexican rule to its own set of laws and court system so that "technically there never was a 'lawless' period." But in Tombstone, where partisan politics would dictate the role of law enforcement, personal feuds, misunderstandings, and greed would lead to a "trail of blood" across the territory, with repercussions throughout the West.

CHAPTER 2

"A Big Camp This with a Big Future"

When the Earp entourage arrived in Tombstone, they rented the only dwelling they could find, a one-room, dirt-floored adobe on Allen Street. Housing was tight because lumber was scarce. Bullwhackers hauled timber from the Chiricahua Mountains fifty miles to the east and the Huachuca Mountains thirty miles to the west; the competition for their loads was so great that men would race out to meet the freighters, claiming the lumber by straddling it on its way into town.

A readier source of timber could be found in the Dragoon Mountains, but hostile Apaches continued to roam these mountains, resisting white attempts to force them onto reservations. Travelers risked their lives simply in passing through the forbidding Dragoons. If a desert sojourner encountered rustlers or border-raiding Mexicans, he at least had "an even break." But against an Apache he didn't have "the ghost of a chance," for "you could never see him, unless possibly he was seen by his victims at the instant of the fatal shot striking them."

So wood was hauled from the Chiricahuas and Huachucas—not only for buildings but for the mines themselves.

Timbering had to be provided for the various deep mining levels; the Comstock, the granddaddy of all silver mines up in Nevada, had swallowed "millions on millions of square feet of timber," so that "in it whole forests have found a tomb." Dick Gird's brother and a partner would almost match Gird's profits from the silver mines with their income from a Huachuca Mountains sawmill.

Water was another precious commodity. One entrepreneur arrived in 1879 to find the liquid being hauled from a site three miles away and selling for two dollars a barrel. He searched out a green spot a mile from town, borrowed fifty dollars from a local merchant to dig a well, and soon undercut the competition. But Tombstone residents still joked that any bather using less than fifty cents' worth had simply had a "spit bath."

The lack of adequate wood and water might pose problems, but Tombstone's climate and desert beauty proved a delight to many. At almost five thousand feet elevation, the community enjoyed generally cool summers and mild winters, with occasional rainstorms giving way to "a clear sky and bright sunshine . . . a well washed land and a balmy pure air." The open desert landscape and nearby hills and mountains provided an ever-changing natural panorama, especially at sunset, when a rosy light suffused the stark Dragoons.

A Tombstonian might pause to admire a vivid blue sky or a magical sunset, but no one forgot for a minute the sole entrepreneurial promise that had brought them all to southeastern Arizona, the glorious lure of mineral wealth. One early resident would recall, "You never heard a hard luck story in Tombstone. Everyone had great expectations. He might not have a dollar in his pocket—but he had millions in sight! He would draw from his pockets a bunch of mining locations, each showing title to fifteen hundred by six hundred feet of untold wealth along some lead lode or vein that only needed a little development to become a second Comstock!"

Jim, Virgil, and Wyatt Earp joined in this speculative excitement only five days after arriving in Tombstone, filing on a mining location with Robert "Uncle Bob" Winders, a former Fort Worth, Texas, saloon proprietor known as a man who "never fails in his undertakings." The brothers would establish at least nine more claims—together, singly, or with another party—in the year that followed.

Two legends survive concerning the Earps' early months in Tombstone. In the first, propagated in 1929 by John Clum and two years later by Stuart Lake in his colorful *Wyatt Earp, Frontier Marshal,* the already legendary lawman Wyatt Earp rode into Tombstone and immediately began clearing out such riffraff as the Clantons and McLaurys, with some minor help from his brothers and with the unanimous gratitude of Tombstone's law-abiding citizens.

In the second, most ably presented in Frank Waters's 1960 *The Earp Brothers of Tombstone: The Story of Mrs. Virgil Earp,* the Earp men merged unnoticed into the lower social and economic strata of Tombstone, with Virgil's Allie and Wyatt's Mattie sewing up tents to keep food on the table. In this version, Virgil was the sole worker of the three. Jim had his bum shoulder, and Wyatt, protecting his long, slender gambler's hands, "had no intention of workin'," instead devoting himself to "sizin' up the town as he said."

In truth, Wyatt and his brothers came as neither heroes nor ne'er-do-wells. Contemporary accounts seem to substantiate the idea that they, like the "cowboys," barely created a ripple in the life of Tombstone at first. The Earps were simply men looking to get ahead, and they attempted to do so by generally respectable means. Virgil had the deputy United States marshal commission, of course; with county and town law enforcers already in place or lined up, the commission didn't translate into much action or money, but it gave him an official status. Then, through the mining locations and town lot purchases, he, Jim, and Wyatt quickly established themselves as property owners. Wyatt pulled off a sweet deal within three months of his arrival in Tombstone by selling a third interest in a mine to Harry Finaty of Dodge for ten thousand dollars. (A Dodge paper reported Finaty planning a trip to Tombstone to check the purchase, which he understood was sitting unworked because of foul air.) The Earp brothers would also soon lease two of their claims to a San Francisco investor for a more moderate six thousand dollars.

So the Earps were playing the mining game with some success. Few of the men spreading across the San Pedro Valley in search of minerals were naive enough to expect to find a claim they could develop and work by themselves. Silver mining almost invariably required technology and industrial equipment beyond their reach. Seldom did a man stumble across any significant quantity of easily removable surface riches, as the Spaniards did in Arizona in the eighteenth century and as John Sutter's workmen did in California to spark the gold rush of '49. After a machine drill powered by air or steam had been introduced to the West in 1870, one observer noted, "If hell is below, it wouldn't take long to go there." But machine drills required capital, as did such other industrial innovations as dynamite, power hoists, and elaborate timbering systems.

Thus, prospectors and their small-time investors hoped for a strike that could be sold for a handsome sum to the "big moneymen," usually East· or West Coast financiers. The Schieffelins and Dick Gird had only developed their San Pedro Valley finds with the financial aid of Tucson gun dealer John Vosburg and his silent partner, former territorial Governor A.P.K. Safford. The Tombstone Mining and Milling Company, encompassing the Tough Nut and related claims, had gone into full swing in August 1879, when the first bullion bar produced weighed in at eighty pounds and was valued at over eighteen thousand dollars. Eastern financiers now had their eyes on the operation.

The future looked sunny indeed for Tombstone; if Wyatt Earp spent a few months sizing it up, there was a lot to size up. Life pulsated along Allen Street day and night. In fact, Tombstone had an air of perpetual busyness—a common feature of mining boomtowns. The New England-bred novelist Helen Hunt Jackson would write of Leadville, Colorado, that "It looked all the time as if there had been a fire and the people were just dispersing, or as if town-meeting were just over," with folks moving restlessly about, talking and gesturing eagerly. In Tombstone, Allie Earp would recall, "It was like livin' at the foot of the Tower of Babel." The streets teemed with prospectors, ranchers, cattle drovers, teamsters, Fort Huachuca soldiers, merchants, miners, and mining men, the elite who ran the mines or provided the money to develop them. The contrasts could not have been greater. On a busy corner might stand a miner in battered felt hat, baggy trousers, and ankle-high brogans, his pallid face reflecting long hours underground, while beside him rushed a pig-tailed Chinaman in Oriental dress. On another corner a sun-baked rancher clad in rough work clothes might pause to count his money, while behind him a gambler, fingers agleam with rings, cut an elegant figure in crisp white shirt and checked trousers. This crowd would periodically be augmented by the latest stage arrivals.

John Pleasant Gray, a recent graduate of the University of California at Berkeley, arrived in such a crowded conveyance in 1880 and later asserted that, far from being deterred by Tombstone's grim name, he and his fellow travelers would have been no less enthusiastic about the town's grand prospects if it had gone by the name of Hell. Jammed stages had begun rolling into the camp as early as fall 1878, when J. D. Kinnear's Tombstone and Tucson Express started weekly service. The ten-dollar ticket, purchased at Rice's Drugstore, Tucson, entitled the holder to a slow, cramped, dusty, and jolting seventeen-hour ride with an overnight stop.

New stage lines quickly sprang up to meet the demand; by early 1880 they were offering thrice-weekly service and shortening the trip to one hard day by using six-horse teams. One stage traveler reported of the journey, "There are no towns and few settlers in route, except a little Mormon affair on the San Pedro River [St. David], the way stations of the stages, and three little places between the Contention mill-site and Tombstone, which three places a fellow passenger assured me rejoiced in the popularly bestowed names of 'Hog-em,' 'Goug-em' [*sic*] and 'Stink-em.'"

At the stage stops, travelers would fill their bellies with beans, that food staple of the frontier. A Chicago *Tribune* journalist traveling from Tucson to Tombstone in the winter of 1880 would witness an indignant traveling salesman refuse yet another meal of beans and call for something—apparently, *anything*—else, only to have a rough dinner companion point a Colt revolver at his left eye and order him to eat the beans. He did, and presumably made it to Tombstone alive.

As each stage rumbled into Tombstone, the driver would invest its arrival with high drama by forcing his team into a teeth-jarring gallop along Allen Street, then pull up with a flourish in front of the Cosmopolitan Hotel, one of the two main hostelries. Here, if a man had money, he could leave "roughing it" behind. Tombstone's popular Russ House didn't even list beans on the menu, instead offering such elegant dishes as "Chicken Fricassee a la Creme" and the dubious "Calf Head in Tortue." Oxcarts brought fruits and Mexican brown sugar from Arizona Territory's southern neighbor, while hunters, taking advantage of the abundance of game around Tombstone, provided the bear, antelope, deer, and wild turkeys found "hanging in front of the best restaurants."

After a traveler had refreshed himself with a good meal and darkness fell, the pace of the town only quickened, with stores, restaurants, and saloons remaining open into the early-morning hours. Melodies from the dance halls and the noise of tired, excitement-seeking men created a hubbub which Gray reported "could be heard miles away by the lonely cowboy or prospector wandering in to join the gang."

"The gang" was usually drinking hard, seeking a little female companionship, and gambling. Most of the men congregating along Allen Street sought any diversion from the hard and dreary lives they led.

Miners, for instance. The deep mining necessary to extract the precious silver from Tombstone mines exposed workers to a variety of uncomfortable and dangerous situations. For a trip into the earth, miners would crowd together on a small platform, called a mine cage, which was lowered down a narrow, uneven shaft at eight hundred feet per minute or more. The slightest movement by one of the workers could mean death, as was the case for a Montana miner who tried with his foot to push his lunch box back from the edge of the platform. A Helena newspaper reported, "In an instant he was being drawn and ground through the narrow opening, but his comrades seized him and held him on the platform. His leg was pulled from its socket and he died soon afterward."

If a miner made it safely to a lower level, he often suffered from inadequate ventilation at best and asphyxiating pockets of gas and dead air at worst, especially when fire broke out. Gases in an 1869 fire in the Comstock mine produced a horrific result: "Dead men were lying on the floor of the level as they fell in the agony of suffocation, with their mouths glued to cracks in the planks or raised over winzes [inclined shafts], turning everywhere for one last breath of fresh air. Their faces were flushed and swollen, but the features of well-known friends were not past recognition."

In addition to this, timbers could suddenly give way, or a man could fall into scalding underground water pools. No wonder a newspaper editor in a Colorado mining town found the miners a gaunt, weary-looking lot, and no wonder they and their fellow western laborers sought a variety of leisure-time escapes.

Many of these escapes were less than respectable. Boomtowns were notorious for their "sinful" character. During the United States' first gold rush of any note, an early 1830's boom in Cherokee Nation, Georgia, a reporter testified, "I can hardly conceive of a more unmoral community than exists around these mines. Drunkenness, gambling, fighting, lewdness, and every other vice exist here to an awful extent." He reported many of the inhabitants worked three days a week, then devoted the other four days "to every species of vice."

By early 1880, Tombstone was acquiring the accoutrements of civilization, including sporadic Sunday church services and schooling for nine students in a dirt-floored building with packing-box desks and plank seats. But the wild and rollicking mining camp character remained. Lawyer Wells Spicer, who was to conduct an inquest on the O.K. Corral shoot-out, wrote in February 1880 that the town boasted "two dance houses, a dozen gambling places, over twenty saloons and more than five hundred gamblers," adding, "Still, there is hope, for I know of two bibles in town."

Drinking was Tombstone's most popular form of recreation; contemporary descriptions of mining towns across the West indicate that most of the inhabitants were fairly pickled in alcohol. "Aurora of a Sunday night," wrote one 1863 observer of the California mining town, "Saloons—saloons—saloons—liquor—everywhere." A visitor to Tombstone would observe in March 1880, "Every house is a saloon and every other house is a gambling hell."

Men drank copiously for a number of reasons. Not only did liquor provide a release from the "heat, dust and drudgery" of their lives, but the men also found in the saloon "what companionship and sense of community life was available among a fluid, shifting population." And they drank simply because the liquor was there.

Alcohol was "high in value in relation to its bulk" and easily transported "on the backs of mules or even men and then watered down on arrival to fatten profits still further." A fellow could start up a bar with as little as ten dollars. Charles F. Bennett of Pinal, Arizona, who borrowed five hundred dollars to buy a big, well-established saloon, recalled his first weeks in the business: "Well do you know there was six weeks I never saw a bed; just slept on the billiard tables; I kept right by the saloon and never closed it night or day. I made $20,000."

The saloonkeeper often matched his customers glass for glass, at least in part to keep the high spirits flowing and the coffers filling. Tucson barman George Hand demonstrated the extent of this participation in a July 1876 journal entry: "Feel tip-top for one who has been drunk for six years."

One western story that reflects this heavy alcohol emphasis involves an old and knowledgeable imbiber who, blindfolded, could identify every variety of liquor put to his lips. Finally, he was given a liquid that stumped him. He sampled the elixir again and again, then gave up—unable to identify water.

Allen English, silver-tongued Tombstone lawyer, perhaps best summed up his fellow citizens' love affair with liquor when he stepped from a saloon to see the moon rising at the end of Allen Street and orated, "Oh, Moon, thou are full, but you ain't a damn bit ahead of me."

A man with amorous yearnings could easily move from wine to women. "Nowhere else does one see prostitutes as he sees them in a new mining town," the Aurora observer had noted in 1863. Frontier newspapers referred to the women by a number of colorful, patronizing terms, including "soiled doves," "fair cyprians," and "frail sisters."

These women were usually young, poor, and uneducated, getting by in an environment almost exclusively masculine.

The nature of western industry was such that it encouraged "a masculine ambiance and a masculine work force." Few jobs existed for women, but men were always willing to pay for feminine sexual favors.

The prostitutes led tumultuous lives, unable to gain any economic security, harassed by local authorities, often abused by their long- or short-term lovers. Such conditions fostered "a population of women notable for the coarseness and violence of their lives" and locked into a cycle of "sordidness and corruption."

Some of these women worked as "hostesses" in the saloons and gambling halls, receiving a percentage on the drinks they could encourage a man to buy. Then, for a price, the drinker could accompany the prostitute to her cramped, drafty shack in back of the saloon. Or the "frail sister" might enjoy the relative security and prestige of a house run by a madam. In Tombstone, their houses occupied a red-light district east of Sixth Street, and the establishments of choice ranged from the rough-and-tumble brothel of former Dodge City denizen Nosey Kate Lowe to the elegant establishment of Blonde Marie. The latter reputedly offered only French damsels, but then, it wasn't too hard to fool an inebriated Romeo with a few *mais oui*'s. In one tony establishment, aptly named the Establishment, girls vied for business as men fought for mining claims, with at least one aggressive businesswoman distributing discreet cards advertising her services: "Elderly gentlemen would do well to ask for Maxine in the upper parlor. She is especially adept at coping with matters peculiar to advanced age and a general run-down condition."

In addition to wine and women, the boomtowns offered gambling aplenty, with faro and keno the favored games. The Tombstone *Daily Epitaph* would report in 1880 that "The Call of 'Free Roll' at the keno game, will collect a bigger crowd in 10 minutes than the cry of 'fire' on a windy night." One Tombstone resident later recalled that the miners would come in from the hills, get baths, new overalls, and a few drinks, then head for the gambling halls, where they would cheerfully lose all their money and, "far from manifesting any regret over the loss," seem "buoyed up by a sense of duty performed."

In the West of the 1870's and 1880's, deft, personable gamblers with good reputations were accorded nearly as much status as bankers or lawyers. Faro dealers in particular ranked high because they had to be especially sharp to deal and handle the bank through the shifting complexities of the faro layout, "with bets placed in all manner of ways and combinations." These men earned twenty-five dollars for a six-hour shift and five dollars an hour overtime at Tombstone's posh gambling palaces such as the Crystal Palace Saloon.

Jim Earp obtained a job dealing faro. He also began tending bar at Vogan's Saloon and Bowling Alley near the corner of Allen and Fifth streets. In the 1880 census, he was listed as "saloonkeeper." Wyatt and Virgil were both listed—ludicrously—as "farmers." In those early months, they were still seeking the right breaks, though Virgil occasionally served as a special officer assisting town Marshal Fred White.

From day to day, Tombstone grew and changed around them. In February 1880, Ed Schieffelin himself came in from a three-month prospecting trip to find his city mushrooming. Tombstone in late 1879 had boasted about a thousand residents; by the end of 1880, population estimates would range as high as seven thousand.

About the same time Ed reappeared, as rough-looking as ever, George Parsons stepped from a Tucson-to-Tombstone stage and began chronicling the town's life in his journal. Parsons had decided to move to Tombstone and hire out as a miner while raising capital to become a mining speculator. To this end, the moralistic, class-conscious bank clerk had spent hours rowing in San Francisco Bay to build his strength for a life of hard mining labor.

Nothing could quite prepare him for the dangerous demands of the job. Hiring on at the Merry Christmas mine, Parsons was soon "double-jacking," holding and turning a hand drill while a fellow worker hammered it with an eight-pound sledge. This was considered more efficient than the single-jacking method, in which a man swung a four-pound sledge, turning the drill with each impact. But double-jacking was fraught with threatening possibilities. "More difficult than I imagined to hold drills properly," Parsons confided to his journal, noting, "One little slip and one's hands, arms or legs might be smashed to a jelly." The business of wielding the sledge he found "equally as ticklish," while the blasting with "giant powder," the popular term for dynamite, "has to be handled carefully" or "cap explodes and one is likely to go flying out of the shaft."

Nothing could quite prepare Parsons for Tombstone itself, either. Parsons, who even objected strongly to cardplaying on Sunday, landed in a mining town where men made no distinction between the Sabbath and other days of revel, with activities that went substantially beyond cardplaying. Of Tombstone's prostitutes, he would write, "I have seen hard cases before in a frontier oil town where but one or two women were tho't respectable but have never come across several such cases as are here." In fact, he would spend almost a month in town before noting the arrival of lawyer Tom Fitch's wife with the words, "About the first lady I've seen in Tombstone."

Respectable women were indeed in short supply in the mining camps; one observer in a Colorado camp noted that there were many young "gentlemen" from good families there, but only one girl of comparable status, the sister-in-law of the camp doctor. "Forty young fellows calling regularly . . . set up rules," he remembered, rules which specified "only 6 at a time . . . 4 minutes on sofa with girl."

Parsons had his own long-distance sweetheart, Nathalie, but the relationship was decidedly unsatisfying. He waited four years for a photo, and finally received it in May 1880 only to note, "Rather curious effect. She's dressed warmly and is taken in a snow storm." Almost a year and a half later he would receive a second disappointing portrait: "Got horrible tin type of Natahlie [sic]. Terrible thing."

Parsons would enjoy some respectable female companionship in Tombstone, but he remained horrified by all the forms of vice prevalent there, repeatedly bemoaning in his journal how quickly a man could go to hell in Tombstone.

Parsons's priggish aversion to the riotous underside of Tombstone life would be accompanied by a cold distaste for those who for whatever reason failed to fit into his view of a civilized social order. Nonetheless, he was an earnest, industrious man who tried to live up to his own ideals, and his journal provides the most detailed record we have of daily life in Tombstone during its boom years.

In a later era, both pro- and anti-Earp forces tended to downplay the amount of actual violence in the town before the O.K. Corral shoot-out, but Parsons's entries show that liquor, greed, and pride often combined to provoke violent or near-violent personal clashes. His entries echo the impressions of many observers of frontier mining towns. Journalist Horace Greeley, visiting Denver in its early days, had commented, "More brawls, more fights, more pistol shots with criminal intent in this log city . . . than in any community of equal numbers on earth."

Such firsthand observations provide corroboration for the findings of a recent study on frontier violence centering on the mining towns of Aurora and Bodie, California. Research found no listing of crimes such as bank robbery and racial attacks, only infrequent instances of robbery, burglary, and theft. However, random shooting, fistfights, and gunfights "occurred with alarming frequency," particularly in Bodie, which boomed at the same time as Tombstone. The combatants had usually been drinking and become piqued over some point of personal pride; they willingly squared off, but often stopped with a simple show of arms.

On the day of Parsons's arrival in Tombstone, February 17, 1880, he wrote, "Shooting this A.M. and two fellows in afternoon attempted to go for one another with guns and six shooters—but friends interposed." Less than two months later, he would report to his journal, "Several more shooting scrapes—but they are of such frequent occurrence that their novelty has ceased."

More controversy was taking place than that found in saloon quarrels, however. When Parsons arrived, "everyone" was going armed, in large part because of the rampant threat of claim jumping. After joining a surveying crew, he reported to his journal, "I was never in a place or business before where there was so much chenanniging [sic] carried on. . . . No one seems to be exempt from talk—to say the least."

The inherent tensions in such a situation, however, did not override his appreciation of Tombstone's bright future. Strolling the town for the first time, Parsons noted happily,

"Very lively camp. Fine broad street. Good restaurants. . . .
Business good here and signs very encouraging indeed." A
month later, he would comment, "Times prosperous here.
Place seems to be forging rapidly ahead."

The Tombstone area silver discoveries had so invigorated
the territory's economy that they drew the Southern Pacific
Railroad farther southward than first planned—not to remote
Tombstone itself, but along a southerly route to its jumping-
off place, Tucson. On March 20, residents of both communities celebrated the extension's completion to Tucson, with
Dick Gird presenting Southern Pacific officials with a silver
spike from the Tough Nut mine and first Tucson Mayor William Oury proclaiming, "We now have no frontier to which
the pioneer may flee to avoid the tramp of Civilized progress."
In Tombstone, horse races led the calendar of festivities.

The Earps enjoyed fast horses; Wyatt and Virgil would
both race favorites during their Tombstone sojourn. Down on
the San Pedro, the Clantons, too, appreciated swift horseflesh.
About this time they put their fastest mare up against a horse
called the Thomas Bald Hornet and lost, forfeiting three hundred head of cattle.

Another horse fancier entered Tombstone in early
1880—the dapper Johnny Behan, who brought with him his
racehorse Little Nell, bought for twenty dollars and destined
to sell for a thousand. Thirty-four-year-old Behan, a native of
Missouri, had long ranged through Arizona Territory, first
marching into it with the California Column during the Civil
War, then working as a civilian at the various army forts. From
1867 onward, he had held a number of responsible positions,
including deputy sheriff and sheriff of Yavapai County, headquartered in Prescott. He also served two stints in the territorial legislature, one as a representative from Yavapai
County and one as representative from Mohave County. With
Tombstone booming, he chose to emigrate to the mining
camp and open a livery stable with a partner, John Dunbar.

If Wyatt Earp was to have a major antagonist in his struggle for power in Tombstone, it would not be Old Man Clanton
or one of his sons, the McLaurys or John Ringo; it would be
Johnny Behan. Many considered Behan an able and proven
public servant. "He was a square shooter, loyal to his friends,

generous to a fault, and there was no question as to his nerve," one area resident would remember. Another would insist, "Johnny wasn't afraid of anybody." Others considered him weak. Clum would write, "Johnny would have been all right, back in his native Missouri, but the Tombstone pace was a bit too fast for him." He had arrived in Tombstone on the heels of an embarrassing incident in Prescott, as described in the *Arizona Weekly Miner:* "Hon. John H. Behan had occasion to call at the Chinese laundry this P.M., when a controversy arose, leading to some half-dozen of the pig-tail race making an assault on him with clubs. He tried to defend himself with a revolver, which, unfortunately, failed to work. He received several severe cuts about the head."

Some contemporaries distrusted Behan's smooth politician's facade and his penchant for the high life. He loved to gamble, and his wife had divorced him in 1875, complaining that he blatantly frequented houses of prostitution. Perhaps in retaliation, she would send their son, Albert, born in 1870, to live with Behan in Tombstone.

If the Earps gained a nascent enemy in Behan that spring, they also gained two very useful friends, Marshall Williams and the returning John Clum. Williams, a former Yuma resident, in April became Tombstone's Wells Fargo agent and would soon hire Wyatt as a shotgun rider.

Wells Fargo & Company, the brainchild of two eastern businessmen named Henry Wells and William G. Fargo, had opened its first express office in San Francisco in 1852 and had taken only three years to become the preeminent express and freighting service in the West. By 1866, the company had gained control of every major stage line west of the Missouri River. However, completion of the transcontinental railroad in 1869 had hurt the company, as people turned to the rails to transport themselves and their valuables. Wells Fargo weathered the change by contracting with the Central Pacific Railroad to provide rail express service and by going into remote places such as Tombstone, where quick, safe transportation of goods was much needed.

In fact, Ed Schieffelin had been unable to find any stage line willing to carry the bullion bars from the Tombstone mills when they first began producing. Everyone was too afraid of robbery. From August until November 1879, Schieffelin himself loaded a wagon with the mill's output and transported it to Tucson with the help of a driver and three guards.

So the presence of the respected Wells Fargo organization was pointed to with pride in Tombstone, as was the arrival of a second newspaper. The *Nugget* had begun publication in October 1879; now Clum jumped into the Tombstone newspaper business. He arrived in April 1880, writing enthusiastically to his wife back in Tucson, "I have just returned from a trip to the Tough Nut mine—was down in several of the shafts and tunnels—Showing is splendid, a big camp this with a big future." On May 1, the first edition of his *Epitaph* appeared, and Clum, with the boosterism which characterized newspaper editors of fledgling American communities, noted, "Tombstone is a city upon a hill promising to vie with ancient Rome upon her seven hills in a fame different in character but no less in importance."

Parsons agreed with Clum's optimistic assessment, though he began to feel the effects of Tombstone's remoteness. Shortly before Clum's first edition appeared, Parsons mused, "This is a terribly out of the way place. It is farthest from N.Y. by rail and telegraph than any other city in the U.S. a fact I was not aware of till recently."

A rail line directly into Tombstone would lessen the isolation, of course. Everywhere across the West, communities eagerly vied for selection as railroad sites and awaited the coming of the steel rails as their most tangible, effective link with the outside world. The Southern Pacific was pushing southeastward from Tucson to the new railroad town of Benson, twenty miles northwest of Tombstone. On April 3, the Arizona and Mexico Railroad and Telegraph Company organized in Tucson, with plans to run a railroad from Benson down the San Pedro to Charleston, then "up the draw" to Tombstone and then on to Dragoon Pass to meet the Southern Pacific line being built toward that point. By May, graders were busy preparing the right-of-way out of Benson.

May 1880 was a particularly volatile month in Tombstone's volatile history. When Clum was serving as Indian agent at San Carlos, he had convinced Mimbres Apache leader Victorio to submit to reservation living. But after Clum's departure from San Carlos, the dissatisfied Victorio had escaped, leaving a bloody trail. Peace was temporarily achieved when the leader and his tribe were briefly allowed to return to their old home of Ojo Caliente, where they behaved circumspectly. But when army troops showed up to escort them back to San Carlos in October 1878, Victorio and his warriors disappeared into the mountains. Victorio came in for a brief stay at the Mescalero Reservation at Tularosa; but misunderstandings and hostilities led to his final break with the whites, and he drew to him angry Apaches from the various tribes.

Now they were harassing the settlers of New Mexico, Mexican Chihuahua, and southeastern Arizona. Under the daring leadership of Victorio, who proved a master strategist in encounters with army troops, the Indians would kill almost a thousand people in these three areas during 1879 and 1880, and their threat was most keenly felt in Tombstone that May of 1880.

On March 3, Parsons had confidently dismissed a prospector's story of having to abandon a claim in the Dragoons because of Apaches. "No danger from them now," Parsons wrote, as "their power was broken with the surrender of Cochise in the Dragoons." But in April, cattlemen from New Mexico had begun driving their herds across the border and into the San Simon, Sulphur Spring, and San Pedro valleys to escape the Indian menace. Now Victorio pushed the exodus farther westward. On May 21, Parsons wrote, "Indian scare increasing. Dragoon people coming in. Much excitement on San Pedro and Gila."

Tombstone would remain untouched, and Victorio would meet his death at the hands of Mexican troops in October of the year. But Victorio's lieutenant Nana would wreak his own vengeance, leading an ambush against the Mexican troops in which a Mexican sergeant with Victorio's saddle and amulets would be chopped to pieces. As this incident demonstrates, the serious Apache threats that would continue to surface throughout the next two years would contribute greatly to a sense of instability in Tombstone.

Another source of instability surfaced within the town itself in the form of conflicting claims to town lots. In mid-March 1879, A.P.K. Safford, J. H. Palmer, and James Clark had purchased the Tombstone townsite and hired a man to lay out the streets, but they failed to get clear patent to the property. As people poured onto the site, laying claim to lots and buying and selling at will, the whole ownership question became snarled. Sometime in 1879, John Pleasant Gray's father, Michael, a former Texas frontier ranger, arrived and bought into the townsite company, joining original purchaser Clark. By May 1880, he had become the local justice of the peace and was trying to exert control over the town lots. On May 5, Parsons noted, "Quite a row in town this a.m. or yesterday. Gray—the justice endeavored with several armed assistants to eject Hatch from the lot opposite P.O. on the SW corner. A crowd gathered and sided with Hatch when Gray and party— after a flourish of pistols retired." Parsons explained that Gray had tried to sell the lot a day previously but "having no patent for a town site—he can't give good titles to property."

Clark and Gray made a move to alter the situation to their advantage on May 9, registering their company with the territorial land office. Federal statutes mandated that the community's mayor hold the townsite company's deed in trust; therefore, Tombstone chief official Alder Randall would receive the patent and have the power to determine what the company could claim. Meanwhile, a "bad state of feeling" persisted in town, with Parsons reporting on May 10 that "shooting and rows of various kinds" could be traced to lot jumping.

Tombstone was not atypical in this regard; social theorists have asserted that the whole story of western community building is one of controversy, shifting social groupings, and political and economic power plays. They have pointed to the varied populaces, the difficulty in establishing social norms, the "absence of a well-defined structure of leadership," and "the uncertainty of the town's economic future" in depicting western communities in general as centers of "social disintegration, conflict, and instability."

Adding further to Tombstone residents' unease was the possibility of fire, the single worst threat in most mining boomtowns. A hellish description of Virginia City, Nevada, shortly after discovery of the Comstock Lode makes the hazard clear:

Frame shanties, pitched together as if by accident; tents of canvas, of blankets, of brush, of potato-sacks and old shirts, with empty whiskey-barrels for chimneys; smokey hovels of mud and stone . . . pits and shafts with smoke issuing from every crevice; piles of goods and rubbish on craggy points, in the hollows, on the rocks, in the mud, in the snow, everywhere. . . .

Virginia City had developed beyond these rude origins by the time it burned in 1875, but the fire nonetheless raged uncontrolled for over five hours, ravaging an area almost a mile long and a half mile wide, killing four people, and destroying two thousand buildings. Fire fighters brought out their engines and hoses only to find the water supply quickly exhausted; they watched helplessly as the flames consumed their equipment.

In Tombstone, May of 1880 began with a fire. The Dexter Corral burned, and news that an adjoining store contained "several tons of black and giant powder" caused people to desert their houses and their meals rather than run the risk of being blown sky-high. Although no injuries resulted, the incident left townspeople feeling at risk, for they still depended on haulers for their limited water supply.

Adding to the volatile mix in Tombstone that month were other new arrivals, including two completely different adventurers, James Reilly and Josephine Marcus, who checked into the Cosmopolitan Hotel about the same time and who would exacerbate tensions in the town. On May 13, the *Nugget* reported that Reilly was ready to practice law in Tombstone, with "collections a specialty."

A handsome man of about fifty with white hair and beard and a dramatic black mustache, Reilly had emigrated from Ireland at age eighteen, served in an army regiment in Texas, and freighted goods across the Southwest. In 1863, he was barred from Mexican Sonora and Lower California for killing a Mexican national. He surfaced in Yuma, where he published and edited a muckraking newspaper and served as district attorney of Yuma County, at least until his bondsmen either backed out or were disqualified. Reilly moved the newspaper to Phoenix, then sold it and moved on to Tombstone. The

Prescott *Miner* in 1878 described the contentious, controversial Reilly as "a man whose hair has been grizzled at the early age of 48 years by the impotent fury and ferocity of his passions." Tombstone would make him a justice of the peace.

The second adventurer was a svelte young woman with yards of dark hair and bold, alluring eyes. Josephine Sarah Marcus of the *Pinafore on Wheels* troupe was returning to Tombstone, by the account in Glenn Boyer's *I Married Wyatt Earp,* as the fiancée of ladies' man Johnny Behan.

As an old woman, up until her death in 1944, Josie showed a puritanical concern for laundering the past, so that researchers have had a time getting her stories to match what was going on in Tombstone. Boyer's *I Married Wyatt Earp* has her placing her arrival—vaguely—a few months later, but the Cosmopolitan guest list includes a "J. Marcus" for the week of May 12, and it is likely she did arrive this early to cast her fortunes in the mining town.

Behan and Marcus had not met in Tombstone; Behan was still working out of Prescott during the *Pinafore* troupe's mining town engagement. They may have met in early 1879, when a Prescott newspaper reported Behan visiting San Francisco, where Josie's family lived. Boyer's *I Married Wyatt Earp*—now widely regarded as partly or wholly fiction on the part of Boyer—has the two meeting in a dramatic scenario soon after Josie ran away from home to join the troupe. In this account [attributed to Josie], the players are en route from California to Prescott, only to find themselves surrounded by Indians and saved by the appearance of an armed posse including the dashing Behan. [Boyer speculated that such an encounter may actually have occurred when the *Pinafore* troupe left their December 1879 Tombstone engagement for Prescott and met a group of trackers, including Behan, on the trail of three Mexican stage robbers.]

Whatever the initial circumstances, the two were soon living together in a Tombstone home, possibly bought with money furnished by Josie's prosperous merchant father back in San Francisco. In *I Married Wyatt Earp,* Boyer has Josie spinning elaborate stories of chaperons and honor preserved at all costs. This is consistent with her later propensity for propriety, but her only chaperon appears to have been Behan's son from his failed marriage,

ten-year-old Albert Behan. His father didn't seem in any
hurry to marry; Josie took care of the boy and began looking
about for a better deal for herself.

Meanwhile, the Earps had settled into separate residences, though still remaining clannishly close. Jim and Bessie
now lived on the south side of Fremont, the broad street running parallel to Allen to the northeast. Wyatt and Mattie resided on one corner of First and Fremont; Virgil and Allie, on
another. Morgan Earp was at the family home in California,
but would soon be staying with Virgil and Allie and sending
for his common-law wife, Louisa Houston Earp, or Lou, a
twenty-five-year-old native of Wisconsin who had cast her fortunes with Morgan in Dodge City and remained with the Earp
parents. Lou was a striking young woman with a refined look
and large, liquid eyes.

Even when this beauty arrived, however, Morgan apparently divided his time between living with her and batching
with a man named Fred Dodge. At least, Dodge himself would
assert that he and Morgan were sharing a cabin off Allen
Street by January 1881, with Wyatt occasionally joining them.

Dodge was a gambler from California who later claimed
to have been an undercover Wells Fargo agent in Tombstone.
He had arrived in town just a few days after the older Earp
brothers and recalled in his memoirs that he dismounted from
the stage to find Virgil and Wyatt scrutinizing him carefully.
They had been waiting for Morgan to arrive, and explained
that Dodge bore a strong resemblance to him. Indeed, as he
talked with the brothers, Dodge heard a passerby comment,
"There is another one of the Earp boys." Dodge happily
aligned himself with his look-alike friends; he grew close to
Morgan and "idolized" Wyatt.

The latter in June 1880 was continuing to "size up the
town." Tombstone was fast gaining the look of a prosperous,
established community. Only one year before, Danner's dirt-
floored tent saloon with plank benches and kerosene lamps
swinging from the tent rafters had served as the camp's center
of conviviality, with two bits charged for all drinks and most of
the patrons knocking back straight whiskey. Now there were
such establishments as the Alhambra on Allen between Fourth
and Fifth, a commodious building divided into gaming rooms

and saloon and boasting a bar "constructed of walnut, mahogany, and rose woods; executed in Wrought and fillagree [*sic*] work, neatly gilded and finished" with elaborate French and Italian bar fixtures and a variety of fine wines and liquors.

Hotel accommodations had improved considerably, too. In July 1879 the Cosmopolitan Hotel had consisted of a tent with bunks; less than a year later it was a two-story brick structure with fifty bedrooms, all "being furnished with bedroom sets of black walnut and rosewood and spring mattresses." And, of course, as the Russ House menu demonstrated, restaurants had come a long way as well. While John Pleasant Gray commented that the Can Can Restaurant was well named because "a can opener was about the only way of arriving at a dinner" in Tombstone, at least one patron compared its cuisine favorably to that of Delmonico's in New York.

Four theaters, too, now lent an air of celebration to the town, with two of them featuring local talent and two being used for traveling troupes, local dances, and miners' meetings.

Then there were the more mundane businesses, which in June 1880 included two bakers, two barbers, two blacksmiths, four boot and shoe stores, three clothing stores, four dressmakers, one furniture store, one gunsmith (who also repaired sewing machines), two "Hardware, Tinsmiths, & Plumbers," three livery stables and corrals, four lumber yards, and four meat markets. There were also six Chinese laundries, signaling the presence of a large community of those Oriental emigrants who moved from California across the West in the late nineteenth century doing whatever work—cleaning, cooking, vegetable peddling, mining, railroad construction—which prejudiced Anglo westerners would allow them to do. The Chinese clung fiercely to their own cultural mores; at least among the first generation, most planned a return to their native country. In Tombstone, four hundred to five hundred Oriental emigrants occupied "Hop Town," an area bordering the western edge of the business district. The Chinese had their own gambling houses and opium dens.

Tombstone possessed a Mexican enclave as well. While the Chinese with their alien culture provoked blatant discrimination and outright hatred across the West, Mexicans were more tolerated yet just as firmly relegated to menial laborer positions.

In addition to the various business enterprises in Tombstone, for professional advice and treatment, the town's citizens could turn to eight lawyers, two dentists, two druggists, and five physicians, one a female listed as Mrs. Marion Webb, M.D.

Everyone looked to the railroad as the final cap to Tombstone's prosperity, but the railroad did not come. Instead, that June, work on it stalled just four miles out from Benson. At about the same time, Southern Pacific trains began rolling regularly into Benson, so at least Tombstone was now only twenty miles from a railroad station. Carriages and wagons began a brisk business carrying passengers and goods from the station to the mining town.

Tombstone's first sensational violence occurred in late June and involved one of its most visible and colorful personalities, Nashville Frank Leslie, known as Buckskin Frank. Leslie, a former Arizona army scout and San Francisco bartender, had drifted down to Tombstone from Fort Grant, reputedly along with well-known army scout Tom Horn and teamster Frank Stilwell. Leslie himself would play only a small part in the drama surrounding the O.K. Corral gunfight, but like many of the principal players, he was a classic peripheral westerner. Billy Breakenridge called him "a very treacherous man when drinking" and saw his jovial, genial side only while riding with him in a posse. Others found him generally intelligent and pleasant, with a showman's skill at mixing drinks in his bartending vocation. His reputation as a mean drunk and a crack shot, however, justifiably caused some apprehension even among those who liked him; he would not limit victims of his shooting prowess to the flies that he reportedly blasted from the ceilings of Allen Street saloons.

A photograph of Leslie shows a neat and impassive man with a handlebar mustache. He dressed well, though accounts vary as to the style. One has him favoring Prince Albert coat, checked trousers, pearl-studded shirt, and gleaming boots, while others state he preferred buckskin suits and silver-mounted pistols. Considering his nickname and the fact that he claimed to have performed in Buffalo Bill's *Wild West Show*, the latter attire seems more likely.

But perhaps he was wearing the Prince Albert coat and pearl-studded shirt a little after midnight on that June evening while he sat on the porch outside his Cosmopolitan Hotel room with his arm around the waist of May Killeen. May's husband, Mike, did not care for this situation, a fact of which Leslie was aware. The suitor carried a pistol in his pocket and had positioned a Colt six-shooter on the floor in front of his chair.

Sure enough, Mike Killeen, armed with a pistol himself, came hunting the couple. Leslie's friend George Perine had suspected such a move and saw the irate husband before Leslie did.

According to Mike Killeen's testimony, Perine called, "Look out, Frank, there is Mike," causing Leslie to rise from his chair "in a half standing position" and pull his pistol. "He fired the pistol at me and I fired one shot at him," Killeen explained.

> I saw I was in for it and I made a jump and caught the pistol and beat him over the head with mine. . . . I happened to look and saw Perine standing in the door with his pistol levelled at me; he pulled the trigger, which he repeated twice, firing in all three shots; by this time I had used up Leslie pretty well; then turned and jumped and caught Perine's pistol, and did the same to him; by this time people commenced to congregate and I dropped this man, not thinking of my own wounds; all I knew was I was shot in the nose somewhere.

Perine told a completely different story, asserting that he had run unarmed to the porch as he saw Killeen step onto it and commence firing and that he arrived to find Killeen and Leslie struggling. "I took one step towards them when Leslie went down on his knees," Perine related, "and Killeen came towards the hallway" with guns in each hand. Perine testified that he grappled with Killeen as the latter tried to point one of the pistols at him. Then Killeen fled, firing a shot back at Perine, whose hat had "got jammed down" over his eyes, blinding him. "Almost immediately," Perine stated, "someone whom I believe was Leslie fired a shot at Killeen and rushed down the hall" after him.

Leslie himself testified that he had struggled with Killeen and followed him down the hallway, but stated he had not seen Perine through the whole incident. In Leslie's version, he was rising to bid May Killeen good-night when he heard someone behind him say, "Take that, you s-- of a b----," and a gun fired, the bullet hitting him on the side of the head. Leslie stood up and faced Killeen; then, as the latter fired again, Leslie dropped to his knees, grabbed the assailant around the legs, and seized the six-shooter he had left lying on the floor. He could not get it cocked. The two men grappled again, Killeen forcing his pistol barrel toward Leslie, Leslie pushing it away just as it went off. "I saw Killeen's face distinctly by the flash. He swore and groaned directly when the pistol went off, saying, 'Oh, my God!' and snuffling as though struck in the face or nose. He staggered back and I sank to the floor of the veranda."

Now, Leslie testified, he drew his pocket pistol and, from a kneeling position, fired at Killeen's upper body. Then he rose and struggled with his adversary once again, firing again. Both fell; then Killeen started down the hall with Leslie in pursuit, "half blind with blood." A deputy city marshal stopped him at the top of the stairs.

May Killeen supported her suitor's testimony, stating that she had not seen Perine either. She had watched her husband fire the first two shots, then had run to the hotel proprietor's room and enlisted his aid.

Leslie was not seriously hurt, but after a few days Killeen died of his wounds, still insisting that Perine had "shot him without cause." Tombstonians would avidly follow the case but were distracted from its details by the latest signs of the city's progress and potential. On July 13, Parsons wrote in his journal, "The telegraph poles reached town today and telegraphic communication with the outside world was opened. . . . [T]he town is making rapid progress. Remarkable changes since my advent. There'll be a boom in the fall and I must make some money out of it in some way."

As Parsons planned to build on his mining dreams, Wyatt Earp was beginning to get some promising breaks. First, Williams hired him as a stagecoach messenger. Second, M. E. "Milt" Joyce opened his Oriental Saloon, providing a place where Wyatt and Morgan and their Dodge City friends would ply their gambling trade. The *Epitaph* breathlessly reported on July 22, "Last evening the portals were thrown open and the public permitted to gaze upon the most elegantly furnished saloon this side of the favored city of the Golden Gate," a combination bar and gaming house with chandeliers and Brussels carpets. In August, Wyatt would buy a quarter interest in the Oriental's gambling concession.

Even better, however, than the Wells Fargo job and the opportunity the new saloon represented was the mid-July appointment of Wyatt as deputy sheriff of Pima County by Tucson-based County Sheriff Charlie Shibell. It was an enviable coup because deputy sheriffs collected and kept a percentage of the county taxes, including the lucrative and easily collected taxes owed by the railroad and mining corporations. Wyatt had received only one month's pay for the Wells Fargo job when he passed the position on to Morgan, arrived from his stay at the Earp parents' home in California.

The new deputy sheriff embarked on a career in Tombstone law enforcement with the well wishes of most of the community. The *Epitaph* editorialized on July 29, "Wyatt has filled various positions in which bravery and determination were requisites, and in every instance, proved himself the right man in the right place."

His Wells Fargo appointment helped, of course, as did his background as a lawman in Dodge. In fact, events in Tombstone can be comprehended only in light of Wyatt Earp's experiences in Kansas. He and the friends who followed him to Tombstone, most notably Bat Masterson and Doc Holliday, came to the mining town with an understanding of frontier society that had been shaped on the prairies, in the saloons and gambling halls of the dusty cow towns and raw frontier forts of Kansas and Texas. Like the cowboy-rustlers with whom they would come in conflict, Wyatt and his friends were tough-natured men who had learned to survive in a series of harsh environments. Neither the heroes nor villains of legend, they would nonetheless learn to cloak themselves in the legends. For they were frontier shootists—men who ultimately lived by the gun—and they received their training in and around Dodge.

CHAPTER 3
The Shootists

Dodge City was originally a buffalo hunters' town. In fact, it was called Buffalo City when it sprang into existence in 1871—one adobe dwelling and a collection of tents catering to the prodigious thirst of the hunters and of the soldiers stationed five miles downstream in a bend of the Arkansas River at the United States Army's Fort Dodge.

Wide-scale killing of buffalo had begun in the late 1860's, when the supply seemed inexhaustible. General George Crook in 1870 estimated there were fifty million of the shaggy animals grazing on the plains. There were stories of herds temporarily drinking creeks and even rivers dry, estimates of buffalo covering up to twelve hundred square miles. Kansas pioneer Bob Wright would testify, "I have traveled through a herd of them days and days, never out of sight of them." Men shot the animals indiscriminately, for meat to feed the emigrants and railroad crews, for winter robes, or simply for sport.

The slaughter gained new impetus in 1871, the year of Buffalo City's birth, with the news that the hides could be treated in the East to make machine gaskets and power belting, as well as clothing. That was also the year twenty-three-year-old Wyatt Earp wandered into the buffalo camps from his brief stint as a Missouri constable and his brush with the law in the Cherokee Nation.

Though a buffalo hunt required planning and hard work, the profits were great. With hides worth at least three dollars each and cartridges costing only twenty-five cents apiece, as one hunter put it, "every time I fired . . . I got my investment back twelve times over." Also, as his statement implies, the killing of the animals was almost ridiculously easy. The hunter could ride his horse to within a few hundred yards of the beasts, then walk into closer range, position his rest sticks on the earth, lay his Sharps buffalo rifle across them, and begin firing. As the wounded animals "pawed the earth, threw blood from their nostrils, then slowly sank to the ground and died," the other beasts would stare uncomprehendingly. Should one buffalo make a move to lead an exodus, the hunter could quickly drop the animal with a shot to the lungs and continue the carnage. Famed hunter Tom Nixon once killed 120 in this way in just forty minutes.

However, despite the ease with which the animals were dispatched, buffalo hunting was not a job for a solitary man. Each camp needed a variety of workers—wagon driver, watchman, stock tender, cook—who could also act as skinners. In the wake of the killing, the crew faced a grisly job: "With razor-sharp skinning knives, they ripped a carcass down the belly and the inside of each leg. A cut was made around the neck and the hide loosened along the incisions. A rope was tied to the skin at the neck, a hitch taken on a saddle horn, and the skin peeled straight back from head to tail. The heavy hides were loaded into the wagons to be taken back to camp and staked out for drying."

The men who did this work had to be tough, not only to wield the bloody implements of their trade but to endure on strong black coffee and wild game for months on end and to survive the harsh prairie winter weather, with snow-and-sand blizzards that swept down suddenly, plummeting temperatures from seventy-four degrees above zero to twenty below within twenty-four hours.

That winter of 1871–1872, as the years of most intense buffalo slaughter began, Wyatt met in the camps a number of the companions he was to know and work with in Dodge. Foremost among them was William Barclay "Bat" Masterson, whose farming family had just migrated to Sedgwick, Kansas, on the edge of the buffalo range. Five years younger than the rangy Wyatt, Bat was smaller, softer-looking with prominent, expressive eyes and full features. But a fellow buffalo hunter would later describe him as "a chunk of steel."

The Kansas buffalo camps offered ample training for the careers of itinerant peace officers and gamblers which Bat Masterson and Wyatt Earp were to assume. The men regularly handled a variety of guns—six-guns for personal defense, shotguns for hunting the abundant small game of the prairie, Sharps rifles for the buffalo slaughter. They had to be able to defend themselves against hostile elements, hostile Indians, and hostile campmates, many of whom drank copiously and wanted to debate with their fists Wyatt's apparently genuine distaste for liquor. The two newcomers learned some of the nuances of the gambling profession from the interminable games that went on while the hunters were in camp. They were nervy, shrewd young men who became more nervy and shrewd on the prairie—and they became fast friends.

With the end of the hunting season in spring 1872, many hunters drifted in and out of Buffalo City. That summer, an Atchison, Topeka and Santa Fe engineer platted a town around the tents, and in September, the first train puffed into the settlement, rechristened Dodge City. The arrival of the railroad, providing transportation for the hides, led to a peak Kansas hunting season the winter of 1872–1873. An estimated seventy-five thousand animals were felled within sixty to seventy-five miles of Dodge. One old-timer later recalled, "The noise of the guns of hunters could be heard on all sides, rumbling and booming hour after hour, as if a heavy battle were being fought." Now there were stories of how one could walk for miles across the prairie without setting foot on the ground, treading instead on the carcasses of the buffalo. Pioneer-turned-merchant Bob Wright recalled that he and a business partner shipped two hundred thousand buffalo hides in that one season, with at least as many more handled by other Dodge middlemen.

It took one more winter for buffalo to be almost completely obliterated from the Kansas plains. The slaughter around Dodge alone in the years 1872 to 1874 has been estimated at from about one and a half million to three and a half million. Gradually, as the great animals grew scarce, the hunters began congregating around the Kansas cow towns, places such as Ellsworth and Hays and Wichita.

The cow towns are places of myth today; to understand the mentality of men such as Wyatt Earp and Bat Masterson, one has to recognize that Dodge and its sisters were places of frontier myth then as well, that westerners moved about the real late-nineteenth-century West well aware of a West of romantic fantasy that already dominated American imaginations. In 1823, when the trans-Mississippi landscape remained the province of native Indian tribes, fur traders, and mountain men, James Fenimore Cooper had drawn upon the legends of Daniel Boone and worked with the hardy frontiersman image already part of America's pioneer consciousness to produce a powerful western icon, a heroic son of the wilderness with civilized sensibilities—Natty Bumppo. By the time the country found itself in the midst of a war between North and South, the New York dime novel industry was producing for a general readership a slew of stories featuring western frontier heroes in the Natty Bumppo mold.

Thus, the idea of the solitary and stalwart frontiersman, occupying the gray area between civilization and wilderness, between restraint and lawlessness, and ultimately casting his lot with the good and the true through heroic feats of daring was already firmly ingrained in America's understanding of itself. The idea was taken a step further with the emergence of the law-enforcing gunman as hero. Colonel George Ward Nichols probably started this trend with his 1867 *Harper's New Monthly Magazine* article depicting Wild Bill Hickok as a stalwart, steel-nerved dispenser of frontier justice. With this portrayal—and with Ned Buntline's 1869 sensationalized life of western scout William Frederick "Buffalo Bill" Cody—the line between real westerner and romantic hero became hopelessly blurred. Both Wild Bill Hickok and Cody soon capitalized on and added to the romantic image of the frontier hero by playing themselves in western shows for eastern audiences.

Like Hickok and Cody, Wyatt Earp and Bat Masterson

would show that they recognized the power of this romantic myth and could use it to their personal advantage. They would discover that journalists and other writers were eager to disseminate the most amazing tales about the frontier lawman and his prowess; the two would gladly provide such tales. Wyatt in particular would do so in such a way as to cast all of his actions in the noblest and most daring light.

Thus, Wyatt Earp's Kansas experiences have become embroidered in a tapestry of myth, begun by Wyatt himself in his own accounts of his life, furthered by Earp champion Clum and a few other old-time admirers, and developed by his biographer Stuart Lake. Lake would build on Wyatt's own claims, appropriate for him the exploits of Kansas friends such as Masterson, and coolly drop him into storied Wild West confrontations to produce in 1931 a biography that presented the ultimate western hero.

So, after the buffalo-hunting season of 1873–1874, the Wyatt Earp of myth was in Ellsworth, Kansas, facing another peripheral man, Texas gambler and gunman Ben Thompson. In Wichita and in Dodge, this mythical Earp repeatedly and miraculously caused Texas cowboys to cringe simply through the force of his commanding presence. In both towns, so the legend goes, Wyatt Earp single-handedly held off anarchy, as represented by the bands of malevolent cowboys and cattle kings who put a price on his head.

None of this is reflected in the newspapers and other documents of the period. Instead, two things can be said of Wyatt's cow town experiences. First, he became a shootist, a member of that loose fraternity of men, good, bad, and in between, who derived strength from their guns and their own willingness to use them, and second, he did have an able but undistinguished career as a Dodge lawman.

Wyatt Earp had walked smack-dab into not only the era of the frontiersman but also the era of the gunfighter. Rangers on the Texas frontier during its republic days had established the gun-toting tradition; forty-niners bound for California had continued it, as had partisans in the fight over "Bleeding Kansas." Then came the greatest impetus to the pistol-packing tradition: the Civil War. This great national bloodletting stimulated gunplay across the West by increasing

American toleration of violence and encouraging "a high respect" for the virtues of physical courage and boldness, "even among criminals." It also contributed to western gunplay by bringing technical improvements in firearms and churning out thousands of trained fighters. Further, it stimulated smoldering prejudices between men of southern origins and Democratic leanings, such as the Texas cowboys, and men from the North with Republican affiliations, such as Wyatt Earp and his brothers.

The annals of the gunfighter era are filled with the names of brothers and cousins, whole male lines of families bound together in a precarious, shifting existence in the West. Ironically, the younger members of an extended family would often prove more violent than would the Civil War veterans. Indeed, a number of the premier shootists of the 1870's and early 1880's, the peak period for western gunfights, would be those who had missed out by chance of birth on the glory and gore of the civil conflict.

The shootists shared a fascination with guns and ammunition, testing and modifying different weapons, experimenting with bullet weights and grades of powder as Colt, Smith & Wesson, and Remington flooded the market with new arms in the early 1870's. Gunfighters wanted something with real stopping potential; many quickly found the 1873 army model Colt revolver, the six-shot, single-action Peacemaker, to their liking. (A legend persists that mythmaking author Ned Buntline himself came to Dodge and presented "Buntline specials" to Wyatt and Dodge's other peace officers, but this idea has been effectively disputed.)

Most of the men who went "heeled" would stick their preferred weapon in a pocket or belt rather than in a holster, though notorious badman John Wesley Hardin "was said to have worn two holsters sewn to a vest" with the pistol butts "pointed inward across his chest." If a man carried two weapons, one usually served as a backup; the ambidextrous fellow with two six-guns blazing is primarily a creature of myth.

Not surprisingly, the gunmen were drawn to jobs requiring firearm possession and use—on one side of the law, as peace officers and range detectives; on the other, as stage, bank, and train robbers and rustlers; in between, as gamblers,

ranchers, and cowboys. Violence-prone southwestern cattleman Clay Allison, a Civil War veteran, coined the "shootist"
term by announcing it as his occupation. Allison, whose exploits included riding naked through Mobeetie, Texas, visited
Dodge on occasion. He knew how to use a gun and liked to
take the law into his own hands to dispense a rather warped
justice. He may well have been psychotic. His notoriety spread
after he decapitated a lynching victim and displayed the head
in Cimarron near Dodge in 1870.

The shootists, whatever side of the law they happened to
fall upon, all shared a tough pride, even arrogance, and a certain disregard for life, expressed in a common tendency "to
kill when provoked." Two gamblers might resort to gunplay,
as might two drunken cowboys. But ominously and increasingly, a line of enmity was drawn in both Dodge and
Tombstone between the men who spent much of their lives in
the saddle—gun-toting ranchers and cowboys with southern
roots and allegiances—and the town-dwelling peace officers
and gamblers, who usually hailed from the northern states.

Whatever their allegiances, the gunfighters' proficiency
has been vastly overrated. While courage and skill were obviously important, the shootists themselves recognized quick
but careful deliberation—cool assessment of the situation and
actions based on that assessment—as the most important at-
tribute of a man about to place his life on the line. Bat Masterson would write in 1907, "I have known men in the West
whose courage could not be questioned and whose expertness
with the pistol was simply marvelous, who fell easy victims before men who added deliberation to the other two qualities."
The best at combining the three qualities, Masterson asserted,
were Wild Bill Hickok and a number of part-time or full-time
denizens of Dodge—Ben Thompson, Wyatt Earp, Doc Holliday, buffalo hunter and lawman Big Bill Tilghman, dance hall
entrepreneur Rowdy Joe Lowe, saloon man Luke Short.

Milt Hinkle, son of Dodge city lawman George Hinkle,
would count Tilghman among the best, but would imply that
Earp and Masterson didn't give men a fighting chance; further, "Both were known as gunmen, and both were known to
have been on the shady side of the fence at times." However,
Dodge resident O. H. Simpson, who often heard old-timers

rate the gunfighters, would admiringly single out Wyatt Earp as a paragon "almost invariably receiving credit for having a mentality that would function under the greatest stress."

But whatever their abilities, nobody was as proficient as the legends claim. Wild Bill Hickok was perhaps the best marksman in the West—many people who had seen him shoot said so—but his prowess was nonetheless inflated and mythologized through word of mouth and the cheap fictionalizations of his exploits. For example, as sheriff of Ellis County, Kansas, in 1869, Hickok reputedly dispatched an obstreperous teamster named Sam Strawhim in a Hays saloon by looking at Strawhim in a mirror and firing without turning around. More realistic accounts show that Strawhim threatened the sheriff with a beer glass and Hickok faced his adversary and shot him in the head.

With other shootists, either contemporaries or their own actions dispute the legends of proficiency. Oklahoma outlaw Al Jennings was reputedly one of the best marksmen in the West, able to "hit a can thrown into the air, or move it over the ground, with well-placed shots." But those who knew him refuted this claim, with one remarking, "I happen to know that Mr. Jennings can't hit a gallon can at twenty yards with aimed fire once out of ten times. I've seen him try."

Often, the legends were proven wrong when two gunmen actually began shooting at each other. Both Charlie Harrison and Jim Levy had reputations as superior marksmen when they engaged in a gun duel in Cheyenne, Wyoming, in 1877, but the two exchanged seven shots with only one connecting. When Harrison finally fell wounded, Levy hurried to the fallen duelist and finished him with one last shot. The chief concern when a gun battle erupted "was not hitting the other man first or in the right spot but just *hitting* him. In gunfight after gunfight . . . men emptied their weapons at their adversaries without wounding them, or inflicting only minor wounds."

Of course, part of the problem with the legends of prowess lay with the guns themselves. Even if a man used a weapon enough to familiarize himself with its peculiarities—particularly the way its sights aligned—he would still find variations based on the type of ammunition and even between one cartridge of a certain kind and the next. With practice and a good match between gun and ammunition, even a good gunman would still experience a range of five or six inches when shooting a Colt .45 cartridge from a distance of fifty yards.*

There were embarrassing accidents, too. When Wyatt Earp was enforcing the law in Wichita in early 1876, the Wichita *Beacon* reported that "policeman Erp [*sic*]" was sitting in the back room of a saloon when "his revolver slipped from his holster . . . causing a discharge of one of the barrels." And Arizona pioneer James Hamilton would recall an incident in George Spangenberg's Tombstone gun store when "I found one of the Earps and companions examining a new Colt .45 in the light of the door.

"Geo. and I were looking over the display of .45's in the glass case on the counter, when we got the surprise of the loud report and the crash of a bullet into the floor just behind me. Looking with surprise at the gun handlers, they met our gaze with a smile and 'beg pardon' for carelessness in letting the trigger slip."

Billy Breakenridge, a crack shot himself, would recall a time when Johnny Behan's gun accidentally discharged, nearly striking the deputy. In all such cases, the solution was to keep one chamber empty and leave the hammer on it, a practice Breakenridge followed assiduously after his close call.

Sometimes the mistakes were not minor but tragic. In 1871 in Abilene, Kansas, Marshal Mike Williams was called to the scene of an evening disturbance. Scheduled to board a train in forty-five minutes in order to see his ailing wife in Kansas City, Williams let famed shootist Hickok go to the scene of the trouble in his stead. As a crowd gathered, Hickok and the leader of a band of drunken Texans exchanged gunshots. Williams appeared and pushed through the crowd to aid Hickok. The latter, seeing the movement, turned and fired. Williams died instantly with a bullet in the head; the stunned and sorrowful Hickok paid his funeral expenses.

Despite such accidents, and despite purposeful attempts on life, the gunfighter seldom actually killed another man.

---

*See Dan Pribilski, "Straight-Shootin' .45s," *The Roundup*, vol. 25, no. 6 (June 1987), pp. 24–25.

When he did so, he did not necessarily adhere to a clear code of western honor. In the same year that Hickok shot Strawhim, he was reported to have tricked Bill Mulrey by calling to someone apparently behind Mulrey's back, "Don't shoot him, boys," then firing on his disconcerted adversary. This story probably has more basis in fact than the mirror trick, simply because a shootist, once he had decided firing was necessary, took the most efficient course he could toward downing his man.

But like the stories of amazing proficiency, the tales of number of kills were vastly inflated. In 1881, a New York newspaper would report that Bat Masterson had killed twenty-six men, leading a Kansas editor to argue that it was "too much for a small man only twenty-seven years of age, and we call for a recount." Subsequently, historians have been able to lay only one killing at Masterson's door, and they are not even completely sure of that.

The violent personal legends of the gunfighters parallel the violent legends about the wide-open towns they frequented. As Dodge evolved from buffalo-hunting center to premier cattle town, it developed such a bloodthirsty reputation that a reporter in July 1878 felt compelled to write, "It is not nearly so awful a place as reports make it. It is not true that the stranger in the place runs a risk of being shot down in cold blood, for no offense whatever." He provided scant reassurance to any nervous tenderfoot. What, after all, might constitute an offense in this strange and volatile environment? Besides, easterners, midwesterners, and far westerners in their relatively stable and established communities remained titillated by tales of sin and bloodshed in these raw frontier settlements. Dodge residents disputed their lurid reputation, but at the same time they enjoyed such stories as that of the drunken cowboy who boarded a train and announced he wanted to go to hell. "All right," replied the conductor, "give me a dollar and get off at Dodge."

Historians have estimated that nine to fifteen men were killed during Dodge's first year of existence. Bob Wright remembered that twenty-five were killed in shooting scrapes that year, leading to the formation of a vigilance committee. But "hard, bad men" got into the organization and used it for their own ends. Major Richard Dodge, Fort Dodge commander, had to step in and establish order in 1873. He mused that "roughs" were taken into vigilante organizations to add strength "until, as I have often seen, a vigilance committee organized by good men in good faith has become simply an organized band of robbers and cutthroats."

Vigilantism would surface in Tombstone, too, and play a part in the tensions and killings there. Even though frontier communities quickly fell under some legal jurisdiction—federal, state or territory, county, and city—the fact remained that residents often perceived indifferent and/or inadequate law enforcement at any or all of these levels.

Thus, men took the law into their own hands, reaping much needed changes—or bloody havoc. "We are the mayor and the recorder, the hangman and the laws," proclaimed one member of San Francisco's 1850 Committee of Vigilance, a group that did perform nobly in halting a band of former American soldiers and Australian toughs who were terrorizing the city's Peruvian and Chilean community. Other committees throughout the West took their cue from the San Francisco group. At their best, the vigilantes acted in the interests of "an overwhelming majority" of citizens, including the community's best members. The men regulated themselves, acted "quickly and effectively," brought about "a more stable and orderly condition," and quietly disbanded when their job was done.

But often "the line between extralegal organizations who claimed to preserve order and extralegal gangs accused of creating disorder was a fine one indeed." Vigilantes frequently became armed forces of one racial, class, or cultural group moving against other groups with opposing interests. And as Major Dodge hinted, a dark bloodlust quickly slipped into many vigilante activities. In 1851, when western vigilantes hanged two men, they did so by gleefully pulling on the ropes, "nearly dash[ing] the brains of the doomed men against the beams from which they were suspended" as a watching crowd cursed, jeered, and told jokes.

More than twenty years later, vigilantes in Phoenix, Arizona, watched silently as a horse team bolted from under the feet of one hanging condemned murderer, then another. The first man sank and slowly strangled. The second jumped high, came down hard, and broke his neck. One observer ended the silence with a wry comment: "Why, the son of a gun must have been hanged before. He knows just how to do it."

Lynching was used as a response to frontier tensions and violence only in isolated instances, however; Dodge would have only two lynchings, Tombstone one. These frontier towns muddled toward a balance between license and restraint with less stringent measures—or gunfire.

From 1873 to 1875, Dodge maintained a tenuous claim on law and order. The buffalo trade was dying, the great animals' bones bleaching beside the railway, but the settlement remained a point of supply for the military garrisons and posts scattered across the prairies and plains, as well as for various ranches, hunters' camps, and settlements. Then, in 1875, Dodge began to develop as a cattle-shipping point. As the country around the cow towns to the east was becoming too well settled, railroad officials looked to the former buffalo-hunting capital in southwestern Kansas as the destination for ranchers and cowhands driving their herds to market from Texas, western Kansas, eastern Colorado, New Mexico, and Indian Territory (now Oklahoma). Dodge would rapidly become "the greatest cattle market in the world," with more than two hundred thousand head arriving on the outskirts of town in a single season.

The largest influx of beeves came from the Lone Star State, driven north by Texas cowboys. These men led both idyllic and incredibly arduous lives on the trail. At its best, the drover's job involved riding over a wildflower-strewn prairie on a balmy day as the cattle flowed forward almost of their own accord. At its worst, the job brought monotony, discomfort, and danger.

The cattle outfits would form in the spring, as grass became plentiful for the herds to fatten on along the way. "Point men" were needed to ride "out and well back from the lead cattle," then move forward and close in to guide the herd in the direction desired. Swing men "rode well out from the advancing column, warding off range cattle and seeing that none of the herd wandered away or dropped out." The drovers brought with them their gaily decorated saddles, their bridles with ornamented bits, and their oiled canvas slickers, but horses were provided by the cattle owner. Each cowboy rotated six to ten mounts during a drive, selecting the steadiest horse of the lot for night guard duty, as the cattle were most likely to stampede during the hours set aside for rest.

The men slept in the clothes they wore during the day, using boots and coats for pillows. Often, they would wake to find the cattle had naturally begun grazing on ahead with the dawn; after a hurried breakfast, the drovers would ride out to spend sixteen to eighteen hours in the saddle, covering perhaps twenty miles with their charges. Water and grass were prime concerns during the day; the men tried to provide a grazing period for the animals in the late afternoon before stopping and bedding them down for the night.

In the darkness, stampedes became a primary concern, for they were frequent enough occurrences that no outfit could hope to escape one completely. Former cowboy Andy Adams vividly described the circumstances in his fictionalized but authentically detailed *Log of a Cowboy*: "A stampede is the natural result of fear, and at night or in an uncertain light, this timidity might be imparted to an entire herd by a flash of lightning or a peal of thunder, while the stumbling of a night horse, or the scent of some wild animal, would in a moment's time, from frightening a few head, so infect a herd as to throw them into the wildest panic."

When such a panic occurred, the drovers spent a grueling night trying to bring the herd under control and often spent days rounding up their wayward charges.

By the time these men hit Dodge, they were ready to relax and to use their hard-earned wages to luxuriate in any riotous excess offered. Their business would bring prosperity to Dodge; their wild ways would keep Dodge citizens on edge.

On Christmas Eve 1875, before the large cattle influx began, a group of Dodge City businessmen met to appoint temporary officials for their just incorporated settlement. In this meeting, a split developed that would widen through Dodge's heyday and be echoed in Tombstone a few years later. Some of the businessmen preferred a laissez-faire attitude toward cowboys and other potential troublemakers who came to Dodge to carouse. These businessmen, conscious of the revenues they could enjoy, felt that the brawling and noisy midnight hurrahs other cow towns had experienced should be tolerated as a generally harmless release of pent-up energies. The law-and-order businessmen, however, argued that stringent laws would have to be enforced to maintain the stability and safety necessary for Dodge to flourish.

Behind these views were assumptions about the character of the revelers themselves. To the wide-open faction of businessmen, the cowboys were basically decent young men out for a good time. To the law-and-order advocates, they were generally low-class and treacherous malcontents who had to be controlled as quickly and forcefully as possible.

In April 1876, a member of the law-and-order faction, George Hoover, was elected mayor in the first municipal election. He appointed three-hundred-pound saloon operator Larry Deger as town marshal and gunman Jack Allen as assistant marshal, then set out to enforce such ordinances as a ban on carrying of firearms in town, extended to all except peace officers.

Allen disappeared almost immediately, but cow towns usually had up to five assistants or city policemen, particularly during the cattle season. Two new Dodge officers surfaced on the heels of Allen's departure—Wyatt Earp and Bat Masterson.

Although Wyatt had just been forced out of Wichita by a city commission charging him with vagrancy, the charge was not necessarily an aspersion on his character. Even Wild Bill Hickok, always associated with the law, had had vagrancy charges slapped on him by nervous frontier townspeople who recognized his shooting prowess, and thus his potential for attracting or causing trouble. Sometimes a shootist's background and reputation worked against him, and sometimes it worked for him, with city officials favoring the tough man who had moved in a wild milieu as one best suited to control it. Wyatt had, after all, spent almost a year policing the wild cow town of Wichita. Wichita newspapers took little notice of Policeman "Erp," but at least one old-timer remembered him as a highly dependable officer, and a Wichita newspaper did note upon his firing, "It is but justice to Erp [*sic*] to say he has made an excellent officer, and hitherto his conduct has been unexceptionable."

Bat had just spent two eventful years primarily in Texas, beginning with a sojourn in the Panhandle that turned into a fight for his life. He was one of twenty-eight buffalo hunters, most part-time inhabitants of Dodge, who had ranged southward and settled into the old Indian trading post of Adobe Walls in the spring and summer of 1874.

The Kiowa, Comanche, Cheyenne, and Arapaho Indians who roamed the Panhandle decided to drive the invaders out under the leadership of half-breed Quanah Parker and at the urging of Comanche medicine man Isati, whose name musically translates into "Rear End of the Wolf." On June 27, 1874, the hunters found themselves under siege, outmanned at least eight to one. But with the help of rapid-fire Sharps .50 caliber rifles, they managed to hold the Indians off and straggle back to Dodge.

Bat found trouble in Texas again in January 1876, when he and Corporal Melvin King got into a dispute over a dance hall girl in Sweetwater. Both King and the girl were killed; legend has it that the latter was fatally wounded when she threw herself in front of Bat. Altercations such as this are told and retold a thousand different ways, with the motivations, preliminaries, and actual shooting changing with each telling. A Jacksboro, Texas, newspaper simply reported that King had been killed by a "citizen."

Shortly thereafter, Bat again returned to Dodge. Now twenty-two, he was no longer a scruffy adolescent prairie hunter, but a dapper, impeccably neat gambler-in-training. His old friend Wyatt at twenty-seven was looking smoother and more mature, too. A photo of Wyatt taken about 1868 shows a young man with a sharply chiseled face and a shock of unruly hair; by his Tombstone years, he would have developed more fully in the face and neatly subdued his hair.

If the two were looking more refined, they were still as tough as their experiences and natures made them. Any troublemaker in the streets of Dodge was quickly "buffaloed," slammed on the side of the head with the three-pound barrel of a revolver by one of the peace officers. Wyatt in particular favored and perfected this method; he also punched and slapped and used whatever force necessary. Bat Masterson would relate that a Dodge city alderman once ordered Wyatt to do something, then, when the deputy hesitated, stormed forward and attempted to rip his badge off. "Wyatt knocked him down as soon as he laid his hands on him, and then reached down and picked him up with one hand and slammed a few hooks and upper cuts into his face, dragged his limp form over to the city calaboose, and chucked it in one of the cells."

One Dodge old-timer described a "typical arrest" to his son. Wyatt had just searched a cowboy in a billiard hall and had taken a knife and shotgun cartridges from him.

> Earp then pushed him towards the door and the cowboy spun about and returned the compliment whereupon Earp punched him in the face and dragged him towards the street, on the sidewalk the prisoner began to struggle telling Earp to let go and cursing him loudly soon they were fighting and Earp butted the man then tripped him, sending him sprawling into the street. Before he got up Earp cracked him over the head with his revolver opening a deep gash.

If the treatment sounds ruthless, most Dodge residents agreed that a degree of ruthlessness was necessary. Bob Wright would later write that cowboys delighted in shooting up and taking over cow towns, but the tough hunters and freighters employed as lawmen—plus a strict gun-checking policy—foiled their few attempts to do so in Dodge.

More telling than the "typical arrest" of the cowboy was Ben Thompson's account of an arrest Wyatt made in Wichita during his year as a city policeman there. In Stuart Lake's Earp biography, Wyatt, with six-guns in holsters, bravely walked up to a gun-pointing Melvin King, the man who would soon be killed by Bat Masterson in Texas, then slapped him, disarmed him, and took him "by the scruff of the neck" to jail. Thompson, however, told a marshal that Wyatt was "covered by two men standing with shotguns behind him" when the incident occurred, that he hit King "across the head with the barrel of his six-shooter four or five times," and that the three then took King to the jail, robbed him, and beat him, "almost . . . to death."

A mutual antipathy quickly developed between Wyatt and the drovers crowding into Dodge. The Texans reportedly called Wyatt, Bat, and their friends the Fighting Pimps because of their affinity for Dodge's brothels and their liaisons with young women of dubious social standing. And Cowboy Pink Simms, who later became a deputy United States marshal, provided support for Thompson by describing Wyatt as "an efficient officer if he could surround himself with a bunch of killers." To Simms, Wyatt "had courage of a foxy type" and was "no lone wolf" but "always the leader of a vicious pack."

If Wyatt's ruthlessness did not endear him to some, he nonetheless forged alliances in Dodge with other shootists, such as gambler Luke Short, "the undertaker's friend" who allegedly "shot 'em where it didn't show." Bat Masterson would recall that Short shot a man in the cheek—certainly a place that shows—in Leadville in the late seventies and also dispatched a number of Sioux braves while selling alcohol to the Indians in Nebraska. However, like that of other shootists, Short's reputation far exceeded his actions. He was a tough customer nonetheless, an unschooled cowhand who had turned to selling whiskey from a barrel in Dodge during its buffalo camp days, then advanced to the gambling trade. If there was liquor or gambling to be found, Short was usually involved; he would run Dodge saloons and gaming tables and go on the western gambling circuit.

Wyatt also had the pleasure of seeing brother Morgan added to the police force when Bat Masterson decided to depart for the Black Hills gold rush to do some gambling. Morgan, too, would get itchy feet and move on to Montana, but Wyatt always liked gathering his brothers around.

Most important, he maintained the goodwill of the respectable people of Dodge, serving as a deacon at Dodge's Union Church and receiving favorable notice in Dodge's county newspaper, the *Ford County Globe* as "one of the most efficient officers Dodge ever had." (Biographer Lake, intent on legend building, merrily changed it to "the most efficient officer" when he quoted the *Globe*.)

The good reputation that Wyatt enjoyed in Dodge resulted at least in part from the fact that he did the dirty work for the town's God-fearing, law-abiding citizens. Many did see him, however, as a courageous, upstanding officer, and an inscription in a Bible presented to Wyatt by the law firm of Sutton and Colburn indicates that some Dodge citizens found him far more saint than sinner: "To Wyatt S. Earp as a slight recognition of his many Christian virtues and steady following in the footsteps of the meek and lowly Jesus."

He also demonstrated a sense of humor not apparent after his departure from Dodge. The cow town was a practical joker's paradise, with the most common victim being the latest tenderfoot who believed all those wild shoot-'em-up frontier stories. Two men would invite the new arrival on an antelope hunt, then surreptitiously unload his gun or substitute blanks while telling him chilling tales of Indian barbarity. When they had ridden a short distance from Dodge, a band of blood-thirsty renegades would appear on cue, sending the terrified newcomer hurtling back to Dodge, where a crowd had gathered to watch his frantic entrance. Behind him would come the other "hunters" and the Indians, Dodge residents dressed in Indian regalia salvaged from the Battle of Adobe Walls. The trick backfired only once, when a newcomer, a jeweler by trade, hedged his bets by secretly packing a second gun, then began firing real bullets at the startled "Indians."

Bob Wright recounted a similar trick played by Wyatt and Bat, returned to Dodge after his gambling trip. An eastern doctor, a specialist in "venereal and private diseases," assumed that such a sinful town as Dodge would have many cases in his specialty, and town jokesters assured him by letter that Dodge was indeed overflowing with diseased specimens. The good doctor arrived, and a lecture was arranged. On the evening of the lecture, Wyatt sat on one side of the speaker, Bat on the other, with other "gun men" clustered close to the stage. As the doctor began to talk, he was interrupted and insulted first by one, then by another skeptical listener. The two seated on the platform threatened to shoot anyone who interrupted; as soon as the next epithet was hurled, they started firing along with one of the gunmen at the front, sending the doctor and most of the audience scrambling into the night.

In such ways, the shootists played with their town's and their own fierce image even as it developed. An itinerant preacher extracted a promise from Mysterious Dave Mather, another gunman and sometime Dodge lawman, to attend a

Dodge revival service. "Dave would not break his word," Bob Wright commented laconically. "He was never known to do that. If he promised a man he would kill him, Dave was sure to do it." Mather's arrival at the evening service sent the preacher and many members of his audience into joyful paroxysms and avowals that they could now die content with "the wickedest man in the country" in the fold. Mather responded by announcing that perhaps dying would be a good idea, as they had professed a willingness and thereby could all avoid backsliding. He proposed to kill himself after killing all the others, then proceeded to fire over the preacher's head. When everyone ducked for cover, he strolled to the door, commenting, "You are all a set of liars and frauds, you don't want to go to heaven with me at all."

Mather drifted on into Las Vegas, New Mexico, where he would work as a lawman and become implicated in a series of train and stage robberies. Wyatt and Bat continued to make Dodge their base. Wyatt found ready employment as an assistant city marshal when he wasn't on gambling trips; he also worked as a faro dealer in Dodge.

Wyatt reportedly gained a reputation in the cow town of Hays in the early 1870's for being "up to some dishonest trick every time" he gambled. On at least two other occasions in his life, too, he would be charged with running confidence games. But he would often work without apparent controversy in that most prestigious of gambling jobs dealing faro. Besides, it was generally accepted that professional gamblers would do some cheating. The skill with which they did it was what mattered. "Tinhorn gamblers" who used marked cards and other cheap tricks were usually regarded with contempt by a frontier town's citizenry. But men such as Dick Clark, the gentlemanly owner of Tombstone's Alhambra Saloon, were admired for their class and cunning. Clark would turn his glittering diamond ring to his palm and use it as a mirror when dealing in a big game. As one Tombstone saloonkeeper later testified, "Wherever skill of the mind or fingers could be employed to bring in the money, Dick Clark and his brethren used what gifts they had."

In short, cheating—if done with finesse—was considered part of the game. The *Daily Nugget,* in reporting on a Boston man who had perfected a faro system that precluded cheating, commented, "Singular as it may seem, nobody who plays the game can be found to favor the new system."

Obviously, when a gambler cheated, he wanted to do so in such a way that he could not be challenged. Professional gamblers had to be men who knew how to avoid trouble, who could move smoothly through the saloon environment, where liquor and bravado often added up to trouble.

As the careers of Wyatt Earp and Bat Masterson attest, a man could be both trouble-attracting gunman and trouble-deflecting gambler. Each role called for nerve and skill, with "dexterity and intuition [developed] to an almost superhuman degree." In Tombstone, "There were several of the two-gun type of gamblers, but these men never made any gun-play while at their games."

Bat Masterson frequented the Dodge gambling tables while working as undersheriff to Ford County Sheriff Charles Bassett. In 1877 he ran against Dodge City Marshal Larry Deger for Bassett's county law position. Announcing his candidacy, Bat stated, "I have no pledges to make, as pledges are usually considered before election to be mere clap-trap." He associated with the wide-open-town faction and ran as its candidate, beating law-and-order candidate Deger by a narrow margin in November; the next month, the Dodge town council removed Deger as marshal and appointed Bat's brother Ed in his place.

Wyatt was gambling in Texas at the time; he did not return until early May, a month after Ed Masterson had been gunned down by a drunken cowboy outside Josh Webb's Lady Gay Saloon. Researchers have tended to portray Ed as weaker, less up to the task of law enforcement than Bat or the Earp brothers, but they seem to base this assessment on the fact that he got killed in the line of duty and the others didn't. Ed was trying to disarm the cowboy when he was shot point-blank through the abdomen, leaving a hole "large enough for the introduction of the whole pistol." He fatally wounded the assailant, shot an accomplice, then walked two hundred yards to Hoover's Saloon, where he announced to the bartender that he had been shot. Losing consciousness, he died thirty to forty minutes later.

Stunned city residents draped their doors in crepe, and former County Sheriff Bassett took over as marshal. He appointed Wyatt one of three assistant marshals when he showed up in May. Dodge was gearing up for its biggest cattle season yet, with thirteen hundred Texas cowhands driving some 265,000 longhorns to town through the spring and summer and establishing temporary cattle camps "that extended for miles along the Arkansas."

Despite Ed Masterson's killing and the cowboy influx, in June 1878 the *Ford County Globe* revealed the generally mundane nature of law enforcement in a wild and woolly frontier town by applauding Wyatt "for his endeavors to stop the bean business [shooting beans through straws at patrons' heads] at the theater the other night." Indeed, western lawmen regularly performed such chores as shooting stray dogs, removing obstructions in the streets, and inspecting flues, chimneys, and sidewalks.

Masterson's death, however, had shown how close the frontier lawman walked to a sudden violent encounter. In July, Wyatt shot and killed cowboy George Hoy to log his only recorded killing in Dodge. Wyatt and fellow assistant marshal Jim Masterson, a second brother of Bat's, were on duty outside the Comique Theater where the celebrated performer Eddie Foy was in the midst of a recital of "Kalamazoo in Michigan." Also inside were Bat Masterson and Doc Holliday, newly arrived from Texas. A group of cowboys were riding by on their way back to camp when Hoy suddenly broke away from his fellows and came toward the theater at a gallop, firing three shots through its wall.

Foy later recalled, "Everyone dropped to the floor at once, according to custom." Despite his suicidal tendencies, Doc Holliday was not overly anxious to end his own existence, for Foy reported that the dentist and Masterson in particular impressed him with "the instantaneous manner in which they flattened out like pancakes on the floor. I had thought I was pretty agile myself, but those fellows had me beaten by seconds at that trick."

Wyatt returned the fire and shattered Hoy's arm; the cowboy would die about a month later, after gangrene had set in. Legend claims Hoy's bullets were intended for Wyatt, the terror of the cowboys, but neither Foy nor Wyatt's friend Bat entertained this possibility, instead speculating that Hoy had had a difference with the theater's proprietor or one of the chorus girls—or that he didn't like Foy's act.

Wyatt claimed another attack on his life about the time of the Hoy incident—an assassination attempt foiled by Doc Holliday, who "saw a man draw on me behind my back. 'Look out, Wyatt!' he shouted, but while the words were coming out [of] his mouth he had jerked his pistol out of his pocket and shot the other fellow before the latter could fire."

This story has not been substantiated in the records of the period, and the account certainly inflates Doc's gun proficiency in light of subsequent confrontations. But such an incident would explain Wyatt's loyalty to his volatile sidekick, particularly when such loyalty would prove costly in Tombstone.

As summer gave way to fall, shootist and cattleman Clay Allison himself came to Dodge, giving rise to a number of legendary stories. He was supposedly gunning for any Dodge City peace officer and George Hoy's killer Wyatt Earp in particular. Depending on which version one chooses to believe, he either cowed the officers into disappearing from the streets until his departure or was met with effective, efficient law enforcement (in the person of Wyatt Earp, of course). One old-timer related that Allison contemplated a rampage but was dissuaded by a ranching friend dispatched by Bat Masterson.

Records show that Allison visited Dodge in early August and again in September but reveal no hint of disturbances. In the latter month, peace officers had their hands full with a real Indian scare. On September 21, the Dodge City *Times* reported "great excitement all week over the news brought in almost hourly of murder and depredations" by Chief Dull Knife's band of Northern Cheyennes who had deserted their Indian Nations Reservation to return to their former Bighorn Mountains hunting grounds. Wyatt received notice in the local paper as one of the leaders in extinguishing a house fire believed to have been set by Indians four miles west of Dodge.

If Allison did not cause trouble that fall, another cattleman certainly did. In July, Wyatt brought Jim Kennedy, son of prominent Texas rancher Mifflin Kennedy, into Dodge police court on the charge of carrying a pistol; the next month Marshal Bassett picked him up on a disorderly charge. Kennedy also had a run-in with Dodge Mayor James Kelley, who became incensed and beat him up. Nursing a grudge against all of Dodge, but against Kelly in particular, Kennedy rode into town under cover of morning darkness on October 4 and fired into Kelley's bedroom.

The mayor, however, was ill and in the army hospital at Fort Dodge. He had lent the use of his home to the popular Varieties theater performer Dora Hand. Jim Masterson and Wyatt came running at the sound of the shot and found Hand lying dead in Kelley's bed with a bullet through her chest. A posse quickly formed: County Sheriff Bat Masterson, Deputy Sheriffs Bill Tilghman and Bill Duffey, City Marshal Bassett, and Assistant Marshal Earp. They caught up with Kennedy, killing his horse and shattering his left arm with gunfire when he attempted to flee. Bat Masterson later reported he could hear Kennedy's bones "craunch" with the impact. To the young rancher's surprise, he was charged not with the murder of James Kelley but with the killing of the lovely Dora. The charge was to make him very unpopular, although he would eventually get off because of insufficient evidence.

As 1878 gave way to 1879, Wyatt Earp began to grow dissatisfied with Dodge. This may have been in part because his young friend Bat seemed to be garnering all the leading roles. In January 1879, Bat would add to his county sheriff title that of deputy United States marshal, and in March and June he would command companies of men en route to Colorado to participate in the Royal Gorge War, a bitter battle between two railroads over which was authorized to build through the gorge toward Leadville.

Then, too, Dodge was getting a little too sedate, losing its "snap," as Wyatt would later relate, and becoming downright boring during the static winter months. There *was* a famous gunfight in April of '79 in the Long Branch Saloon that provided some excitement and proved how farcical such fights could be. Freighter Levi Richardson, a former crack shot buffalo hunter, came up against gambler Cock-eyed Frank Loving in a dispute over a woman. Richardson fired and missed; so did Loving. Richardson fired three more times, all misses;

Loving responded with three as well, two of them hits, and got his man.

The gunfight provided fuel for numerous discussions among the shootists as to how Loving had carried the day. But a number of Dodge's gunmen had moved on, restless and looking for new opportunities. Even Doc Holliday, who had been regarded as "a sort of grouch" in Dodge, had cleared out in less than a year, going to Trinidad, Colorado, where he reportedly wounded "a young sport named Kid Colton," then followed Dave Mather and another former Dodge lawman, Josh Webb, to Las Vegas, New Mexico.

Somewhere there was a town where Wyatt Earp could really make his mark, and all the latest talk was of Tombstone, that city of silver dreams developing in the Arizona desert. Brother Jim came up from Fort Worth to join Wyatt, and the latter resigned his assistant marshal position to head for Las Vegas, then Arizona. The *Ford County Globe* on September 9 reported his departure. It also reported a recent "Day of Carnival," with "slugging & wrestling" and water, slop, and rotten-egg slinging: "The 'finest work' and neatest polishes were said to have been executed by Mr. Wyatt Earp."

Wyatt left such jocularity behind. He took with him an antipathy for cowboys, a penchant for quick and violent responses to threatening situations, a rigid loyalty to his brothers and Doc Holliday, and a desire to grab a bigger share of the political and economic pie the next time around. All of these modes of thinking and acting would lead him into trouble in Tombstone, where by midsummer 1880 the Earp brothers were firmly establishing themselves in the fabric of town life and Wyatt was wearing a star.

CHAPTER 4
"A Pretty Hard Reputation"

No sooner had Wyatt Earp captured the prized deputy sheriff job in Tombstone in July 1880 than an incident occurred which brought the Earps into opposition with Frank McLaury. It began when thieves stole six government mules from the army's Camp Rucker, situated on the White River east of Tombstone and south of the rustler headquarters of Galeyville. Lieutenant J. H. Hurst quickly arrived in Tombstone with a contingent of soldiers; armed with the intelligence that the animals might be hidden on the McLaury ranch, he recruited Wyatt, Virgil, Morgan, and Wells Fargo agent Marshall Williams to go with the troops to the site on the Babocomari.

Demythologizing critics of the Earps have questioned what business the three brothers had accompanying the soldiers, but Virgil was, after all, a deputy federal marshal, and Wyatt a deputy sheriff. Further, both Virgil and Wyatt would appoint Morgan a special officer as the need arose.

So at least two of the brothers rode onto the McLaury ranch on the morning of July 25, 1880, with the power of the law behind them. Frank McLaury either failed to recognize or to acknowledge this fact when he recounted that Lieutenant

Hurst "came to my ranch with an escort of soldiers accompanied by several citizens" and informed him of the theft.

Wyatt Earp would later state that the searchers had tracked the mules to the ranch and found a branding iron used to alter the government brand. He also would complain that he and his brothers were dismissed by Hurst after the latter "made some kind of a compromise" with McLaury's friend and fellow rancher Frank Patterson in order to retrieve the animals.

Despite the parlay with Patterson, the lieutenant returned empty-handed. On July 30, he published a notice in the *Epitaph* promising rewards for the "arrest, trial and conviction" of the thieves and for the return of the animals. In the *Epitaph* he stated, "It is known that the stolen animals were secreted at or in the vicinity of the McLaury Brothers ranch on the Babacomari [*sic*] river on July 15th, 1880; and it is also believed that they were there branded on the left shoulder over the Government brand U.S., by the letter and figure D 8."

The notice identified the thieves as "PONY DIEHL, A. T. HANSBROUGH, MAC DEMASTERS" and charged that Patterson and Frank "M'Lowry" were among those who helped them hide the cattle. Frank only acknowledged that Hurst had identified the thieves to him as Diehl, "Hahsbrough," and "McMasters."

Two of the alleged rustlers' names bear special note. Pony Diehl, or Deal, and Sherman McMasters were to reappear—at least once more as partners—in the annals of southeastern Arizona crime during this period. Yet overall, Diehl associated with the rancher/rustler faction, while the short, red-faced McMasters would become an Earp confederate.

Meanwhile, Frank McLaury was fuming over Hurst's identification of him as an accomplice to rustlers. On August 5, in the pages of the *Weekly Nugget,* the rancher charged that Hurst was "a coward, a vagabond, a rascal and a malicious liar" who had possibly stolen the mules himself. "My name is well known in Arizona," McLaury wrote, "and thank God this is the first time in my life that the name of dishonesty was ever attached to me. . . . I am willing to let the people of Arizona decide who is right."

Despite the harsh accusations on both sides, the incident was apparently never resolved. Hotheaded Frank McLaury now had reason to look with disfavor on the Earp brothers who had accompanied the "malicious liar" Hurst, just as the Earps as law enforcers now had reason to look with suspicion on McLaury.

To place McLaury's protestations of innocence in perspective, it is necessary to understand the relationship between rustlers and ranchers in southeastern Arizona in 1880. The rustlers who ranged between western New Mexico and eastern Arizona were primarily Texas cowhands. Some had become outlaws in Texas and moved westward only one step ahead of the Texas Rangers. Some had driven cattle to Kansas and frequented the cow towns in the late 1870's. Some had participated as gunmen in the bloody 1878 warfare between political and economic factions in Lincoln County, New Mexico. Some had done all three of these things.

The rustlers generally roamed between Charleston on the San Pedro and distant Shakespeare, a bleak little mining town in western New Mexico. The landscape they occupied was "rough and mountainous," but possessing "well watered canyons and extensive valleys that afford the finest sort of range for cattle." A group could often be found at the Double 'Dobes, two rude adobe structures perched high in the Animas Mountains of New Mexico, or at the community of San Simon, across the Arizona line. But Galeyville, on the eastern slope of the Chiricahua Mountains, became their favorite haunt. The picturesque little mining center, with a smelter employing "some thirty or forty men," occupied a high mesa bordered on the north and south by the two branches of Turkey Creek. The rustlers occupied the side canyons and gorges, establishing squatters' claims and building corrals that became holding pens for stolen cattle destined to be purchased by the ranchers and other cattle buyers of Arizona. Billy Breakenridge estimated that sixty or more rustlers headquartered at Galeyville. Their leaders, most pioneers of the area later agreed, were John Ringo and a fellow named Curly Bill Brocius.

The rustlers' principal business was twofold: to raid into Mexico for horses and cattle, and to ambush Mexican smugglers who crossed the border with Mexican silver for trade.

Sharing in the extended history of racial prejudices and outright enmity between Texans and Mexicans, the raiders "had no compunction about stealing from [the Mexicans] or shooting and robbing them whenever they got an opportunity."

If the rustlers were rightly hated by their Mexican victims, they received sympathy and respect from many citizens of southeastern Arizona. Like the James and Dalton-Doolin gangs of the Middle Border, the rustlers enjoyed the status of "social bandits," maintaining ties to the local community, avoiding "directly harming local people" and even providing small kindnesses to the citizenry. Social bandits paid well for services rendered and adhered to a code of honor, displaying admirable masculine attributes. Such men were "brave, daring, free, shrewd, and tough, yet also loyal, gentle, generous, and polite. They were not common criminals." In fact, they attracted significant support among rural dwellers and stood in daring opposition to an increasingly "industrialized, bureaucratized world."

The key point to many was honor. Billy Breakenridge would say of Brocius, "I learned one thing with him, and that was that he would not lie to me. What he told me he believed, and his word to me was better than the oaths of some of whom were known as good citizens." And John Pleasant Gray, who came into contact with many of the rustlers when he and his brother Dick established an isolated ranch in the Animas Mountains, later remembered them as having a moral code—at least in their dealings with Anglos: "[Even the toughest usually] had a strain of honor in their hearts which placed them several notches ahead of our present day criminals. For one thing, they would not kill an unarmed person as so often occurs in our civilized world of today; nor would they rob the hand that fed them."

Pioneer James Hancock similarly found many of the rustlers possessing some honor, asserting that they "never molested the small ranchers." A natural sympathy often existed between the small ranchers and the rustlers; they generally shared Democratic southern origins, cattle-droving backgrounds, and the challenges of living and working in a harsh natural environment. The rustlers' willingness to pay and courtesy were remarked upon as well. A doctor who treated members of Curly Bill's band on occasion was pleased with his quick and generous remuneration, commenting, "I will say that I never lost a cent by a man I attended for Curly Bill." Robert Boller, one of a group of men en route to Tombstone on New Year's Day 1881 to make their fortune in the mines, reported that the rustlers at San Simon "were very kind to us."

Nonetheless, the rustlers *were* gunmen—often lawless gunmen—and their presence usually carried a threat. A rancher might gladly welcome a group of hungry cowboys into his home; he might also welcome them reluctantly, knowing that his hospitality was all that kept his cattle from being stolen.

By the same token, the rancher might gladly accept rustled stock into his holding pens, buying them cheaply or taking a cut of the night's action. Or he might accept the stolen animals simply because by acceding to the rustlers' wishes he guaranteed his own survival. As Gray later commented in explaining his own hospitality toward rustlers, "Your livestock, and in fact, all your possessions were at the mercy of any enemy, and your one and probably your only sure protection was your reputation for fair dealing with your fellow man, and your willingness to play the good neighbor role."

That meant offering a bed and food to any traveler—and not asking questions. Boller, who became a freighter hauling goods between Tombstone and other isolated Arizona communities, explained, "One night we might share our bed with a Deputy Sheriff, the next with an outlaw, with a price on his head."

Some ranchers suffered solely from guilt by association. Two cattlemen in the San Simon Valley were accused of "grand larceny," the common charge for rustling, simply because "they were unfortunate in having their ranch in San Simon Valley, which was the hang-out for all kinds of rustlers and outlaws."

The McLaurys did hold stolen stock. Breakenridge himself, tracing a stolen horse to the McLaury ranch, would warn Frank that either the horse would be returned or "you will have to quit ranching here and turn out with the rest of the rustlers."

However, the McLaurys were no desperadoes. Breakenridge later pointed out that neither was ever charged with a crime in Arizona, nor have any records been uncovered to show that they engaged in any illegal activity before arriving in the territory. They enjoyed a reputation among some southeastern Arizonians as personally honest and hospitable ranchers. Tom McLaury acted as a frontier banker, handling money for other ranchers and rustlers. And John Pleasant Gray would write of the brothers, "These boys were plain, good-hearted, industrious fellows. They may have harbored passing rustlers at their ranch, but what rancher did not? and it would have been little of a man who would have turned away any traveler in that land of long trails and hard going."

On a trip to Lordsburg, New Mexico, to get supplies for his Animas Valley ranch, Gray himself heard someone refer to him as "the fellow who feeds all the rustlers." Years later, he would comment, "In a settled and law-abiding community you might get by with a so-called lofty stand of virtue and declare your house was your castle, turning a deaf ear to any undesirable, and ask him to move on." But it was an attitude the smaller ranchers simply could not sustain. Through sympathy or through the desire to survive or through both, the McLaurys opened their home to and associated with the rustlers.

In addition to the McLaurys and other small ranchers, there was yet another class to consider: the owners and operators of large spreads. Men such as pioneer Sulphur Spring Valley rancher Henry Clay Hooker tended to align their economic interests with those of the businessmen in town, and Hooker and others were more likely to lose stock to the rustlers both because of their allegiances and because the very size of their operations made them appear fair game.

It is tempting to think in terms of the lawless element operating free of restraints in the desert and the law-abiding, respectable people gathered in town. But most of the trouble in Tombstone itself was generated not by "cowboys" but by Tombstone inhabitants. A few days before the Earps and Lieutenant Hurst journeyed to the McLaury ranch to look for stolen mules, a "sporting man," or gambler, who had resided in Tombstone for several months was killed by a friend in a senseless dispute over a shirt.

T. J. Waters had just bought the garment, which boasted

blue and black checks. When he entered the saloons along Allen Street wearing it, the fashion arbiters of Tombstone ridiculed his choice and put him in an ugly frame of mind, made worse by liquor. Waters emerged from a saloon and encountered an "intimate friend," E. L. Bradshaw, with whom he had prospected and shared a cabin.

All unaware, Bradshaw, too, made a mildly joking remark about the shirt, and the infuriated Waters attacked him with fisticuffs. Bradshaw left, returned armed, and asked, "Why did you do that?" Waters made some remark, and Bradshaw, described as "very reserved and peaceable," pumped four shots into his friend, apparently from the rear, as two entered the center of the back, one struck the left arm, and one hit the head and ranged downward. The *Epitaph* either showed a wry sense of humor or a blissful ignorance in running its account of the killing next to an ad for a local merchant who "has just received a large supply of checkered shirts."

As deputy sheriff, Wyatt Earp took Bradshaw to the county jail in Tucson; a Tucson jury would later acquit the irate gunman. Whether Bradshaw himself was drunk or just fed up remains unclear. If the former, the whole incident demonstrated the truth in the words of a Bodie, California, man who refused to identify a friend who had shot at him in a drunken argument. "He's a first rate fellow when he's sober," the man explained, "but he'd shoot his best friend when he's drunk."

Physical violence on the frontier was not limited to a lower socioeconomic class. Mining town professional men also turned to fisticuffs. In Tombstone a few weeks after the Bradshaw-Waters confrontation, new Justice of the Peace James Reilly and lawyer Harry Jones came to blows in a courtroom, with Wyatt Earp caught in a farcical no-win situation as peacemaker.

The case under consideration was that of George Perine, Buckskin Frank Leslie's friend who had been present when a jealous Mike Killeen was killed outside the Cosmopolitan in June. Leslie, of course, had taken the blame for the shooting, claiming self-defense, but some Tombstonians still remembered Killeen's dying statement and felt the evidence pointed to Perine. On August 14, Parsons reported in his journal,

"Warrant issued for rearrest of Perine implicated in the Killeen killing and he hid at our house today. [Deputy] Sheriff [Wyatt Earp] took him between Chinaman's and our house. Lively times."

Three days later, attorney Jones, Perine's counsel, criticized Reilly for remaining on the bench to judge a case on which he had worked as counsel prior to his July appointment. Reilly responded by warning Jones not to come to court for the hearing the next day.

The following morning, Jones appeared beside Perine as the case commenced. Reilly, "with the majesty which would have shamed a Roman emperor, thundered forth, 'Mr. Jones,' and pointed a massive finger in an unmistakable manner toward the door." Jones didn't budge. Reilly then ordered the officers of the court, including Deputy Sheriff Earp, to evict the defense lawyer. As they mulled this strange order, the glowering justice of the peace himself descended from the bench. Jones responded by pulling a gun. The officers relieved him of it, and Reilly lit into the attorney. As the two scuffled, Reilly choking Jones and Jones striking Reilly in the face, Wyatt "cut the gordian knot of doubt by declaring both parties under arrest."

Reilly nonetheless resumed his seat on the bench, while Jones went to Justice of the Peace Michael Gray's courtroom and was released on his own recognizance. Back he went to Reilly's courtroom, where the latter slapped a twenty-five-dollar fine and twenty-four-hour jail term on him. Wyatt Earp was instructed to take Jones all the way to Tucson to serve out the one-day sentence.

The deputy deposited Jones at the stage depot to wait for the Tucson stage, then returned to the courtroom. He was met by a still-angry Reilly, who demanded that he appear in the courtroom the next day on a contempt charge for failing to obey Reilly's initial order to remove Jones. Wyatt pointed out that he wouldn't be around the next day, since Reilly had ordered him to Tucson with Jones. Besides, he reminded the cantankerous justice, Reilly himself needed to appear in Gray's courtroom after ending his own court day to answer assault charges filed by Jones.

The whole incident reflects the view of Allen English, the

drunken Tombstone lawyer who orated to the moon. Fined twenty-five dollars for contempt when he appeared in court inebriated, English commented, "Your honor, $25 wouldn't pay for half the contempt I have for this court."

Actually, the Reilly-Jones scuffle was tame in relation to some courtroom dramas. In Prescott in 1883, two adjoining ranch owners went to court over water rights. The plaintiff's lawyer called the defense lawyer a liar, and the defense lawyer responded by throwing an inkstand and grabbing his opponent by the throat. The courtroom then erupted in confusion as the rancher being defended jumped up with a knife and began slashing in every direction. The bloody melee ended when the plaintiff's son shot the crazed defendant in the back.

The upshot of the Tombstone incident was that more than one hundred Tombstone citizens signed a petition calling for Reilly's recall. "We deem you incompetent to discharge the duties of your office," read the petition, "and a man of such ungovernable temper and poor discretion that you are unsafe with official power." Wyatt and Morgan signed it; so did Mayor Randall, City Marshal Fred White, James Vogan (Jim Earp's boss at the saloon and bowling alley), and Coroner H. M. Matthews. So, too, did men whose names were to surface in opposition to the Earps, such as Oriental owner Milt Joyce and mine claimant Peter Spencer.

Reilly weathered the public outcry and nursed a grudge against Wyatt. He would eventually get a chance to act on that grudge.

Meanwhile, Tombstone continued to boom. By the end of 1880, the area mills would be putting out half a million dollars monthly in bullion and the number of claims located in the area would top three thousand, although only fourteen of the mines had complete hoisting works. By the late summer of 1880, water flowed through pipes into Tombstone from a Dragoon Mountains reservoir eight miles to the east, though it still remained in scarce supply. A church was being erected, and owners of hotels, restaurants, and saloons continued to outdo each other in providing luxuries. The Grand Hotel opened in September, its upstairs described by the *Epitaph* as "a perfect bijou of costly furniture and elegant carpeting known as the bridal chamber." Parsons dined at the Grand on the fifteenth and pronounced it "the best place I've seen thus far in the territory. . . . Best meal yet and best served."

According to Frank Waters's account of the Earps in Tombstone, the Earp women dwelt far from all this comfortable grandeur, continuing to take in sewing in their cramped homes on Fremont Street and listening to an occasionally expansive Wyatt detail the glories of Tombstone's ornate places of entertainment and refreshment. In this narrative, Virgil's Allie and Wyatt's Mattie once ventured downtown and inside the elegant Occidental dining room, only to have Wyatt react with fury to Mattie's "show[ing] her face on the streets."

Waters's portrayal is colored in part by Allie Earp's obvious dislike for her brother-in-law, reflecting a mutual antipathy from their first meeting. This inauspicious encounter took place in Dodge City in 1876, when the Earp family entourage headed by Nicholas and Virginia Earp arrived in Dodge on their move westward. Allie was sitting in the back of the family's wagon when Virgil brought Wyatt and Morgan to meet her. "My shoes were off, and when Wyatt and Morg reached out to shake hands I stuck out a bare foot. I never did grow up, I reckon. Size or noway else. Wyatt gave me a cold and nasty look, and turned away. But Morg pinched my toes real friendly."

Allie was a scrappy little Irish fighter with a pert face and a sharp tongue; Wyatt's Mattie, by contrast, was a quiet, retiring woman with square features and a docile nature. Even though Wyatt named a Tombstone mining claim after her, Mattie is a shadowy or absent figure in most accounts of his life, the "woman done wrong" and forgotten. But fierce little Allie would later want her hardworking companion remembered as "as fine a girl as ever lived."

That late summer and fall of 1880, as Allie and Mattie continued their sewing and limited domestic routine, the Earp men moved more firmly into the fabric of Tombstone life. Wyatt in August obtained his one-fourth interest in the Oriental gambling concession from three fellow investors: Alhambra owner Dick Clark, Lou Rickabaugh, and William H. "Bill" Harris, all of whom had gained glittering gambling reputations on the circuit from Dodge to California. And in September Wyatt became secretary and charter member of a

Tombstone volunteer fire company, a position of some prestige within the community. The Earps' success in leasing two
mining claims was duly reported in the *Epitaph,* as were Wyatt's and Virgil's improvements on their town lots. "The
Messrs Earp are erecting on their property at the foot of Fremont St. a number of frame dwelling houses," the paper reported in October. "Four have been completed and a fifth is
under way."

The Earps were also frequently mentioned in the newspapers in connection with law enforcement. A typical story appeared in the *Epitaph* of August 14, 1880, which reported that
Virgil and Morgan, out looking for five horses stolen from a
storekeeper, had encountered a Fort Grant sheriff searching
for a stolen mule and had helped him locate the mule and the
thief. The latter, the *Epitaph* reported, gave up "when a six-
shooter was run under his nose by Morgan Earp."

Morgan apparently did not participate in his brothers'
business activities, but Wyatt and Virgil often delegated law
enforcement responsibilities to him. For example, in September "Special Deputy Sheriff Morgan Earp" took a prisoner
to Tucson. At the same time, he continued his Wells Fargo job.
On September 7, the *Epitaph* reported that a stage to Benson
on which Morgan was riding shotgun had lost two bullion bars
when the hind boot broke open; Morgan and the driver re-
traced their route in the dark and recovered both.

Such reports helped establish all of the Earps as honest,
hardworking Tombstone citizens. Trouble materialized, however, in the form of Wyatt's tubercular gunfighting friend Doc
Holliday.

Fresh from a string of skirmishes with the law in Las
Vegas, New Mexico, Doc had arrived in Tombstone during
the summer. In October, he started getting into trouble in
Tombstone.

The dentist and his mistress Big Nose Kate Elder had actually traveled part of the way to Tombstone with the Earp
entourage the previous fall. By some accounts, Wyatt had
picked up his crony in Las Vegas; by others, Doc had sought
out Wyatt along the route after hearing he had left Dodge.
Kate Elder later said that she and Doc had gone to Prescott
with the Earps and stayed there after Virgil and Allie joined
the party bound for Tombstone.

The record, however, places Doc primarily in Las Vegas between his departure from Dodge and his arrival in Tombstone. Doc had first joined former Dodge lawman Josh Webb in a Las Vegas saloon venture. However, neither of the two men could stay out of trouble. In March 1879, Doc became entangled in a series of minor problems with the Las Vegas law, with charges ranging from keeping a gaming table to carrying a deadly weapon. His killing of a drunken and dangerous Mike Gordon outside the Holliday-Webb saloon in July 1879 caused few repercussions with the authorities, but he later got into a less clear-cut altercation with another former Dodge resident, Charley White. The two exchanged shots in a barroom, with White receiving a superficial wound.

Meanwhile, Webb was fast becoming one of the West's most pronounced examples of a duplicitous lawman, or at least a lawman gone bad. In September 1879, he was arrested for a Las Vegas area train robbery; six months later, he was charged in Las Vegas with complicity in the robbery and murder of a cattleman. Dodge friends raised money to help Webb. He also got assistance from another direction. The saloonkeeper had become friends with a well-known desperado, Dave Rudabaugh, whom he had helped arrest in 1878. Now Rudabaugh broke into the jail, killed a jailer, and offered to spring Webb. The prisoner apparently felt optimistic about his chances in court, for he declined. A few months later, convicted of murder and sentenced to hang, Webb had second thoughts and staged his own bloody escape from the Las Vegas lockup.

By this time, however, his former saloon partner Holliday was in Tombstone. One Las Vegas newspaper writer certainly considered his departure a case of "good riddance," later remembering him as "a shiftless, bagged-legged character, a killer and a professional cutthroat" and his lover Kate as "a Santa Fe tid-bit" who "surrounded her habiliments with a detestable odor."

On October 11, 1880, Doc began arguing with one John Tyler in the Oriental Saloon. The *Daily Nugget* of October 12 identified both as "well-known sports"; Tyler has also been identified as a professional gunman hired to make trouble in the Oriental by rival saloon owners and as a shady manipulator trying to force the concession owners to give him an interest. In fact, according to some sources, Wyatt had gained his quarter interest in the gambling concession because the other concession owners needed protection against Tyler's racketering. Whatever the underlying situation, friends disarmed both men, and Tyler departed. If Tyler was the troublemaker, Oriental proprietor Milt Joyce nonetheless remonstrated with Holliday about causing a disturbance. Holliday was not the type to accept criticism; his response resulted in Joyce's ordering him out of the saloon. Holliday returned for his pistol, which had been placed behind the bar. When it was denied him, he departed but soon appeared again. The *Daily Nugget* reported what followed:

> [Holliday] walked toward Joyce, who was just coming from behind the bar, and with a remark that would not look good in print, turned loose with a self cocker. Joyce was not more than ten feet away and jumped for his assailant and struck him over the head with a six-shooter, felling him to the floor and lighting on top of him. Officers White and Bennett [city assistant marshals] were near at hand and separated them, taking the pistols from each. Just how many shots were fired none present seemed able to tell but in casting up accounts Joyce was found to be shot through the hand, his partner, Mr. Parker, who was behind the bar, shot through the big toe of the left foot, and Holliday with a blow of the pistol in Joyce's hands.

Doc was fined for assault and battery, and he and Joyce embarked on an enmity that was to extend to their friends. Increasingly, such enmities broke down along political party lines. A Republican organizational meeting had been held in Tombstone in September, with George Parsons attending and commenting, "Republicans haven't much show in this territory. They will make a gallant fight though."

Doc Holliday, with his who-gives-a-damn outlook on life, was apolitical, but the Earps were not. They would align themselves with the leading Republicans—men such as Clum and Parsons—while Joyce would become a prominent Democrat.

Party divisions were forming in anticipation of county elections in November. Meanwhile, sporadic violence continued in Tombstone itself, with a real criminal element entering in. "Our town is getting a pretty hard reputation," Parsons had written in July. "Men killed every few days—besides numerous pullings and firings of pistols and fist fights. One man in town now with a $1200 reward for him. Others known to be convicts." In August, while traveling to the nearby mining camp of Richmond, Parsons encountered a nervous man with a "huge pistol" on the trail. "Seems from his account there are about 25 men in town who wouldn't hesitate to cut a man's throat for $2½," Parsons commented.

In short, then, there were two facets to Tombstone's crime problem in the fall of 1880. First, men such as the late E. L. Bradshaw got drunk and touchy and picked fights. The toll in this type of situation tended to be high because at this time men were allowed to carry weapons in town as long as they were not concealed. Second, a petty criminal element was operating in Tombstone, an element that operated best in urban situations. Melvin Jones, the rancher who had worked with Frank McLaury near Camp Grant, would later identify this group as the "tinhorn gamblers," who avoided the hard labor of the cowpuncher and the respectable citizen in order to work a variety of scams, from cheap card tricks to outright thieving. Both the Earp faction and the cowboys would have ties to this group, but the cowboys themselves—the rustlers and their allied ranchers—did not enter into the Tombstone crime problem until the end of October, when Curly Bill Brocius shot and killed Tombstone City Marshal Fred White.

The pages of the *Nugget* and the *Epitaph* give no hint to this point that the rustlers had frequented the town or posed a law enforcement problem. The *Epitaph* in reporting the fatal shooting even got Curly Bill's last name hopelessly muddled. But, then, Curly Bill has been the subject of much confusion over the years, as he apparently shared some adventures with a Curly Bill Graham. The information on both is meager and tends to overlap. Breakenridge described Curly Bill Brocius as "fully six feet tall, with black curly hair [thus the name], freckled face, and well built." Melvin Jones called him "a typical west-Texas cowboy," while James Hancock remembered him as affable but dangerous when drinking, like his friend John Ringo.

Like Ringo, Brocius cloaked himself in mystery. He told Hancock that his earliest memories were of being on the Kansas plains with an old buffalo hunter who said he was his father, that the two had become separated, and that he had gradually found his way into Arizona. He probably entered the territory driving a herd of cattle to the San Carlos Indian Reservation. Breakenridge first encountered him in a San Simon saloon. Curly Bill was lounging on top of a card table; spying the saloonkeeper with a cup of water in his hand, Bill raised up and fired a bullet at the cup, laconically commanding the saloonkeeper not to drink that "pisin."

The bullet went through the wall and killed Curly Bill's horse. Bill's luck was like that. And despite his status among the rustlers, he lived in relative obscurity until the night of October 27.

The *Epitaph* of the next day reported the evening's events:

> A lot of Texas cowboys, as they are called, began firing at the moon and stars on Allen Street, near Sixth. City Marshal White, who happened to be in the immediate neighborhood, interfered to prevent violation of city ordinance, and was ruthlessly shot by one of the number. Deputy sheriff Earp, who is ever to the front when duty calls, arrived just in the nick of time. Seeing the Marshal fall, he promptly knocked his assailant down with a six-shooter, and as promptly locked him up, and with the assistance of his brothers, Virgil and Morgan, went in pursuit of the others. That he found them, an inventory of the roster of the City Prison this morning will testify.

By other accounts, White, a United States Army veteran, had called on the assistance of Virgil Earp when he went looking for the troublemakers. The two found Curly Bill on the street and attempted to disarm him. There was a struggle. Bill's six-shooter fired, and a bullet ripped into White "four inches below and three inches to the left of the navel," penetrating downward and backward and "piercing the small intestine and making its exit from the pelvis."

The incident occurred at the rear of the cabin shared by

Fred Dodge and Morgan Earp. Dodge later recalled that he and Morgan arrived on the scene almost immediately, finding Wyatt already there holding Curly Bill and bullets being fired from a nearby arroyo. In a slightly different version, which he gave to Lake, Dodge remembered that Wyatt first ran by him and borrowed a pistol, warning both Dodge and Morgan to "Look out for yourselves now."

The close-range gunshot had set Fred White's clothes on fire; Dodge recalled the confusion—and his own value to the Earps over Fred White: "Wyatt said, 'Put the fire out in Fred's clothes.' My name was Fred also and they thought it was me. The guns clicked fast and they would have shot Curley [sic] Bill, had I not spoken and said, 'It's Fred White, not me.'"

As deputy sheriff Wyatt disarmed and arrested Brocius, whose gun was found to still have five cartridges. The six-shooter fully loaded at the time of the attempted arrest seemed to indicate that Bill had not been one of the shootists, but he was now facing far more serious charges. White died of peritonitis within a few days, after calmly saying good-bye to gathered friends.

Accounts as to what actually happened in the struggle differ. Curly Bill himself testified at his trial in Tucson that Virgil had seized him from behind, causing the hair-trigger pistol to fire. John Pleasant Gray later speculated that Bill had filed off the safety catch of the pistol so that he could "fan" the hammer and produce six shoots in rapid succession. A story circulated at the time that Bill had offered White the pistol butt first, then spun it into his own hand and cocked it as White reached for it. In fact, this trick became known as the Curly Bill spin, and the rustler was skilled at it, as Breakenridge attested:

> [Curly Bill] was a remarkable shot with a pistol, and would hit a rabbit every time when it was running thirty or forty yards away. He whirled his pistol on his forefinger, and cocked it as it came up. He told me never to let a man give his pistol butt end toward me, and showed me why. He handed me his gun that way, and as I reached to take it he whirled it on his finger, and it was cocked, staring me in the face, and ready to shoot. His advice was, that if I disarmed any one to make him throw his pistol down.

However, Melvin Jones later recalled Curly Bill's grumbling that there wouldn't have been any trouble if Virgil hadn't grabbed him and claiming that he had been struck over the head by one of the Earps while surrendering to White. White himself, before he died, said the shot was accidental. Some even pointed a finger at the Earp brothers. James Hancock later alleged that a number of citizens believed Virgil Earp, anxious to make his own bid for power, "done [sic] the actual killing."

Such a Machiavellian move on the part of the Earps, particularly on Virgil's part, seems unlikely, but the shooting did nonetheless benefit the Earp brothers, with Virgil immediately appointed assistant city marshal, actually acting marshal, by the town council.

The incident had other effects as well. Virgil Earp would later refer to a vigilance committee itching to hang Brocius at the time, although records show vigilante organization efforts a few months later. Whether there was any concerted vigilante threat or not, the killing did stimulate ill feeling among the townspeople against Brocius and his friends. This ill feeling was quickly extended to "cowboys" in general by the proper Republican portion of Tombstone's population, the citizens who favored strict law-and-order measures. They defined "cowboy" in broad terms, including most of the men who rustled, ranched, or just roamed outside the settlements. One Tombstone resident would later recall that to staunch Republican John Clum "just about any farmer who was from the South who happened to be a Democrat was automatically a 'cowboy.'"

Increasingly, an influential segment of Tombstone's citizenry would look at the cowboys rather than at the town's criminal element when trying to pinpoint the main source of outlawry. Curly Bill, acquitted of the murder charge, maintained a low profile, but he still quickly became what Parsons called "our chief outlaw at present," with the cowboys—or the cowboy influence—blamed for sundry criminal acts. This tendency to look outside the town for sources of trouble also reflected an attitude expressed by one Dodge City resident, who recalled that that town's gunfighters "fought among themselves and fleeced and sent many guests of this western Monte

Carlo to 'Thy Kingdom Come,' and too often the law was a dead letter. But the violators were home folks, they were part of us."

About the time White got shot in Tombstone, a cowboy in a Shakespeare, New Mexico, saloon heard that President Rutherford B. Hayes was going to be traveling through the Southwest by train and remarked, "Suppose we go and stop the train and make Old Hayes give us a speech when he comes along." The idle comment sparked a mobilization of army troops and armed citizens to guard the President, while the cowboy apparently went on about his business unaware of—or delighted by—the furor his remark had created.

Actually, whether he was bent on criminal activity or not, the free-roaming "cowboy," the man who lived and worked or simply ranged outside the settlements, represented a threat to frontier communities simply because he chose not to be a part of them and thus thumbed his nose at the social order they represented. However he might escape the established order, though, he still had to make accommodations to it. Thus, John Ringo in March 1880 wrote apologetically to Pima County Sheriff Charlie Shibell that he could not make a scheduled appearance before the Pima County grand jury because he had been shot through the foot and could not travel. "If you get any papers for me, and will let me know, I will attend to them at once as I wish to live here. I do not wish to put you to any unnecessary trouble, nor do I wish to bring extra trouble on myself. Please let the Dist-Atty know why I do not appear, for I am very anxious that there is know [sic] forfeiture taken on the Bond."

Nobody could completely disregard the law, not even the rustler leader. But individuals and groups could try to control it. One way, of course, was by winning a law enforcement appointment. Melvin Jones complained that the "tinhorn gambler" element was "forever trying to get to be deputy sheriff or constable or deputy anything so they would have the authority to carry a six shooter," and he placed the Earps in this class.

Another obvious way to mold the law to one's liking was to get one's favorite into power. The rustlers carried off a blatant fraud in this regard when county elections were held a week after White's shooting. Democratic County Sheriff Shibell was being challenged by Republican Bob Paul, a veteran Wells Fargo stagecoach guard. The rustlers, with their southern Democratic sympathies, fully backed Shibell and controlled the voting at San Simon. John Ringo was serving as one of two precinct judges for the election; the "J. C. [sic] Clanton" listed as voting inspector was probably Joseph Isaac, or Ike, Clanton. Curly Bill Brocius was out of jail and rounding up the scattered inhabitants of the San Simon Valley, including women and children, to vote repeatedly for Shibell. Then the rustlers "voted all their horses and a dog or two and a stray cat, and finally to make sure no one had been neglected and not been given a chance to cast his ballot, they voted everyone again."

John Pleasant Gray, who was one of the tally clerks for the election in Tombstone, reported that the contest between Shibell and Paul was close, but the Democrats seemed confident of victory. Sure enough, Curly Bill came riding down Allen Street with the returns from San Simon, "one hundred straight Democratic votes for Shibell" and "one lone Republican ballot for Bob Paul, to show as Bill said that the vote was on the square!" The *Epitaph* reported the vote at 103 to 1, with the odd vote attributed to a Texas cowboy eager to demonstrate that there was no intimidation at the San Simon precinct.

Vote fraud was nothing new in Arizona; both Democratic and Republican candidates often benefited. In 1868, the *Arizona Miner* had reported "hundreds of non-citizens of Mexican origin at Tucson, Tubac, and other places" voting for the same United States congressional candidate "as many as three times in one day," and the paper stated that United States Army troops stationed in Arizona were doing the same. In 1870, the news that members of an Arizona City merchandise firm had paraded four hundred ineligible Indians, male and female, through the voting process had led one observer to sarcastic comment: "We believe in the right of women to vote . . . but it would appear more gallant . . . had they first extended this right to the white ladies of Arizona City and compelled the squaws to remain for next season."

In the Pima County election of 1880, the San Simon vote

provided Shibell's margin of victory, and Paul contested the results. Meanwhile, a third method of controlling the law was developing in Tombstone. Maybe a man could grasp a law enforcement position or see to it that a favorite got it, but he also could become the law if he had enough of a power base; he could become a vigilante.

On October 13, 1880, two days after the Holliday-Joyce altercation at the Oriental, the *Daily Nugget* had reported receiving "two anonymous communications, evidently for publication, warning certain parties now in this city to leave town before a certain time, or the peaceful citizens of Tombstone would not be responsible for their safety. Evidently the vigilantes are organizing." The next day, the paper editorialized against such activity, but it is clear from Parsons's journal and other first-person accounts that vigilante justice was frequently considered by inhabitants of Tombstone.

The first hint comes in Parsons's journal entry of June 27, 1880, after the shooting of Mike Killeen: "Killeen dying tonight and Perine up for firing fatal shot. Some talk of going for Lester [Leslie] by miners if K dies which he will tonight." In early August, after encountering the scared, gun-toting traveler on the Richmond trail, Parsons commented, "Tombstone is getting a pretty hard name. Men killed shot—stabbed suiciding etc. every day or two. This thing must be stopped." On August 25, in recording a shooting death, he wrote, "This last shooter will probably be hung if caught by the boys. Something must be done. Lynch law is very effective at times—in a community like this." And after White's death, he recorded, "Vigilantes will probably take care of the next assassins."

Soon Parsons would be writing more cryptically yet more forcefully of the need for vigilante justice: "Peculiar organizations of a certain character are very necessary at times under certain circumstances for a maintenance of right and paving the way to the highest order of civilization."

Part of the problem, of course, was the fact that having a court system did not ensure that crime would be effectively dealt with. First, frontier justice of the peace courts were not known for their efficient and evenhanded dispensation of justice. Almost from their inception, local frontier courts "emerged as special interest agencies staffed by officials notable for their lack of judicial training, unhampered by a sense of tradition and judicial protocol, influenced by political ties, and susceptible to financial shadiness."

In the Tombstone area, Charleston was particularly notorious as a place both of wild wickedness and of uneven judicial administration. Here Justice of the Peace Jim Burnett, who operated a livery stable, "held court wherever he happened to be, using a double-barreled shotgun as bailiff, keeping all fines he collected, and growing quite prosperous in the process." In the remote settlements of the territory, magistrates dispensed their own self-serving (and self-saving) brands of justice.

There were also problems at the county court level. Exactly a week before Fred White's death, the *Epitaph* had complained about witnesses failing to appear in a case against two Mexicans under Grand Jury indictment.

> It appears to us that about enough of this kind of business has been going on in Pima County. Men are shot in the streets and the killers are turned loose because no evidence is brought before the Grand Jury to indict them; men are found dead in various places and a newspaper item is all that is known of the matter; indictments are found and no witnesses are at hand to convict.

The same issue carried a complaint from the Republican County Committee asserting that the incumbent Democratic Pima County district attorney, up for reelection, was not doing his job. The notice cited twenty-five homicides in the past year, with only fifteen suspects incarcerated, one tried, and no convictions. In addition, the committee pointed to the rustling problem:

> Quite a number of cattle thieves have been bound over to appear before the Grand Jury, and they have not appeared, and the Grand Jury left in ignorance of the evidence against them. There are cases where indictments have been made against cattle thieves and receivers of stolen cattle, and the indicted persons have not even been assigned and the indictments left to slumber in the pigeon holes of the clerk's office until time and dust have hidden them from view.

Overall, the complaints in the *Epitaph*—and similar ones made by other western papers of the era criticizing laissez-faire attitudes—actually pointed up a bigger impediment: the difficulty any authority faced, whatever its political coloring, in imposing the legal machinery of civilization on a far-flung and fluid frontier. This difficulty had been reflected in a *Weekly Nugget* note of October 1879: "Our Justice of the Peace, Mike Gray, has been kept quite busy since his appointment, but has not had as much criminal business as he ought, only for the reason that the parties have not been brought before him." Collecting evidence and getting witnesses to appear and testify were no small feats in such a sprawling, wide-open territory.

So the vigilantes *would* eventually organize, but their efforts would only add to the confusion over how to tell a good guy from a bad, how to enforce the law on the frontier, and how much law was necessary. "Will be a bad winter I'm afraid," Parsons mused. It was.

CHAPTER 5
Games of Chance

In Tombstone, talk of Fred White's death and the results of the Pima County elections quickly gave way to renewed discussion of the townsite ownership question. Not only were Clark and Gray of the Tombstone Townsite Company still pressing their claims to town lots, but the Gilded Age Mining Company was also claiming the land on which Tombstone was built and had brought suit against the townsite company. With its first issue in October 1879, the *Weekly Nugget* had noted the effects of this legal imbroglio: ". . . there is a great deal of feeling in the community [concerning the case], and as it is to be brought before the district court at the present session, we hope it will be summarily disposed of. As a controversy, it has done no little damage in retarding business improvements in that locality, as those who purchase ground don't care to buy a lawsuit also." Now Clark and Gray secretly convinced Mayor Alder Randall, by law the holder of the town patent, to deed the patent over to them when it arrived.

Tombstone residents were kept in the dark about the situation, but rumors soon flew to the effect that Randall was going to release the patent to Clark and Gray. The news sparked a demonstration on November 6, 1880, when protesters placed lanterns and candles around a public stand, then built a bonfire at the corner of Fifth and Allen. Here "determined men spoke determined words," championing the rights of individual lot holders. The next day, Randall promised a citizens' meeting that he would follow the wishes of the town council in the matter; however, one council member reported that the mayor was not to be trusted and had been dealing privately with Clark and Gray.

The controversy led to the formation of a Tombstone Citizens League headed by a number of town-oriented Republican businessmen, such as Clum and Parsons. Meanwhile, Tombstone law enforcement remained in a state of flux.

Although Virgil Earp had received the acting city marshal appointment, a special election was scheduled for November 12 to fill the position through the end of the year. "V. W. Earp announces himself as a candidate for constable, subject to the suffrages of the people of Tombstone," reported the *Daily Nugget* on October 30.

He seemed a logical choice, with a record of reliability during his more than three years' residence in the territory. In Prescott to the northwest, Virgil had worked as a night watchman, as a stage driver transporting bullion from the Gillette mines, and as an elected constable. He had made a name for himself in this territorial capital by his actions as a member of a posse tracking two men accused of shooting up the town. The two, camped at a nearby ranch, began firing on the posse when it came into view; Virgil took a Henry rifle and made his way up a creek bed to a spot where he could see one of the gunmen "crouching under an oak tree reloading his gun." The man fell dead at a blast from the Henry rifle, the cigarette which he had been smoking still clenched between his teeth.

Not surprisingly, then, when Virgil had decided at Wyatt's urging to move from Prescott to Tombstone in the fall of 1879, Arizona's Federal Marshal Crawley Dake had handed him the deputy United States marshal appointment which had turned out to be an on-call position helping county and city officials and providing little or no pay. The territorial marshal's office was run on the basis of fees collected and whatever special funds the marshal could extract from the federal government; in the case of Dake, a minor government functionary from Michigan, most monies collected in this piecemeal way went straight into his private bank account.

So Virgil Earp's prestigious federal marshal appointment continued to provide little real power and less money. The Tombstone city marshal, on the other hand, enjoyed a regular income of a hundred dollars a month, plus a percentage on city taxes, and daily held a position of authority within the community.

Virgil was not alone in seeking the job, however. Two part-time Tombstone policemen, James Flynn and Ben Sippy, also jumped into the running. "Ben Sippy is making a good canvass for the Marshalship and it looks as though he would be a formidable competitor to Flynn and Earp," the *Daily Nugget* reported on November 7, concluding, "All the three candidates have warm friends." A few days later, the paper reported Flynn dropped from the race, leaving Virgil Earp and Sippy, both "well qualified for the office."

Sippy showed himself to be a savvy campaigner, running repeated advertisements for the vote in the pages of the *Daily Nugget* on election day. He also served as one of six special policemen working under Virgil during the election. The final tally was Sippy, 311; Earp, 259.

Virgil's stint as acting city marshal had been all too brief. Even worse for the future of the Earps as law enforcers, Wyatt on November 9 had resigned his position as deputy sheriff of Pima County, paving the way for Johnny Behan to take control of Tombstone area law enforcement.

Why Wyatt Earp relinquished the job at this point remains open to conjecture. His one-sentence resignation letter stated obliquely, "I have the honor herewith to resign the office of deputy sheriff of Pima County."

He may have been asked to relinquish the job. Earp detractors hint at this possibility by painting a picture of a swaggering Wyatt unsuited to the position. More likely, if he was asked to resign in favor of Behan, it was because Behan shared with Shibell a Democratic affiliation and a long background in Arizona politics and government.

Wyatt may well have quit Democratic Sheriff Shibell's employ in order to throw his support to Republican Bob Paul for the office. However, Wyatt Earp wasn't the type to work on behalf of another man unless it provided a ready road to power for himself. Already, there was talk of carving out a section of the vast twenty-eight-thousand-square-mile Pima County, with Tombstone becoming the center of a new county. That meant a political battle over the sheriff's job, and by getting out of Democratic employ Wyatt was alliance-building with such prominent local Republicans as Clum and such prominent county Republicans as Paul.

Besides, there were other routes to riches and power. The quarter interest in the popular Oriental gambling operation was proving profitable. Also, Wyatt was continuing to establish and deal in mining claims; during the period surrounding his resignation, he was particularly active in this area. On October 23, the *Epitaph* reported, "The Mr's Earp and [A. S.] Neff received notice yesterday that the purchase money for the Grasshopper mine was in the bank subject to their order." On November 3, it announced that Wyatt and Neff had deeded their interest in the Comstock mine to R. H. Emmanuel for five hundred dollars. The next day, with Chris Bilicke and Albert Steinfield, Wyatt filed an Ole Bull mining claim. In mid-November, Wyatt served as flagman surveying a promising claim belonging to the Earp brothers and R. J. Winders, the north extension of the Mountain Maid claim.

Meanwhile, Johnny Behan stepped into the deputy sheriff position, with the *Daily Nugget* lauding both Wyatt's performance and the choice of Behan to replace him. One of the new deputy's first duties was to take former City Policeman James Bennett to Tucson for a jail sentence. Bennett, who had helped break up the Holliday-Joyce altercation, fought on getting into the stage and finally departed manacled. "A fine record for an aspirant to the office of Marshal," sniffed the *Epitaph*.

Nonetheless, things remained fairly peaceful on the crime front. "Town quiet these days," Parsons noted in his journal entry of November 22. The town lot issue, however, continued to simmer. On the evening of December 4, Clark and Gray gathered "a force of working and reputed fighting men" and moved a house sitting on disputed property halfway into the street. New marshal Ben Sippy stopped them, "being compelled though to take off his coat and show he meant business." A crowd had quickly gathered. "A few of us on the piazza of our house which directly faced the whole thing cried out 'put her back' some distance," Parsons recounted. "Much artillery was on hand and I expected shooting at one time but nothing serious to date."

John Clum led in winning an injunction against the Tombstone Townsite Company. His wife, Mary, wrote to her mother-in-law on December 5, after the house had been moved back, "There is a great excitement here over the Townsite question. . . . It is a great outrage this trying to move people off there [sic] lots by main force."

As the issue worked its way through the territorial courts, it would continue to add an extra degree of instability to the fortunes of Tombstone citizens. Most were aware what a gamble the whole property issue was anyway. Too many mining towns had boomed and busted. For instance, the discovery of gold on the Gila River upstream from Yuma had signaled a pell-mell rush to establish Gila City in 1861. Men "hurried to the spot with barrels of whiskey and billiard tables . . . traders crowded in with wagonloads of pork and beans; and gamblers came with cards and monte tables," so that Gila City in a few months boasted "everything . . . but a church and a jail." Three years later, however, with the gold depleted, a traveler passing the spot reported that "the promising Metropolis of Arizona consisted of three chimneys and a coyote."

Similarly, at the same time Tombstone was developing, the mining town of Irwin, Colorado, spiraled into heady existence. "I have never seen a community where money was so plentiful," reported one mining engineer, adding, "We averaged about $40 a day a piece, besides several large sums from sale of town lots. We each always had several thousand dollars in bills in our money belts and more hidden in our cabin." The boom lasted only three months.

So the buying and selling, the prospecting and investing were all part of a particularly dicey game of chance. Even life itself was tenuous, and not only because of drunken shootings or criminal activity. In her letter to her mother-in-law describing the town lot situation, the pregnant Mary Clum wrote happily of Tombstone's salubrious climate. "I never felt so well in my life as I do now," she asserted. Less than two weeks later, she was dead, having succumbed to a fever after the birth of a daughter. "Very, very sad," wrote George Parsons. "Half of the present female population or more could be better spared than she."

Only a month and a half before, Fred White had been buried with great ceremony, his rosewood casket followed by members of his fire-fighting company and a crowd of Tombstone citizens. Now Tombstonians jammed into the Clum home to pay their last respects to the mistress of the house; even the *Nugget* editor and his wife appeared, despite the fact that the *Nugget* and *Epitaph* already exhibited a pronounced rivalry.

Tombstonians turned from such sobering activities as Christmas approached, however. The "Tombstone Driving Park" provided entertainment on Christmas Day, with both Virgil and Wyatt Earp entering horses in a trotting match for a one-hundred-dollar prize. Johnny Behan's name did not appear on the advance list of entrants; perhaps he was temporarily a bit wary, for in early December his own "fast mare" had bolted while pulling him in a sulky, "fortunately doing no damage to herself or much to the vehicle."

As the year drew to a close, Virgil Earp again challenged Ben Sippy for the city marshal's job, up for grabs in January 1881. The mayor's spot was open, too, with Alder Randall discredited over the town lot question. Democrat Mark P. Shaffer announced for the position, and George Parsons nominated as the Republican candidate the widowed Clum, who enjoyed both sympathy over his loss and prestige as a leader of the opposition to Clark and Gray. On January 4, 1881, Clum won an overwhelming victory, garnering 532 votes to Shaffer's 165. Virgil lost once more to Sippy.

Thus, the Earps had a friend in the new Republican mayor but remained shut out of the important law enforcement jobs in Tombstone. Jim didn't care. He was about to open his own Sampling Room on Allen Street. Morgan seemed happy riding stages, doing odd jobs, and dealing faro at the Oriental. But Virgil was angry about his second election loss, and Wyatt was watching closely for the sheriff job that was about to materialize. Youngest brother Warren had ar-

rived, too, from the Earp parents' home in California. Like
Morgan, twenty-five-year-old Warren was amenable to anything that promised a little action, and he liked the idea of
perhaps getting to wear a star and carry a gun. Allie Earp
later recalled that he "was always asking Virgil when things
were going to start to happen." The handsome, dark-haired
young man, easily distinguishable from his look-alike light-
haired brothers, often frequented the Oriental, watching Morgan and Wyatt at the faro tables.

Brother Wyatt stood ready to clinch the sheriff's position
with the creation of the new county, seven thousand miles
square, in late January. It was named Cochise, in line with the
idea that the only good Indian is a dead Indian, although the
moniker still drew fire from at least one Arizonian who bit-
terly recalled "that bloodthirsty savage." The position of
Cochise County sheriff was one of the best-paying around.
Breakenridge placed the annual income at forty thousand dollars a year, "as the sheriff was also assessor and tax collector,
and the board of supervisors allowed him ten per cent for collections," including the easily gathered mining corporation
and Southern Pacific taxes.

Deputy Sheriff Behan was in the running, too, and had
many backers across the territory. But prominent local Republicans wanted "a two-gun man for sheriff of the new county"
and recommended Wyatt to Governor John Charles Frémont.
The ruddy-faced, white-haired Frémont had won national ac-
claim as "the Great Pathfinder" for his western explorations in
the 1840's, had been the Republican candidate for United
States President in 1856, and had served as a major general in
the Civil War. Notwithstanding these varied impressive cre-
dentials, he was proving a disaster as territorial governor. But
he was, after all, a Republican, and therefore more likely to
appoint a Republican county sheriff.

In later years, Wyatt was to portray himself, with glaring
inaccuracies, as the reluctant hero on whom law enforcement
openings were thrust. For example, in an 1896 interview, he
was quoted as saying that when he first picked up Virgil in
Prescott en route to Tombstone, United States Marshal Dake
"had heard of me before, and he begged me so hard to take
the [federal] deputyship in Tombstone that I finally con-

sented." Thus, with the creation of Cochise County, biographer Lake had Wyatt at first rejecting the idea of the sheriff's appointment because he was already a United States deputy marshal—and Wells Fargo rider to boot. The truth, of course, is that Virgil was the deputy United States marshal and Wyatt had long since relinquished the Wells Fargo job. He later claimed, with some justification, that he had "continued in the service of the express company as a 'private man.'" Wells Fargo general cashbooks show him twice receiving expenses for chasing stage robbers in months to come and twice receiving an apparent monthly salary. But the employment was sporadic at best.

Wyatt clearly wanted the Cochise County appointment, and conflicting sources show that Johnny Behan approached him to discuss their competition for it. In Lake's version, building upon an accusation against Behan by the Earps' counsel at the hearing following the famous gunfight, Behan argued that Wyatt's unwanted nomination might keep them both from getting the job, with a compromise candidate being selected instead. Lake provided Behan with a persuasive appeal: "You telegraph your friends at Prescott to withdraw your name and I'll get the job, sure. I'll appoint you under-sheriff. I'll run the civil business; you can run the criminal end and appoint your own deputies. We'll hire a clerk to handle all collections and split even. Somebody's going to earn this money and it might better be us than a stranger. Is it a deal?"

The smooth politician Behan was certainly capable of offering such a deal, but the whole passage echoes a patently false scene in the biography, with Wyatt being offered the assistant marshalship in Dodge with the understanding that he would actually function with full marshal's powers and make more money than the real marshal. The records of the city during this period show this to be untrue and make one suspicious of subsequent stories of secret offers of power.

But Behan himself admitted offering to make Wyatt undersheriff. In his own self-serving version of the scene, he simply told Wyatt that he hoped to be elected and would make Wyatt undersheriff, but didn't want his competitor to stop running or to feel obligated to return the favor. "He said it was very kind of me, that if he got the office he had his brothers to provide for, and could not return the compliment if he got it. I said I asked nothing if he got it, but in case I got it, and I was certain of it, I would like to have him in the office with me."

Behan won the lucrative position, with Frémont apparently bowing to general Democratic sentiment across the territory. Both Behan and his livery stable partner John Dunbar were former territorial representatives, and thus likely to have some political clout.* Whatever the reason for his success, the victor appointed Harry Woods, *Nugget* editor, as undersheriff, by his own admission reneging on his promise to Wyatt because of an incident that had occurred shortly before the election.

As he later told it, Behan as deputy sheriff had a subpoena for Ike Clanton relating to Bob Paul's contesting of the November election results. He would testify that he did not know where Clanton lived and got the information from Virgil Earp, then proceeded toward Charleston. When he was halfway there, "one man dashed by me on horseback, on the run; and about five minutes afterward another passed me on the run." He thought the first to be Virgil, the second Doc Holliday. Reaching Charleston, Behan gave the subpoena to a man headed for the Clanton ranch and encountered not Virgil but Wyatt and Doc Holliday, ostensibly in Charleston looking for a horse stolen from Wyatt.

Horse stealing was considered the most reprehensible of crimes on the frontier; to be horseless was to lose one's mobility and perhaps one's very livelihood. John Pleasant Gray would remember that he and other cattlemen "took more pride in our saddle horse herd than even in improving the grade of our cattle." Town dwellers such as Wyatt Earp took equal pride in a fine specimen of horseflesh.

By comparison, human life was often cheap. One pioneer would wryly recall, "In those early days—human life didn't count for much. It seemed nothing to shoot a man down—but if anyone stole a horse he could expect to be hung if caught."

This assertion was borne out by an incident at Camp

---

*Also, Glenn G. Boyer has noted that Dunbar, a native of Bangor, Maine, had remained friendly with United States Senator from Maine and Republican party power James G. Blaine, who may have pulled some strings.

Thomas in 1881, when Texas cattle drover Dick Lloyd killed the owner of a saloon and mounted a prized bay Thoroughbred belonging to Joe Hill, frequent companion of Curly Bill Brocius and John Ringo. As the story goes, the drunken Lloyd careened into another saloon on the animal, where he was "shot out of the saddle" by a band of poker-playing cowboys. His killing of the saloon owner might not have sealed his fate, but "when he stole a horse—Joe Hill's horse at that—it was too much, and he died because of his lack of judgment."

In the same vein, and reflecting attitudes toward minorities and women of easy virtue as well, a man arrested for killing a black prostitute near an army fort stated that he found a horse-stealing charge more threatening than the murder charge, as "the punishment for horse thievery exceeded that for murdering prostitutes."

Sometimes the thievery was regarded humorously, if the victim was far enough away. A cowboy from New Mexico rode into Tombstone on a fine horse, stabled it at the O.K. Corral, then went broke and offered the animal for sale at a bargain price. The buyer who grabbed the opportunity paid up and asked about the ownership title. The cowboy responded, "The title is perfectly good as long as you go west with him, but don't take him east; it is not so good in that direction."

Wyatt would later state that he had heard the Clantons had his steed, that he did not know the way to their ranch, and that a friend told him the messenger sent by Behan was riding the horse in question. (He would also charge that on a subsequent trip he found the horse in a Charleston corral and successfully disputed with Billy Clanton over its ownership.)

Behan himself would testify that he returned from the subpoena trip to Tombstone without incident but "a few days afterward" in Tucson encountered Ike Clanton, who informed him that he had come close to "a hell of a scrape. . . . He, Ike, said Earp sent him word that I had taken a posse of nine men down there to arrest him and send him to Tucson, and then he told me he had armed his crowd and was not going to stand it."

Thus, either Behan had double-crossed Wyatt, or Wyatt had tried to double-cross Behan. Or both. Now Behan pointedly ignored the Earps and gathered a group of deputies, in-

cluding Billy Breakenridge, former stage driver and teamster
Frank Stilwell, and the respected Dave Neagle, a longtime
mining man who had resigned superintendency of a Mexican
mine to come to Tombstone in summer 1880. How Wyatt
Earp felt about the situation can be assessed by the fact that he
was already unofficially running for sheriff by March.

Meanwhile, an event occurred that spurred the organiza-
tion of a Tombstone vigilante group. On January 14, a young
gambler named Johnny O'Rourke, popularly known as Johnny-
Behind-the-Deuce, shot and killed mining engineer W. P.
Schneider in Charleston. By one account, Schneider was the
loser in an all-night poker game and pulled a knife, leading
Johnny to produce a pistol and shoot him. By another, Johnny
bumped into Schneider on the street and pulled his gun when
Schneider told him to watch where he was going. By yet another,
Schneider, upset over a break-in at his cabin, ran into Johnny in
the Queen Saloon at lunchtime and exchanged words with him,
provoking the gambler to violence.

The *Daily Epitaph* explained that Schneider entered the
restaurant and remarked to a friend that it was cool. Johnny
interposed, "I thought you never got cold."

"I was not talking to you, sir," said Schneider, provoking
an explosive "God damn you, I'll shoot you when you come
out." *Epitaph* editor Clum had a penchant for purple prose
which would manifest itself in other situations as well. Now,
according to the paper, as Schneider departed the restaurant,
"true to his promise, the lurking fiend, who had seated himself with hell in his heart and death in his mind, drew deadly
aim and dropped his victim dead in his tracks."

Well. More important than the motive or the details, however, was the community response to the crime. Schneider was
no common laborer with a penchant for drink and fighting,
nor was he a law officer killed in the line of duty. Manager of
the Tombstone Mining and Milling Company's San Pedro
smelter, he was one of those respected citizens to whom such
things were not supposed to happen. Charleston residents
were ready to lynch Johnny, and the local constable hustled
him toward Tombstone.

A number of people in and around Tombstone would recall the day's events in dramatically different ways. Fred

Dodge later stated that Virgil Earp was on the Charleston road near his Last Chance claim, where he was having assessment work done, when the Charleston constable approached with his charge—and followed by an angry mob. The constable, in this version, turned Johnny over to Virgil, who brought him on his fast racehorse to Vogan's, where Jim was still tending bar. Lake's version resembles Dodge's, except that in it Virgil took Johnny to the Wells Fargo office, where Wyatt and Morgan were. Allie Earp's grandniece later recalled her aunt telling a similar story, with Virgil exercising his horses on the Charleston road and being pressed into service to convey Johnny to Tombstone ahead of the crowd. The *Epitaph*, however, simply reported that the constable allowed Johnny to ride ahead to escape the mob, and the murderer reined in in front of Vogan's looking for protection.

At least four old-timers who claimed to be present later insisted that Johnny arrived and then left under custody in a spring wagon without incident. James Hancock, for instance, flatly asserted that no mob followed the gambler from Charleston and summed up the reception in Tombstone: "When Johnny was brought in it naturally attracted a bunch of idly curious who gathered around to see what was going on. Just a bunch of harmless 'rubber-necks'—I was one of them myself—no one was armed and there was no demonstration of any kind. They put him in the buggy and drove off towards Benson as quietly as if they were going to a picnic."

Reports immediately following the incident told a different story. George Parsons and a business associate, walking along Allen Street, suddenly found themselves in the midst of a confrontation between miners and law officers holding Johnny.

> The officers sought to protect him and swore in deputies—themselves gambling men—(the deputies that is) to help. Many of the miners armed themselves and tried to get at the murderer. Several times, yes a number of times rushes were made and rifles leveled causing Mr. Stanley and me to get behind the most available shelter. Terrible excitement. But the officers got through finally and out of town with their man bound for Tucson.

The *Epitaph* reported in a similar vein, identifying Marshal Sippy, Sheriff Behan, and Virgil Earp as leaders in protecting the unfortunate gambler, whom Allie Earp described as "only about nineteen years old and awful shy." Allen Street "was jammed with an excited crowd," with more pouring in, when Sippy obtained a light wagon and placed the prisoner in it under the guard of Sippy, Virgil Earp, Behan, and "a strong posse of well armed men."

> Moving down the street closely followed by the throng, a halt was made and rifles leveled on the advancing CITIZENS, several of whom were armed with rifles and shotguns. At this juncture, a well known individual with more adverdupois [*sic*] than brains, called to the officers to turn loose and fire in the crowd. But Marshal Sippy's sound judgment prevented any such outbreak as would have been the certain result, and cool as an iceberg he held the crowd in check.

Over the years following the incident, Wyatt Earp—not even mentioned in either Parsons's or the *Epitaph*'s accounts—became the hero of this scenario. Certainly, he must have been one of the men assisting Sippy, brother Virgil, and Behan, but at the time, Sippy was recognized as the man most deserving of praise. "No one who was a witness of yesterday's proceedings," the *Epitaph* editorialized, "can doubt that [but] for his presence, blood would have flown freely."

Yet by the time he produced his memoirs in the late 1920's, even Billy Breakenridge would be repeating as fact a story of Wyatt Earp's almost single-handedly standing off the crowd. Parsons, writing to Lake in 1928, would depart from his initial record of "the officers" and their success in favor of a story about how Wyatt "backed his horse down the street fronting the mob and lowered his rifle every now and then when a rush was attempted." In Lake's biography, the mining mob became a horde of cowboys led, improbably, by John Ringo and mine founder Dick Gird—with Wyatt standing "One man against five hundred."

In truth, Officers Sippy and Behan, with former marshal Virgil Earp and a number of other deputies, had successfully insisted on upholding a system of law. But many Tombstone residents had grown impatient with the law, as evidenced by Parsons's comment on the whole affair: "This man should have been killed in his tracks. Too much of this kind of business is going on. . . . The law must be carried out by the citizens or should be when it fails in its performance as it has lately done. . . . Tonight I was requested to attend a strictly private gathering and went."

The gathering was a secret vigilante meeting. The men who attended were both honest in their desire to make the Tombstone area safer and possessed of political and socioeconomic prejudices that colored their understanding of law enforcement problems. Despite the fact that they had formed in reaction to the crime of a small-time gambler, this group would see cowboys as Tombstone's crime problem, and ruthless suppression as its solution. Significantly, they did not have the first thing they needed to be a truly effective force: the support of "an overwhelming majority" of citizens.

Parsons's journal for the early months of 1881 does reveal some problems with "cowboys." On January 10, a few days before the Johnny-Behind-the-Deuce incident, he recorded an apparent hurrahing of the area by the rustlers: "'Curly Bill' and others captured Charleston the other night and played the devil generally—breaking up a religious meeting by chasing the minister out of the house—putting out lights with pistol balls and going through the town. I think it was tonight they captured the Alhambra Saloon here and raced into the town firing pistols." On January 21, after the vigilante committee had formed, Parsons commented, "Cowboys bad again. All of us awakened by shots. Town unsafe—some decisive steps should be taken. Out again tonight. *Meeting*." A few weeks later, he reported, "Trouble in town today with cowboy. Bad man. Meeting tonight."

However, the journal soon went back to reporting altercations in the saloons and on the streets between residents and/or individual fortune seekers temporarily in Tombstone. Most of Tombstone's immediate crime problem continued to come from within.

In a significant way, though, the rustlers, their buyers, and their Mexican counterparts did provide an indirect problem for Tombstone without even entering the town. First, rustling activities were increasing on the United States side of the border; cattle dealer T. W. Ayles would complain in a March 1881 letter to the *Epitaph* that he and his neighbors on the San Pedro were repeatedly losing stock to unknown cattle thieves. The robbers' border activities were hampering both development and United States-Mexican relations.

As early as December 1878, the Mexican Legation had notified the United States secretary of state of horses being stolen in Arizona and sold in Mexico by unspecified Arizona bands. Governor Frémont, intent on his own mining speculation, refused to recognize any problem, and the United States government responded to Mexican reports by shuffling them through the bureaucratic maze of the State, Justice, Interior, and War departments. In July 1879, two Pima County deputy sheriffs had reported to Chihuahua cattle rancher Ramón Lujan that a "strong and well organized band" of rustlers, mostly Mexican, were selling cattle from Mexico to "a number of well-known Americans about fifty miles north of the border." The two offered to trace rustled stock for six dollars a day, two-dollars-a-day expenses, and 20 percent of the animals returned.

Lujan apparently took them up on the offer, for in September 1880 the Mexican Legation reported to the United States secretary of state that the deputies had found stolen stock in the possession of a beef contractor at Fort San Carlos—and that Lujan wanted reimbursement for his stolen cattle and expenses incurred in trying to locate the thieves. That same year, the commander at Camp Rucker complained that an organized band was "stealing and running horses across the Sonora, Arizona, New Mexico, and Chihuahua lines."

Mexican raiders and smugglers had established a rendezvous at the old Brunckow mine, with the smugglers periodically traveling to Charleston to purchase "calicos, jewelry, and everything that would carry a revenue in Mexico." Estimates of the number of their Anglo-American counterparts ranged from about twenty-five to about four hundred. One area rancher later recalled coming across Ringo and more than seventy others "camped among the deep pine groves" of the Chiricahua Mountains one morning. The rancher, owner of a small herd, "had lost no cattle to the rustlers and he, in turn, observed a strict and understood code of silence." Ringo offered breakfast, and the newcomer dipped into "a thick pool of pancake batter [that] lay in the deep sag of a tarp that was loosely suspended by its four corners to four trees." He "tossed his flapjacks, ate, and moved on."

Tom and Frank McLaury heightened their involvement with the rustlers by moving in late 1880 twenty-five miles southeast of Tombstone, to Sulphur Spring Valley. They located on the White River about four miles south of Soldiers Hole, a rural crossroads and watering hole for military troops. At this new site, the McLaurys provided a holding pen for stolen cattle driven across the valley from Agua Prieta and Naco. The Clantons also maintained a holding pen and almost certainly participated directly in the rustling. Sam Aaron, who knew them in Charleston, stated that they "would not hold up a stage, [or] bother the mail, but would steal as high as 2,000 cattle at one time in Mexico. They would start in Sonora, Mexico, and would drive forth everything they could lay their eyes on," later selling the cattle at three to four dollars a head.

New County Sheriff Behan and his deputies quickly developed a friendly relationship with the rustlers and their associates. Whether this was simply good policy or inappropriate cozying up to outlaws depended upon one's perspective. Billy Breakenridge argued for the former view, pointing out that, by enlisting Curly Bill to help him collect taxes from the rustlers and their associates, he had both improved the collection rate and headed off any trouble that might have erupted.

In *I Married Wyatt Earp*, Glenn Boyer had Josie Marcus reporting that her erstwhile lover Behan built a political alliance with Brocius, Ringo, the Clantons, and the McLaurys by inviting them home to play poker and have mysterious talks in the backyard. The characterizations of the visitors which Boyer attributes to Marcus are more balanced than many of the recollections in the volume and provide vivid portraits of these somewhat shadowy figures, although we cannot know their accuracy. Curly Bill is presented as "the most likeable of the crew," a fellow who "might have amounted to something if he'd had the chance" and whose "dark, ferocious appearance" was relieved by his frequent laughter and polite conduct. John Ringo is presented as much more reserved but equally gentlemanly, especially when he apologized for keeping his hat on indoors by explaining that this was his good-luck charm while playing poker. "I doubt, on my own observation, that Ringo was as wantonly murderous as some have tried to portray him," Boyer has Marcus comment, "though he was admittedly a killer." Tom McLaury is portrayed benignly as "quiet and pleasant toward everyone," a reserved young man with "a reputation as the hard worker in the family."

However, Frank McLaury is depicted as a troublemaker, a cocky "little strutter" who fancied himself a ladykiller. Ike Clanton, a "blowhard," is presented as "eating with his mouth open, smacking his lips" and being messy in chewing tobacco. In this account, Billy Clanton was simply a "big, loutish boy" who made inept passes at Marcus.

Arizona old-timers and researchers have over the years debated the degree and nature of Behan's actual association with these men, as well as the degree and nature of the Earps' association with them. Like Behan, Wyatt Earp had political reasons to cultivate their acquaintance and, despite his enmity with cowboys in his Dodge days, would soon be deal making with Ike Clanton.

Meanwhile, Wyatt was involved in trouble on another front. The Oriental Saloon, where he dealt faro and held a gambling interest, was getting a reputation as "not a very safe place if a man was known to have money on him"—in fact, as "a regular slaughter house." Even Allie Earp would comment that in her one journey downtown with Wyatt's Mattie, "We didn't loiter in front of the Oriental as some people said it was gettin' a bad name."

Wyatt maintained that the trouble was caused by men hired by rival saloonkeepers and gamblers jealous of the Oriental's popularity. Indeed, competition among saloons was fierce. While just about anyone could set himself up in the liquor-and-gaming business, the failure rate was high. Generally, one to three saloons "came to dominate the liquor trade in a town." In Tombstone, "not a single [saloon] owner listed in the 1880 census . . . appears in a business directory three years later."

Through most of the town's brief heyday, however, the Eagle Brewery—later known as the Crystal Palace—and the Oriental predominated. Although many continued to refer to the brewery by its more pedestrian name, it was transformed into the Crystal Palace in early 1881, becoming an elegant mirrored pleasure hall and boasting a distinguished-looking faro dealer who went by the name Napa Nick. Nick periodically retired to Napa, California, where he was known as Judge Nichols, leading citizen and patron of worthy causes.

Assisting Nick at the faro layout was a young, refined-looking woman who enthralled spectators with her faro-dealing skills. They would watch in amazement as the dark-haired girl wearing "magnificent diamonds" idly divided the chips into two stacks, raised them slightly from the table with thumb and forefinger, and "let them slip through her fingers in such a manner . . . that the chips would fall one on top of the other in rotation."

At the Oriental, Buckskin Frank Leslie mixed drinks with a showman's skill while the Earps and their friends dealt the cards. By mid-February 1881, former Dodge City denizens Luke Short and Bat Masterson had joined the dealers—simply following Wyatt Earp to this new action spot or responding to a call for gunmen to help control activities at the Oriental or both.

Bat had led a peripatetic existence since shortly after his friend's September 1879 departure from Dodge. In November of that year, while brother Jim Masterson had gained the Dodge City marshal appointment, Bat had lost his Ford County sheriff reelection bid. The defeat stemmed in large part from voters' dissatisfaction with Bat's association with gunmen such as Ben and Bill Thompson and Doc Holliday.

The former buffalo hunter turned in his deputy United States marshal badge as well and departed for Leadville, Colorado, where he spent a few months gambling. He returned briefly to Dodge to act as a delegate to the Ford County Republican Convention, then again packed his cards for Colorado. In June 1880, he responded to a request for help from Ben Thompson in Ogallala, Nebraska, by traveling to Ogallala and helping spirit away trouble-prone brother Bill, who had aroused citizens' ire by engaging in a gunfight with a saloon

operator over a woman known as Big Alice. Using Dodge as
his base once more, Bat headed for Tombstone in early February 1881.

An account of Masterson's passage from Dodge to Tombstone provides a glimpse of the state of western transportation
during this period of rapid development. First, Masterson was
able to take a train to Trinidad, Colorado, where he boarded
the new Santa Fe line—a caboose attached to the railroad construction train. Another passenger on the same caboose later
recalled climbing aboard to find "a small band of determined-looking men all armed to the fullest extent" against possible
Indian attack—all, that is, except one who wielded only a silk
umbrella. The umbrella-toting William H. Stilwell, new associate judge for Arizona, was a "fine-looking gentleman" who
"wore a silk hat—the first one to be tolerated in New Mexico
without a few shots being taken at it."

The Santa Fe line halted abruptly in open country, so the
passengers moved to an overland coach to journey through
Apache country to the Southern Pacific line at Deming, New
Mexico. Bat Masterson, carrying a Sharps rifle and two Colt
revolvers, was "by common consent . . . given the seat beside
the driver as our best fighting man." Reaching Deming without incident, the travelers boarded a Southern Pacific work
train to Benson, where Masterson caught a stage to Tombstone.

He arrived in mid-February and joined his friends dealing cards at the Oriental. Masterson was soon attempting to
maintain the peace at the saloon and gambling hall, but without success. For trouble surfaced between two gambler-gunfighters—one of them Luke Short himself.

In the early morning hours of February 25, Short exchanged words at the gaming tables with Charlie Storms, who
had dealt cards in mining towns from Deadwood to Tombstone. Storms "was what the men of the West call 'gritty,' and
had been in a number of shooting affairs, in all of which he
showed plenty of nerve." But, then, Short had no mean reputation himself.

Bat Masterson, considering himself a friend of both men,
separated the two and accompanied Storms to his room.
Storms didn't have the sense to stay there. He reappeared on

the street with a gun. Finding Masterson talking to Short on
the sidewalk, the drunken gambler pulled Short into the street
and tried to shoot him at close range. Short then "stuck the
muzzle of his own pistol against Storms' heart and pulled the
trigger." Parsons related to his journal what followed:

> I seized hat and ran out into the street just in time to see
> Storms die. . . . [Storms] was game to the last & after been
> [*sic*] shot through the heart by a desperate effort steadying
> revolver with both hands fired four shots in all I be-
> lieve. . . . Short very unconcerned after shooting—proba-
> bly a case of kill or be killed . . . the Faro games went right
> on as though nothing had happened. . . .

The doctor summoned to attend to Storms, a surgeon
lately out of army service named George Goodfellow, showed
Parsons a portion of bloody handkerchief driven into the
wound by the .45 caliber bullet. A few days later, affairs got so
bad in the gambling section of the Oriental that Milt Joyce
shut down the games.

Troubles were mounting outside the town as well. On
February 21, in an address to the Eleventh Territorial Legislature, Governor Frémont acknowledged a grave problem
with border outlaw bands and asked for "earnest attention" to
the fact that "life and property on both sides of the [Arizona-
Mexico] line are insecure," causing a "risk of serious complica-
tions with the government of the United States." Just a few
weeks later, a Mexican rustler was hanged by a group of
Graham County residents—two thirds of them Mexican—
from whom stock had been stolen. Reports of the incident
sparked a protest from the Mexican government, which in
turn roused the United States government to request a report
from the field.

Adding to the southeastern Arizona crime problem was
the growing threat of stage robbery. Ever since California gold
rush days, men of nerve and few scruples had waylaid stages
for the money boxes and bullion they contained, and often for
the personal valuables of the passengers as well. These robbers quickly learned that it was wisest to accost the stage driver
"from the front at well-selected spots; at the top of a steep hill

when the horses were tired, or at a narrow turn where the team had to come almost to a stop." They didn't want to be behind the stage, unable to get a shot at one of the horses and unable to prevent the driver from proceeding forward at breakneck speed.

Many robbers worked alone, although chances of success were enhanced if it looked as if one had confederates. Thus, an Idaho bandit known as Stove Pipe Sam reportedly rigged dummies to look like fellow robbers, while Arizona outlaw Bill Brazelton, working north of Tucson in an area known as the Cactus Forest, took advantage of the fact that the huge saguaro cacti could be mistaken for a phantom band. The most famous solitary bandit of all was Black Bart, a gentlemanly operator who left poetry at the scenes of his crimes and managed to relieve Wells Fargo stages of about forty thousand dollars over a nine-year period, working primarily in northern California. He would not be caught until 1883, when a nineteen-year-old deer hunter who had hitched a ride on a stage winged him in the midst of an attempted holdup. Bart escaped but, gentleman that he was, unknowingly dropped a silk handkerchief at the scene. Wells Fargo detectives were tired of looking like fools when it came to catching Bart; they traced him through a laundry mark on the handkerchief, and the bandit—known as respectable businessman Charles E. Boles—was sent to San Quentin.

Bart and most of his fellow highwaymen conducted their business without bloodshed, but there were violent exceptions. Probably the most bloody stage robbery of the frontier West occurred in Idaho in July 1865. A Wells Fargo stage, carrying seven or eight passengers and bullion worth seventy-five thousand dollars, was waylaid in a canyon by seven robbers with shotguns and blackened faces. Passengers unwisely fired on the bandits, unleashing a brutal attack. Two of the travelers were killed as they emerged from the stage; a third was wounded, then dragged across the road by his hair and finished with a second bullet. The driver, too, was fatally shot. One passenger escaped into the brush of the canyon. There are two accounts of survivors using subterfuge to stay alive. By one, a passenger played dead as the robbers kicked his prostrate form. By another, a traveler "lay on the floor of the coach in the midst of his dead comrades" uninjured but so bloodied that the bandits "honored his pleas to let him die in peace" and agreed to leave alive the man still breathing beneath him to share his dying moments.

Generally, however, stagecoach riders simply complied peaceably with the bandits' demands and endured whatever delay and humiliation resulted. In 1867, passengers on a stage near Virginia City, Nevada—including Professor Josiah D. Whitney of the California Geological Survey—were herded into a barn and tied up by highwaymen. A contemporary newspaper painted a mournful picture of the seven unfortunates sitting in the barn debating their helplessness, with the professor, "ever ready with a theory where rocks and other formations are concerned," groaning in the face of the fact that "the fellows with shotguns were no fossils."

Wells Fargo and other carriers tried to combat the threat of robbery, but shotgun riders were not always available for a stage run, and even if they were, they could often provide a limited defense at best. In 1878, the Black Hills Stage Company tried a different method of safeguarding its cargo by introducing a "Treasure Coach," a special Concord model with steel plates more than one-third inch thick, designed to deflect rifle slugs "fired from as close as fifty feet." This innovation didn't last long. In September, bandits ambushed the stage, picking off the outside guard with a rifle bullet, then shooting through the unarmored top of the coach and injuring one of two inside guards. The driver and the second inside guard quickly fled, leaving the robbers to remove twenty-seven thousand dollars from the strongbox at their leisure.

Not every robbery haul was that rich, of course, but stages across the mining West carried both tempting loads of bullion and tempting sums of hard cash, including payrolls for workers at the big mines. Nonetheless, the Tombstone area remained relatively free from stagecoach robbery attempts—until the early spring of 1881.

On February 26, Parsons noted a stage holdup near Contention, "but only $135 in W F & Co's box it being the off night. Passengers undisturbed." Two and a half weeks later, however, the bungled robbery of one of pioneer stage entrepreneur J. D. Kinnear's coaches on the road to Benson ended in murder and ignited hostile suspicions between factions in and around Tombstone. From the moment three bandits stepped out of the evening shadows to stop the Kinnear stage north of Contention on the night of March 15, Tombstone would be split wide open by distrust.

CHAPTER 6
"A Most Terrible Affair"

Bud Philpot was driving the stage from Tombstone to Benson that night; Bob Paul, still awaiting the reversal of the Pima County election results, rode shotgun to guard the approximately twenty-five thousand dollars' worth of silver aboard. First, the stage jolted the eight miles northwest to the mill town of Contention on the San Pedro River. Here—unexpectedly—Philpot and Paul exchanged places before following the San Pedro northward to the railroad town. A number of the passengers reported the driver incapacitated with "cramps in his Bowels." If such was the case, the cramps killed him.

For as Paul guided the stage across a dry wash and up an incline a short distance north of Contention, a man "stepped into the road from the east side and called out 'Hold.'" The highwayman was immediately joined by an indeterminate number of comrades, "and a shot was fired from the same side of the road instantly followed by another." Bud Philpot fell with a bullet "almost through the heart." In the fusillade from the bandits that followed, passenger Peter Roerig, who was seated in a rear dickey seat on top of the coach, was mortally wounded by a .45 caliber slug through the back.

Paul managed to return fire, but he had his hands full.

Philpot's body was slumping downward, about to fall into contact with the heels of the horses closest to the front wheels. Fred Dodge later reported that Paul used his left hand, still holding three reins, to grab Philpot and pull him into the front boot as the team broke into a "Sure Enough runaway." The experienced Paul then "Steadied them out and kept the Road till he had the team under Control."

By other accounts, Paul lost the reins and had to ease down on the pitching wagon tongue to retrieve them. When he brought the stage under control, he hurried onward to Benson with the wounded Roerig, bypassing a nearby stage stop called Drew's Station. The men at the station, hearing the shots and the coach's rapid escape, ran out to "the scene of the tragedy, where they found poor 'Budd' [sic] lying dead in the road, and by the bright moonlight saw the murderers fleeing rapidly from the place."

When the news of the "most terrible affair," as Parsons termed it, reached Tombstone later that evening, it touched off a flurry of activity. Parsons and a companion named Abbott were playing chess when Dr. George Goodfellow burst in, looking for a gun. "Abbott finally—let him have his upon Doc's assurance he didn't want to kill anyone. I stopped our chess—got revolver and followed him up—not wishing him to get hurt if I could help it. Men and horses were flying about in different directions."

A large posse rode out into the night: Behan and his deputies, Virgil, Wyatt, and Morgan Earp, Holliday, Masterson, Marshall Williams. The less rough-and-ready Parsons, Abbott, and Mayor Clum contented themselves with futilely "shadow[ing] several desperate characters in town, one known as an ex stage robber."

The posse followed a trail from the holdup site to the ranch of Len Redfield. Here they found two hard-ridden horses and a man desperately trying to hide. His name was Luther King; he confessed to holding the horses during the attempted robbery, and identified as the bandits three members of the rustler crowd—Billy Leonard, Harry Head, and Jim Crane.

The Earps and their friends from this point onward would argue that stagecoach robberies were simply a new and ugly extension of the cowboy problem, a situation exacerbated by county law enforcers' friendliness with the likes of Curly Bill. They asserted that Len Redfield (later a rider with an outlaw gang) and his brother Hank were rustler associates and that Behan and Breakenridge were giving the cowboy element every break, letting King confer with the Redfields before being taken in.

However, a rumor quickly surfaced in Tombstone that "the hunters were hunting themselves"—that Marshall Williams, Doc Holliday, and even the Earps were implicated in the attempted robbery. Some Tombstonians saw robberies as the natural extension of the activities of the tinhorn gambler element, as represented by Holliday and the Earps. To some, the tinhorn gamblers were "the worst outlaws," men who preferred not to do hard cowboy work or even own a horse, instead renting a horse from a corral when they wished to "make a run out in the country and rob a stage or hold up someone who they had been informed by some of their pals had some money." One Tombstone area resident would later charge that "The Erbs [*sic*] and their combinations would commit depredations, and immediately blame it on the Clantons," who stuck to rustling.

Still others perceived an unholy alliance between the Earp "gang" and the cowboys. Mining engineer Robert A. Lewis later charged that Wyatt and Doc "were at head of a gang, with Ike Clanton and a bunch of cowboys, to do stage holdups just below the town of Contention whenever they were tipped off that the valuables would be thrown out and nobody hurt." John Pleasant Gray would assert that Leonard, Head, and Crane had arrived at Gray's Animas Valley, New Mexico, ranch after the robbery, with Crane telling him "the whole thing had been planned by the Earps. Morgan Earp was to go out that night as messenger, and he had given the tip that about twenty thousand dollars was in the Wells Fargo strongbox." James Hancock presented a similar theory:

> Nearly all old-timers believed it was [Marshall] Williams who tipped off the Earps as to shipments. . . . I have heard it stated that the money was not put in the box, but was held out in the office and the stage holdup pulled off as a

blind. They were afraid that if the outlaws got the box they would pull out for Mexico and leave the Earp crowd to make the best of it. A smooth scheme—the money could be kept in the office and the Earps stay in town.

The problem with this theory, as various Earp researchers have argued, is that the robbery was bungled, so an empty strongbox would have been exposed. But Marshall Williams was indeed a suspicious character. Even Earp supporter Dodge would call him a crook who was stealing from his employer, Wells Fargo. Soon after the attempted stage robbery, Parsons would report to his journal that Williams was "not agreeable" and was to be replaced by "an old stock broker." Nonetheless, Williams would remain in the position for months, then disappear, leaving a string of debts.

Thus, the friendship of the Wells Fargo agent was a liability to former Acting Town Marshal Virgil Earp and former candidate for county sheriff Wyatt Earp, both eager to capture the jobs next time around and anxious to dispel the pall of suspicion settling around their heads. Rumors of the existence of a mysterious fourth highwayman did not help, particularly when the prime suspect for the role quickly was identified both publicly and privately as Doc Holliday.

There were various reasons for suspecting the avuncular dentist. For one thing, he was known to associate with Billy Leonard, one of the identified bandits. Leonard had come to the frontier a skilled watchmaker, reportedly of New York origin. He had set up shop in Las Cruces in south-central New Mexico by June 1879. When he soon opened a shop at nearby Mesilla as well, a Las Cruces newspaper reported approvingly: "We can assure the people of that village that he does first class work. He has done a large amount in this town while here and has given general satisfaction. He makes a specialty of repairing and cleaning fine watches and adjusting them to heat, cold, and position, and has with him an assortment of fine movements which he will put into cases to suit his customers."

However, Leonard made a different kind of impression in the town of Las Vegas to the northeast. Here, while Doc Holliday was running his saloon in that summer of 1879 and the town was reeling from a string of stagecoach robberies, the watchmaker was charged with assault to kill. He moved on westward, claiming ranchland in the mountains of southwestern New Mexico where the rustlers held full sway. Soon he had become a leader among the rustlers.

John Pleasant Gray remembered Leonard as "a man much above his fellow rustlers in intellect and education." Leonard performed a service for the rancher, converting Gray's long-barreled Winchester into a carbine for a saddle gun and using only a table knife and a three-cornered file as tools. The rustler received in payment a copy of a book chronicling the life of Wild Bill Hickok, who had died in Deadwood in 1876, victim of an assassin's bullet through the back. The delighted Leonard gathered his fellow rustlers around "and then spent the rest of the day reading to them," with the result that Hickok was "the hero, henceforth, of the rustlers."

This image of Leonard as a sort of innocent Peter Pan reading stirring stories to the Lost Boys is undercut, however, by a letter in the Tucson *Citizen* complaining that a horse-stealing charge against Leonard had been corruptly thrown out of court on a technicality and that the owner of the stock had been intimidated into dropping the charges rather than lose all of his stock to the cowboys. The letter identified the rustler as "Billy the Kid" Leonard, but all young outlaws named Bill automatically became "Billy the Kid" during this period. (The "authentic" Billy the Kid Bonney, veteran of the Lincoln County Wars in New Mexico, was at the time of the Benson stage robbery about to embark on his final spree, shooting his way out of a Lincoln County jail in April only to have Lincoln County lawman Pat Garrett track him down and kill him in July.)

Leonard has also been depicted as putting his jeweler training to use by establishing a small, remote reduction plant where he could extract gold and silver from stolen bullion and melt down stolen precious metal items.

Whether or not Leonard was this versatile, he was clearly running on the wrong side of the law, and Tombstonians understood that he and Doc were old friends from Doc's Las Vegas days. Even Wyatt Earp's adulatory chronicler Lake asserted that the two had become "good friends" in Las Vegas and resumed the relationship in Tombstone. And among the staunchest Earp admirers, a criminal Leonard-Head connection was perceived; Fred Dodge would later write that Doc "was a full fledged member of the gang that Leonard was in with."

Such surmises were bolstered by Doc's disagreeably volatile—some said treacherous—temperament. Although Allie Earp "never could stand him," other women seemed to like him; his mistress, Kate Elder, who visited him periodically in Tombstone, called him quiet and gentlemanly, with "a fine set of teeth," while according to Boyer, Josie Marcus found him pleasant to be around, with "a sense of humor and a sense of fun as well." But Bat Masterson, who certainly knew him well, asserted that Doc "seemed to be absolutely unable to keep out of trouble for any great length of time" and had "few real friends anywhere in the west"—with good reason. He "never played square with anyone" in the Tombstone area, Fred Dodge charged, while Masterson judged him a man of "mean disposition" and "ungovernable temper," "hot-headed and impetuous and very much given to both drinking and quarrelling." Within a year, a Tucson paper would describe him as "generally known as a desperado of the first order," while a Las Vegas paper would pointedly comment that the gaunt, prematurely graying dentist was "not a whit too refined to rob stages or even steal sheep."

So both Holliday's association with Leonard and his own reputation worked against him. Even more damning, however, were the actions attributed to him on the afternoon and night of the crime. The *Daily Nugget* at first simply referred to a fourth unnamed suspect still in Tombstone who had appeared armed with a Henry rifle and a six-shooter at a Tombstone livery stable, rented a horse there about four o'clock, and announced that he might return that night or might be gone for seven or eight days. The Tucson *Weekly Star* soon picked up the story:

> He started toward Charleston, and about a mile below Tombstone cut across to Contention, and when next seen it was between ten and eleven o'clock riding into the livery stable at Tombstone, his horse fagged out. He at once

called for another horse, which he hitched in the streets, for some hours, but did not leave town. Statements attributed to him, if true, look very bad, indeed, and if proven are most conclusive as to his guilt, either as a principal actor, or an accessory before the fact.

Earp supporters would later charge that *Nugget* editor and Undersheriff Woods had maliciously planted the seeds of suspicion against Holliday in the paper. Holliday had ridden for Charleston that afternoon, but had witnesses to attest to his return by six-thirty that evening. However, he had reportedly ordered a second horse during the evening and been seen by a number of witnesses—including Ike Clanton and the two McLaurys—riding hell-for-leather toward Tombstone after the botched robbery. For example, a telegraph worker said he and a companion had been stringing lines between Charleston and Tombstone. ". . . we heard the report of a rifle and in a few minutes saw Doc Holliday on the 'Dunbar horse' headed toward Tombstone. (It was a noted race horse and anyway we knew people's horses in those days.) Then we saw two or three men on horseback about one-fourth of a mile farther up the hill."

The worker stated that the "consensus of opinion" at Drew's Station was that Holliday was "at the bottom of it" and had shot Philpot "because he knew too much."

Suggestions of a criminal link between Holliday and the Earps would come from an unlikely source—Virgil's Allie, at least as represented in Waters's book. The account includes a dramatic scene in which Big Nose Kate Elder visits Wyatt and Mattie's home and goads the Earp women to recognize what their men are involved in. "It's that sneakin' con man husband of yours what's the trouble!" she tells the unfortunate Mattie.

Then it happened. Kate had been leanin' against the closet door, her hand on the doorknob. As she flipped around, the door flew open. . . . Out of the closet tumbled a big suitcase, spewin' out on the floor. . . . Wigs and beards made of unraveled rope and sewn on black cloth masks, some false mustaches, a church deacon's frock coat, a

checkered suit like drummers wear, a little bamboo cane—
lots of things like that!

Kate contemptuously identifies the paraphernalia as "Wyatt's
disguises," moved from Doc's room at her insistence, and
charges that "two-bit tinhorn" Wyatt is a troublemaker who
will soon have "that stupid Virge under his thumb like Morgan!"

Kate herself in later years would give a slightly different
account, stating that she was visiting Mattie Earp when Wyatt
opened a trunk and produced from it a false mustache and
beard. "He held it between finger and thumb," she related,
"and turned toward me and said, 'Mrs. Holliday, do you know
what these are?' I said, 'Yes, I think I do.'" Nonetheless, in this
narrative produced near the end of her life, Kate proved enig-
matic on the subject of Doc's and the Earps' participation in
the stage robbery.

In the Waters account, after the Benson stage robbery a
whiskey-swilling Kate tells Allie that Wyatt heads the stage-
coach-robbing gang and that Doc was the fourth highwayman,
gunning for Paul but hitting Philpot instead. Such a view is
bolstered by the fact that Kate would soon be identifying her
lover in an arrest warrant as the murderer of Philpot.

But, then, Kate was as mettlesome in her own way as Doc
was in his. Wyatt Earp used to tell a story of how she sprang
Doc from a Texas jail by starting a fire in a shed to distract
attention, then holding a six-shooter on the local marshal. The
tale has not been substantiated, but Kate certainly did proceed
through life on her own terms. A native of Budapest, Hungary, she was originally Mary Katherine Horony or Haroney,
a child emigrating with her family to Davenport, Iowa. After
both parents died during her adolescence, Kate ran away
from her guardian and assumed the name Fisher. She later
stated that she had married and had a baby son, but when
husband and son died, she "headed West." She frequented the
Kansas cow towns in the 1870's, working at a Wichita "sporting house" and a popular Dodge dance hall.

Kate claimed to have married Doc in his native Georgia in
1876. The two volatile personalities often quarreled and often
parted. According to Kate, when Doc in Prescott received a

letter from Wyatt urging him to come on to Tombstone, she had announced, "If you are going to tie yourself to the Earp Brothers, go to it. I am going to Globe." She nonetheless periodically stayed with Doc in his rented room in Tombstone and used the name Kate Elder.

On her second visit, the Benson stage robbery occurred, and Doc rode off with the posse, first to the robbery site near Drew's Station, then to the Redfield ranch, where they found King. By at least one pro-Earp account, Bob Paul and Wyatt Earp scared King into talking by telling him that the flurry of shots had killed a woman—Doc's mistress, Kate. Later in the year, Wyatt would simply note of his part in King's capture, "I safely say, if it had not been for myself and Morgan Earp they would not have got King, as he started to run," heading for a patch of brush on the river, "and would have got in it, if [it] had not been for us two."

Behan and Breakenridge brought King in while the Earp coterie—Marshall Williams, Doc Holliday, Bat Masterson, and Virgil, Wyatt, and Morgan Earp—continued the hunt for Leonard, Head, and Crane. Soon Behan and Breakenridge rejoined the hunt, accompanied by Buckskin Frank Leslie. "Another party started out today for robbers," Parsons penned in his journal on March 22, "just 3 or 4 men but amongst them two of best trailers and plainsmen in U.S. so said. F. Leslie and Breakenridge."

Leslie has sometimes been identified as a member of the Earp coterie, apparently because he happened to work as a bartender and bouncer at the Oriental. However, the flamboyant shootist remained independent of both the Earp and Behan factions—so much so that both sides would later charge he was in cahoots with the other. Earp biographer Lake asserted that as a "broken old vagabond," Leslie told Wyatt that Behan had hired him to throw the Earp party off the robbers' trail, while in the Waters account, Kate Elder revealed to Allie that Leslie was "the trailer for Sheriff Behan's outfit just to lead 'em off the trail."

Whatever Leslie's allegiances, a wary Breakenridge found the bartender surprisingly good company. The "life of the party," Leslie "had a good voice and sang well, told good stories, never complained of being tired, was always ready to go.

He was a much better companion out in the country than he
was in town."

The first posse soon began losing members, despite the
enticement of a thirty-six-hundred-dollar reward offered by
Wells Fargo. According to the Earp version of events, Marshall
Williams had already accompanied Behan and his prisoner
back to Tombstone to ensure that Luther King did not escape.
Bat Masterson and Doc Holliday, too, soon gave up the chase.
Wyatt himself came in early, ostensibly to track King, who escaped from the Tombstone jail almost as soon as Behan had
gotten him deposited.

King had been left in the charge of Undersheriff Woods.
Woods's *Daily Nugget* reported the escape on March 19 by
bringing in Doc Holliday's name as well:

> [King] escaped from the sheriff's office by quietly stepping
> out the back door while Harry Jones, Esq., was drawing up a
> bill of sale for a horse the prisoner was selling to John Dun-
> bar. Under-sheriff Harry Woods and Dunbar were present.
> He had been absent but a few seconds before he was missed.
> A confederate on the outside had a horse in readiness for
> him. It was a well-planned job by outsiders to get him away.
> He was an important witness against Holliday.

The Tucson *Star* also hinted at an accomplice, reporting that
"a certain person" had been overheard informing King "that a
fresh horse would await him at Helm's ranch" in the Dragoons. Parsons simply wrote, "King the stage robber escaped
tonight early from H. Woods who had been previously notified of an attempt at release to be made. Some of our officials
should be hanged. They're a bad lot."

Indeed, a charge that Woods was deliberately throwing
blame on Holliday included an assertion that Undersheriff
Woods had let the prisoner go and had laughingly concocted a plot to incriminate Holliday in a move so brazen that
lawyer Jones in disgust became an Earp partisan.* But
whether or not Woods did plant the reference to Holliday

---

*Jones was soon given a deputy sheriff commission—Glenn G. Boyer has speculated
possibly as a bribe.

to make trouble for the Earp faction and to deflect criticism from his own poor performance, the dentist's name nonetheless sprang easily to many lips.†

Meanwhile, Leonard, Head, and Crane were rumored heading for a cattle ranch used by rustlers in the Cloverdale area of New Mexico, so the reduced Earp posse—Virgil and Morgan, accompanied by Bob Paul—and the Behan posse—Behan, Breakenridge, and Leslie—worked their way through the rustler haunts east of Tombstone, trailing through Galeyville, the San Simon Valley, the ranch of rustler associate Joe Hill, and the Double 'Dobes in New Mexico's Animas Mountains. The two groups traveled separately and camped together at night. All they found after passing through the mountains were surveyor's stakes showing the future course of the Atchison, Topeka and Santa Fe Railroad between New Mexico and Benson.

Later accounts of the degree of cooperation between the two parties vary greatly. Biographer Lake painted a picture of Virgil, Morgan, and Bob Paul almost famishing on the New Mexico plains, with Virgil's horse dropping dead under him, while the sheriff's posse, carrying food it did not offer to share, rode merrily along on relatively fresh steeds. According to this narrative, when the parties gave up and turned westward, with Behan, Breakenridge, and Leslie reaching Joe Hill's ranch first, the three even failed to send back much-needed provisions.

Breakenridge naturally gave a different account:

> Our horses were tired and we did not know the way, or where there was a ranch at which we could get aid, and after a consultation I decided that my horse was as able to carry me back to the San Simon Cienaga that night as he would be in the morning. Behan and Leslie thought the same, but the marshal's [Virgil's] posse decided to wait until morning. We saddled up and struck out after dark, and reached Joe Hill's ranch about daylight. We got Hill's people up and hired a man to take some provisions back to the

---

† Holliday biographer Pat Jahns has dismissed the idea that Doc was actually involved, but has noted, "it is quite possible that [he] was an accessory before the fact."

marshal's party. He met them on the way and they were glad to see him.

Considering the distance covered and the lack of provisioning places, it had been a long, tough trip for all concerned. The men finally reached Tombstone on April 3.

Aside from King's escape, little had been happening in town, though the *Daily Epitaph* on March 22 had carried an intriguing note: "What action if any did the Coroner take looking to an investigation of the human arm which was found on the street the other day. It surely demanded some attention." April Fool's Day had sparked some levity, with Clum attempting to startle Parsons by pretending to spot the now infamous Curly Bill Brocius on the street. Another April Fool's prank related by Parsons and depending either on a dummy or a free-falling risk taker shows how Tombstone, like Dodge, could play with the hard reputation it was developing: "I was lolling back in my chair in front of Grand Hotel after my dinner there when a loud report at the 'Cosmopolitan' startled the hundreds of people on the street, and at same instant a man's body fell from roof to the ground. A moment of suspense preceded the general laugh and hilarity. . . . Best thing of the kind I ever saw."

The Earps, however, had little to laugh about, for after Virgil's and Morgan's return they continued to be taxed with the uncomfortable Leonard-Holliday connection. In fact, Ike Clanton would later charge that Virgil had spent the seventeen days trailing in the mountains and desert in order to keep Paul and other posse members *away* from the robbers' real escape route into the San José Mountains in Mexican Sonora.

> Virgil told me to tell Bill Leonard . . . not to think he was trying to catch him when they were running him and told me to tell Billy that he [had] thrown Paul and the posse that was after him off of his track . . . and that he had taken them on to a trail that went down into New Mexico, and that he had done all he could for him, and that he wanted them to get those other fellows that were with him—Crane and Head—out of the country, for he was

afraid that one of them might get captured and get all of his friends into trouble.

Virgil would flatly deny this accusation as a self-justifying story on Ike's part. He and his brothers, with the backing of Clum and other prominent Republicans—bankers, mining men, mercantile managers, real estate speculators—insisted that they were simply stalwart law enforcers hamstrung by the lax attitudes toward rustlers demonstrated by the county sheriff's office and by a good portion of the population of Tombstone and vicinity.

But a powerful opposition was operating as well, a Democratic coalition dubbed the County Ring. Behan was not the only Democrat to profit from the formation of Cochise County. His livery stable partner, John Dunbar, had received the county treasurer appointment, while Oriental owner Milt Joyce, still smarting from his October run-in with Doc Holliday, had become chairman of the county board of commissioners. Then, of course, Harry Woods served not only as undersheriff but as editor of the Democratic *Nugget*. The powerful men in the County Ring tended to have accumulated many years in the territory and to favor the fellows from the ranches, legal and illegal, over the gamblers and part-time lawmen who surfaced in the mineral boomtowns. To many of the Democrats who had lived and worked in the territory for a long time and shared a ranching orientation, such men as the Earps were carpetbaggers, as were Clum and the Republican businessmen whose interests ran to speculation in mining and town lots.

On the other hand, the Earps, Clum, and many of their friends had arrived in the early days of Tombstone's development and made a strong commitment to the tenuous town. To newcomers stepping off the stage that spring of 1881, such men were old-timers. And there were always recent arrivals to make one feel like an old-timer in that fast-changing environment. In March, the Southern Pacific Railroad building eastward had met the Atchison, Topeka and Santa Fe at Deming, New Mexico, opening up a second transcontinental railroad and stimulating travel to the Southwest. The new rail line cut by four days travel time to or from New York, while continued improvements in travel from the West Coast meant much traffic into Tombstone from California. On March 24, Parsons had written, "San Franciscans are flocking in now. Stages are crowded." About a week later, he noted, "Town filling up with strangers. A boom is upon us."

Tombstone lost at least one short-term resident in early April, however, when Bat Masterson departed for Dodge. If he was happy to leave the Earp-Holliday troubles in Tombstone behind, he headed into another explosive situation. Brother Jim Masterson was embroiled in a dispute with business interests in Dodge and had just been relieved of his city marshal's badge. When Bat alighted from the train on April 16, he immediately spied two men who had been making threats against Jim. He pulled his gun and began firing; the resulting shoot-out became known as the Battle of the Plaza. No one was killed, but the recklessness of Bat's action cost him an eight-dollar fine and the loss of the goodwill of many Dodge citizens. He and Jim left town; wisely, they chose not to go to Tombstone.

In that silver town, speculation over the Benson stagecoach murders was giving way to controversy over mining claims. Across the West, the first rush to a mining boomtown was followed by fierce and often violent disputes. In Tombstone, 1881 and 1882 would prove to be not only the years in which other tensions surfaced but the peak period for ownership disputes and litigation.

The whole question of mineral ownership was made more complex by the nature of lode mining. Eager prospectors could tap into a lode at different geographical points, then argue forever as to who had the right to mine the vein. The problem had first surfaced in California, where an Apex Law developed as a result. The law mandated that "ownership of the surface part of the vein, or apex, gave the miner the right to follow that vein, together with all its 'dips, spurs, angles, and variations,' as deep and as far as it led him, even if it took him below another man's claim."

However, in application, the law fell apart. For example, some veins narrowed and disappeared, then reappeared at another point. John Pleasant Gray, whose father, Michael, had a following-the-vein claim in Tombstone that languished in the courts, later wrote that the issue "has often resulted in the absolute ruin of both litigants."

Adding to the confusion and animosity was the unscrupulous practice of fractioning. A fellow would locate and claim a few square feet of unclaimed land between two good working operations. As the operations moved closer to his patch of earth, he would start threatening litigation over vein ownership and collect a settlement from one or both of his neighbors.

In Tombstone in April 1881, two mining disputes erupted. The first centered again on the Gilded Age Mining Company, which "was perpetually involved in litigation for everything from failure to pay grocery bills to unsettled boundaries." The unsettled boundaries remained the most incendiary issue, with the two partners in the Gilded Age venture now trying to take over occupied town lots. On April 22, Parsons reported "much excitement in town" over the controversy. The next day, he observed that one of the partners had been threatened "with pictures of coffins, bloody hands, gallows, etc." and almost shot. On April 27, he noted, "'Gilded Age' excitement abating somewhat." The threatened partner was venturing onto the street only with a bodyguard.

No sooner had the Gilded Age furor dwindled, with the issue again going to the courts, than rival claimants of the Mountain Bay mine came close to a showdown. Wyatt Earp was deputized by the sheriff and placed at the head of four other special deputies to stand armed at the mine entrance.

Wyatt continued his own mining-related activities. He and Doc had filed extensive water rights with two partners in the Huachuca Mountains in February; in May, Wyatt, Virgil, and Jim, along with partner R. J. Winders, filed for a patent on their First North Extension of the San Francisco-owned Mountain Maid mine.

While the Earps continued to build on their mining opportunities, Wyatt still chafed under the mantle of suspicion engendered by the rumors after the Benson stage robbery. Leonard, Head, and Crane remained free, and Doc Holliday's name remained before the public as he responded to the pressure by getting charged with "threats against life" and indicted in a shooting incident.

The month of May 1881 nonetheless passed peacefully enough in Tombstone. Up in Galeyville, Curly Bill Brocius took a bullet in the cheek from drifter Jim Wallace, a veteran of the Lincoln County Wars. Wallace had approached the visiting Billy Breakenridge and tried to pick a fight. Curly Bill stepped in and made Wallace apologize to the deputy. This, of course, did not sit well with Wallace, who continued to joust verbally with Curly Bill, then shot him as the cowboy was mounting his horse. Breakenridge reported, "The bullet hit him in the cheek and knocked out a tooth coming through his neck without cutting an artery." James Hancock, who also claimed to be present, later said that "every one thought that Bill was dead, and he could not talk anyway as the bullet had partly paralyzed the vocal cords in his throat."

A number of Curly Bill's friends disarmed and arrested Wallace. They were holding him in a corral when Breakenridge came to claim him. The *Arizona Weekly Star* reported that the cowboys were threatening to lynch Wallace, but Breakenridge recalled that they turned him over easily. He explained to the group that armed men would not be welcomed at the justice of the peace's when the case was considered and got a reply both nonchalant and chilling—"that they did not care to go down, for if Curly died they would hunt Wallace up, and if Curly lived he could hunt him up himself."

The *Weekly Star,* commenting on the shooting, editorialized, "A great many people in southeastern Arizona will regret that the termination was not fatal to one or both of the participants." In mid-May, four cattle-"buying" cowboys—actually a Galeyville butcher, two other Anglos, and a Mexican—in attempting to fulfill a beef contract with Fort Bowie were killed near Fronteras, Mexico. Newspapers reported they had been surrounded by Mexicans and had answered a demand to surrender with gunfire. The incident was destined to have repercussions.

That same month, the case against Luke Short in the Storms killing was dismissed in Tucson, and Short left Arizona Territory soon thereafter. James Earp and his Bessie, too, departed Arizona, but only on a visit to the Earp parents in Colton, California. On May 6, the *Daily Epitaph* reported, "J. C.

Earp & wife left for Colton, California last evening. He expects to be gone about a month or 6 weeks."

According to various anti-Earp accounts, such trips were the occasion for transporting stolen money, but these conjectures are impossible to substantiate. The historical record does not show frequent Earp departures from Tombstone, and even if the brothers were depositing money in California, they had other sources of income: James, Virgil, and Wyatt were involved in mining, business, and real estate, while James, Wyatt, and Morgan were skilled gamblers able to increase their fortunes at the gaming tables.

In short, the Earps had many reasons for wanting to stay in Tombstone and maintain a good reputation. Wyatt Earp decided to go on the offensive against the rumors linking Doc Holliday, and thus the Earps, with the Benson stage robbery. In early June, by his own later testimony, he approached Ike Clanton, Frank McLaury, and Joe Hill to see if they would lure the Benson stage robbers into the Tombstone area for capture. "I told them I wanted the glory of capturing Leonard, Head, and Crane," Wyatt explained, "and if I could do it, it would help me make the race for sheriff at the next election. I told them if they would put me on the track of Leonard, Head, and Crane, and tell me where those men were hid, I would give them all the reward and would never let anyone know where I got the information." Wyatt also stated that he mentioned to Ike the suspicions against Doc Holliday and reasoned "that if I could catch Leonard, Head and Crane, I could prove to the citizens that he knew nothing of it."

Ike Clanton told a different story. Wyatt had approached him alone, swearing him to secrecy and offering both the reward money and money from his own pocket—six thousand dollars total—if he would "help put up a job to kill Crane, Leonard and Head." Ike gave a different motive, too, for Wyatt's request:

He said that his business was such that he could not afford to capture them. He would have to kill them or else leave the country. He said he and his brother, Morg, had piped off [stolen and passed on] to Doc Holliday and Wm. Leonard the money that was going off on the stage, and he said he could not afford to capture them, and he would have to kill them or leave the country, for they [were] stopping around the country so damned long that he was afraid some of them would be caught and would squeal on him.

Ike provided a noncommittal ending to the interview: "I then told him I would see him again before I left town. I never talked to Wyatt Earp any more about it." Wyatt, however, insisted that Ike responded favorably to the scheme, confiding that he wanted to get Billy Leonard "out of the way" because Leonard owned a certain New Mexico ranch that Ike was trying to claim. According to Wyatt, Ike's only reservation was whether Wells Fargo would pay the reward for the three if they were brought in dead, as "Clanton said that Leonard, Head and Crane would make a fight, that they would never be taken alive." Wyatt asserted that he obtained a telegram through Marshall Williams from a San Francisco Wells Fargo superintendent agreeing to pay for the three live robbers or three corpses. He showed the dispatch to Ike and Joe Hill, later relaying the contents to Frank McLaury.

Virgil Earp, in his own later testimony, affirmed his brother's version of events, explaining that Ike had approached him after talking with Wyatt and announced, "I am going to put up a job for you boys to catch them." Virgil wanted an assurance that Ike could be trusted, and Ike responded with the story of the coveted ranch claim, concluding, "Now you can see why I want these men either captured or killed and I would rather have them killed."

"Here are three of you and there is only three of them," Virgil said he responded. "Why don't you capture or kill them, and I would see that you get the reward?"

By this account, Ike reacted vehemently—"Jesus Christ, I wouldn't last longer than a snowball in hell if I should do that!" The "rest of the gang" would think they had done it for the reward. No, Ike insisted, "As soon as Wyatt gets a telegram he is going to send for, in regard to the reward dead or alive, and they will give it dead or alive, we'll start right after them, to bring them over" either to the McLaury ranch or to Willow Springs southeast of it.

With the telegram in hand, Wyatt would recall, a plan was

laid. Hill would go to the New Mexico hideaway of Leonard, Head, and Crane and tell them that they were needed to pull off the robbery of a paymaster en route from Tombstone to Bisbee. Through this ruse, Hill would lure the three to the McLaury ranch in Sulphur Spring Valley, where Wyatt would be waiting with a posse. In Wyatt's account, then, Hill rode eastward after giving his watch and chain and "between two and three hundred dollars" to Virgil Earp for safekeeping.

Leonard and Head foiled any plans by getting themselves shot to death in the Hachita, or Hatchet, Mountains of New Mexico on June 6. Newspapers reported that the pair were ambushed by the two Hazlett brothers, part-time miners and stockmen, who suspected Leonard and Head of being assassins hired by Tombstone Justice of the Peace Mike Gray to obtain the Hazletts' ranch. Gray's son John Pleasant provided a different motive, of course, stating that the Hazletts hid beside the road near the town of Hachita and shot the two in order to collect the Wells Fargo reward.

The Hazletts didn't live long to tell their version. Jim Crane gathered a number of rustlers and went gunning for the brothers. "The Hazlett boys were game," reported the Tucson *Star*, as they "made a brave fight, killing two and wounding three of the Crane party, but being over powered and finally killed." In Kansas, the Topeka *Capitol* soon reported the Hazletts' father en route to New Mexico. In an account that foreshadowed a similar one involving another pair of brothers, the paper stated, "Mr. Hazlett had received a letter from the boys a short time since saying that they had sold their stock and were coming home, and the next news that came was a telegram yesterday informing him of their death."

According to Earp legend, Billy Leonard had lived "some hours" after his shooting, long enough to confess to the Benson stage robbery and conveniently absolve Doc Holliday of any participation. Purportedly, Morgan Earp rode to New Mexico and got the particulars of Leonard's confession before Jim Crane arrived to fill the Hazletts full of lead. However, the Earps were too ready with claims of deathbed confessions, as will become apparent later in the narrative.

As it was, the death of Leonard and Head did nothing to

allay jealousies and suspicions between the factions in Tombstone, and the summer would bring new reasons for enmity and insecurity. June started, appropriately, with a temperature of 104 degrees in the shade, ushering in a series of further unsettling events.

CHAPTER 7
Fire, Flood, and Friction

On June 6, 1881, Tombstone City Marshal Ben Sippy departed the town on a two-week leave of absence, providing an opportunity for Virgil Earp to step into local law enforcement again. The city council quickly appointed Virgil interim city marshal; one of his first acts was to intervene between Ike Clanton and Fred Dodge's partner, "sporting man" Denny McCann, after McCann slapped Clanton and the two armed and drew guns in front of the Wells Fargo office. The *Daily Epitaph* approvingly reported that Virgil had prevented one funeral, and perhaps two. At about the same time, the *Daily Nugget* noted that the number of cases in the local peace court had increased and concluded, "Probably the new Chief of Police has something to do with the revival of business."

Sippy's departure was swiftly understood to be permanent. By June 11, Clum's paper was reporting a rumor that he had skipped town indebted to the city for one thousand dollars. The city auditor denied the charge, but the *Daily Nugget* also reported the marshal indebted to creditors, with one displaying a picture of the departed accompanied by the sarcastic comment "Though lost to sight, in memory dear." The paper added: "Two hundred dollars worth."

Sippy may have had other troubles as well, for he had been repeatedly listed among eighteen squatters on Vizina Consolidated Mining Company property in the public notice columns of the *Daily Nugget*. He also had received a reprimand from the city council for being absent without leave in January, and was called on the carpet in May for "his action in regard to releasing certain prisoners." In December, he had experienced a minor embarrassment, as evidenced by his *Daily Nugget* advertisement of the twelfth offering a ten-dollar reward "for the return to the undersigned of an ivory-handled revolver he lost yesterday." But he had garnered praise for his handling of the town lot and Johnny-Behind-the-Deuce affairs.*

Now, in mid-June, the *Daily Epitaph* reported that Sippy had passed through Lamy, New Mexico, traveling eastward, and concluded, "It looks very much as if the ugly reports about him are true. If so, it is his too confiding friends that suffer and not the city."

At the same time, Clum's paper did not miss a chance to laud Virgil. "Mr. Earp is filling the position of Chief of Police with credit to himself and satisfaction to the people," the *Daily Epitaph* editorialized on June 15. "There is no perceptible increase in stature, dignity nor self-importance since his elevation to his present honorable and responsible position." A week later, the paper reported that it "seems to be accepted Sippy will not return." The vacancy would be filled thirty days after the expiration of his leave.

The weather in Tombstone through June continued hot and uncomfortable. Although the nights were often cool, Parsons reported the temperature rising to 108 in the shade during the day, and dust storms added to the misery. "A terrible wind blast this afternoon," Parsons wrote on June 15, "and worst whirlwind I ever saw. Lasted some time. . . . Couldn't see teams in the St for dust."

Then, on June 22, a real catastrophe occurred that made the normal vagaries of the weather seem minor. In midafternoon, with the temperature 100 degrees in the shade, pro-

---

*Ben Traywick has speculated that Sippy simply tired of the stringent demands of the job, particularly as the factions within town became more pronounced.

prietors Alexander and Thompson of the Arcade Saloon on Allen Street trundled a barrel of bad whiskey out front, preparing to send it back to its distributor. Alexander tried to measure the contents and accidentally dropped his gauge rod into the barrel's depths. An Arcade bartender then stepped forward with a wire to retrieve the rod.

He either lit a match or held a lighted cigar in his mouth, and the barrel exploded in flames, giving birth to Tombstone's first great fire. "In less than three minutes," the *Daily Epitaph* reported, "the flames had communicated with the adjoining buildings and spread with a velocity equalled only by a burning prairie in a gale."

Tombstone residents had tried to anticipate this threat. For example, in April the city council had appointed a committee to study the proposal of the Sycamore Springs Water Company to furnish water free for fire fighting, provided the company was not taxed. In May, the council had adopted a resolution "instructing tax collector to remit $7.56 each night from license of Prof. Taylors performance provided he give a benefit for the fire department of the city of Tombstone." City water tanks were in place; in fact, three days before the fire, Parsons had stayed at the home of a friend whose bathroom was connected to the water tanks and had recorded "my first good bath in Arizona." But the water supply was woefully inadequate for fire fighting, and the voluntary fire companies had no engine. Mayor Clum himself was on a trip to the East to purchase one.

Ironically, Clum was returning from this trip on a train bound for Benson when he and the other riders saw "a great column of smoke rising over the hills to the south." Clum tried to convince his fellow travelers that "we had a live volcano over there," but on arrival in Benson he learned "that Tombstone was burning."

There was little serious threat to life; business owners rushed to save their money, records, and other valuables. Although at least one account had Milt Joyce of the Oriental salvaging a barrel of liquor and receiving princely prices for its contents, the *Epitaph* reported that he "did not save a farthing's worth of anything" and could not unlock his inner safe to save his own cash and deposits before the flames swept through the saloon.

On the other hand, George Parsons's friend Milton B. Clapp, manager of Safford, Hudson & Company's bank, responded by placing "all money and valuables" *in* his (apparently fireproof) inner safe, then calmly locking everything that normally required safeguarding within the building. "While locking the outer door the plastering began to fall around his head," reported the *Epitaph*, but the dutiful manager made good his decorous escape.

Parsons, working in the Sycamore Springs Water Company office with another man when they heard the cries of "Fire," first rushed to assist Clapp. "The flames were lapping the Oriental when we reached the cor[ner] of 5th and Allen and I immediately ran into the bank to help Milton. Everything was hurry and confusion and the flames were making fearful headway. . . . I took place in line and passed flour and provisions out of Fitzhenry's store."

Parsons soon became the injured hero of the day. The fire-fighting citizens, knowing that awnings, porches, and other building protuberances were "the great elements for spreading the flames," swiftly began demolishing these extensions. Parsons attempted to cut a balcony loose, only to have the roof collapse on him. His face bore the brunt of the impact; as he reported to his journal, "the worst wound was caused by a stick going through my upper lip cutting a round hole and going thence through everything up through the left side of my face. Piercing the nasal cavity by bridge of the nose." Dr. George Goodfellow in an extended series of treatments would devise a nose splint, place a wire through the nose, and perform plastic surgery so that Parsons eventually presented an unblemished visage to the world.

Fortunately, his was the worst injury received. Unfortunately, however, Tombstone's business center was devastated, with sixty-six businesses, stores, saloons, and restaurants burned and losses estimated at from $175,000 to $300,000. Lawyer Wells Spicer, who saved official and private papers, had ordered his frame office destroyed to impede the fire's spread, but the sacrifice had gone for naught. By 6:00 P.M., only "the charred and ghastly skeletons of the adobe buildings" stood in the business district, "while here and there thirsty tongues of flame would break forth as if the greedy element, not satisfied with having consumed everything in its course, still craved for more."

The fire was the occasion for lot jumpers to make their move, and Acting City Marshal Virgil had to organize a posse to drive off these opportunists and restore the original owners to their property. Many of the jumpers established themselves in "little round Tents" on the lots they claimed, and horsemen would appear in the middle of the night, lasso the tent pole, and gallop away, pulling the tent from its moorings and leaving the claimant lying exposed.

Boomtowns rebuilt almost as fast as they burned. Teams hauled wood from the Huachucas, new frame and adobe buildings materialized nearly overnight, and soon the town was busier and livelier than ever. On June 28, Virgil won an unanimous endorsement from the city council to become permanent chief of police in Sippy's absence; he was instructed to enforce the fire ordinance, to see to rubbish removal, and "to prevent the use of fire works within City limits on July fourth." The Fourth would be celebrated in relatively subdued fashion. "Due to the Late Disastrous Fire there will be no General Parade," the *Daily Nugget* of July 1 announced, but there *would* be a fire company procession to the new opera house, a patriotic program including an oration by Tombstone lawyer Thomas Fitch, and a "GRAND BALL IN THE EVENING AT THE THEATRE."

As the holiday approached, fireworks were igniting on a number of fronts. First, Wyatt Earp and Johnny Behan's live-in lover Josephine Marcus had discovered each other.

Just when the Earp-Marcus affair began is difficult to pinpoint, but as late as June 11, Josie was going under the name Josephine Behan in receiving a receipt for twenty-five dollars sent to San Francisco. By Boyer's account, Josie had come to see Behan as a "pompous little dandy" bent on self-advancement. "He did me just one favor," the account states. "Through him I met Wyatt Earp."

Wyatt was still maintaining a residence with Mattie Blaylock; they would eventually mortgage their home as husband and wife. Allie Earp would remember a forlorn Mattie leaving a candle burning for the straying Wyatt in the window every night and faithfully washing, ironing, and starching his shirts so that he could cut a fine figure with the tantalizing Josie on his arm. As related in the Waters narrative based on Allie's reminiscences, a spot on one of those shirts led Wyatt to reject it and led Mattie to her only display of anger, with Allie finding her crying and beating the shirt against a fence post. "'He tore it off because it had this little spot on it after I washed and starched it so careful!' She burst out into sobs again. 'Me washin' and ironin' shirts for him to show off in to that—that—' She fell on the ground and began beatin' the fence post with her bare fists."

Mattie was not the only one affected. Johnny Behan might not care enough about Josie to marry her, but neither was he thrilled when she took up with his chief political rival. Josie remained in the house she and Behan had shared, but now Wyatt spent much of his time there. Josie would later recall that Wyatt was away one night when Behan appeared to demand that she get out or move the house, as the lot was in his name. Morgan Earp had thoughtfully shown up to protect her in Wyatt's absence, was occupying a makeshift bed in the parlor, and flattened the demanding Behan. Why the chivalrous Morgan was so concerned about Josie and not his own wife, Lou, remains problematic. But, then, Morgan and Wyatt both seemed to have a number of places to light, between the domiciles of the various women and Fred Dodge's cabin.

The pairing of Wyatt and Josie was fact, but the Waters narrative contains speculation regarding another romantic liaison destined to have negative consequences. Jim Earp's stepdaughter, Hattie, was of an age to have her own affairs of the heart; one evening, according to this account, she was spotted escaping through a window and climbing into the buggy of a "cowboy swain." Jim, Virgil, and Wyatt waited for her, strapping her "to a finish" when she returned. Waters quoted Allie Earp as saying that she never learned who the suitor was, but "I always thought she was sweet on one of the McLaury brothers."

In addition to such explosive affairs of the heart, the summer brought other problems. Ike Clanton and Wyatt Earp regarded each other with increasing wariness, both feeling vulnerable because of their previous dealings. Ike would later swear repeatedly in court that he had not entered into an agreement with Wyatt concerning the deceased Leonard and Head and the still very much alive Crane, but the Earps would tell a different story: that he had, and that Marshall Williams, not privy to the agreement, had nonetheless suspected something of the kind, had gotten drunk, and had said enough to Ike to frighten him and to make him doubt Wyatt's promise to keep the plan secret. In this version of events, Ike was worried about the consequences to himself if other rustlers found out about the attempted double cross of the highway robbers, and he suspected both the unreliable Williams and the equally unreliable Doc Holliday of knowing too much.

Doc was having his own troubles—with Big Nose Kate. On July 6, the *Daily Nugget* reported an interesting development:

Important Arrest

A warrant was sworn out yesterday before Judge Spicer for the arrest of Doc Holliday, a well-known character here, charging him with complicity in the murder of Bud Philpot, and the attempted stage robbery near Contention some months ago, and he was arrested by Sheriff Behan. The warrant was issued upon the affidavit of Kate Elder, with whom Holliday had been living for some time past.

Spicer immediately released the defendant on five thousand dollars' bail, with Wyatt Earp, J. Meagher and J. H. Melgren acting as sureties.*

Kate Elder appears to have been motivated by a desire for vengeance. The Waters account indicates that the volatile dentist used her as a punching bag when the going got rough. Even if he did not, the two independent, touchy personalities were bound to clash. Kate was no Mattie Blaylock.

The Earps and their supporters charged that Johnny Behan, Milt Joyce, and other members of the County Ring had gotten Kate drunk in order to procure the affidavit. Kate her-

---

*Meagher and Melgren were proprietors of the Alhambra, where Doc dealt faro, and Wyatt has been identified as a silent partner in the gambling operation there.

self in later recounting events would demonstrate a handy amnesia regarding the incident. Within a few days, Judge Wells Spicer ordered the charges dropped, on the recommendation of the district attorney, who had examined witnesses and concluded "there was not the slightest evidence" on which to build a case.

Kate had overplayed her hand. On July 7, the *Daily Nugget* reported her tribulations in the unfeelingly light tone western newspapers adopted for women of easy virtue: "Miss Kate Elder sought 'surcease of sorrow' in the flowing bowl. She succeeded so well that when she woke up she found her name written on the Chief's register with two 'd's' [drunk and disorderly] appended to it. She paid her matriculation fee of $12.50, took her degrees and departed." However, Kate also picked up a conviction on a "threats against life" charge and faced an appearance before United States Court Commissioner T. J. Drum on a writ of habeas corpus. For her defense, she acquired the services of Wells Spicer, who had heard her charges against Doc.

Spicer wore a number of hats in Tombstone. His newspaper advertisements proclaimed him an attorney, mining broker, notary public, and "Commissioner of Deeds for the State of California," with "Particular attention paid to Mining Suits, and Mining Matters Generally," including "Mines surveyed, and Maps, Charts, Diagrams with detailed descriptive reports furnished." He also was partner with Wells Fargo agent Marshall Williams in a tobacco and stationery store, dealing in "the Choicest Brands of Imported Key West and Domestic Cigars, Tobacco, Pipes, Stationery, Etc." And, of course, he had become a justice of the peace.

At forty-nine, Spicer had a long personal history in the frontier West. He had worked for years as an attorney and mining engineer in Salt Lake City, Utah. In the former capacity, he had defended Mormon Indian agent John Lee in federal court for his part in leading the 1857 Mountain Meadows Massacre, when Mormon settlers joined Indians in murdering members of an emigrant train passing through southwestern Utah. The crime was so heinous and the evidence against Lee so compelling that Lee received a death sentence. While the Mormon leader waited for execution, Spicer, ever the entrepreneur, convinced Lee's wife, Emma, to outfit a gold-seeking expedition in a move that prompted the condemned Lee to write, "Let Judge Spicer make his fortune independent of us. . . . I owe him nothing."

In 1878, Spicer arrived in Tucson looking for mining opportunities. It was not surprising that the Tombstone boom would lure the balding lawyer southeastward. He would become known as friendly to the Earp faction, but that didn't keep him from successfully defending Kate Elder. Commissioner Drum considered all the points in her case and ordered her set free and the writ dismissed. Commenting on the origin of Kate's legal troubles—her own charges against Doc—the *Daily Nugget* of July 9 concluded, "Such is the result of a warrant sworn out by an enraged and intoxicated woman." Kate didn't waste much time catching a stage for Globe.

The Lake biography of Wyatt Earp states that Doc had offered to leave town and was told by Wyatt, "You send that fool woman away and I'll be satisfied." Doc paid his mistress to disappear, and "as far as Wyatt Earp ever knew, she and Doc Holliday parted company forever." In reality, Kate would return to witness, if not participate in, further troubles in Tombstone.

Another threat to Doc Holliday and to the Earps, according to some of those unsympathetic to them, was Benson stage robbery participant Jim Crane, who still roamed near the Mexican border after avenging his friends' death in Hachita, New Mexico. Crane often stopped in for a meal at John Pleasant Gray's Animas Valley ranch that summer, and Gray repeatedly urged him to give himself up, confident that Crane's account of the Earps' involvement in the robbery would give him "a good chance for a light sentence."

Buckskin Frank Leslie came to the ranch that summer to arrest Crane. Leslie had been given police powers in the Oriental Saloon in November of the preceding year; now he carried a deputy sheriff appointment from Behan. The *Daily Nugget* of July 3 reported the new deputy departed "for a trip of several weeks duration to the country eastward of us." Gray would remember that Leslie rode up to the ranch one morning, looking for the outlaw in order to take him in. Gray informed him that the man he sought would probably appear for lunch, but "I did not think he would be able to arrest Jim without killing him, and . . . I objected to any such method being sprung at our house."

After a short time, Crane did come in, carrying a short Sharps rifle, and joined Leslie and Gray in an uneasy meal, sitting down "on Leslie's right with the gun across his lap and the muzzle in Frank's direction." Leslie did not even mention his mission, soon announced his intention to start for Tombstone, and, on departing, muttered, according to his host, "Tell Jim if they want him, someone else will have to serve the warrant." Gray concluded, "I heard later that Leslie had reported back to his office that he could not find his man."

In town, people were still anxious over the threat of fire; in July, Virgil collected subscriptions for a hook and ladder company. There was a close call on July 11, when a blaze started in a dry goods store, but it was quickly extinguished "by the prompt action of one of the parties in the store who however was severely burned."

Actually, flood rather than fire would threaten the routines of Tombstone citizens through July and August. The Fourth of July holiday had brought with it a heavy rainstorm, and the month continued increasingly wet. On July 24, Parsons noted, "It never rains but it pours now." Two days later he reported Tough Nut Gulch "a foaming torrent ten feet wide," and on the twenty-seventh he recorded that the rains had caused "great damage to railroad and mills," with a dam swept away on the river and "No mail. We're completely isolated." By August 9, floods were an almost daily phenomenon, and by the middle of the month, parts of town buildings were collapsing under the watery onslaught, with the San Pedro periodically unfordable.

Despite this natural disruption, Tombstone itself was sedate enough. In mid-July, a miner was wounded in a gunfight and brought to Dr. Goodfellow, who performed abdominal surgery and stitched the bullet holes in the intestines—a revolutionary procedure for the time. Despite this incident, another shooting, and a rash of arrests for drunkenness, by August 1, Virgil was advising the Tombstone council that "the city was at present remarkably quiet" and that the police force could be reduced to three men. The council acted accordingly, retaining James Flynn and A. G. Bronk and appointing John Bowman a special policeman without pay. Unlike brother Wyatt, Virgil seemed unconcerned with working his relatives onto the police force. In July he had submitted a list of nine possible police officers to the city council, but the brothers were not among them.

Earp researchers have speculated that both Wyatt and Morgan were busy working undercover for Wells Fargo, but the company's cash books indicate that at this point, Morgan had been off the payroll since February, picking up $4.15 in May and $72 in June for his part in the pursuit of the Benson stage robbers. Wyatt had received only three Wells Fargo payments—$125 and $95.82 the previous August and, like Morgan, $72 in June. However, in August and September 1881, Wyatt's name *would* appear under "General Salary" for the amounts of $100 and $95.82.

If things were quiet in town as Virgil reduced the police force, trouble continued to build along the border. The May killing of the Galeyville butcher and his three companions on their cattle-"buying" expedition near Fronteras, New Mexico, had sparked rumors of a revenge raid by their confederates in Arizona Territory, with a Tucson paper in June reporting seventy cowboys en route to Fronteras, and with Mexican officials organizing a Fronteras military force to meet the potential threat.

Governor Frémont's response to such problems remained minimal, despite the fact that he *had* called the attention of the Eleventh Territorial Legislature to the matter in February. However, the governor was like many political appointees of his era. Handed a job as a political plum, he regarded it primarily as a means of self-advancement with the powers back in Washington, and remained either unaware of or unconcerned with the regional complexities of government administration.

Frémont's generally lackadaisical attitude was exacerbated by the fact that he had clashed with the territorial legislature over the few ideas he did offer in regard to making Arizona a prosperous territory. The gulf between the mostly Democratic Eleventh Territorial Assembly and the governor was so strong that after the body had adjourned in March, Frémont had sent a telegram to President Garfield complaining about the members and asking if they had requested he be removed. By the time border troubles heated up again, Frémont had departed on another extended jaunt to the East, and residents of southern Arizona were voicing their displeasure with his performance. Tombstone resident J. W. Moorhead fired a sarcastic letter to the United States attorney general in late May:

> [Frémont's] actions have resembled those of a hen on a hot griddle. When he was first appointed he was so long in getting out to the territory that everyone supposed that he was one of the lost sheep of little Bo-peep; but like those patient but errant quadrupeds of the nursery rhyme, he turned up, after a great while. Since then he has been popping up from Arizona to New York and Washington, and from those cities back to Arizona, in a bewildering manner. It has never been safe to assume that Governor Frémont was in Arizona. . . .

Meanwhile, American officials continued to note the problems in the southeastern section of the territory. United States Attorney E. B. Pomery in Tucson complained on June 23 that the outlaw element in the region was "augmented by the exiled ranger from Texas, the hunted stage robber from Montana, the murderer from Idaho, the desperate criminal of every class from every place," and he surmised that their depredations could quickly lead to "an open rupture" between Mexico and the United States. Bob Paul, now Pima County sheriff, commented on the hanging of the Mexican rustler in March in a June 30 letter to the Mexican consul in Tucson by portraying the situation in similar terms: "The south-eastern portion of the Territory has been under control of the worst and most desperate class of outlaws, both American and Mexican, and an example was needed in order to put an end to so deplorable a state of affairs. I do not know of a single instance in which an innocent person has been hung or killed by good and law abiding citizens."

As for the leading rustlers, Curly Bill was still recovering from his face wound. Melvin Jones later recalled that he and his brother were establishing a ranch on the Gila River that summer when Curly, looking thin and wan, rode up, accompanied by a group of prospectors and a fellow named Russian Bill Tettenborn, or Tattenbaum.

Russian Bill has become a mythic figure in the annals of southeastern Arizona and southwestern New Mexico, his exotic nickname lending an air of romantic adventure to his life. Tales have grown of his connections to Russian nobility, but memoirs of people who claimed to know him and factual accounts rob Bill's story of its glamour. He was simply a would-be rustler whose father was reportedly a Russian subject in a Baltic port. Bill told people that he had been an attaché at the Russian Legation in Washington D.C., but "if he had ever been anybody of importance he had long since degenerated into a trifling way of living." The lanky blond drifter hung about the unpopulated areas of southern New Mexico and Arizona, attaching himself to groups of prospectors and rustlers. The prospectors found him a shiftless braggart, and "even the other rustlers avoided him as being mean and cowardly." He was not "the regulation type desperado," but apparently aspired to be one. His large yellow streak kept him from it. John Pleasant Gray and his brother Dick once encountered Bill in the Animas Mountains and scared him into dropping a chunk of freshly rustled beef and taking off in panicked flight by yelling that Mexicans were coming.

Russian Bill would soon reach a bad end, as would another associate of Curly Bill's. In early July 1881, Tom Harper was hanged in Tucson for a September 1880 killing, and a newspaper reported, "His demeanor on the scaffold was cool and jaunty. He made no confession, but left a letter to Curly Bill, a well known desperado, admonishing him to take warning from him and not to be too handy with his pistol and 'to stand a heap from a man before you kill him.'"

Curly continued to range southeastern Arizona, but perhaps profiting from Harper's advice, he maintained a low profile. Not so with John Ringo, who in early August made the newspapers by holding up a poker game in which he was participating in Galeyville.

Ringo was drunk and losing; he and a companion, David Estes, pulled guns and forced the other participants from the room, then scooped up the approximately five hundred dollars on the table and stole a horse. Billy Breakenridge later made light of the incident, reporting that the rustler leader soon felt bad and returned the money to the players, who "were satisfied, as they all liked Ringo." But the *Daily Nugget* reported, "Some of the [poker] party were so frightened that they broke for the woods where they remained concealed until daylight."

Charges would be brought against both Estes and Ringo. The disposition of Estes's case, like that of Billy the Kid Leonard on the horse-stealing charge, brought an anonymous complaint printed in the Tucson *Star* and the *Arizona Citizen* and directed to Acting Governor John Gosper, at the helm of Arizona affairs in Frémont's extended absence. The judge in Galeyville, the writer complained, had dismissed the charges on the technicality that the victims could not specifically identify which parcel of money was whose. Furthermore, the letter charged, Estes had offered the deputy sheriff who brought him in five hundred dollars to be released, but the court ruled the testimony of the deputy irrelevant. "Thus you see," the letter writer commented with bitter humor, "a single pair in Galeyville wins five hundred dollars."

So Ringo and Estes experienced only temporary mild inconvenience for their crime, and Ringo continued to enjoy the status of the social bandit and to have his apologists. One pioneer Arizonian remembered, "He was a pretty nice fellow and came from a good family but he was wild, used to get on some awful drunks, and become very despondent." An anonymous stage driver recalled that "you would not take him for a bad sort except when he was drinking and gambling and losing, then he was pretty mean."

The stage driver also recollected working at a Lordsburg, New Mexico, corral where Ringo would leave his horse—sometimes without paying. The proprietor told his worker, "I had rather have Ringo's friendship than his hatred beside[s] some day when he has the money he will come in and pay." And cattleman A. F. Franklin wrote of two instances in which he claimed Ringo actually deflected trouble by his presence. In the first, an armed saloon patron was harassing Franklin when Ringo walked in, placed his money on the bar, and announced, "All of Franklin['s] and my friends have a drink." No one cared to "insult him by refusing"—certainly no one who had heard of the December 1879 incident with the bar patron in Safford. In the second incident, Franklin reported a crowd of men about to erupt into violence in a store when Ringo appeared, "slam[med] his gun on the counter," and announced, "if there is going to be a row I think I would like to be in on it." Those present "suddenly decided they had business elsewhere."

Ringo, like his compatriot Curly Bill, was considered highly skilled with a gun; Franklin claimed that the rustler could perform a three-quarter spin, shoot necks off beer bottles, and demonstrate 40 percent accuracy when firing into the open bottle necks.

The marksman and his rustling friends were targets of an *Epitaph* campaign that August. On the thirteenth, the newspaper reported two incidents—an attempt to steal cattle on the San Pedro near Charleston and an attack on three Mexican military men departing Tombstone with supplies and gold and silver. In both cases, the *Epitaph* identified the perpetrators as "murdering cowboys" driven from West Texas and Lincoln County, an organized gang making southeastern Arizona their haven and posing a threat so great that in the absence of effective law enforcement, "the people are justified in taking the law into their own hands and ridding themselves of the dangerous characters who make murder and robbery their business."

This call for vigilante justice was followed the next day by a story of stock run off from the edge of town by "two cowboys," with the comment "Now isn't it about time the people organized?"

However, two days later, the paper remarked facetiously, "Cowboys don't seem to visit our city very much. Don't they like the climate? We feel slighted."

Nor did the newspapers have new stage robberies to report, contrary to the accounts of many writers eager to show either the cowboys or the Earps as embarking on a coach-robbing spree. Tensions were building between the Earp and Behan factions in town, but August, too, passed fairly peacefully, if soggily. On August 19, Parsons recorded, "Floods have been something terrible. Cañons flooded and all roads and trails washed away—completely obliterated." On the twenty-fifth, he noted, "We're in a bad way in town. Eggs and potatoes gone and flour getting scarce owing to the washouts. No mail at all. . . ."

Meanwhile, rustling-related violence along the border had reached new heights with two bloody episodes in early August. The first became known as the Skeleton Canyon holdup. A Mexican smuggling packtrain wending its way through the Peloncillo Mountains on the Arizona-New Mexico border near Mexico was attacked by as many as twenty rustlers. Estimates of the number of Mexicans attacked ranged from four to nineteen; the Mexican Legation informed the United States State Department that nine Mexican citizens were missing as a result of the raid. Joseph Bowyer, manager of the Texas Consolidated Mining and Smelting Company in Galeyville, would report that the raiders had killed three members of the party, but the surviving victims were reluctant to report the crime because of their own illegal activities. The incident provoked Governor Luis Torres of Sonora to write to the absent Governor Frémont requesting that something be done by American authorities.

There seems no question that some of the men known as cowboys were the attackers, but which cowboys remains unclear. Wyatt Earp would testify at the inquest that he was "satisfied" Frank and Tom McLaury were involved, and the whole Earp faction would follow this line by placing Curly Bill, the Clantons, and the McLaurys at the scene. However, James Hancock reported that three other members of southeastern Arizona's free-floating desert population, Milt Hicks, Jim Hughes, and Jack McKenzie, staged the holdup. "No one knows how much the boys got," he recalled, "but Milt told me afterwards that the Mexican that was leading the heaviest packed mule got away 'and us a shootin' at him.'" Hancock reported Galeyville "flooded with new Mexican silver dollars that looked like they had just come out of the Mint." Bowyer relayed to Gosper that one of the cowboys who participated in the raid said they had gotten "the d——st lot of truck," including some silver bullion, about four thousand dollars in Mexican coin, mescal, horses, and cattle.

Only a few days after this incident, a party of Americans bedded down for the night in Guadalupe Canyon, where Arizona, New Mexico, and the Mexican states of Sonora and Chihuahua all meet. According to John Pleasant Gray, whose brother Dick, or Dixie, was among the number, the men were accompanying rancher Billy Lang, also known as Will, who was driving one hundred beef cattle from his New Mexico ranch to market in Tombstone. Dick, who had just turned nineteen, simply wanted to go to town. Cowboys Charley Snow and Billy Byers were along to help herd the cattle. Milk cow buyer Harry Ernshaw was returning to Tombstone. Old Man Clanton, who maintained his own ranch in the Animas Valley, had freighted supplies to some of the valley ranchers and now was returning to the Tombstone area as well, cooking for the party and carrying its bedrolls and camp equipment in his wagon. Outlaw Jim Crane completed the group; according to Gray, the stage robbery participant was ready to turn himself in and reveal the Earps' involvement.

The presence of seven men so close to the border with known rustler Clanton among them has naturally led some to conclude that the group was not moving cattle legally owned by Lang.*

There is also the possibility that the men had recovered stolen cattle from Mexican bandits, for on July 20 Mexicans had filtered through the Guadalupe Pass into the Animas Valley and helped themselves to stock belonging to Lang, Clanton, and Michael Gray. The *Daily Nugget* of August 3 reported that ranchers and cowboys had followed the bandits into Mexico and recovered the stock.

Whatever their reason for being in the canyon, the seven travelers camped in the middle of three low hills, near the stone monument marking the United States-Mexican boundary. Lang and Snow arose the next morning to find the cattle moving about uneasily. Rancher Lang suspected the presence of a bear, and as Clanton and Ernshaw also rose, he instructed Snow to get his gun and check for the animal. Crane, Gray, and Byers remained in their bedrolls as Snow rode his horse up one of the three inclines.

He had not gone far when gunfire erupted from behind

---

*For example, Ben Traywick in his *The Chronicles of Tombstone* says that the herd, three hundred head, had been rustled by Curly Bill and sold to Old Man Clanton at fifteen dollars a head.

the hills. Snow was immediately cut down; so was Clanton. Dick Gray and Jim Crane were hit and killed in their sleeping bags. Survivor Byers, a small, light-haired cowhand from Kansas, would describe the scene to a Tucson newspaper.

> When they first fired and killed Charley Snow I thought the boys were firing at a bear, jumped up out of my blankets, and as I got up the boys around me were shot. As soon as I saw what was up I looked for my rifle, and not seeing it I grabbed my revolver, and seeing them shooting at us from all sides, started to run, but had not gone forty feet when I was shot across my body, but I didn't fall, and in a few more steps was hit in my arm, knocked the pistol out of my hand and I fell down.

Byers saw Ernshaw and Lang run by him; he saw Lang fall, "shot through the legs," and fire his revolver at the attackers, who turned out to be Mexican soldiers, directed by three commanders on one of the hills. The cowhand thought Lang managed to kill one soldier and wound another. Soon he saw the attackers "coming from the direction Will and Harry had run, wearing their hats." He wisely played dead.

> When I saw the Mexicans begin stripping the bodies, I took off what clothes I had, even my finger ring, and lay stretched out with my face down, and as I was all bloody from my wounds, I thought they would pass me by, thinking I was dead, and had already been stripped. I was not mistaken, for they never touched me, but as one fellow passed me on horseback he fired several shots at me, one grazing my head, and the others striking at my side, throwing the dirt over me. But I kept perfectly still and he rode on.

One can only echo the Tucson newspaper's comment on this account: "Byers certainly displayed wonderful nerve in pretending to be dead and lying still while they were shooting at him."

Meanwhile, milk cow buyer Ernshaw had escaped and begun walking the fifteen miles to the Gray ranch. He reached it at dusk. Gray and a companion quickly saddled up, gave

Ernshaw a mount, and rode to a newly established mining camp, Gillespie, on the west slope of the Animas Mountains twenty miles away. Here they found twenty-five miners who "nobly responded" to their request for help by joining them. Mounted on horses and mules, the members of the party traveled in the night darkness, with muddy stretches slowing them down. They reached the massacre site at dawn to find the buzzards gathered over the naked bodies of Gray's brother and the other victims. "The only thing left of the camp outfit," Gray wrote, "was the buckboard standing near the ashes of the campfire," the vehicle having been too large to haul into Mexico over the mountain trails.

Gray and the miners found Billy Byers about five miles away, walking around dazed, "completely out of his head," with a bullet hole through his abdomen. The rescuers dressed Byers's wound. They buried Charley Snow where they found him, about a half a mile from the others—his body "was too far gone to be moved." The wounded cowhand and the other bodies were loaded into a wagon and taken to the Gray ranch. Here the men tore up flooring to make coffins and buried Dick Gray, Old Man Clanton, Jim Crane, and Billy Lang on a nearby knoll.

The Guadalupe Canyon incident dramatically focused the attention of residents of southeastern Arizona and of territorial officials on the border problems. Byers, who brought into Tombstone the buckboard pierced with thirty bullet holes, thought the Mexicans who attacked the Lang party were troops from Fronteras. This conjecture was shared by others. The *Arizona Weekly Star* reported on August 25, "It is known that a company of soldiers, under the command of Capt. Carillo, were scouring the country in the vicinity of the scene of the massacre in search of a party of cowboys who had been depredating on Mexican soil."

Some saw the whole affair as fitting retribution against the cowboys for the Skeleton Canyon incident, particularly because the names of Jim Crane and Old Man Clanton excited suspicions. Parsons's journal entry reflects the attitude of the law-and-order Republicans in Tombstone: "This killing business by the Mexicans, in my mind, was perfectly justifiable as it was in retaliation for killing of several of them and their robbery by cow-boys recently this same Crane being one of the number. Am glad they killed him, as for the others—if not guilty of cattle stealing—they had no business to be found in such bad company."

Naturally, John Pleasant Gray presented a different view, commenting, "[L]ittle did we think that revenge would strike us and not the guilty rustlers who were probably well out of the way by this time."

Some have rejected the newspaper accounts of the incident in favor of a scenario in which the Earps killed or engineered the killing of the Lang party. For example, Oriental owner Milt Joyce reportedly surmised that the Earps, anxious to silence Jim Crane before he got to Tombstone, were behind the ambush. And Earp researchers have speculated that the Earps tried to arrest Crane in Guadalupe Canyon, then, encountering resistance, engaged in a shoot-out with the Lang party.

Nonetheless, the Guadalupe Canyon massacre was generally regarded as an example of border conflict between Mexicans and residents of Arizona Territory, and it was followed by yet another incident when a train of wagons owned by both Mexicans and Americans was stopped at Soldiers Hole and only the Mexicans' property taken.

Meanwhile, County Sheriff Behan and Assistant Federal Marshal and City Marshal Virgil Earp were increasingly having trouble working together with all the enmities built up between their factions. Behan had the sheriff's appointment Wyatt wanted; Wyatt had Behan's girl. Behan's backers were pointing at the Earps and Holliday as instigators of the attempted Benson stage robbery; the Earps and their backers were pointing at the cowboys as instigators and decrying Behan's friendly attitude toward them.

Acting Governor Gosper arrived in early September to survey the situation and quickly got an earful from Tombstone's leading citizens concerning the cowboy threat outlined by the *Epitaph*. He found county law enforcement, as represented by Behan, and city/federal law enforcement, as represented by Virgil Earp, very much at odds. Gosper reported to United States Secretary of State James G. Blaine that Behan "gave me but little hope of being able in his department to cope with the power of the cowboys." One of the most recent complaints against them had come from an American employee of a Sonoran gold mine, who reported the waylaying of "every merchant and courier who is sent up from here." Now Gosper related to Blaine the complete lack of law enforcement cooperation which he found:

> [Behan] represented to me that the Deputy U.S. Marshal, resident of Tombstone, and the City Marshal for the same, and those who aided him seemed unwilling to heartily cooperate with him in capturing and bringing to justice these out-laws.
>
> In conversation with the Deputy US Marshal, Mr. Earp, I found precisely the same spirit of complaint existing against Mr. Behan (the Sheriff) and his deputies.

The acting governor warned that either the cowboys would gain free rein or secretly organized vigilantes would impose their own brand of order. At the same time, like the *Epitaph,* he did favor a form of vigilantism. Despite the paper's appeals, few steps had been taken to renew a concerted vigilante effort such as that which had arisen after the Johnny-Behind-the-Deuce incident. Now Gosper encouraged Tombstone's businessmen in such a move, and the Citizens League which had existed to fight for individual town lot rights was revived as a Citizens Safety Committee.

The idea of a cowboy threat was still disparaged by some. The *Daily Nugget* of September 7 commented dryly, "We know not whether all the crimes laid to the 'cowboys' have been committed by them or not, but certain it is, they have a large number of grievous sins to answer for if they are guilty of one half they are accused of." And two days later, the paper printed a letter of complaint from J. J. Chandler, who had a milk ranch east of Tombstone. The *Epitaph* had run a story asserting that a traveler had narrowly missed being attacked and robbed in the ranch's vicinity; Chandler argued that the traveler had mistaken two of his youthful helpers for desperadoes and asked, "Who was it that saw 'a thief in every bush'?"

It is tempting to speculate that many town dwellers found in the "cowboys" a convenient enemy, a repository for all the fears and uneasiness inherent in the risky business of casting one's fortunes in the middle of the Arizona desert. "Cowboy" sympathizers, however, were too quick to gloss over the very real problems created by the rustlers' border activities. And the whole question of whom to trust in the unstable mining communities of Cochise County, in the canyons, washes, and dry hills of the territory, remained almost impossible to answer. Another stage robbery would only make answers harder to discover.

CHAPTER 8
"I Expect to Record Several Killings"

The Sandy Bob stage, so named after its operator, Charles "Sandy Bob" Crouch, departed Tombstone for Bisbee on the evening of September 8, 1881, with no guard and twenty-five hundred dollars in the Wells Fargo & Company treasure box. Driver Levi McDaniels guided the horses along the southerly trail toward the booming copper mining town located in the Mule Mountains just a few miles north of the Mexican border, passing through the small mining community of Hereford. A short distance out of Hereford, the lead horse veered to the right of the road, and a voice called out of the late-evening darkness, "Hold on." Two men appeared, handkerchiefs covering their noses and mouths. One held a double-barreled shotgun; the other, a six-shooter.

They ordered McDaniels to throw out the mail sack, then the Wells Fargo chest and everything in the boot except a few blankets. As the driver did so, the two lined the passengers up on the other side of the stage and took their valuables, relieving one unfortunate traveler of almost six hundred dollars cash. This accomplished, the man with the six-shooter motioned to McDaniels and the passengers to resume their journey, but the fellow carrying the shotgun climbed up to

McDaniels's seat, speculating, "May be you have got some sugar." The bandit went through the driver's pockets, then allowed him to proceed.

This robbery occurred at about 11:00 P.M., but news did not reach Tombstone until 9:30 the following morning, when two messengers rode into town and reported to Marshall Williams. He in turn notified the sheriff's office. Within a few hours, a group of trackers had gathered, ready for a search. The *Daily Epitaph* on September 10 reported "Deputy Sheriff Breakenridge, Wyatt and Morgan Earp" en route to the holdup scene. Breakenridge was soon joined by his fellow deputy, Dave Neagle, while the Earp brothers were joined by Marshall Williams and Fred Dodge, and the posse split in two, with Breakenridge and Neagle pushing onward to Bisbee first.

Members of the two posses would later tell vastly different stories as to who deserved credit for tracking and arresting the stage robbers. All the men started with a valuable clue. The shotgun-wielding bandit's reference to money as "sugar" focused suspicion on Frank Stilwell, who was well known to refer to money in this way.

Stilwell, brother of well-known army scout Simpson "Comanche Jack" Stilwell, had traversed Arizona as a teamster, stage driver, and miner before arriving in Tombstone during its early boom days, reportedly along with Frank Leslie and another well-known scout, Tom Horn. Stilwell had opened livery stables in rough-and-tumble Charleston and in Bisbee; he had also gained a deputy sheriff appointment in each place. A surviving photo of him shows a broad-faced and clean-shaven young rogue sitting jauntily on a stool with a pipe between his teeth. *I Married Wyatt Earp* would later describe him as "act[ing] like a daring, wild boy playing cops and robbers," and Stilwell apparently craved the excitement of both roles. Breakenridge would call him an efficient officer with no known crime record, but the *Daily Nugget* would run an item indicating that teamster Stilwell had killed a Mexican cook four years earlier. "Stilwell at that early day smoked cigarettes, wore a broad brimmed Texas or Mexican hat and buckskin pants trimmed with fringe," the report noted.

At the time of the Bisbee stage robbery, he apparently favored high-heeled boots, for he left prints from such boots at the scene of the crime, then went into Bisbee and immediately had a shoemaker replace the heels with low ones.

Breakenridge claimed that he and Neagle followed the trail to Bisbee, interviewed the stage passengers, obtained Stilwell's old heels from the shoemaker, and established that they matched the prints at the scene of the crime. Fred Dodge, however, claimed that Breakenridge and Neagle had parted from the Earp party at a cattle crossing where the trail was lost and that he personally rediscovered the trail and found an actual bootheel, "one like all Cowboys and men who were much in the saddle used," near the summit of one of the Mule Mountains. According to Dodge, the Earp party then headed for Bisbee, where Wyatt looked up the shoemaker and Dodge found Stilwell at a corral wearing new bootheels. Both posses also learned that Stilwell had ridden in with his Bisbee livery stable business partner, Pete Spencer.

Spencer, often referred to as Spence, was a Tombstone resident; he and his young Mexican wife, Marietta, and her mother lived on the southeast corner of First and Fremont, directly across the street from the home occupied by Virgil and Allie. The Spencers had married only the previous month, but they apparently lived together before that; Glenn Boyer later related that on Josie Marcus's initial trip to join Behan in Tombstone she had enjoyed talking with Marietta, en route to join her husband, Pete. And Allie Earp would remember the Spencers living across the street through most of the Earps' Tombstone stay, although the Earp men instructed their women not to associate with their nearest female neighbor.

Pete Spencer was something of a chameleon. He was rumored to have Texas origins and was generally labeled a cowboy. Yet he lived in town and engaged in mining speculation, going so far as to advertise in the *Daily Nugget* against anyone buying any portion of the Franklin mining claim "as said mine is my property." Melvin Jones, friendly to the cowboys, called Spencer a tinhorn gambler and "one of the most treacherous and low down robbers and murderers that ever was let live in any town." Nobody really appears to have liked the lean, dark-haired man with the flowing black mustache, though one New Mexico peace officer reputedly called him "the hardest working man I ever knew." Even Marietta would give him up as a bad bargain before long.

In Bisbee, Spencer wound up being arrested along with Deputy Stilwell. In Breakenridge's version, he and Neagle collected the evidence and turned it over to Earp posse member and Wells Fargo agent Williams so that he could get a federal warrant charging the two with robbing the mail and express. When Williams failed to do so, County Deputy Neagle went and got a warrant. Only then did the Earps prevail upon Williams to obtain the federal warrant.

Dodge, on the other hand, wrote emphatically to Stuart Lake in 1930 that neither Neagle nor Breakenridge "had anything to do" with the detection or the arrest, also handled by the Earp party. Breakenridge and Dodge agreed on only one thing: that the two posses banded together to convey the prisoners to Tombstone. But Dodge added that both Stilwell and Spencer vowed to get the Earp posse—Wyatt, Morgan, Marshall Williams, and Fred Dodge. Wells Fargo general cashbooks show that Wyatt, Morgan, and Dodge got twelve dollars each for their trouble.

In Tombstone, the two suspected robbers went before Judge Spicer and were admitted to bail at seven thousand dollars each—two thousand for robbing the cash-carrying passenger and five thousand for robbing the mail. They quickly raised the money; part of the amount was put up by Ike Clanton, indicating that Stilwell and/or Spencer indeed had rustler ties.

Wyatt Earp would later contend while facing charges of murder in the deaths of the McLaurys and Billy Clanton that the McLaurys became incensed over the arrest of Stilwell and Spencer, with whom they were "always friendly." But friendliness does not explain the intensity of Frank McLaury's reaction, as described by Wyatt. Wyatt claimed the elder McLaury confronted Morgan Earp on the street in front of the Alhambra soon after the posse's return to Tombstone.

> . . . Frank McLaury commenced to abuse Morgan Earp for going after Spence and Stilwell. Frank McLaury said he [would] never speak to Spence again for being arrested by us.

He said to Morgan, "If you ever come after me, you will never take me." Morgan replied that if he ever had occasion to go after him, he would arrest him. Frank McLaury then said to Morgan Earp, "I have threatened you boys' lives, and a few days ago I had taken it back. But since this arrest, it now goes." Morgan made no reply and walked off.

Varied sources fail to show any clear connection between McLaury and the two accused, aside from Earp faction claims and an apparent mutual association with Ike Clanton. Virgil Earp in his later testimony gave a better reason for Frank McLaury's anger: the idea that the cowboys were spooked by rumblings concerning the new vigilante organization efforts, with the Earps as enforcers. According to Virgil, mention of the vigilante movement had in September sparked a conversation between him and Frank, who approached him one day near the Grand Hotel.

"I understand you are raising a Vigilance Committee to hang us boys."

"You boys?"

"Yes, us and [the] Clantons, Hicks, Ringo, and all us cowboys."

Virgil recalled that at this point he asked, "Frank, do [you] remember the time Curly Bill killed White?"

"Yes."

"Who guarded him that night and run him to Tucson next morning, to keep the Vigilance Committee from hanging him?"

"You boys."

"Now do you believe we belong to it?"

"I can't help but believe the man who told me you do."

"Who told you?"

Virgil testified that Frank both identified the man as Johnny Behan and asserted, "I'll tell you, it makes no difference what I do, I never will surrender my arms to you. I'd rather die fighting than be strangled."

One must remember that at the time they recounted these conversations, both Wyatt and Virgil were trying to exonerate themselves, brother Morgan, and friend Doc Holliday. However, Virgil's account points up the tension growing between the cowboys and the Earps as agents of a town-dwelling faction. Frank's antagonism probably remained fueled by the mule-stealing incident in summer 1880 and was further provoked by the general ill feeling between the factions.

While Virgil's testimony pointed to Johnny Behan as a catalyst for trouble, some believed that the Earps in September were setting up a showdown with the McLaurys. Breakenridge later related that shortly after the arrest of Stilwell and Spencer, Virgil warned him the McLaurys were threatening to kill anyone who participated in the apprehension, and further urged the deputy sheriff to shoot the brothers on sight or be shot by them. But when Breakenridge saw Tom McLaury a few days later, Tom told him "he was sorry for them [Stilwell and Spencer], but it was none of his fight and he would have nothing to do with it, as he had troubles enough of his own."

Either the Earps were responding to real threats made by Frank McLaury, in which case he was talking himself into an early grave, or they were purposely creating suspicions against the McLaurys. If the latter, they may have done so because the McLaurys had potentially damaging information on the Earps and Holliday concerning the March stage robbery or simply because any violence or threatened violence on the part of the rancher/rustlers gave Wyatt Earp a chance to perfect the law-and-order stance that he hoped would win votes in the first Cochise County sheriff's election. This second possible motive is supported by an account that Wyatt, still looking for a way to win recognition and erase any lingering doubts about the March stage robbery, approached Ike Clanton with the idea of staging a fake robbery after the Stilwell-Spencer affair. Ike and some of his friends would be the highwaymen, of course, with the Earps and Holliday the heroic law enforcers who would scare them off. No one was supposed to get hurt or arrested, but Ike reportedly couldn't quite relax as to the results of this scenario and declined.

Whatever the situation between the Earps, Clantons, and McLaurys at this point, suspicions and tensions were heightened in September by the fact that Stilwell and Spencer could move about freely, awaiting trial in Tucson. Pete

Spencer and the Earp brothers continued to live in close prox-
imity, and the *Epitaph* observed mildly on September 13 that it
had "no desire to pre-judge the case," but if Frank Stilwell was
indeed guilty, "it would seem to be in order for Sheriff Behan
to appoint another deputy."

The stage robbery and subsequent arrest of a deputy
sheriff had a number of individuals nervous, but more pressing to many citizens that early fall was the renewed Indian
menace. Victorio's successor, Nana, had been raiding nearby
in New Mexico, and in late August a new threat had erupted
from the normally peaceable White Mountain Apaches living
between the San Carlos Reservation and Fort Apache, on the
Salt River to the north.

The White Mountain Apaches had rallied around medicine man Nakaidoklini, who predicted that a new age was
dawning for his people and that dead leaders would be returned to life. Nakaidoklini became known as the Prophet and
devised a powerful religious dance that coalesced his followers
into a threat to white rule. Early in August, military commanders sent a half Indian chief of scouts, Sam Bowman, to
observe one of these dances near Fort Apache. He returned in
an agitated state of mind and tried to resign, reasoning, "That
kind of dance always meant trouble, and he didn't want to get
mixed up in it."

A corollary to the idea of a new age for the Apaches was
the notion that the whites, or pindahs, would be disposed of
or conveniently disappear. Nakaidoklini had white authorities
worried, particularly when he ignored the summons of the
San Carlos Indian agent and Fort Apache commander to
come in and talk. In late August, that commander, General
Eugene A. Carr, went out with a force to bring the medicine
man in. They managed to start for the fort with Nakaidoklini,
but at a spot where the soldiers camped for the night, fighting
broke out, with some of the army's own Indian scouts siding
with the Apaches.

On September 4, Parsons wrote, "Terrible news of Indians today. Exaggerated probably. Massacre of Genl. Carr and
command reported at Camp Apache. Globe threatened and
other places and much fear felt here."

The report *was* exaggerated; Carr had lost only a few

troopers, while his men had killed six rebellious Indian scouts and approximately twelve of the White Mountain Apaches, including Nakaidoklini himself. But the Apaches had then begun killing whites in the Fort Apache area and even attacked the fort itself, a rare occurrence in the frontier West, despite the evidence of many a Saturday matinee.

In Tombstone, anxious citizens gathered in Schieffelin Hall, a two-story adobe theater completed only months before. Whenever Apache troubles arose, the defiant Indians, killing and stealing, would flee across southeastern Arizona into the relative safety of Mexico. Through the afternoon and evening, Tombstone area residents attending the Schieffelin Hall meeting debated what to do about this sudden threat from what had been the friendliest of Arizona Apaches. Attorney Tom Fitch argued successfully for a wait-and-see attitude and faith in the government to handle the situation, hitting home by reminding those present "what result would be to Tombstone if this scare got abroad."

The United States Army would quell the White Mountain disturbances in a show of force that simply touched off a more serious Indian threat. Department of Arizona Commander Orlando Willcox forced the White Mountain Apaches' surrender and "paroled" them to Camp Goodwin, a San Carlos subagency where the Chiricahua Apaches were uneasily living, near Camp Thomas. When Willcox, in an "exceptionally stupid move," changed his mind a few days later and sent troops to move the White Mountain band, the unnerved Chiricahuas bolted for Mexico under the leadership of Cochise's son Naiche, Geronimo, Juh, and Chatto. Army troops pursued them to the Pinaleno Mountains bordering the northeast end of the Sulphur Spring Valley, but the Indians staged a successful dusk attack, then "quietly killed any animals that could give them away," including "dogs, who might bark, and the horses light enough in color to be seen clearly in the night." The escapees then disappeared into the canyons, mountains, and deserts of southeastern Arizona.

During the first week of October, Billy Breakenridge and a companion were riding through the middle pass of the Dragoon Mountains when they discovered the body of a wood hauler killed by the fleeing Chiricahuas. The two hurried to town, and a posse was quickly formed. Predictably, it included Johnny Behan, Breakenridge, Marshall Williams, and Virgil, Wyatt, and Morgan Earp. Not so predictably, it also included Clum and Parsons and a number of other townsmen. Though Clum later stated there were thirty-five posse members, Parsons reported to his journal that "20 odd of us dashed through town thoroughly armed and equipped," on the outskirts choosing Behan as captain and "Earp" as first lieutenant.

The party started following the Indian trail eastward, passing through the Dragoons and entering the Sulphur Spring Valley. "A terrible rain storm set in after leaving [the] road," Parsons recorded, "and it seemed to me as though it never rained harder and such a continuous heavy rain I never knew before in Arizona." Some of the posse members gave up, quietly turning their horses westward. Others fell back; Parsons and Clum were left "some distance behind," experiencing "hard work to get along, the ground was so soft and boggy, horses going in nearly up to their knees at times." Finally, the remaining posse members joined their speedier fellows at the ranch of a man named Frink (later referred to as Major Frink), not far from Frank and Tom McLaury's spread. Here the posse learned that the Indians had stolen twenty-seven horses from the two ranches.

The seventeen men crowded into Frink's cabin for an uncomfortable rest cut short by a 3:00 A.M. departure. Accompanied by their host, they then rode through the moonlight following the Indian trail to Leslie Cañon, the mouth of Horseshoe Pass in the Swisshelm Mountains to the southeast. Here, according to Parsons, they saw few signs and "none of a large force." Frink and Breakenridge scouted ahead and found Indians herding the stolen horses, but when Breakenridge returned to Leslie Cañon, he discovered the rest of the party, intent on breakfast, had gone to the McLaury ranch, or the "McLoring" ranch, as Parsons garbled it.

There is a special irony in the scene—Virgil, Wyatt, and Morgan Earp sitting down to eat in the home of the men they would kill less than three weeks later. Neither Breakenridge's nor Parsons's account makes clear whether Frank or Tom were in, though John Pleasant Gray recalled passing through about the same time period and encountering both. "They treated me to the best they had," he would remember, "a good meal and a fresh horse for my remaining twenty-five-mile ride to Tombstone." The McLaurys may have fed the posse themselves; they may have employed a cook, as did Gray at his Animas Valley ranch. Parsons took no note. He did take note of whom the posse happened to meet at the ranch, however.

"At McL's was Arizona's most famous outlaw at the present time 'Curly Bill' with two followers," Parsons commented in his journal. "He killed one of our former marshals and to show how we do things in Arizona I will say that our present marshal [Virgil] and said 'C Bill' shook each other warmly by the hand and hobnobbed together some time, when said 'CB' mounted his horse and with his two satellites rode off."

Almost forty years later, Parsons would elaborate on this scene in a letter to Stuart Lake: "The best of feeling did not exist between Wyatt Earp and Curly Bill and their recognition of each other was very hasty and at some distance. Virgil Earp at that time was on better terms with Curly Bill and he (Virgil) and I walked up to him and had a chat, while the others rested and took things easy for a little while. It was a rather tense situation."

An odd one, too, considering the solidarity of the Earp brothers and the fact that Wyatt would claim to cut Curly Bill in half with a double load of buckshot a few months later.

Parsons on this meeting judged Curly Bill "not a bad looking man" but "very determined" and "not fully recovered from the Galeyville wound." He complained in his journal that a pair of spurs belonging to a member of the posse had disappeared with the departure of the rustler and his two minions, but acknowledged that "'CB' was polite and considerate enough . . . to sharply wheel his horse to one side of my bridle which I had accidentally dropped."

While the posse members were filling their bellies and encountering the noted outlaw, rancher Frink was recovering his stolen animals single-handedly, stationing himself at a point in the hills between the Apache warriors and the Indian women driving the horses, then rushing out and stampeding the horses back into the Sulphur Spring Valley without Indian pursuit. Perhaps they admired the crazy pindah. He certainly had guts.

At the same time, one cannot be too hard on the civilian posse, although they gave up after breakfast, with part of the group returning directly to Tombstone and the other part to Soldiers Hole to turn the matter over to the army troops there. The Tombstone men wound up traveling 125 miles in just under forty-eight hours and had endured a lot of discomfort in the process on the trail of the elusive and dangerous Apaches. The posse had guts, too.

Few would say the same for the professional soldiers who directed military operations in southeastern Arizona. Most residents felt nothing but exasperation with the army role in quelling Indian depredations. Parsons, who was one of the men dispatched to Soldiers Hole, watched the military depart in pursuit of the Indians on the morning of October 7, "bugles blowing an hour before hand to notify all Indians to get out of the way." Breakenridge, too, noting that the soldiers were camped at Soldiers Hole waiting for the ground to dry so that the horses could follow more easily, commented, "The army horses always seemed to need rest when they came near the Indians."

John Pleasant Gray told a similar story when he and some cowboys were in pursuit of Apaches driving stolen stock. Encountering a cavalry troop hunting Indians, the trackers requested assistance and were told that the soldiers' horses were "badly fagged" and the encumbrance of a packtrain made further pursuit impractical. "It was the old, old story so often put up by so many army men. When an Indian trail got hot some such excuse was made for turning back. True, there were exceptions, especially among young officers, but the old, grizzled line captains had, with Arizona ranchers, become a byword for failures in fighting the Apache."

Thus, Gray reported, the Apaches acted confidently in the face of army pursuit and at least one army general chose ranchers or their cowhands to deliver important messages rather than delegate them to soldiers, many of whom had been recruited in cities and knew little of frontier life. "One cavalry troop which was stationed at Rucker all one summer could make the best bread you could wish for. They came from San Francisco—and had enlisted during a baker's strike!

But a cowboy once said they couldn't follow a wagon track and were constantly getting lost."

There were other factors in the army's lack of success: a large and difficult terrain to police with a small number of men; meager finances; cultural understandings of how war should be waged; ineffective and inappropriate command. The more capable officers sought the glamour of the "national theater," prizing those posts in which they could help subdue the Plains Indians, and the more capable commanders put them there. As mining, emigration, and railroads began to expand in the Southwest, military leaders did began to take more notice of the area and deploy some of their better men. But the upshot of it all was that a citizen of southern Arizona in 1881 could expect little or no protection against the Indians from the troops.

Nor could the troops provide any real assistance in quelling the continuing border troubles involving rustlers. A rider appended by the Democratic party to an army appropriation bill in 1878 specified the military could not act as part of a posse comitatus. Both General of the Army William Tecumseh Sherman and Arizona Commander Willcox wanted troops to intervene in the border strife, but they could not by law do so.

The law itself remained inadequately applied both at the local justice of the peace level and at the county court level, with few criminal cases of any type being pursued to conviction. Sometimes, however, the machinery moved inexorably forward, as it did that October of 1881, when the trial of Frank Stilwell and Pete Spencer began in Tucson. Virgil and Wyatt reapprehended the two on the thirteenth, with Virgil accompanying them to Tucson. According to Boyer's account in *I Married Wyatt Earp*, Marietta Spencer and Josie Marcus had been on friendly terms since their chance arrival in Tombstone together, and Marietta agitatedly informed Josie in mid-October that the "Rustlers" were plotting to get the Earps—that certain cowboys were encouraging Ike Clanton and Frank McLaury to shoot it out with the Earp brothers. The rustlers promised to back the two up, but "had no intention" of doing so, instead planning to let the men get their comeuppance for having dealt with Wyatt Earp in the first place.

This account was intent on showing the cowboys as

the villains of the upcoming gun battle. Later events, including Marietta Spencer's own testimony, would reinforce the idea that Pete Spencer was indeed eager to take his revenge on the Earp brothers, but when he planned to and whom he planned with would remain matters open to debate.

Meanwhile, he and Stilwell were facing incriminating testimony in Tucson. Virgil returned to Tombstone, then journeyed back for the opening of the judicial proceedings with his good friend Johnny Behan. Marshall Williams, too, traveled to Tucson and testified he had put $2,500 in the express box. Driver Levi McDaniels recounted the robbery experience, and passenger S. W. Rhea stated in court that the gunmen had relieved him of $593. Shoemaker R. P. Dever explained that he had changed the heels on Stilwell's boots after the robbery. Bisbee butcher D. W. Weldt gave testimony "as an expert in identifying the tracks of men and animals." The star witness, however, was John Hiles of Bisbee, who testified that he had heard Stilwell and Spencer planning to hide the robbery money before their arrest.

The Cochise County sheriff and the Tombstone city marshal did not stay for the full examination, returning home on the twenty-first. The town had settled down somewhat since the last Indian scare.

Along the Arizona-Mexico border and in the rustler enclave of Galeyville, however, troubles persisted. Galeyville mine manager Bowyer had written to Gosper on September 17 that the rustlers continued to raid "along the line of Sonora and Arizona" and to shoot up Galeyville, "going to the length of shooting the cigar out of one's mouth: this of course produces a nervous feeling among visitors especially." He further complained, apparently referring to John Ringo, that "A notorious cowboy known as John R. offers to sell all the mutton the town can consume at the rate of $1.00 per head. No secrecy is observed in this kind of transactions [sic]."

In his own reports to Washington, Gosper pointed out that Mexican bandits were causing severe troubles as well and that "mere rumor and false statements often for a time creates [sic] an uneasiness which a knowledge of the facts quickly dispels." But he was upset by the situation he had found in Cochise County, and he was exasperated over the continuing absence of Governor Frémont. On October 6, as the Tombstone posse was following the Apache trail, Gosper recommended to Secretary of State Blaine that the wandering Pathfinder be ordered to his post or resign. On October 11, Frémont followed the latter course. Meanwhile, Crawley Dake's Tucson deputy, J. W. Evans, notified the governor of Mexican Sonora that he believed two hundred to three hundred armed and organized cowboys had established a headquarters in Mexico. How much this was an honest assessment and how much simply a Dake-like ploy for funds are open to debate. Either way, Evans couldn't get a response from Washington on the matter.

The men known as cowboys continued either to stay away from Tombstone or to behave decorously enough to avoid censure while in town, but their presence outside the settlements sparked anxiety in some town-dwelling travelers. Parsons, returning to Tombstone from a mill operation in the mountains in early October, took a route to avoid cowboys, whom he defined singly in his journal as "a rustler at times . . . and rustler is a synonym for desperado-bandit outlaw and horsethief." His cabinmate, Nick Stanton, was accosted about the same time by a cowboy "on the Charleston road 3 or 4 miles out." The cowboy demanded Stanton's horse; the two men struggled, and Stanton escaped with the animal. On hearing the news, Parsons obtained a permit for his friend to carry firearms in the city limits, noting with a touch of dark and not wholly facetious glee that "I expect to record several killings by him before long."

The day after this entry, the *Daily Nugget* ran another view of the cowboy—an elegiac article written by a man who had spent much of his life on the range. "The cowboy is healthy and cheerful," he wrote, "No one is more hospitable, and his bravery is proverbial. But he is a relic of barbarism, and must go, and the places that have known him will not mourn his departure, for he is too much addicted to 'whooping 'em up.'"

Civilization was on the march, and the cowboy did not fit in. At his best, he was a hard worker who possessed a clear code of honor and who liked to kick up his heels now and then. At his worst, he was a dangerous and dissolute drifter, a threat to both individuals and the social order.

John Pleasant Gray admired many of the Texas cowboys with whom he came in contact on the Arizona frontier. He cited their willingness to work long, hard hours under tough conditions for a meager wage—all without complaining or quitting—and their intimacy with the natural order.

> I know of no other following that can show the loyalty of the old time cowboy under every condition of endurance or hardship. Many of them were almost illiterate yet they had a knowledge of Nature which stood them in hand. They could tell time by the stars almost to the half hour if not closer. . . . On even the darkest night I have followed them to camp when I had lost all sense of direction, but they could always locate the camp wagon, even when all landmarks were blotted out in stormy weather.

Obviously, however, not all of the men called cowboys were such noble primitives. Some had no staying power, and some were downright mean. Rustler Sandy King reportedly stole an old man's horse near Soldiers Hole; when the man protested being left afoot, King grazed his head with a bullet. According to a *Daily Nugget* news item, King also appeared in Lordsburg, New Mexico, and ordered goods at a local store. When the clerk asked to whom he should charge the order, King replied, "To this!" and produced a pistol. "It is not good," replied the clerk, drawing a pistol of his own and shooting the would-be thief through the neck.

The story sounds suspiciously like one told of King's confederate Russian Bill Tettenborn, who reportedly entered a Shakespeare, New Mexico, store, selected a number of loud silk handkerchiefs, and, displaying a big Colt pistol, directed the clerk to "charge it to Russian Bill." This clerk, too, had a pistol handy and used it to crease Bill's neck. The similarity in stories may reflect the fact that Sandy King and Russian Bill rode together—and died together. Soon after the store-robbing incident or incidents, the two were charged with horse and cattle theft. King was lodged in the four-by-eight-foot

Shakespeare jail; Russian Bill made it to Lordsburg on an apparently stolen horse, but was apprehended and joined his confederate in the claustrophobic clink. Local citizens then lynched the two from the rafters of the eating room of the local stage stop. King, so the story goes, asked for and received a shot of whiskey, shaking off the mortal coil with a flip "Here's seeing you later boys." The gangly Bill hung with his toes brushing the floor.

The next morning, a stage arrived, and the passengers entered the dining area to find the two bodies still dangling. "What did you hang them for?" one traveler asked the proprietor.

"Well," he is said to have replied, "Russian Bill here, stole a horse and Sandy King was just a damned nuisance."

Back in Tombstone at about the same time, the local caboose was housing Milt Hicks, Charlie Thompson, and Jim Sharp. Sheriff Behan had arrested Hicks at the Grand Hotel on October 22 on a grand larceny charge involving cattle theft. Thompson, too, was being held for grand larceny, while Sharp was accused of killing a Mexican at Charleston. Late in the afternoon of Monday, October 24, a boy entered the men's cell to remove the slops while the jailer held the door for him. Hicks, one of the rumored participants in the Skeleton Canyon raid, immediately grabbed the jailer and announced, "We have been in here for some time, come in and try it yourself awhile." The three then made a clean getaway.

Once again, all the familiar posse members would gather for the chase. Behan, Breakenridge, the three Earps, and Frank Leslie followed the trail the first night, returning when darkness set in. Then, later that evening, a second posse, consisting of Behan, Virgil Earp, Dave Neagle, Breakenridge, and "some citizens," rode out to check the ranches where the escapees might have gone "for horses, arms, and food."

Hicks would be sighted in Shakespeare, but the three would fade away, replaced by more sensational events. On October 18, the *Daily Nugget* had related that a pistol shot had been heard the night before coming from behind the Alhambra or Occidental Saloon, leading to the supposition that "some despondent wretch" had committed suicide. But no one was found, and therefore, the newspaper remarked facetiously, "[W]e are disappointed in not having a dead man for breakfast." Again, on the twenty-third, a *Daily Nugget* advertiser joked, "We haven't had a man for breakfast for some time, but you can get all the butter, eggs and poultry for breakfast you want at the Boss Store." Soon— very soon—a man for breakfast would cease to be a joking matter.

CHAPTER 9
"Let the Ball Open"

On Monday morning, October 25, 1881, Ike Clanton and Tom McLaury breakfasted with their brothers Billy and Frank at J. J. Chandler's ranch about twelve miles east of Tombstone. Chandler had selected a picturesque location for his operation, which supplied milk to the mining community. Surrounded by stately cottonwood trees, the two-story adobe ranch house sat comfortably near a water source, Antelope Springs, on a low, level spot in the rugged yet undulating terrain at the foot of the Dragoon Mountains.

While Billy and Frank rounded up cattle near Stockton Hill, Ike and Tom were planning to head into Tombstone for supplies. Tom also would be transacting cattle business with a Tombstone butcher. He and Ike hitched up a light wagon, tied a saddle horse behind, and proceeded through the dry arroyos and over the brush-covered hillocks toward town, arriving in the late morning.

Tombstone was bustling with arrivals and departures. The *Daily Nugget* of this date listed "M. Williams," probably Marshall Williams, among those leaving on the stage. George Parsons was away, on an extended visit to a Huachuca Mountains mining camp. The second posse hunting Hicks, Thompson, and

Sharp remained out, with Breakenridge staying on the trail, but at some point on the twenty-fifth both Johnny Behan and Virgil Earp returned. Prominent local lawyer Tom Fitch and wife had just returned from a trip, and both Pima County Sheriff Bob Paul and former Pima County Sheriff Charlie Shibell were newly arrived in town. According to the *Daily Nugget*, Doc Holliday and Morgan Earp had returned from Tucson on Saturday evening, the twenty-second.

Doc was still facing the felony robbing-the-mails charge to come up before the district court convening in November. Morgan, without any significant business interests, ranged more freely than did his older brothers. He spent part of his time at the railroad town of Benson in particular, where he was identified both with law enforcement and with a dangerous tinhorn gambler element. In August, Morgan had assisted a deputy sheriff in the Benson apprehension of two well-known tinhorn gamblers; he had also been identified by a Tucson newspaper as a member of leading tinhorn gambler Ed Byrnes's gang of Benson "top and bottom" thieves, men who used loaded dice to trick the gullible into betting against the possibility of the tops and bottoms of three rolled dice adding up to twenty-one. Since the tops and bottoms would add up to twenty-one every time with unloaded dice, this was known as a real sucker trick.

Morgan may have been gambling in Tucson. Doc was. His on-again, off-again traveling companion Kate would later recall that he was "bucking at faro" at the annual Tucson San Agustin Feast and Fair when Morgan appeared and told him, "Doc, we want you in Tombstone tomorrow. Better come up this evening." Kate put the date of this conversation as the twenty-fifth. She said Morgan did not want her to go back to Tombstone with Doc, and Doc himself tried to dissuade her. But tag along she did, riding the freight train with the two men to Benson, then changing with them to an open buckboard for the last stage of the journey.

So the newspaper had Morgan and Doc returning on the twenty-second, while Kate had them journeying back to Tombstone on the twenty-fifth. Whatever their comings and goings beforehand, the two went out together about 10:30 P.M. on the twenty-fifth. A couple of hours later they encountered Ike Clanton sitting down to order a meal at the Occidental Lunch Room, which was attached to the Alhambra Saloon. Now hostilities commenced in earnest. From this point on, those favorable to the cowboys would see events as part of a Holliday-Earp plot to provoke a fight. Earp supporters would argue that the Earps and Holliday were simply keeping a lid on things in the face of a clear cowboy threat.

Ike and Wyatt would be the only ones to testify at the hearing conducted by Justice of the Peace Wells Spicer as to the scene in the lunchroom that night. In Ike's version, Doc, incensed over an erroneous idea that Ike had made threats against the Earps, stood with "his hand in his bosom" apparently resting on a pistol and immediately began cursing him as "a son of a bitch of a cow boy" and urging him to go for his gun. When Ike replied that he was not armed, Holliday taunted, "You son of a bitch, if you ain't heeled, go and heel yourself." Meanwhile, Morgan Earp sat with his feet over the lunch counter and his hand "in his bosom also," coolly regarding Ike. Now, as the latter rose to leave, Morgan added his threats to Doc's: "Yes, you son of a bitch, you can have all the fight you want now!" He, too, urged the cowboy to come back on the street armed. Virgil was standing on the sidewalk outside; so was one of his deputies, Jim Flynn, for Virgil instructed his brother and Doc to leave Ike alone "while Jim was there." Wyatt Earp also appeared but said nothing. "I walked off and asked them not to shoot me in the back," Ike concluded.

Wyatt's account, of course, is different in tone but also in detail. He was sitting at the lunchroom counter eating when Holliday came in and confronted Ike about the secret pact to capture the Benson stage robbers. If Ike had been saying that Wyatt had betrayed a confidence and told Doc about the arrangement, Doc insisted, then Ike was "a damned liar." Ike denied that he had made such a charge, and a quarrel ensued. Wyatt called Morgan over from the Alhambra bar and had him intervene by taking Holliday's arm and leading him into the street.

Wyatt explained that he had called on Morgan to take care of the matter because the younger brother was a police officer. Virgil, too, would testify that Morgan had been acting as a sworn special policeman, with badge, for almost a month. Only the week before, the council had approved a twenty-dollar claim made by him.

Wyatt, too, intermittently worked as a special, controlling potential disruptions within the drinking and gambling halls. Enforcers were often given powers within specific saloons, as evidenced by Frank Leslie's special appointment at the Oriental. In addition to this type of limited appointment, however, Virgil had made Wyatt acting city marshal when Virgil went to Tucson for the Stilwell-Spencer trial. In relating an incident that occurred only half a day after the lunchroom encounter, Wyatt would state that he had acted as deputy city marshal, still holding the temporary appointment after Virgil's return. However, that evening in the lunchroom he turned to Morgan as the representative of the law.

In Ike's version of the missed midnight meal, he departed first. In Wyatt's, Ike followed Morgan and Doc outside, and the quarrel recommenced in Virgil's presence, with Virgil threatening to arrest both Ike and Doc if they did not stop.

Wyatt Earp often embroidered accounts in favor of himself and his brothers, but the record shows that Virgil would not hesitate to arrest friend as well as foe. He had arrested Mayor Clum for "fast riding" on city streets in August. True, Milt Joyce had lodged the complaint, but Virgil carried out his duties and imposed a fine. In June, he had brought Wyatt himself before the local court on a charge of disturbing the peace and fighting; Wyatt had pleaded guilty and paid the twenty-dollar penalty.

Only once had Virgil's performance in making arrests invoked mild criticism in the press, and that was in September when he let Sherman McMasters, still wanted on the February Globe stage robbery charge, get away. Bob Paul was holding the other suspect, Pony Diehl, when McMasters was spotted in Tombstone. Virgil telegraphed Paul asking whether McMasters was still wanted. Meanwhile, McMasters received warning; he was riding out of town by the time the marshal came looking for him with confirmation of his "wanted" status. Virgil fired five shots after the fugitive, and Johnny Behan went in pursuit. The officers should have "arrested him when they first met him in the street," the *Daily Nugget* observed. There are hints McMasters was back in town as the Earps and Ike Clanton headed for a showdown; he would soon be riding openly with Wyatt.

Wyatt himself stated that after the middle-of-the-night lunchroom encounter, Morgan went to the Oriental, Ike went to the Grand Hotel, and he himself went to the Eagle Brewery (Crystal Palace), where he was in charge of a faro game then in operation. When he stepped back onto the street a few minutes later, Ike was there wanting to talk. "He told me when Holliday approached him in the Alhambra that he wasn't fixed just right. He said that in the morning he would have man-for-man, that this fighting talk had been going on for a long time and he guessed it was about time to fetch it to a close."

Wyatt argued that Holliday didn't want to fight but only to "satisfy" Ike that Wyatt had not talked about the Benson stage robbery pact. Holliday's actions tended to prove otherwise, but, then, what does one tell a man with a six-shooter (Ike had armed himself in the trip to the Grand) making threats against one's friend at one o'clock in the morning?

However, by Wyatt's account, Ike threatened not only Holliday but the Earps as well. "I will be ready for you in the morning," Wyatt quoted him as saying, and again, after their conversation ended and Ike followed him into the Oriental: "You must not think I won't be after you all in the morning."

Clanton's desire to go one-on-one with Holliday is understandable, but this is ludicrous, suicidal talk—to warn one of four skilled gunmen, including at least two with police authority, that you will "be after" them in the morning. If Ike Clanton did indeed make these statements—and he would soon be making similar statements to others—he was very foolish, very drunk, or both.

The response Wyatt said he gave is significant and lends credence to the view that he wasn't particularly interested in a gunfight: "I told him I would not fight no one if I could get away from it, because there was no money in it." After the second dead-end conversation with Ike, Wyatt took possession of his faro bank money, met Holliday on the street between the Oriental and Alhambra, and walked with him westward on Allen Street, with Doc going to his room for the night and Wyatt to his house.

They got more sleep than did Ike, Virgil, and Tom Mc-Laury. Ike would say nothing about talking with Wyatt, but would simply report that about a half hour after the lunch-room incident, he entered the Occidental and engaged in an all-night poker game. The other participants were Tom Mc-Laury, Virgil Earp, Johnny Behan, and "another gentleman, I don't know his name."

Curiouser and curiouser. The acting governor has visited Tombstone and found a crippling lack of cooperation between Sheriff Behan and Marshal Earp, yet the two sit all night playing cards together. Ike Clanton has just had a run-in with the Earps, yet he and Tom McLaury gamble till dawn with one of them.

Of course, one does not have to like the people one gambles with. Each of these men had reason to be wary of the others; maybe they just wanted to keep tabs on each other all night long.

Neither Behan nor Virgil divulged information about the poker game in their hearing testimony, and Ike simply complained that Virgil kept his pistol in his lap the whole time. When Virgil got up to leave at daybreak, he stuck the weapon in his pants. Ike followed him out and complained about his treatment earlier—Virgil's telling Doc and Morgan to leave him alone when Jim Flynn was present—and about Virgil playing cards with a six-shooter in his lap. In light of these incidents, Ike announced, "I thought he stood in with those parties that tried to murder me the night before. I told him if that was so, that I was in town. He said he was going to bed."

The only point that Virgil agreed on in remembering this conversation was the business about going to bed. He testified that Ike stopped him and asked him to carry a message to Doc Holliday: "The damned son of a bitch has got to fight."

"Ike, I am an officer and I don't want to hear you talking that way, at all. I am going down home now, to go to bed. I don't want you to raise any disturbance while I am in bed."

Virgil began walking, and Ike called, "You won't carry the message?"

"No, of course I won't."

"You may have to fight before you know it."

Virgil concluded, "I made no reply to him and went home and went to bed." Allie was waiting, wanting to know if anything was up. Virgil told her that he had been trying to keep Doc and Ike from killing each other.

"Why didn't you let 'em go ahead?" she replied. "Neither one amounts to much."

Virgil got a few hours of sleep; Ike didn't. Chafing at Doc's and Morgan's taunts of the night before, tired and probably hung over, Ike wandered the morning streets, looking for a fight. Barkeeper E. F. "Ned" Boyle, heading home after all-night duty, encountered him first, at about 8:00 A.M. in front of the telegraph office. "His pistol was in sight and I covered it with his coat and advised him to go to bed. He insisted that he wouldn't go to bed: that as soon as the Earps and Doc Holliday showed themselves on the street, the ball opened—that they would have to fight."

Boyle detoured to Wyatt Earp's residence and informed him of the situation before going home to rest. Wyatt himself remained in bed. Meanwhile, Ike headed for Julius Kelly's Saloon, entering and calling for a drink with a fellow named Joe Stump. Kelly overheard Ike telling Stump about his run-in with Holliday and the Earps. "I asked Clanton what trouble he had been having. He stated that the Earp crowd and Doc Holliday had insulted him the night before, when he was not heeled; that he had now heeled himself, and that they had to fight on sight. I cautioned him against having any trouble, as I believed the other side would also fight, if it came to the point, or words to that effect."

About this time, Virgil Earp's brief rest was interrupted by the appearance of one of his deputies, A. G. Bronk, who stopped by the house to get a commitment on a jail inmate and to inform the marshal that he needed to get up, as "There is liable to be hell," with Ike threatening to kill Holliday and "counting you fellows in, too." Virgil had been active at least two nights in a row—the first as a member of the posse trailing the jail escapees, the second as a gun-ready member of the card game. He stayed in bed.

Ike continued his peregrinations, appearing at Hafford's Saloon on the northeast corner of Fourth and Allen, known as Hafford's Corner, with rifle in hand. He repeated his litany to proprietor R. F. Hafford: that he had been insulted the night before, that he had been unarmed at the time, and that he was now ready to fight. He also complained that Holliday and the Earps had agreed to meet him before twelve o'clock noon, but it was already five after. Hafford corrected him: "I said, 'It is ten minutes past,' looking at the clock, 'and you had better go home. There will be nothing of it.' In two or three minutes he went out. . . ."

Soon Ike materialized at the rooming house where Doc Holliday boarded, an establishment fronting Fremont Street and belonging to frontier photographer Camillus Fly and his wife. Like his friends, Doc was sleeping in. But Kate was up. Fly had his photo gallery in a separate building at the rear, and Kate was idly examining the pictures when a man with a rifle came in, looked around, and then went into the boardinghouse dining area. Mrs. Fly soon entered the gallery and informed Kate that Ike Clanton had been looking for Doc. Kate went to her lover with the news: "Ike Clanton was here looking for you and had a rifle with him."

"If God will let me live long enough, he will see me," John Henry Holliday said, and got up.

By this time, Virgil and Wyatt had arisen and emerged from their homes into the unusually cold air. Snow was on the way. Both men wore mackinaws against the chill. Virgil would later testify that he encountered a man named Lynch on the street. Lynch warned the marshal that Ike was hunting him and threatening to kill him on sight. Then Virgil met Morgan and James Earp; they told him, "He has got a Winchester rifle and six-shooter on and threatens to kill us on sight." Virgil instructed Morgan to come with him, and they began looking for Ike to "arrest and disarm him."

Meanwhile, according to Wyatt's testimony, he was approached by lawyer and Deputy Sheriff Harry Jones, who asked, "What does all this mean?"

Wyatt responded by asking Jones what he meant.

"Ike Clanton is hunting you boys with a Winchester rifle and six-shooter."

Wyatt said, "I will go down and find him and see what he wants."

The three "fighting Earps" met up and then parted again, with Wyatt searching along Allen Street and Virgil and Morgan looking along Fremont. The latter two found Ike emerging from yet another saloon, the Capitol, at the southwest corner of Fourth and Fremont, still carrying his Winchester. As he moved along Fourth Street toward Allen, they quietly moved up behind, buffaloed, and disarmed him.

John Clum had only moments before innocently greeted the cowboy on the corner, then begun conversing with Charlie Shibell about any news the former sheriff might have for the *Epitaph*. Virgil and Morgan walked past with six-shooters in hand.

"What does that mean?" Shibell inquired.

"Looks like real trouble," Clum replied. He and Shibell watched as Virgil disarmed and arrested Ike.

R. F. Coleman, a mining man, witnessed the incident as well and testified at the coroner's inquest: "I saw [the] city marshal, Earp, speak to [Ike], but I did not hear what he said. The marshal made a grab and took the rifle out of Clanton's hand. There seemed to be a little scuffle by both of them when Clanton fell. I did not see the marshal strike him but I saw Clanton fall, and they took his revolver from him, and took him to the police court."

Coleman did not see any blows, but Virgil had knocked the cowboy off his feet with a six-shooter slammed against the side of the head. Ike later stated that when the incident occurred, he was walking along with District Judge William Stilwell, he of the silk hat who had arrived in southeastern Arizona with fellow train-and-coach passenger Bat Masterson. The rough Ike and the elegant jurist Stilwell were certainly odd companions; one wishes that Stilwell had been called to testify concerning the incident, but he was not.

Ike did readily admit that he was looking for Doc Holliday. He testified that he was suddenly struck from behind by the marshal and recovered to find Morgan with a pistol cocked and pointing at him. Virgil himself stated that he didn't think he spoke to Ike, that he simply walked up to him and grabbed the cowboy's rifle in his left hand as Ike started to turn. At this point, Virgil testified, Ike reached for the six-shooter protruding from his waistband, and the marshal buffaloed him. "I asked him if he was hunting for me," Virgil related. "He said he was, and if he had seen me a second sooner he would have killed me."

Wyatt Earp placed himself at the scene of the action as well, though the others did not. Wyatt stated that he was approaching Ike from the opposite direction, that he "walked up to him and said, 'I hear you are hunting for some of us.'" Ike responded in this version by throwing his rifle around toward Virgil, who grabbed it and buffaloed him.

The cowboy was charged with carrying a concealed weapon, and the Earps hauled him into the nearby recorder's court in the Gird Block, three two-story buildings butted together in a row on the northwest corner of Fourth and Fremont. The recorder's court occupied the first floor of the center building; the complex built by Dick Gird also contained county offices and the mining exchange, with the whole structure sometimes going by the name Mining Exchange Building. Just across the street was the Capitol Saloon, whence Ike had emerged.

Ike sat down on a bench, a handkerchief against the cut he had received on the side of the head from Virgil's six-shooter. The courtroom was crowded, but Judge A. O. Wallace was not there. Virgil left to locate him, and Morgan leaned against the wall, facing the prisoner and holding Ike's Winchester and six-shooter. The two men were heatedly discussing the buffaloing and arrest when R. J. Campbell, clerk of the Cochise County board of supervisors, entered right behind Wyatt Earp. Wyatt sat down beside Morgan, facing Ike.

Soon, Campbell remembered, Wyatt looked at Ike and announced that the cowboy had threatened his life "two or three times" and he wanted it stopped. Ike made no reply. As Wyatt rose and lit into Ike verbally, Campbell recounted the conversation that transpired.

"You cattle thieving son-of-a-bitch, and you know that I know you are a cattle thieving son-of-a-bitch, you've threatened my life enough, and you've got to fight."

To this, Ike Clanton defiantly replied, "Fight is my racket, and all I want is four feet of ground." Campbell also at one point heard Ike tell Morgan in "an ordinary tone of voice" that "if you fellows had been a second later, I would have furnished a Coroner's Inquest for the town."

Wyatt himself testified that he cursed and challenged the prisoner, giving a fuller rendering than did Campbell: "You damned dirty cowthief. You have been threatening our lives and I know it. I think I would be justified in shooting you down any place I should meet you. But if you are anxious to make a fight, I will go anywhere on earth to make a fight with you—even over to the San Simon, among your own crowd."

The various testimonies show that the Earps actually offered Ike a weapon with which to make a fight. In Wyatt's account, Ike had started the hostilities by telling him, "I will get even with all of you for this. If I had a six-shooter now I would make a fight with all of you." To this, Wyatt said, Morgan responded by holding out Ike's own six-shooter and saying, "If you want to make a fight right bad, I will give you this one." Ike got up to take it, but was stopped by a deputy sheriff named Campbell, who said "he would not allow any fuss."

A slightly different version of this incident was given to the *Daily Epitaph* by an anonymous eyewitness, who reported that Ike turned to Virgil (out looking for Judge Wallace, according to the defense) and said, "You fellows haven't given me any show at all today. You've treated me like a dog." Immediately one of the Earps proffered a Henry rifle, and "in less than half a minute everybody [in the courtroom crowd] was about a block away." When they heard no shooting, the onlookers returned.

Ike himself would testify that Wyatt and Morgan began abusing him, with Virgil soon joining in the taunting and Morgan offering to pay Ike's fine "if I would fight them." Ike agreed, and Wyatt offered the rifle "muzzle first, the muzzle pointed down as he presented it." Ike then decided he didn't like the odds. "I saw Virgil Earp put his hand in his bosom, this way [shows the motion]. Morgan Earp stood over me and behind me on the bench in the rear. Wyatt Earp stood to the right and in front of me, and then I told them I did not want any of it that way. Wyatt Earp asked me where I wanted to fight, and as well as I remember I told him I would fight him anywhere or any way."

Judge Wallace finally appeared and fined the cowboy twenty-five dollars "and costs of this action" on the concealed weapons charge. Ike immediately paid. Coroner's inquest witness Coleman would relate that at this point—after the trial—words passed between Virgil and Ike, with Virgil offering Ike his rifle in challenge and provoking Ike's statement "all I want is four feet of ground!" He did not take the rifle, however. Virgil gave a different account, stating that after the trial he simply asked Ike where he wanted his arms left. "Anywhere I can get them, for you hit me over the head with your six-shooter," he quoted Ike as replying. Virgil took the arms to the Grand Hotel and left them with the barman there.

The next run-in involved Wyatt and Tom McLaury. Wyatt would imply in his testimony that he walked out of the court after the fining of Ike and almost immediately ran into Tom. Other witnesses testified that Wyatt was walking toward the court, and one testified that Tom was coming from the court, leaving open the possibility that Wyatt had already departed and Tom had just stopped in on hearing of Ike's trouble.

Butcher A. Bauer was walking along Fourth Street with a cattleman when the two saw "both Mr. Earp and McLaury [walk] pretty near solid together, face to face." Bauer and friend stopped and watched as Wyatt and Tom exchanged words which Bauer could not hear. Tom had his hands in his pants pockets. Suddenly Wyatt "raised his left hand or fist-like and run [sic] it into Tom McLaury's face."

"Are you heeled or not?" Wyatt demanded.

"No," answered Tom, "I am not heeled. I have got nothing to do with anybody." The cowboy backed away, but Wyatt followed, pulled a pistol from his coat pocket, and hit him "two or three or maybe four blows" on the shoulder and on the left side of the head. Tom fell on his right side in the middle of the street, grabbing his left ear. When he was lying on the street, Bauer reported, the cowboy "opened his eyes up large and trembled all over."

Bookkeeper J. H. Batcher also witnessed the scene. He saw Wyatt speak to Tom, and testified "about that time I thought it was time to get out of the road and I left." Despite this retreat, however, Batcher heard Tom "speak rather loud" and tell Wyatt "that he had never done anything against him and was a friend of his," but that "whenever he wanted to fight, he was with him [ready to fight as well]."

At this point, Batcher, too, heard Wyatt ask, "Are you heeled?"

The observer did not hear the answer but saw Wyatt pull his gun as he asked, and he saw him slap the cowboy across the face with the palm of his hand, then strike him once on the side of the head with the pistol. Both Batcher and army surgeon J. B. W. Gardiner saw Tom fall; carpenter Thomas Keefe testified that he fell again: "I saw Mr. Earp knock McLaury down with his pistol, twice—I saw him fall twice—McLaury threw his arms up to knock the blows of the pistol off."

According to Wyatt himself, Tom said, "If you want to make a fight, I will make a fight with you anywhere," and Wyatt responded with "All right, make a fight right here." At the same time he slapped Tom "in the face with my left hand and drew my pistol with my right." Wyatt alleged that Tom "had a pistol in plain sight on his right hip, in his pants," but no one else stated that Tom was visibly armed, and if he had been, Wyatt could have run him in.* Nonetheless, in Wyatt's version, he instructed Tom, "Jerk your gun and use it." When Tom made no reply, either lacking a gun or calculating whether to go for a hidden one, Wyatt buffaloed him.

Wyatt would recall that he then strolled down to Hafford's Saloon on the corner of Fourth and Allen and bought a cigar. Bauer stated, however, that as Wyatt left the prone cowboy, he said, "I could kill the son of a bitch." Tom unsteadily arose, "staggered and walked toward the sidewalk and picked up a silver band or roll, to put on his hat again, that was knocked off." He walked in the opposite direction from his adversary, toward the post office on the southeast corner of Fourth and Fremont.

After the buffaloing, Bauer saw Tom in the Capitol Saloon "about 1 or 2 o'clock." Andrew Mehan, apparently working at the Capitol at the time, would testify that Tom checked a pistol with him "between one and two o'clock." If the timing is correct, it appears that Tom McLaury had been carrying a hidden pistol when he was buffaloed, but then quickly disposed of it.

Two other witnesses, however, asserted that they thought Tom *procured* a weapon at about 2:00 P.M. Albert Bilicke, son

---

*See Alford Turner, *The O.K. Corral Inquest* (College Station, Texas: Creative Publishing Company, 1981), p. 172.

of the proprietor of the Cosmopolitan Hotel and a friend of the Earps, explained that he was standing on the sidewalk in front of the hotel on Allen Street and saw Tom enter the Eagle Meat Market, also known as Everhardy's, across the street. Bilicke testified, "When he went into the butcher shop his right-hand pants pocket was flat, seemingly nothing in it. When he came out his pants pocket protruded, as if there was a revolver therein." J. B. W. Gardiner, who was standing with Bilicke, gave a similar testimony, pronouncing himself "sorry to see Tom McLaury had gotten his pistol." However, Ernest Storm, who was running the market, would state that Tom, "bleeding on the side of the head," came in "about 2 or 3 o'clock" without weapons and "did not get any in there that I saw."

Meanwhile, Frank McLaury and Billy Clanton rode into town from Antelope Springs, arriving about two o'clock. With them was an older man referred to variously as Frick and Major Frink, apparently the McLaurys' neighbor who had recovered his own horses from the Indians a few weeks before.

Lawyers for the Earps and Holliday would later try to establish that Ike Clanton had sent a telegram to Charleston or possibly to some other location to enlist the aid of Frank and Billy. Ike had been in front of the telegraph office when E. F. Boyle encountered him that morning. But a telegram seems an easy enough matter to check, and no evidence was brought forward to substantiate this charge. Furthermore, the two men came not from Charleston but from the opposite direction; they apparently arrived unaware of the trouble; and even if we allow that Ike did want to marshal his brother and friends for a fight, the chances of getting a telegram delivered to the free-ranging men and getting them to town, all within a brief span of hours, are quite slim. Ike would explain under oath that Frank and Billy came in at neighbor Frink's request; other testimony would show that Frank McLaury, like his brother, had business to transact with a local butcher.

The new arrivals appeared on Allen Street, heading for the Grand Hotel. Then occurred a curious incident. Billy Allen, a friend of the cowboys, later testified that as they neared the Grand, "Doc Holliday went out and shook hands with one of them in a pleasant way and said, 'How are you?' or something of that kind." Ike Clanton, too, asserted that "Doc Holliday met Billy Clanton about 20 minutes before [the fight] and shook hands with him and told him that he was pleased to meet him." In other words, Doc went out of his way to be pleasant to a young man whose brother had been hunting him with a gun. Doc's action has led to speculation that he was "deliberately misleading the cowboys as to his intentions."

After Holliday passed on and Frank, Billy, and Frink continued to the Grand Hotel, Allen joined them. They were "about to take a drink," and invited him along. "I called Frank off to one side," Allen testified, "and asked him if he knew what was going on.

"After I told them what I had heard, that Tom McLaury had been hit on the head by Wyatt Earp, Frank says, 'What did he hit Tom for?' I said I did not know. He says, 'We won't drink.' That is the last words I ever heard him say. They got on their horses and rode off. Before that he said, 'I will get the boys out of town.' The glasses were on the counter when he said this. They did not drink."

Now events began to move swiftly, if erratically, toward a confrontation. Another friend of the cowboys, Billy "the Kid" Claiborne, who had accompanied Ike to the doctor to get his head dressed, now encountered Frank and Billy, looking for Ike on Fourth Street. According to Claiborne's testimony, Billy announced, "I want to get him to go out home," and stated that he personally had not come to fight anyone "and no one don't want to fight me."

The various testimonies given at both the coroner's inquest and the Spicer hearing do not make clear where Frank and Billy met Ike, but one good possibility is that they found him in George Spangenberg's Gun Shop, on Fourth between Fremont and Allen and up the street from Hafford's Saloon. Wyatt Earp remembered that he saw both sets of brothers enter the gunshop together, but other testimony indicates that Ike was in the gunshop alone and was joined by Billy and Frank.

Ike himself recalled that he was in the gunshop when Billy and Frank appeared, Frank asking where he could find Tom. Ike, who repeatedly glossed over his own actions and intentions on this troubled day, nonetheless provided a forthright explanation for his presence in the shop: "I went in there and asked for a pistol. The gentleman that runs the shop remarked that my head was bleeding, that I had been in trouble, and he would not let me have it. My physical condition was that from the blow I received from Virgil Earp, I felt very sick."

Indeed, laundry operator P. H. Fellehy saw Ike in the gunshop a little after 2:00 P.M. "with his hand under his jaw, kneeling on the counter." Fellehy also saw "a large crowd of people" near the store. Word of Ike's morning threats, of the buffaloing of both Ike and Tom, and of the arrival of their brothers had led anyone who was out and about in Tombstone to expect some kind of clash.

As the cowboys gathered at the gunshop, Wyatt Earp did a nervy thing. Frank's horse was on the sidewalk "with his head in the door of the gun shop," in violation of city ordinances, and Wyatt chose this moment to revive his temporary marshal appointment and remove the animal onto the street. Whether he did it to goad the cowboys further or simply to enforce the law and remind them of its authority, he was taking a chance.

Virgil was around the corner on Allen Street when Bob Hatch, proprietor of Campbell and Hatch's Saloon and Billiard Parlor, rushed up and said, "For God's sake, hurry down there to the gunshop, for they are all down there and Wyatt is all alone. They are liable to kill him before you get there."

Virgil turned the corner and saw Wyatt move from the edge of the sidewalk in front of the gunshop into a crowd of "a dozen or more" people and "shoo" a horse off the sidewalk. According to Wyatt's testimony, this brought Frank McLaury, Billy Clanton, and Tom McLaury to the door of the shop, Billy with his hand on his six-shooter. Frank "took hold of the horse's bridle and I said, 'You will have to get this horse off the sidewalk.' He backed him off into the street."

Frank reentered the gunshop, where Virgil saw him helping Billy Clanton put cartridges into Billy's belt. The two Earps moved away, Virgil taking a position in the doorway of a vacant store with a double-barreled shotgun, probably a ten-gauge, which he had obtained from the Wells Fargo office. One witness, laundryman Fellehy, saw Ike silently pass the marshal without looking at him. Fellehy heard someone ask Ike, "What is the trouble?" and receive Ike's reply: "I don't think that there will be any trouble." The cowboy passed on to the Occidental Saloon on Allen. Soon the McLaurys and Clantons, as well as Billy Claiborne, proceeded along Allen Street to the Dexter Livery and Feed Stables, also known simply as the Dexter Corral.

Both Billy Claiborne and Ike would testify that Billy Clanton had asked his brother to leave town. Claiborne reported that Billy, who wanted "to go to some other corral [the West End] to get his brother's horse," told Ike "that he wanted him to go and get his horse and come home to the ranch, and his brother told him that he would go directly." Ike testified that Billy had asked him to leave town and he had responded by asking "the corral man, where my team was," to harness the animals. First, however, they went to the Dexter establishment to "get something my brother had left there" before departing town.

Mining man R. F. Coleman saw the Clantons and Mc-Laurys in one of the Dexter stalls "in deep conversation," and noticed J. Doling, the proprietor of the Occidental, speaking to Ike there. The Dexter Livery and Feed Stables were owned by Johnny Behan and John Dunbar. Sheriff Behan himself had been conspicuously absent to this point, having by his own testimony slept until "about one or half-past one o'clock." By the time he got up and settled into a chair at Barron's Barber Shop for a shave, the men in the shop were avidly discussing the morning's events. He heard one person present say, "There is to be trouble between the Clanton and the Earp boys," and he asked the barber to hurry with the shave so that he could go disarm "everybody who had arms, except the officers."

He found Virgil standing on Hafford's Corner, still holding the shotgun and accompanied by Doc Holliday. Doc was clad in "a heavy overcoat, shaggy, light-colored gray," reaching below his knees. From Hafford's, the three men could look half a block westward on Allen to the Dexter Corral; at about this time, the cowboys crossed the street and entered the O.K. Corral. "[I, Behan] asked him what was the excitement. . . . He said there were 'a lot of sons of bitches in town looking for a fight.' I don't think he mentioned any names.

"I said to him, 'You had better disarm the crowd.' He said he would not, that he would give them a chance to make a fight. I said to him, 'It is your duty as a peace officer instead of encouraging a fight to disarm the parties.'"

Fellehy witnessed at least part of this exchange, and his account resembles Behan's. The laundry operator saw the sheriff approach the marshal at Hafford's Corner; pushing to the front of the crowd, Fellehy heard Behan speak and Virgil respond.

"What is the trouble?"

"Those men have made their threats. I will not arrest them, but I will kill them on sight."

The two continued to talk as Behan invited the marshal into Hafford's to have a drink with him and with Charlie Shibell.

Virgil remembered the conversation quite differently. By his account, he called on Behan to help him go disarm the cowboys, but Behan declined, arguing that they would not surrender their arms to Virgil without a fight. Instead, Behan announced that he would go alone "and see if I can't disarm them," as he felt confident the cowboys would not hurt him. "I told him that was all I wanted them to do," Virgil stated, "to lay off their arms while they were in town."

While the two men were talking, a stock and mining broker named William Murray approached and called Virgil aside. According to Virgil's testimony, one committee of citizens—miners whom he did not know by name—had already approached him about the situation. Now Murray told him, "I have been looking into this matter and know you are going to have trouble. I can get 25 armed men at a minute's notice." Virgil told him that "as long as [the cowboys] stayed in the corral—the O.K. corral—I would not go down to disarm them; if they came out on the street, I would take their arms off and arrest them."

Witness Coleman also approached the marshal with a warning. Coleman had been standing in front of the O.K. Corral, noting the cowboys in conversation across the street, when they came toward him. "Billy Clanton was on horseback. Frank McLaury was leading his horse when they came up to where I was standing. Billy Clanton remarked to me it was very cold. He asked me where the West End corral was. I told him it was on Fremont Street.* Frank McLaury had passed on before this talk between me and Billy Clanton. Ike Clanton fetched up in the rear."

Coleman moved toward Hafford's and met Behan. He told the sheriff "that he should go and disarm those men," as "I thought they meant mischief." Behan asked where they had gone. Coleman told him and proceeded a few steps, meeting Virgil and repeating his message. The marshal "said that he did not intend to disarm them." This statement can be interpreted as a variation on Virgil's assurances that he would not disarm the cowboys if they stayed in the corral—or as an intention to fight. Coleman certainly anticipated a fight, as his subsequent actions would reveal.

A visitor to town who would become the star witness for the defense at the Spicer hearing, train engineer H. F. Sills, also approached Virgil after seeing the cowboys in the O.K. Corral. He later testified that he had stood for "three or four minutes" within "four or five steps" of them and heard them threaten to kill Virgil Earp on sight. "Some one of the party spoke up at the time and said that they would kill the whole party of the Earps when they met them," Sills stated. Two of the men had pistols "in plain sight." After hearing their talk, Sills inquired of a passerby who Virgil Earp was, found him, and delivered a warning.

Meanwhile, the cowboys passed through the O.K. Corral from Allen to Fremont as Coleman and Billy Allen stood together watching. Allen later testified that he knew something was about to happen: "After seeing them pass through the O.K. corral . . . I stood on the sidewalk a while with Mr. Coleman, then told him I did not want to see it. He said, 'Come on, let's go see it.' And so I went into the O.K. corral and passed through it with Coleman onto Fremont Street."

At this point everybody, with the possible exception of some of the participants in the gunfight, knew what "it" was. The corral alleyway bordered Bauer's Meat Market on Fremont. Here Frank and Tom McLaury stopped to talk with butcher James Kehoe. Kehoe would testify, "There was a little

---

*Actually, the office entrance was between Allen and Fremont on Second, a fact Ike should have known since his team was there. Billy's asking the location of a bystander indicates that the brothers may have been at cross-purposes.

misunderstanding between [Frank] and me about some money we owed them; Frank was in debt to our firm and we owed some money to Tom." Kehoe was standing at the door talking with the brothers when Johnny Behan came up. Tom did not appear to be armed; Frank was. The butcher related the conversation that transpired between Behan and Frank McLaury.

"Frank, I want you to give up your arms."

"Johnny, as long as the people in Tombstone act so, I will not give up my arms."

Behan then told Frank he would take him to the sheriff's office to "lay off" the arms, and Frank replied, "You need not take me. I will go."

"Well, come on," said Behan, and the two proceeded up the street, pausing where the Clantons and Billy Claiborne stood in a vacant lot between Fly's Rooming House and a private house belonging to Tombstone lumber dealer and City Councilman W. A. Harwood.

Behan and others mentioned only Frank being at the butcher shop, holding his horse, with Tom standing on the vacant lot two doors down with the others. In his testimony, Behan related that he told Frank "there was likely to be some trouble and I proposed to disarm everybody having arms." Frank demurred, stating that "he would not, without those other people [the Earps and Holliday]" being disarmed, that "he had done nothing and did not want to make any fight," and that "he did not intend to have any trouble." Nonetheless, Behan reiterated that he must "give [up] his gun, all the same, or his pistol." The sheriff then noticed Ike and Tom standing between Fly's and the Harwood house, and instructed Frank to "come along with me."

There are indications that another person was in on the conversation between Behan and Frank McLaury. Tombstone lawyer Marcus Aurelius Smith, destined to become one of Arizona's first United States senators, has been identified by researchers as the "tall man" to whom housewife Martha King saw Frank talking after she arrived at Bauer's to do her grocery shopping. When King arrived at the butcher shop, she found "quite a number of men standing in a group together on the sidewalk by the door of the market," and when she went inside, "the parties in the shop were excited and did not seem to want to wait upon me." When she asked what was happening, they told her "there was about to be a fuss between the Earp boys and the cow boys." She looked out to see Frank McLaury leading his horse and telling the "tall man," "If you wish to find us, you will find us just below here." Smith would later be excused from testifying at the coroner's inquest and would not appear at the Spicer hearing.

Why the cowboys had positioned themselves "just below here" remains open to conjecture. To the question asked at the hearing, "How come you and Billy Clanton and the McLaurys to be there?" Ike would respond, "My reason for going there was to get mine and Tom McLaury's team. By mutual understanding Billy Clanton and Frank McLaury were going out with us to the ranch. I and Tom McLaury had given orders to have our team hitched up." Billy Claiborne would state that the Clantons and McLaurys had gone "down there" because the McLaurys had "business at the butcher shop to attend to," and the Clantons "went there to get their horses to go out home."

These testimonies make it sound as if the men were standing in the corral where the team had been left, the West End Corral, but they were not. They *were*, as Ike also stated, "on our road to the corral" located on Second between Allen and Fremont, but they could have as easily gone up Fremont as Allen if the McLaurys had not had business with the butcher. None of the responses satisfactorily explains why they were stopped in a vacant lot next to the boardinghouse where John Henry Holliday roomed.

The cowboys may have been hoping for a confrontation with Doc, the one who had started the trouble the night before. More likely, they were divided at this point, both between each other and within themselves. Ike obviously would have loved to "get" the Earps and Holliday, but he had been up all night with little or no sleep; he had been drinking, suffered a blow to the head, expended his energy roaming around seeking vengeance in the morning, and forfeited his weapons. Tom was also hurt and (depending on whom one believes) weaponless. Frank was certainly the type to get angry at his brother's buffaloing, but he also had more sense than Ike did concerning challenges to officers of the law on their home turf. At nineteen, Billy may well have been young and unthinking enough to go after a man who had humiliated his brother; he also seemed anxious to avoid trouble in much of the admittedly biased testimony.

As Johnny Behan attempted to take the cowboys in charge, Virgil Earp was still on Hafford's Corner less than two blocks away and probably not feeling too chipper himself after two or three hours' sleep. He and Doc had been joined by Wyatt and Morgan. Now, according to Virgil's testimony, a man named J. L. Fonck came to the marshal and pledged ten men to assist him. Virgil told Fonck what he had told Murray: that he would not "bother" the cowboys as long as they were in the O.K. Corral. "Why, they are all down on Fremont Street there now," Fonck responded.

Virgil stated at the hearing, "Then I called on Wyatt and Morgan Earp, and Doc Holliday to go with me and help disarm them." Fellehy was watching and reported, "When this gentleman [Fonck] got through talking to marshal Earp, his two brothers, with Doc Holliday, all went down Fourth St. together." Wyatt would testify that Morgan brought up the matter of horses; if the cowboys had horses, they could make "a running fight." "No," Wyatt responded, "if they try to make a running fight we can kill their horses and then capture them."

Virgil, reasoning that "I did not want to create any excitement going down the street with a shotgun in my hand," passed the gun to Doc to conceal under his long coat and took Doc's cane in exchange. Doc probably wasn't too thrilled with the exchange because with his reed-thin frame he generally avoided the "punishing recoil" of a shotgun. The dentist tucked a nickel-plated pistol in his pocket as well. Virgil, Morgan, and Wyatt all had six-shooters, Morgan's in a right-hand pocket and Wyatt's either in his hand or, according to one observer, "pushed down in his pants on the right side a little." Thus armed, Virgil instructed the others to "Come along."

Around the corner and up Fremont Street in the vacant lot, the five cowboys stood with Johnny Behan. He asked how many of them were together, and they responded, "Four." Claiborne explained that "he was not one of the party, that he was there wanting them to leave town." He continued talking with Billy Clanton beside the latter's horse as Behan conversed with Ike, Frank, and Tom. William Cuddy, theatrical manager at the nearby Schieffelin Hall, had heard rumors of trouble and strolled down to the lot. He would testify that Billy Clanton, seeing him approach, "put his hand on his pistol, as if in fear of somebody," but then recognized Cuddy and relaxed. Behan had his back to the newcomer and did not initially see him as the conversation continued.

"I won't have no fighting. You must give me your firearms, or leave town immediately," Cuddy heard the sheriff say.

"They will have no trouble with us, Johnny. We are going to leave town now," Ike replied.

Behan himself would testify that Ike told him he was not armed, and "I put my arm around his waist to see if he was" and "found that he was not." Tom McLaury pulled his coat [actually, his vest] open to show that he had no weapon; Ike would remember his saying, "Johnny, I have no arms on." Under cross-examination, Behan would state that he was certain Ike was unarmed and that he was "satisfied" that Tom was, though he "might have had a pistol and I not know it." Could he have had a pistol in his pocket? No, as "I examined him very closely with my eye."

Billy Clanton remained armed, justifying not checking his gun by stating that he was headed out of town. Frank McLaury continued to insist that the Earps be disarmed as well. According to Ike Clanton, Frank told Behan "he would leave town and keep his arms, unless the sheriff disarmed the Earps." In the latter case, "he would lay off his, as he had business to attend to in town which he would like to attend to before he left."

Behan looked eastward along Fremont. The Earps and Holliday had rounded the corner and were moving along the street toward the cowboys. "Wait here," the sheriff said, "I see them coming down. I will go up and stop them."

Were the Clantons and the McLaurys under the sheriff's arrest at this point? Behan would tell the coroner's inquest jury that he had announced, "I have to arrest you all" before wrangling over who was leaving town and who would and would not give up arms. In a statement reflecting his painful ineffectiveness in taking in hand these ticklish matters between the city marshal and the out-of-towners, Behan would remark to the jury, "At the time I left the McLaurys and Clantons . . . I considered the Clanton party under arrest, but I doubt whether they considered themselves under arrest or not, after I turned to meet the other party."

By his own testimony, Behan also told the Clantons and McLaurys that he was going "to disarm the other party." Witness Coleman walked up to Fly's just as the sheriff left. "You need not be afraid, Johnny," he heard one of the cowboys call, "you need not be afraid, Johnny, we are not going to have any trouble." But in fact, the Clantons and McLaurys were already standing on "the field of battle."

CHAPTER 10

"I Am Shot Right Through"

"The gunfight at the O.K. Corral" has a ring to it which "the gunfight in the vacant lot between Fly's and Harwood's" clearly lacks. However, the fact is that the famous confrontation took place on Tombstone's Lot 2, Block 17, fronting on Fremont Street, while the O.K. Corral fronted on Allen and extended to the rear edge of Fremont Lots 5 and 6. These two lots were occupied by Bauer's Butcher Shop and the Papago Cash Store, with an alleyway exit to the O.K. Corral between them. The cowboys had moved through that exit, turned left, and passed three buildings—Bauer's, an assay office, and Fly's—before reaching the vacant lot. Now the Earps and Doc Holliday walked along the left-hand side of Fremont, passing the Papago Cash Store and the corral outlet only ninety feet from the vacant lot in which the cowboys were standing, with Frank McLaury and Billy Clanton still holding their horses' reins.

Johnny Behan met the Earp party just past the corral exit, in front of Bauer's. The sheriff would testify that he told the Earps, "I was there for the purpose of disarming the party" and "did not want any trouble, and would not allow it if I could help it, and not to go down." The four did not respond. He tried again.

"Gentlemen, I am sheriff of this county, and I am not going to allow any trouble, if I can help it." They brushed past. Behan stated he followed "probably a step or two in the rear" and "expostulating with them."

Both Billy Allen and R. F. Coleman, now standing at Bauer's, would testify that they heard the sheriff tell the Earps and Holliday not to proceed, although Allen would observe in contrast with Behan's testimony that he "did not use any very great exertions." Butcher James Kehoe would give a slightly different version, stating that he heard the sheriff say, "You are an officer," or, "I am an officer," but like the other witnesses, Kehoe heard no reply. Ike Clanton would remember that Behan held up his hands when he got close to the Earp party "and told them to stop, that he had our party in charge."

Wyatt, however, would recall that Behan approached the group with the admonition "For God's sake, don't go down there or you will get murdered."

"I am going to disarm them," Virgil replied.

Then, Wyatt would maintain, as Virgil moved past and Wyatt and Morgan came even with the sheriff, Johnny Behan announced, "I have disarmed them." Wyatt noted, "When he said this, I took out my pistol, which I had in my hand, under my coat, and put it in my overcoat pocket."

This gun was most likely the one Wyatt had used earlier to buffalo Tom McLaury. Witness Bauer would call the weapon "an old pistol, pretty large, 14 or 16 inches long, it seemed to me," a description that has led researchers to classify it as a Colt single-action "Peacemaker" with a 7½-inch barrel or a Peacemaker with "an extra long 10 or 12 inch barrel." A Smith & Wesson No. 3, .44 American with an 8-inch barrel has also been mentioned as a possibility, but the solid Colt packed more of a wallop and could be used in repeated buffaloings, while the Smith & Wesson cylinder would fly out and the barrel bend the first time it was put to such a use.*

Johnny Behan would repeatedly deny that he had told the Earp party he had disarmed the cowboys. The words attributed to him by Wyatt do seem inconsistent—first warning the Earps and Holliday that they will get murdered if they go further, then stating that the cowboys are disarmed. If the sec-

---

*See Turner, *The O.K. Corral Inquest,* pp. 124–25, for a discussion of Wyatt's weapon.

ond remark can be regarded as a deception, the first remark indicates that Behan was not consciously setting the Earps up for attack. As the sheriff testified that he *did* tell the Earps and Holliday he was there to disarm the cowboys, perhaps Wyatt simply misunderstood the statement. At any rate, Behan didn't help matters. While one can give him credit for trying to step in and stop an explosive confrontation, his attempts were almost ludicrously ineffectual at best.

Housewife King, still trying to get a cut of meat for supper in Bauer's Butcher Shop, did not see Behan attempt to halt the Earp party. She did, however, hear someone at the door announce, "There they come!" as the butcher finally filled her order. She moved to the doorstep and saw Holliday, whom she knew, and three men whom she did not know passing by on the sidewalk, with Holliday "on the inside," closest to the buildings. The men were traveling at a "leisurely" pace, "as any gentleman would walk, not fast, or very slow." But Doc's coat was blowing open, revealing the shotgun, although he was trying to keep it covered. "And what frightened me and made me run back," she would relate, "I heard this man on [the] outside—[he] looked at Holliday and I heard him say, 'Let them have it.' And Doc Holliday said, 'All right.'"

Within seconds the four reached the edge of the fifteen-foot-wide lot. No one present could later agree as to the exact positions of the members of both parties, but the Earps and Holliday apparently stood in a row, Wyatt on the lot next to the corner of Fly's Rooming House with Virgil, Morgan, and Doc aligned to his right, Doc still partially on Fremont. In truth, there was little room on the small patch of vacant ground for the newcomers. Again, the positions of the other cowboys vary according to the teller, but Billy Clanton had joined Tom and Frank McLaury in a row in front of the wall of the Harwood house, Billy at the corner directly opposite Wyatt, Tom and Frank on Billy's right. Behind the three men were Billy's and Frank's horses. Billy Claiborne would testify he was still standing with his friends, his back to the Harwood house, too. Ike Clanton had moved close to Fly's corner, near Wyatt, as the Earps and Holliday came up. Nine men and two horses added up to a tight fit—not the ideal situation for a gunfight.*

---

*Ben Traywick, in conversation with the author, has pointed out the cramped nature of this encounter.

Testimony would be divided as to whether the Earp party had guns in hand or drew them when they stopped. Both Ike Clanton and Billy Claiborne recalled that the Earps and Holliday were holding pistols when they arrived at the corner of the lot; Behan stated that the four drew their weapons "when they got to the party of cow boys." Wyatt insisted that he had pocketed his six-shooter when he understood Behan to say the cowboys were disarmed. Actually, the weight of evidence suggests that Virgil was holding only Doc's cane, though he was carrying a six-shooter, and that both Doc and Morgan were holding revolvers, Doc's a nickel-plated one that appeared bronze in the afternoon light. Wyatt may or may not have been brandishing his pistol; although he said that he had placed it in his overcoat pocket, he may have adopted a popular practice of the 1880's, grasping the gun in his waistband through a slit in the top of his pocket.*

As for the cowboys, both Billy and Frank were carrying Colt single-action army revolvers; they also had Winchester rifles in scabbards on their horses. Ike's Winchester carbine and Colt .45 caliber pistol were still sitting behind the bar at the Grand Hotel where Virgil had left them after the buffaloing and court appearance; by Ike's own admission he had tried and failed to rearm at Spangenberg's Gun Shop. Tom McLaury had left his Winchester carbine in the West End Corral on Fremont and his six-shooter with saloon man Andrew Mehan.

As soon as the Earp party paused, they issued a verbal challenge. Ike Clanton, Johnny Behan, Billy Claiborne, and Billy Allen would all testify that one or more of the newcomers said, "You sons of bitches, you have been looking for a fight and you can have it." Behan said he thought Wyatt Earp uttered the words. Claiborne was unsure but believed Virgil was the speaker; he also indicated there was more than one by adding, "They both said the same thing at the same time." In line with this assertion, Ike Clanton would testify that Wyatt and Virgil both delivered the taunt. Billy Allen heard it but simply attributed it to "the Earp party." R. F. Coleman, about thirty feet away, heard the term "sons of bitches" used, "by which party I could not say."

Immediately on the heels of this remark, Virgil Earp

---

*See Turner, *The O.K. Corral Inquest,* p. 125.

called on the cowboys to "Throw up your hands!" Almost everyone present in the lot and nearby heard and reported this command; some stated that it was followed by a second statement. Johnny Behan recalled that Virgil added, "We are going to disarm you!" Wyatt Earp, who made no mention of the sons of bitches remark in his testimony, agreed, reporting Virgil's words as "I have come to disarm you!" Saloonkeeper Robert Hatch, watching from nearby, reported the declaration, "We have come down here to disarm you and arrest you." Virgil himself recalled his words as "Boys, throw up your hands. I want your guns."

At this crucial moment, the various members of the two parties were very close—from three or four to ten or twelve feet apart. Coleman, who had talked Billy Allen into coming to see "it," now turned to get out of the way, later explaining, "I then thought I was a little close." It is unfortunate that he did so, for testimony as to what happened next veered into two diametrically opposed accounts, with those favoring the cowboys—Claiborne, Fuller, Allen, Ike Clanton himself, and later on, old-timers who claimed to have seen the fight—insisting that the four men were responding in an unresisting manner and with Virgil and Wyatt Earp insisting that the Clantons and McLaurys initiated the violence.

Johnny Behan, Ike Clanton, Billy Claiborne, and Billy Allen all would testify that Tom McLaury responded to Virgil's command by throwing open his coat and announcing, in one way or another, "I have got nothing." Claiborne reported that Tom said, "I haven't got anything, Boys, I am disarmed." Ike alone recalled an Earp party remark following this, a variation of the previous one: "You sons of bitches, you ought to make a fight!"

Behan also would remember that as Tom showed he was unarmed, Billy Clanton cried, "Don't shoot me. I don't want to fight." Billy Allen gave a similar account, stating that the youngest Clanton held his hands out in front of him and announced, "I do not want to fight!" A third witness testifying to Billy's statement was his friend Wesley Fuller, who had been on his way to warn Billy to get out of town when he saw the confrontation develop from a position in the alley behind Fly's. He heard Billy tell the Earp party not to shoot, that he did not want to fight, and he saw Billy throw up his hands.

Furthermore, Fuller would testify, Billy was in this position when the Earp party started the shooting a split second later. Allen would contend that Billy still held his hands in front of him as the gunfire started. Both Ike Clanton and Billy Claiborne would insist that the Clantons and Frank McLaury had their hands up, while Tom McLaury was still holding his coat open.

Wyatt and Virgil reported a completely different scene. In Wyatt's account, both Billy Clanton and Frank McLaury responded to Virgil's command to throw up their hands by putting their hands on their six-shooters. Seeing the action, Virgil responded, "Hold, I don't mean that! I have come to disarm you!" At this, Billy and Frank started to draw, while Tom McLaury threw his hand to his right hip, threw open his coat, and jumped behind a horse. (Everyone persisted in referring to Tom's coat, although witness James Kehoe would report he was clad only in dark pants, long, lightweight blouse, and vest, a description supported by Coroner H. M. Matthews's testimony.)

Virgil related that Billy and Frank already had their hands on their six-shooters and that Tom had his hand on the Winchester on one of the two horses before Virgil even told the men to put their hands up. When he did so, he testified, "Frank McLaury and Billy Clanton drew their six-shooters and commenced to cock them, and [I] heard them go 'click-click.'" Virgil raised his hands, still holding the cane in his right—or shooting—hand, and said, "Hold on, I don't want that!" As he did so, Billy Clanton "threw his six-shooter down, full cocked."

The approach, the challenge, and the response—whether submission or defiance—had all taken only a matter of seconds. Martha King would reveal just how brief a time it was. When she heard one of the Earps tell Holliday to "Let them have it!" and heard Holliday respond affirmatively outside the butcher shop, she fled toward the back wall. But she would state that before she reached the middle of the shop, she heard firing. Butcher Kehoe, too, would testify that less than a minute after the Earps passed the sheriff on Fremont, "I heard two shots in quick succession."

All witnesses and surviving participants would agree that two shots were initially fired, so close together that they almost sounded like one report and could not have come from the same weapon. Mining man C. H. Light, in his room at the Aztec Rooming House at the northwest corner of Fremont and Third Street when the shooting started, summed up the general consensus: "There was not time enough for a man to draw a pistol to fire a shot, between the first two shots. They must have been from two pistols. The man who fired the second shot must have been prepared to fire when the first shot was fired."

Who fired these shots? Billy Clanton and Wyatt Earp, according to Wyatt himself, Virgil Earp, and railroad engineer Sills, the out-of-towner who said he had heard and reported cowboy threats. Remember that in the scenario provided by Wyatt and Virgil, Billy Clanton already stood with his pistol cocked. Wyatt would testify, "The first two shots were fired by Billy Clanton and myself, he shooting at me and I shooting at Frank McLaury. I don't know which was fired first. We fired almost together." Wyatt claimed to have hit Frank in the belly. Virgil Earp would state that Billy was aiming his pistol "kind of past me" and two shots went off simultaneously, with Billy's one of them. Sills would say that he saw Virgil speak to the cowboys, but "by that time Billy Clanton and Wyatt Earp had fired their guns off."

There are two basic problems with this testimony concerning the firing of the first shots. First, there is Wyatt's alleged response. He asserted that "I never drew my pistol or made a motion to shoot until after Billy Clanton and Frank McLaury drew their pistols." When he drew, he explained, even though Billy was aiming at him from a few feet away, he chose to go for Frank McLaury, whom he knew as the most skilled and dangerous of the four.

Wyatt Earp was nervy and good with a gun. Nobody was that good with a gun. Weapons authorities have established that the reaction time of even the most skilled gunman will make him the loser if his reasonably swift opponent has even started to draw first. As testimony would show, Billy Clanton and Frank McLaury were both considered swift, efficient shooters. If they were already standing there with pistols cocked, intending to shoot, Wyatt Earp could not have drawn and fired almost simultaneously with one of them.

The second problem with the testimony of Wyatt, Virgil, and Sills is the fact that most of the other witnesses—including two who had warned the Earps about the cowboys—would state they saw Billy in the act of drawing his pistol *after* the fight was under way.

In fact, a number of witnesses would assert that the Earp party fired both shots, with Billy Claiborne and Ike Clanton flatly identifying Doc Holliday and Morgan Earp as the shootists. Claiborne provided a vivid eyewitness account: "Then the shooting commenced, right then in an instant, by Doc Holliday and Morgan Earp—the two shots were fired so close together it was hard to distinguish them. I could not. I saw them shoot." Billy Allen, behind the Earps on Fremont, saw Doc Holliday swing his hand up and saw smoke come first from in front of him but was unsure as to which other member of the Earp party fired as well. Johnny Behan simply testified that whoever was holding the nickel-plated pistol had fired first. R. F. Coleman, turning to get out of the way, "had the impression" the shots came from the marshal's group.

Thus, one interpretation of the fight is based on the premise that Doc Holliday and Morgan Earp "opened the ball," Doc wounding Frank McLaury and Morgan hitting Billy Clanton, with Wyatt and Virgil later lying to protect the two less respectable members of their party.

The trouble-prone Doc was a likely initiator. Ike Clanton in his testimony placed the gambling dentist-turned-enforcer about six feet from the McLaurys at the time the gunfire commenced; another witness, Addie Bourland, placed him closer. Dressmaker Bourland, who watched the beginning of the confrontation from the window of her establishment almost directly across Fremont Street from the vacant lot, would testify that she saw "a man with a long coat on" [Doc] walk up to "the man who was holding the horse [Frank McLaury] and put a pistol to his stomach." He then "stepped back two or three feet, and then the firing seemed to be general."

Bourland would prove to be a most unsatisfactory witness, though a useful one to the Earps. Despite the fact that she had viewed the crucial opening moments, her statements would remain extremely vague; she *would* testify, however, that she had seen no one with his hands up.

With Doc's bullet in his belly, Frank McLaury staggered onto Fremont Street, drawing his six-shooter and still leading his horse by the reins. Butcher Kehoe would note, "I saw Frank McLaury running out on the street from the vacant space, drawing his pistol" as the shooting became "general."

Meanwhile, at the corner of the Harwood house, witnesses testified Morgan had shot Billy Clanton in the chest near the left nipple. "How do you know that Morgan Earp shot Billy Clanton?" Ike would be asked. His reply: "Because I see [sic] his pistol pointed within two or three feet of his bosom, saw him fire and saw William Clanton stagger and fall up against the house and put his hands onto his breast." Billy Claiborne was equally explicit; Morgan had fired from approximately a foot away, and Billy "fell up against the window and slid down against the house."

Reports as to whether he slid all the way to the ground or immediately regained his footing are confused. Fuller testified he saw him first draw his gun "in a crouched sleeping [sic] position, leaning against the house." Coleman reported him in a crouched standing position: "Billy Clanton had his hand on his pistol, which was in the scabbard. His hand was on his left hip, as if in the act of drawing. This was after the first two shots were fired." There were indications that Billy also received a wrist wound almost immediately, possibly even before the breast hit. At least one witness thought that Billy had been the initial target of both Doc and Morgan.

Others believed that Doc first hit Tom McLaury, not Frank. Claiborne was "positive" that Doc's first bullet found Tom, as the latter "staggered backward after the first shot." Billy Allen on Fremont testified, "I saw Thomas McLaury when the first two shots were fired slap his hand on his breast, like this, and went onto the vacant lot by Fly's building, where I could not see him."

The contrast between this account and Virgil Earp's could hardly be greater. Virgil had testified that Tom stood at the beginning of the encounter with his hand on the Winchester in the scabbard on Billy Clanton's horse. Now, Virgil would state, Tom grabbed for the Winchester and missed as the horse shied away at the sound of the first two gunshots. Tom then "followed the movement of the horse around, making him a kind of breastwork, and fired once, if not twice, over the horse's back."

For Tom McLaury to have fired over the horse's back, he would had to have been using a weapon concealed up until this point. At the Spicer hearing, the Earp forces would try to establish that he did have such a weapon, although none was found on or near him after the fight. Significantly, the Earps would be the only ones at the hearing to claim to have seen Tom in the act of shooting, although the *Epitaph* would later carry an account by a mine superintendent's wife who stated that she had been nearby and had seen a cowboy using a horse as a barricade and firing under its neck. Modern Earp researchers still entertain the possibility that Tom was armed, citing the long blouse that could have hidden a weapon and speculating that Johnny Behan could have removed a gun immediately after the fight.

The confusion over Doc's shooting of the McLaurys stems from the fact that he apparently shot both within the first few seconds of the melee, first firing the nickel-plated pistol at Frank, then, after Morgan fired, swinging the shotgun up and hitting Tom with a load of buckshot. Witness after witness would testify that they didn't actually see a shotgun used in the fray, but there was Tom staggering in the vacant lot, then, full of buckshot, wobbling a few paces westward on Fremont and falling at the corner of Fremont and Third. Billy Allen said he heard a shotgun; he identified it as producing the second, instantaneous report generally attributed to Morgan's pistol and stated that Tom threw his hands to his breast immediately afterward.

Despite Allen's testimony, the shotgun blast was probably one of the two or three shots fired after the slight pause that followed the initial two. County Probate Court Judge J. H. Lucas, in his office on the second floor of the Gird Block, heard the first two shots, followed in a moment by two more "in quick succession," then by sustained rapid firing. Johnny Behan would testify, "After the first two shots, there were two or three shots fired very rapidly—I couldn't tell by whom." Claiborne could. He said he was looking at the Earp party as one or another of them fired the three shots "one right after another."

I Married Wyatt Earp tells an odd story concerning the opening moments of the fight, asserting that after Doc shot Frank and Morgan shot Billy, the shooting might have stopped if someone—Ike Clanton, Johnny Behan, or Billy Allen—had not fired from between the lodging house and the photo gallery, distracting the Earps' attention and allowing Tom McLaury to shoot and hit Morgan. In addition to the fact that Clanton, Behan, and Allen were all on or beside Fremont at this point, the story simply does not fit with any of the testimony in a number of respects, except to support the Earps' contention that Tom McLaury did have a gun and fired from behind a horse.

Various witnesses would testify that the Earp party fired from five to ten shots before either of the armed cowboys, Billy Clanton and Frank McLaury, could respond. Claiborne, who had left his own arms at Kellogg's Saloon the day before, put the number at six to eight shots at the Spicer hearing. Ike Clanton was adamant that Virgil fired the third shot and Wyatt the fourth. Virgil, of course, had been holding Doc's cane in his right hand; both he and the watching Sills would testify that he switched it to the left hand and drew. By Ike's testimony, Virgil would have had to do so in the brief moment's pause. Ike's testimony also places Wyatt as the last of the Earp party to fire rather than the first. Whatever the order after the initial shots, Virgil and Wyatt apparently quickly followed suit. Johnny Behan would state, "I suppose there was [*sic*] as many as eight or ten shots before I saw arms in the hands of any of the McLaury or Clanton party."

Some of the witnesses didn't wait around counting that long. Wyatt Earp would charge that Billy Claiborne broke and ran when the order to throw up hands was given, and "I never saw him afterwards till late in the afternoon, after the fight." Claiborne himself would testify that Behan "caught me by the shoulders and shoved me in the door" of the lodging house, but maintained that he had witnessed most of the violence, with Behan pushing him to safety only after approximately sixteen shots had been fired and after Claiborne had taken a bullet through the pants leg. By contrast, Billy Allen testified that he ducked into Fly's after the first two shots. Ike Clanton saw only the first four or five before breaking and running.

During that brief period between the order to throw up hands and the fifth or sixth shot, a side drama was being enacted between Ike and Wyatt. Ike would testify that Wyatt had "shoved his pistol up against my belly," told him to throw up his hands, and announced directly to him, "You son of a bitch, you can have a fight." Ike responded by turning, "taking Wyatt Earp's hand and pistol" with his left hand, and using his right hand to grasp him around the shoulder "for a few seconds." In this version, as Ike held him, Wyatt's gun went off. Ike then pushed his opponent around the corner of Fly's and jumped into the front door. (Although he identified it as the front door of the gallery, he clearly meant the entrance of the rooming house on Fremont.)

Wyatt remembered matters quite differently, stating that "after about four shots were fired, Ike Clanton ran up and grabbed my left arm." Seeing no weapon in the cowboy's hand, Wyatt admonished him to "Go to fighting or get away," as "the fight has commenced." He pushed Ike off with his left hand, and the latter ran down the side of the rooming house, ducking in between it and the photograph gallery to the back.

No one else could testify to the confrontation between the two men, although others saw Ike running. Behan's testimony as to location supports Wyatt's, for the sheriff last saw Ike "at the back corner of Fly's house" and guessed that from there he had run into the photograph gallery. Some confusion was created by the fact that other witnesses besides Ike appeared to refer to the rooming house simply as Fly's gallery; Claiborne and Coleman had Ike running into "Fly's photograph gallery," but their testimony actually placed him at the front corner and entering the front door of the rooming house, dodging bullets as he ducked out of sight.

Ike himself claimed that he was fired upon as he ran: "As I jumped into the door of the photograph gallery, I heard some bullets pass my head. As I went by an opening [apparently the opening between the rooming house and gallery], I heard some more bullets pass by me. . . . I heard some bullets strike the building ahead of me [apparently the gallery itself]."

Coleman stated that as Ike ran into the front door of Fly's, "one shot fired at him came pretty near to me, and struck a wagon standing in front of Bauer's shop. There was a second shot fired in that direction."

These shots have been attributed to Doc Holliday. They may, however, have been stray ones fired by Ike's own brother and friend—if indeed, they had yet drawn their weapons. Billy probably responded more quickly than did Frank. Both were hampered by the slugs they had received—Billy in the breast or wrist or both, Frank in the belly—but while Frank began moving with the horse, Billy maintained his position at the corner of the Harwood house and started firing. It was probably he who wounded Virgil in the leg; Sills's testimony even indicates that he may have done so before Virgil fired. According to Sills, the marshal pulled his revolver out as the firing commenced and fell down, apparently hit, then "got up immediately and went to shooting."

Robert Hatch would also suggest in contrast with most testimony that Billy shot in the early seconds. Hatch, accompanied by Behan's deputy sheriff and jailer Billy Soule, had followed the Earps down Fremont; as the firing began, he told Soule, "This is none of our fight. We had better get away from here." Turning to flee, he saw Billy Clanton "standing near the corner of the building below Fly's house [the Harwood house] with a pistol in his hand, in the act of shooting" after "there had probably been three or four shots fired."

Wes Fuller would testify that Billy, with wounds in his right wrist and breast, drew with his left hand only after six or seven shots by the Earp party.

Despite the two debilitating injuries, Billy alone apparently managed to inflict real damage on the Earp party, for Coleman also credited him with hitting Morgan Earp, the most seriously wounded of the marshal's group. Coleman remembered seeing Billy fire "two or three shots while in a crouching position" and seeing one of the shots hit Morgan, who "stumbled or fell," then stood up and began firing again. Behan and Hatch, too, saw Morgan fall, though they did not mention if they saw who shot him. Saloonkeeper Hatch heard Morgan exclaim something like "I am shot!" or "I am hit!" and watched him rise and begin shooting again—at Frank McLaury.

After his initial wounding of Billy, it appears that Morgan, along with Doc, was concentrating on Frank, while Wyatt and Virgil were trying to dispatch Billy. Witnesses would remember Billy in a variety of postures—standing, leaning, crouching, lying down, getting up, and lying (or sliding) down again. Coleman saw him crouching and firing with his pistol across his knee, then rising up and falling down. Claiborne would testify that Billy lay on the ground firing with the six-shooter steadied on his leg after he was initially hit. Behan reported him "lying on the ground with his legs crossed and his pistol resting on his knee."

Judge Lucas arrived at his hall door after hearing six or seven gunshots. He would testify that from this vantage point he could see Billy Clanton and no other participant.* Billy was standing and firing. "I saw from his movements that he was wounded," Lucas would relate.

Meanwhile, Frank had moved with his horse out into the middle of Fremont. Kehoe saw him running onto the street, holding the animal's reins and drawing his six-shooter. Claiborne would state that he did not see a gun in Frank's hand until the wounded man reached the middle of the street; Fuller would testify that Frank did not get his gun drawn until he was a little *past* the middle of the street. (Fuller would also testify that Frank tried to get the Winchester from the horse as he made his way onto the street, but the horse kept jumping away.) Johnny Behan had Frank firing at Morgan Earp with "one hand to [his] belly and his pistol in his right" *before* he got halfway across the street.

Whether Frank drew as he ran onto the thoroughfare or after reaching the middle, his reaction was slow, almost certainly because of the heavy-caliber slug in his belly. Fuller would remember that Frank was staggering and acting dizzy as he drew, and Behan would state, "The first man I was satisfied was hit was Frank McLaury. I saw him staggering and bewildered and I knew he was hit."

C. H. Light's testimony reflects the confusion of the whole affair but gives a good overall picture of the scene at this point. Light, looking out the side window of his room at the

---

*As the gunfight was spilling onto Fremont, and Lucas was looking out across Fremont to the scene of the trouble, it is odd that he would only see Billy Clanton.

sound of gunshots, first saw "several men in the act of shooting" and saw Tom McLaury "reel and fall" on the corner of
Fremont and Third. Then he observed "three men [of the
Earp party] standing at an angle about 10 or 15 feet apart,
about the center of the street, facing Fly's photograph gallery." He also saw another man—Billy Clanton—leaning
against the corner of the Harwood house, and a man with a
horse—Frank McLaury.

Now Frank McLaury's animal broke and ran, leaving him
facing his opponents, Morgan and Doc. "I have got you now!"
witness Coleman heard Frank call to Doc as he fired at him.
Hatch heard the statement as well, and Doc's response: "You
are a good one if you have," or something similar. The bullet
hit the scabbard on Doc's hip, leaving a superficial wound.

Coleman clearly was getting the show he had come to see,
and he even entered in at this point by "hollering" to Doc,
"You have got it now!"

"I am shot right through!" Doc hollered back, as Frank
approached him quartering, or passing his Colt back and
forth in front of him.

Meanwhile, Billy Clanton was going down for the last
time, as Lucas's testimony shows: "His body seemed to bend a
little and his pistol was up above his head as he seemed to be
in the act of falling. I think he caught his hand against the
window or wall and turned partly around. He continued to
struggle until he got clear down on the ground. About the
time he got to the ground, the firing ceased."

Others would state that Billy continued shooting and trying to shoot even after he hit the ground for the last time—
this despite the fact that he had taken a third bullet, under the
twelfth rib on his right-hand side. C. H. Light saw Billy, after
sliding down the side of the house, lie with his head and
shoulders against the structure and "place a pistol on his leg
and fire two shots." Light explained, "He tried to fire a third
shot but he apparently was too weak. The shot went into the
air."

The fact that Billy went down fighting would elicit praise
even from John Clum, who would refuse to waste any sympathy on the youngest Clanton but would measure him against
one of the highest standards of the West and find him not

wanting. The cowboy "made an unwise decision, but, if the record of his part in the street battle is correct, Billy was game—for he continued to fight as long as his strength and ammunition lasted."

Frank McLaury, too, apparently continued trying to end with a direct hit as he made his way to the opposite side of Fremont. Claiborne would testify he saw him "bent down in a stooping position, with his hand on his belly" as the shooting neared an end, but Hatch would recall that Frank stopped at the corner of an adobe building across the street "and stood with a pistol across his arm, in the act of shooting—his pistol in his right hand and resting on his left arm." At about the same time, Hatch noticed Doc and Morgan both firing in Frank's direction, and Frank fell to the ground "as though he was shot."

In contrast, both Behan and Claiborne observed Frank hurrying away. "I looked then in that direction and saw Frank McLaury running," Behan would explain, "and a shot was fired and he fell on his head, and I heard Morgan Earp say, 'I got him.'" Claiborne would report that the elder McLaury "was not exactly running, but was getting around pretty lively when he was shot the last time. He was going away from the Earp party."

Whether Frank was hit by Morgan or by Doc, whether he was shooting or running or both, he took a bullet in the head about the same time Billy Clanton's strength failed him. Suddenly, all guns fell silent. The whole affair had lasted only twenty or thirty seconds, with twenty-five to thirty shots fired.

Billy Clanton was still conscious, lying on his back with his head raised slightly and trying to cock his gun, as tall, grim-faced Camillus Fly, clad in black, emerged from his rooming house with a Henry rifle. Coleman called to the photographer to take the pistol away. Fly apparently didn't relish the job because, according to Robert Hatch, he threw out the same order: "Take that pistol away from that man!" C. H. Light heard Fly threaten, "Take that pistol away from him or I'll kill him." Hatch responded as one who didn't relish the job either: "I said to Mr. Fly, 'Go and get it yourself if you want it.' Fly walked towards Clanton and I was right beside him. Fly reached down and took hold of the pistol and pulled it out of his hand. As Fly did so, Billy Clanton said, 'Give me some more cartridges.'"

Billy was "rolling around on the ground in agony" as Wes Fuller and others picked him up and carried him to the dwelling just past the Harwood house, on the corner of Fremont and Third.

Outside this building, Tom McLaury still lay as carpenter Thomas Keefe came running along Third from Allen in response to the fusillade. Keefe knelt down, raised Tom's head, and called to two or three others, "Let's pick this man up and take him in the house before he dies." The carpenter related that Billy Clanton was already inside when they entered with Tom. "We brought [Tom] in the house and got a pillow and laid him on the carpet and made him as easy as I could. I asked him if he had anything to say before he died, and he made no answer. He could not speak. Then I unbuttoned his clothes and pulled his boots off and gave him some water. . . ."

Billy Allen, too, acknowledged picking the younger McLaury up and carrying him inside. "I pulled his shirt down to see where he was shot," Allen would relate. "He was breathing yet." Billy Claiborne would testify that he saw Tom being brought into the house "about four or five minutes after the shooting had ceased." Claiborne and Allen both were adamant on one point: They observed no arms or cartridge belt on the stricken cowboy. Keefe, too, repeatedly testified that "there were no ammunition or arms on Tom [when he found him lying on the ground], nor on the ground near or about him, nor on his person, nor was there any belt on him."

As Keefe attempted to make Tom McLaury comfortable, Billy Clanton was not going gently into that good night. He was "halloing so with pain" that a doctor was called to give him morphine. The young Clanton had asked Wes Fuller to "Look and see where I am shot." When Fuller saw the serious belly and breast wounds, he told Billy he could not survive them. Billy's response: "Get a doctor and give me something to put me to sleep." When a doctor arrived, Keefe held the cowboy down as the physician injected morphine from two full syringes, "about the thickness of a small sized lead pencil about two inches long." Billy "was turning and twisting and kicking in every manner, with the pain. He said, 'They have murdered me. I have been murdered. Chase the crowd away from the door and give me air.'"

When Johnny Behan stopped in, he heard the youth say, "Go away and let me die." Behan did, and Billy continued to gasp for air. Keefe remembered Billy's last words as "Drive the crowd away!" The youth lingered, now mute, until after Coroner Matthews arrived eight or ten minutes later. Tom quietly died within six or seven minutes of being carried into the house; the doctor did not even treat him.

Meanwhile, Frank McLaury was sharing in his brother's fate. As the gunfight ended, laundryman Fellehy approached the man whom he had seen fall on the sidewalk across the street from the vacant lot and offered to pick him up. Like his brother, Frank could not respond; he could only move his lips. Fellehy retrieved the revolver lying five feet away and laid it at Frank's side, then stepped outside the gathering crowd to see Doc Holliday running with a revolver in his hand toward the prone cowboy and asserting, "The son of a bitch has shot me, and I mean to kill him."

He—or Morgan—already had. Frank died on the sidewalk; Coroner Matthews would stop and examine the body, picking up the revolver, on his way to the house where Billy and Tom lay.

Ike Clanton, the one who had responded to the Earps' and Holliday's intimidation with rash threats, was still running. Theatrical manager William Cuddy, who had only moments before greeted Johnny Behan as the sheriff talked with the cowboys in the vacant lot, was walking on Allen Street when he heard the gunshots. "I looked towards where I had left the sheriff and the party of four men and I seen [sic] Ike Clanton exit through the back door of the little house next to Fly's. In a minute or [a] half he passed me on Allen Street and run [sic] across, into the dance house."

Ike himself would testify that he had run through the lodging house to the space between it and the photo gallery, then veered into another lot and through to Allen Street and the dance hall. He was confused about his route, unsure whether he had run part of the way through the O.K. Corral that he and his companions had passed through only a short time before. Johnny Behan later found him on Tough Nut

Street, "at Judge Lucas' old office." Ike was temporarily taken into custody and jailed, "being guarded by a number of citizens to prevent lynching."

So Ike was not present when Coroner Matthews arrived to examine his dying brother and their comrades. Matthews found Frank with two pistol wounds, "one wound penetrating the cranium beneath the right ear; another penetrating the abdomen one inch to the left of the navel." Matthews concluded, "I should say the wound beneath the ear caused instant death."

Tom had twelve buckshot wounds on the right side; the coroner "laid the palm of my hand on them; it would cover the whole of them, about four inches in space." Billy had suffered one fatal wound "underneath the twelfth rib on the left-hand side" and another "about two inches to the left of the left nipple." The latter was oozing blood from the lung. Keefe and Fuller also noted the wrist wound which had forced Billy to draw and shoot left-handed. Keefe stated that the shot had entered on the inside of the wrist almost in line with the base of the thumb and had exited diagonally on the back of the wrist, breaking the arm with its impact. Keefe even pushed his finger into the wound, "feeling the bone." The carpenter also helped Matthews search the body of Tom McLaury; they found no weapons, but did discover a hefty sum, as Matthews's coroner's report attests: "From the body of Thos. McLaury, I recovered in certificates of deposit in the Pima County Bank, checks and cash in all the sum of $2,943.45— From the body of Frank McLaury one Colts six shooting pistol, with belt and cartridges—From the body of William Clanton, one Colts six shooter, with belt and cartridges and one nickel watch and chain."

While the dead men were being tended to, armed vigilante Tombstone businessmen supporting the city marshal were gathering in front of the *Epitaph* office on Fremont, led by attorney William Herring and George Parson's friend, bank teller Milton Clapp. In later accounts by myth builders, the Earps and Holliday were even being feted by an enthusiastic crowd. In Boyer's *I Married Wyatt Earp*, "jubilant vigilantes" picked up the shafts of a wagon into which the wounded Virgil and Morgan had been deposited and gleefully hauled them home. Wyatt Earp's friend John Flood would carry this scene to absurd lengths in Wyatt's "auto-biography" prepared in the 1920's; here "a surging, jumping, shouting mob" enveloped the Earps with hurrahs, while "the leader of a dozen of the town's most prominent men" mused aloud at the wondrous defeat of the aggressive cowboy marauders.

"How do you suppose they did it?"

The response from a member of the celebrating citizenry: "Just nerve, I guess, and cool headedness."

Well, it makes a nice story. In reality, the mood was more grim and matter-of-fact. Allie Earp would recall arriving on the street to find a doctor probing Virgil Earp's leg for Billy Clanton's bullet. (Actually, the bullet had passed through the calf.) As she remembered in Waters's narrative, men simply loaded Virgil into a hack and sent him home to recuperate. Behind the vehicle came another hack, carrying Morgan Earp with his serious shoulder wound. The bullet which hit Morgan in the right shoulder had penetrated across the back, chipping a vertebra, barely missing the backbone, and exiting through the other shoulder.

Doc Holliday stepped into Fly's and went to his room, where a curious scene transpired, if one is to believe Kate Elder's account: "[He] sat on the side of the bed and cried and said, 'Oh, this is just awful—awful.' I asked, 'Are you hurt?' He said, 'No, I am not.' He pulled up his shirt. There was just a pale red streak about two inches long across his hip where the bullet had grazed him."

Wyatt Earp alone remained unscathed. The admiring Fred Dodge arrived on the scene to find his friend "as Cool and Collected as usual," supervising the removal of Virgil and Morgan. Wyatt and Dodge then started down Fremont and were met by Johnny Behan.

The sheriff was later asked in court to recall the ensuing conversation: "Wyatt Earp said, 'Behan, you deceived me,' or, 'threw me off. You said you had disarmed them.' I told him he was mistaken, I did not say anything of the kind. Then I related to him what I had said. I said, 'Earp, I told you I was there for the purpose of arresting and disarming them.' He said he thought I said I had disarmed them."

However, both Coleman and Cuddy testified, and Dodge would later recall, that the sheriff approached Wyatt with the words "I will have to arrest you."

"I won't be arrested. You deceived me, Johnny, you told me they were not armed," Coleman recalled Wyatt's saying, followed by "I won't be arrested, but I am here to answer [for] what I have done. I am not going to leave town."

Cuddy remembered another man, S. B. Comstock, interposing before Wyatt's reply, "There is no hurry in arresting this man. He done just right in killing them, and the people will uphold them."

Then, Cuddy explained, Wyatt responded, "You bet we did right. We had to do it. And you threw us, Johnny. You told us they were disarmed."

Dodge, looking back adoringly through time, remembered Wyatt staring coolly at the sheriff, then telling him "more forceably than I had Ever heard Wyatt talk before— that any decent officer could arrest him. But that Johnny Behan or any of his Kind must not try it." In fact, Dodge would later add, Wyatt told his political foe that "if he was God Almighty himself he could not arrest him then."

Johnny Behan soon confronted—or tried to confront— the two injured Earps as well. Virgil and Morgan, both still in pain, were sharing a bed in Virgil's home with their wives attending them. In Waters's account, Allie recalled that she saw the sheriff coming toward the house and innocently remarked on the fact, causing Virgil to "roar" for his Winchester. When Allie reiterated that "it was only Johnny Behan," Virgil repeated his command and had her stack a mattress in front of the window. Wyatt soon appeared with the news that Behan planned to arrest the brothers and Holliday. After he left, Allie remembered, Morgan told her, "If they come, Al, you'll know they got Wyatt. Take this six-shooter and kill me and Virge before they get us." Allie and Lou responded in this version by locking the doors, barricading the windows with mattresses, and sitting up all night with a six-shooter.

However, at the trial, both Behan and another visitor, new Deputy District Attorney W. S. Williams, would testify that the sheriff met with the marshal at home as "the three Misses Earp," James Earp, and another man—probably Sherman McMasters—milled about in the room. Williams would remember Johnny Behan's entering and sitting down at the foot of Virgil's bed as Williams himself sat on a sofa near the head of the bed.

> Sheriff Behan said, speaking to Virgil Earp, with reference to the affray that had taken place a few moments before, "I went down to the corral to disarm them, and I could not (or "they would not," I don't know which expression was used). I then met you and your party and spoke to you. You did not answer. I heard you say, 'Boys, throw up your hands! I have come to disarm you.'" One of the McLaury boys said, "We will," and drew his gun and shooting then commenced.

Johnny Behan would remember the visit differently. Upon his arrival, he would testify, Virgil greeted him with the warning "You better go slow, Behan, and not push this matter too far." In this version, Virgil accused the sheriff of deceiving his party as to whether the cowboys had been disarmed and of trying to get a vigilance committee not to commend the Earps and Holliday but to hang them. Behan denied both charges: "In the conversation he told me he was my friend. I told him I had always been his friend. That seemed to settle the matter about the Vigilance Committee. I suppose I told him that I heard him say, 'Throw up your hands.' I never told him I heard McLaury say anything or that I saw him draw a pistol."

Meanwhile, the McLaurys themselves, along with Billy Clanton, had been transported by wagon to the "death house," a cabin behind Dunbar's stables on Fifth Street, where a hastily organized coroner's jury called to determine the cause of death viewed the bodies. Then the three were taken to the establishment of Ritter and Ream, City Undertakers. When corpses were lacking, the partners worked repairing and constructing furniture and "setting up, levelling and repairing billiard tables." Now they had their hands full, preparing for one of Tombstone's biggest funerals.

The coroner's jury removed to their respective homes to mull matters until morning, and tensions and anxieties swelled within the town. The morning of October 27 brought no reduction of tension, as George Parsons quickly learned when he meandered in that day from his extended stay at the mountain mining camp. Some residents expected a cowboy reprisal against the town itself and apparently viewed the bank-clerk-turned-miner, a bit rough around the edges from his mountain sojourn, as the first of the threatening horde. As Parsons reported to his diary, "My cowboy appearance and attire was not in keeping with the excited mind. Loud talking or talking in groups was tho't out of place. Had to laugh at some of the nervousness. It has been a bad scare and the worst is not yet over some think."

Indeed, as everyone struggled with that most basic yet complex of questions—why?—distrust and animosities would continue to prove more explosive, more destructive, than the flames which had consumed the Tombstone business district in June.

Rancher Frank McLaury had a hot temper and a number of rustler connections; whether he was spoiling for a fight with the Earps is still a matter of debate. *The New-York Historical Society, New York City*

Rancher Tom McLaury didn't want any trouble but had the wrong friends. *The New-York Historical Society, New York City*

Rancher/rustler Ike Clanton drank too much and talked too much, then got caught without a gun. *Arizona Historical Society*

Rancher/rustler Newman Haynes "Old Man" Clanton died in a Guadalupe Canyon ambush two and a half months before his son Billy went down shooting beside the Harwood House. *Arizona Historical Society*

Right: A tough, aggressive gambler, business entrepreneur, and sometime-lawman, Wyatt Earp had supporters and detractors across the West. *Arizona Historical Society*

Below left: Virgil Earp, Tombstone's marshal at the time of the famous gun battle, maintained a respectable record as a lawman but made the mistake of taking his brothers and Doc Holliday to confront the cowboys. *Arizona Historical Society*

Below right: Morgan Earp, an affable faro dealer and part-time law enforcer, didn't get out of Tombstone "when the gettin' was good." *Arizona Historical Society*

Dentist-turned-gambler Doc Holliday attracted trouble as naturally as a frontier saloon attracted drinkers; he has been charged with starting the shooting in the famous gunfight. *Western History Collections, University of Oklahoma*

Left: Ed Schieffelin discovered the silver bonanza he dreamed of and put southeastern Arizona on the map, but he remained a perennial prospector. *Arizona Historical Society*

In 1879, Tombstone was spreading across Goose Flats and evolving from mining camp to town. This view is from the Tombstone Hills. *The Bancroft Library*

Allie Sullivan Earp, Virgil's common-law wife, was fiercely devoted to her "Virge" and distrustful of brother-in-law Wyatt. *Arizona Historical Society*

Celia Ann "Mattie" Blaylock lived with Wyatt as his wife in Tombstone, but lost him to Sheriff Johnny Behan's former lover, Josie Marcus. *Arizona Historical Society*

Rustler John Ringo, champion of the Clantons and McLaurys, lived a checkered life and died a mysterious death. *Jack Burrows*

San Francisco bank clerk George Parsons chronicled the life of Tombstone in his journal, became a mining speculator, and had his picture taken by Tombstone photographer Camillus S. Fly. (This photo has also been erroneously identified as a portrait of newspaper editor John Clum, who shared Parsons's perspective on the troubles in Tombstone.) *Arizona Historical Society*

Above: Loading ore at a mine in the Tombstone district in the early 1880's was no easy matter, as this photo taken by photographer Fly shows. *Arizona Historical Society*

Below left: Cochise County Sheriff Johnny Behan was the Earps' chief rival for political power and had his own strong critics and defenders. Below right: Behan's deputy Billy Breakenridge preferred his boss's style of law enforcement to the Earps' and said so in a popular 1928 book that incensed Wyatt Earp. *Arizona Historical Society/Western History Collections, University of Oklahoma*

The Oriental Saloon, where one could often find Wyatt or Morgan Earp, was a popular nightspot with a troubled reputation and a bar valued at $120,000. *Arizona Historical Society*

Below left: Oriental bartender Frank Leslie played only a tangential role in the events surrounding the O.K. Corral gunfight, but contributed greatly to Tombstone's wild and woolly image. Below right: Gambler, shootist, and lawman Bat Masterson forged a friendship with Wyatt Earp in the Kansas buffalo-hunting camps and later joined him for a brief time in Tombstone. *Arizona Historical Society/The Kansas State Historical Society, Topeka*

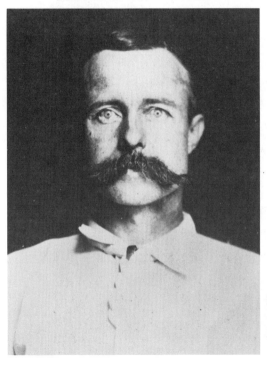

Above: Front Street, Dodge City, still had a raw look in 1879 when Assistant City Marshal Wyatt Earp decided the town was losing its "snap" and moved on. *The Kansas State Historical Society, Topeka*

Below: The victims of the "gunfight at the O.K. Corral"—Tom McLaury, Frank McLaury, and Billy Clanton—were given an elaborate send-off. *Arizona Historical Society*

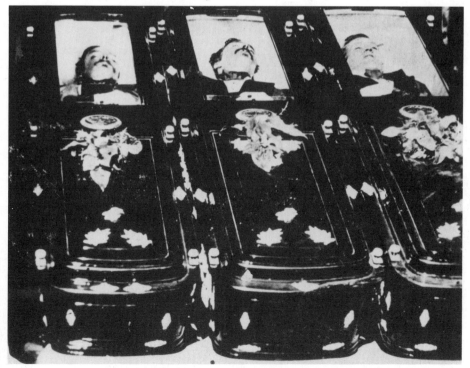

THE PACIFIC COAST.

Desperate Street-Fight in Tombstone.

Cowboys and a Marshal's Posse the Combatants.

Three Men Killed and Two Wounded in the Affray.

Meeting of the Mussel Slough Monument Committee—Big Fire at San Andreas—Coursing.

[SPECIAL TO THE EXAMINER.]

Deadly Work in Tombstone.

TOMBSTONE (A. T.), October 26.—The liveliest street battle that ever occurred in Tombstone took place here at half-past 2 o'clock this after-

Opposite page: The San Francisco *Examiner* carried the story of the gunfight on page 3 the day after the battle.

Right, Justice of the Peace Wells Spicer conducted a tense hearing into the murder charges against Wyatt Earp, Virgil Earp, Morgan Earp, and Doc Holliday. *Utah State Historical Society*

Below: The Spicer hearing was conducted in the "Gird Block," often identified as the Mining Exchange Building but actually a set of three buildings constructed by Dick Gird and containing the mining exchange and county offices and courtrooms. *Arizona Historical Society*

The Bird Cage Theater reverberated with music, laughter, and the clink of well-filled glasses as boomtown Tombstone itself began to fade. *Arizona Historical Society*

CHAPTER 11

"I Think We Can Hang Them"

In displaying the finely clad remains of Billy Clanton and Frank and Tom McLaury in the funeral parlor window on October 27, 1881, Tombstone's citizens were practicing a common ritual of the late-nineteenth-century American frontier. The people of the West displayed and photographed corpses in a variety of ways in those days: propped against a rough wooden or adobe wall; lying in repose on a narrow cot; supported in a coffin by a couple of handy chairs. The two groups most often coming in for this type of treatment were outlaws and young children, the former as indictment on their way of life and a warning to others, the latter as an elegy on an innocent existence ended too soon. Thus, the ritual attending the death and burial of the three cowboys satisfied both those who felt justice had been served and those who felt the three had been wantonly cut down.

Resentments against the marshal's party ran deep, as the sign accompanying the display, MURDERED IN THE STREETS OF TOMBSTONE, indicated. Although the *Epitaph* reported that Frank McLaury had initiated the violence by attempting to draw, only to be plugged by Wyatt Earp, many refused to believe it. A mining engineer who claimed to have seen Billy

Clanton and the McLaury brothers raise their hands as instructed before being shot down, recalled that his own father, also watching, "was wild over what he saw," crying out, "That cold blooded murder!" and wanting "to take my shotgun and go into the scrap."

The son's response is significant: "This is nothing but a bunch of stage-robbers splitting, and killing one another to keep any evidence from getting out." Indeed, rumors continued to fly that the whole episode was the result of illegal dealings gone sour—or of one or more of the cowboys' simply knowing too much about the Earps' and Holliday's involvement in stage robbery. Will McLaury would embrace the latter theory when he arrived to seek reasons for his brothers' death, and the Fort Worth *Democrat* would report in referring to former Fort Worth resident Doc Holliday that "many shrewd guesses [are] heard on the streets, that go to prove that it was not altogether unconnected with the robbery that the shooting occurred, Clanton suspected of knowing too much about the affair."

Tombstone old-timers after the turn of the century would convince one interviewer that the marshal's group seemed "to have deliberately brought on the quarrel for the purpose of getting rid of the Clantons and McLaurys." Melvin Jones was one of the pioneers who later advanced this theory: "It has been my belief for the past many years that Frank McLaury knew something on the Earps and it was him especially they wanted out of their way. Through the drunken talk Ike Clanton made and urged on by Doc Holliday, the Earps got their chance to get rid of the McLaury boys."

Another pioneer would state, "The showdown is supposed to have come as a result of one of the Clantons intimating that they intended telling on the Earps, for the holding up of the stage and the murder of Bud Philpot." And James Hancock would claim that Billy Breakenridge told him "nobody ever did know the real cause but it must have been over the stage robberies and the Clantons and McLaurys knew too much."

A Tombstone mining man interviewed in the Denver *Rocky Mountain News* put a slightly different twist on matters by identifying the Earps and Holliday as part of a large class of aggressive "Bunco-steerers" favored over the cowboys by "the better class citizens, including the business and moneyed men" of Tombstone. The cowboys, he reasoned, didn't have much money to spend in town and only caused trouble when there, while the bunco steerers were quiet and peaceful and, "outside of their bad habits of lying and stealing, would make respectable Sunday School superintendents." The bunco steerers used physical violence against any perceived enemies, either "slugging" them or dispatching them on "a sudden trip to eternity by means of a knife or bullet." The cowboys, he concluded, "have been treated very treacherously."

However, as Earp supporters pointed out, Virgil *was* the city marshal, and had appeared to be a pretty fair and even-handed one up to this point. Ike Clanton *had* been making threats against the members of the Earp party, and more than one person had suspected the cowboys of plotting vengeance in the wake of the buffaloing of Ike and Tom. To law-and-order proponents such as John Clum, the issue was simply one of effective law enforcement. "Was the police force of Tombstone to be bullied and cowed?" he would ask in reviewing the situation years later. Furthermore, the Earps and their backers would repeatedly insist the cowboy threats on October 26 were simply part of a larger rustler effort to get rid of the Earp brothers, who represented law and order far better than did the lackadaisical Behan and his assistants.

It is difficult to gauge what percentage of Tombstone's population favored the cowboys, what percentage favored the Earps, and what number didn't care either way or considered both equally corrupt. The vigilante group backing the Earps claimed almost a hundred men ready to meet the cowboy menace, if necessary, on the day of the gunfight. Among these were the most powerful businessmen in the community. However, the ground swell of bitterness against the Earps and Holliday from other residents was still palpable in the early twentieth century, when historical researchers interviewed the old pioneers. Cowboy sympathizers would assert that the size of the Clanton-McLaury funeral, with an estimated two thousand people in attendance, indicated the general feeling in favor of the Clantons and McLaurys, but a line attributed to Josie Marcus had a point: "A funeral in those times was like a circus; the people weren't primarily mourners but spectators."

A funeral did bring color and spectacle and the temporary abandonment of everyday cares to frontier dwellers. Perhaps the most lavish funeral ever recorded in a rough-around-the-edges boomtown was that of Cripple Creek, Colorado, madam Pearl De Vere in the 1890's. De Vere, who ran the most elegant whorehouse in gold-crazy Cripple Creek, had mysteriously taken an overdose of morphine in her room while an extravagant Christmas Eve party was going on below. Her sister from the East, learning upon Pearl's death that she was not the dressmaker the family understood her to be, refused to handle any funeral arrangements. So the people of Cripple Creek produced an extravagant funeral procession— the obligatory local band playing the death march; the hearse carrying a lavender casket covered with red and white roses; black horses pulling a red-wheeled rig behind, with a cross of pink carnations on the seat; and members of the various Cripple Creek lodges following decked out in "red fezzes, feathered helmets and gold braided scabbards."

The Clanton-McLaury funeral was about that elaborate, with its fancy hearses and splendid caskets and long line of marchers. One account even mentioned fireworks. It was certainly a good show.

The good show, however, was followed by the difficult coroner's investigation. The coroner's jury included S. B. Comstock, who had intervened in Behan's attempt to arrest Wyatt Earp after the gunfight by asserting, "He done just right in killing them, and the people will uphold them." It also included future prosecution witness R. F. Hafford, who had encountered Ike the morning of the gunfight complaining that the Earps and Holliday had failed to appear for a scheduled showdown.

Now Coroner Matthews, Comstock, Hafford, and eight other jurors heard the testimony of nine witnesses. Johnny Behan first gave his version of events, relating his efforts to take the cowboys in charge and stop the Earp party and the misunderstanding over whether he had disarmed the cowboys. His testimony immediately cast doubt on the actions of the Earps and Holliday, as he asserted that he was satisfied both Ike and Tom were unarmed, that Tom was holding his coat open when the firing began, and that one of the Earp party shot first.

Billy Claiborne testified that the younger Clanton had been trying to get Ike to go home when the Earps approached, with Virgil announcing, "You sons of bitches, you have been looking for a fight and now you can get it!" Claiborne claimed that the Earps already had pistols in their hands, that Billy, Frank, and Ike had their hands up and Tom held his coat open when Doc and Morgan began firing, and that Billy cried, "Don't shoot me, I don't want to fight."

Attorney Marcus Smith, who reportedly had been talking to Frank McLaury minutes before the gunfight, was then called but excused. He was followed by William Cuddy, who remembered seeing Behan talking to the cowboys on the vacant lot, noticing Billy nervously put his hand to his pistol as Cuddy approached, and hearing Ike promise the sheriff there would be no trouble, as they were about to leave town. C. H. Light then explained to the jury that he had gone to his window at the sound of the first shots and had seen what appeared to be six parties firing.

Light's testimony concluded the first day of the two-day proceeding. On October 29, P. H. Fellehy led the parade of witnesses, recalling that, shortly before the gunfight, he had seen Ike walk by Virgil without speaking, that Ike had responded to a passerby's question by responding that there would be no trouble, and that Virgil had told Behan he would kill the threatening cowboys on sight.

Ike Clanton, who acknowledged that he had been laying for Holliday in the morning after taunts from the dentist and Morgan Earp the night before, gave an account resembling Claiborne's. He, Billy, and Frank McLaury all had their hands up and Tom was holding his coat open when Doc and Morgan started firing at them. Billy had been trying to get him to leave town; neither Frank nor Billy had been sent for, but had come in at the request of their traveling companion Frink.

Martha King followed Ike, testifying to the chilling exchange she had heard between Doc Holliday and one of the Earps—"Let them have it!" "All right."

The last inquest witness, R. F. Coleman, recalled seeing Ike's buffaloing, viewing the cowboys conversing at Dunbar's Corral, and warning both Johnny Behan and Virgil that he thought the four meant mischief and should be disarmed, a suggestion that Virgil rejected. Coleman heard one of the cowboys tell Behan that there would be no trouble and watched the Earp party's approach. Although he was turning as the shooting began, he thought the marshal's group fired first. He saw Billy Clanton apparently in the act of drawing after the first two shots were fired.

In the face of these testimonies largely damning to the city marshal and his brothers, the jurors took the safe route by simply concluding that the three cowboys had died of gunshot wounds inflicted by the three Earps and Holliday. Here is the *Nugget*'s full comment on that conclusion:

GLAD TO KNOW

The people of this community are deeply indebted to the twelve [*sic*] intelligent men who composed the coroners jury for the valuable information that the three persons who were killed last Wednesday were shot. Some thirty or forty shots were fired, and the whole affair was witnessed by probably a dozen people, and we have a faint recollection of hearing someone say the dead men were shot, but people are liable to be mistaken and the verdict reassures us. We might have thought they had been struck by lightning or stung to death by hornets.

As the coroner's jury issued its report, Mayor Clum and Virgil Earp were requesting troops of Acting Governor Gosper and Arizona military commander Orlando Willcox, citing a potential outlaw threat against the town. The McLaurys and Clantons were known to associate with John Ringo and other rustlers; a portion of the townspeople, as George Parsons's comments have shown, remained highly nervous about the connection. Gosper would soon be reporting to the United States secretary of the interior, "Some of the observing and easily frightened citizens of the county place the number [of cowboy desperadoes] at 100 or more," though his own estimate was much less. He refused to send troops, considering the vigilantes themselves capable of meeting any threat that might materialize.

The idea of a concerted cowboy menace certainly tended both to justify and to draw attention away from the actions of the Earp party in dispatching Billy Clanton and the McLaurys, but the Tombstone city council nonetheless suspended Virgil's city marshal appointment on October 29. He was still confined to his bed. Only the day before, he had been reported "resting easily" and able to "attend to his duties" in a few weeks. He continued to hold the United States marshal appointment he had brought with him to Tombstone.

Ike Clanton was not content with giving his statement to the inquest jury. Now he set out to extract retribution by filing charges against the Earps and Holliday for the killings.

Thus, as the coroner's jury brought in its nonverdict and the city council suspended the marshal, warrants were issued for the arrest of Virgil Earp, Morgan Earp, Wyatt Earp, and Doc Holliday on a triple murder charge. Because they remained in bed with injuries, Virgil and Morgan were spared the serving of the warrants. Morgan remained in serious pain. The *Daily Nugget* reported that cloth may have been carried into his shoulder with the bullet, "and it will be necessary to open the wound and extract all foreign matter."

Meanwhile, Wyatt and Doc were brought before Justice of the Peace Wells Spicer, who "denied bail as a matter of right, but upon a showing of facts by affidavits, bail was granted and fixed in the sum of $10,000 each."

The two quickly raised far more. Eight men put up money for Doc, including Fred Dodge ($500), Earp mining partner R. J. Winders ($1,000), and James Earp ($2,500). Wyatt Earp contributed almost half of the dentist's $14,500 total, kicking in $7,000. (Kate Elder later stated that she gave Doc $75 out of the $100 she possessed and left for Globe.)

Wyatt's own individual total stood at $27,000, with ten contributors. Dodge, James Earp, and R. J. Winders gave the same amounts as they had for Holliday; A. C. Bilicke (either Albert or father Chris) of the Cosmopolitan Hotel gave $1,000, and Lou Rickabaugh, the gambler from San Francisco who held a part interest in the Oriental gambling concession, contributed $5,000. Four others chipped in a total of $7,000.

But the largest contribution to Wyatt's cause—$10,000—came from the man who became his defense attorney, Thomas Fitch.

At forty-three, Fitch had compiled an enviable record in western legal and political affairs. Like Clum a native New Yorker, Fitch had spent his early adult years as a newspaper reporter and editor in Wisconsin, California, and Nevada. A staunch Republican who had marched in party torchlight processions at age eighteen, Fitch also served as a California legislator and as a delegate to the convention to form a state constitution for Nevada. In Nevada in the 1860's he began practicing law and was elected to Congress. He spent the first years of the next decade in Utah, where he managed criminal and civil litigation for the Mormon Church and helped create the Utah state constitution. From Utah he moved to San Francisco and eventually—in 1877—to Arizona, where he had served as a member of the territorial legislature from Yavapai County in 1879. Fitch possessed political clout, oratorical skills, and high respectability; the Earps were in good hands.

The hearing to determine whether the defendants should be bound over to the grand jury was quickly scheduled to begin on October 31 at 3:00 P.M. in the Gird Block courtroom where Ike had been fined for carrying a concealed weapon. Justice of the Peace Spicer would preside. Assisting Fitch, as Doc Holliday's counsel, would be United States Court Commissioner T. J. Drum. Prosecuting attorney Lyttleton Price would be assisted by a number of lawyers, including—significantly—the firm of Goodrich and Goodrich.

Ben Goodrich was in the process of becoming just as prominent legally and politically as Thomas Fitch, but on the other side of the political fence. Goodrich was a native of Texas, a former Confederate lieutenant, and a strong Democrat. He also was a rare phenomenon in Tombstone, a man who neither drank nor gambled, a situation so puzzling that the town "hardly knew what to make of him."

With Fitch on one side and Goodrich on the other, support was breaking along predictable lines. The prosecution would attempt to show that the Clantons and McLaurys had been drawn unwillingly into a confrontation for which they were ill prepared. The defense would try to establish that these men had been making threats against the Earps for a long time, were gunning for them on that particular day, were all armed, and provoked the violence by going for their guns.

On the day the hearing began, George Parsons recorded in his journal, "Met Wyat [*sic*] Earp in hotel who took me in to see Virgil this evening, he's getting along well. Morgan too. Looks bad for them all thus far."

H. M. Matthews testified first, recalling that when he arrived at the scene, Frank and Tom were dead and Billy was dying, all of gunshot wounds. The next day, the eyewitness prosecution testimony began, with Spicer placing a gag rule on the *Nugget* and *Epitaph* by directing them not to publish the witnesses' statements.

Billy Allen and coroner's inquest juror R. F. Hafford gave their depositions on November 1. Allen acknowledged that he "knew all the participants, in one degree or another," Tom McLaury only by sight. He insisted that in his two years in Tombstone his relations with the Earps had been "the best, always—always friendly," but his sympathies were clearly with the cowboys. He related seeing Frank and Billy and "an old gentleman" ride into town and watching Doc Holliday greet them pleasantly. Asked to take a drink with the cowboys, Allen informed them of the troubles of the morning, leading Frank to change his mind about drinking and announce that he would "get the boys out of town." As for the gunfight itself, Allen supported at least part of Ike's and Billy Claiborne's coroner's inquest testimony by stating that Tom was holding his coat open and Billy had his hands out when one of the Earp party, possibly Doc, began shooting.

The defense attempted to establish Allen's unreliability as a witness by cross-examining him about his alleged arrest for larceny under an assumed name in Colorado. Spicer overruled defense attempts to make the witness acknowledge such a record; as for name changes, the unemployed Allen gave a response wonderfully indicative of the fluid nature of identity on the frontier: "I have never had any other name than Wm. Allen. They have called me other names but this is my true name here. A man gets a nickname around the mountains."

Liquor dealer Hafford followed, testifying that he had encountered the armed Ike looking for the Earps and Holliday at ten minutes after twelve on the day in question. Ike announced that these men had insulted him the night before and had agreed to meet him before twelve; Hafford told him to go home.

In the defendants' favor, the liquor dealer's testimony established that Ike was gunning for the Earp party, but it also provided an immediate cause, the insults of the night before, and hinted that Ike's adversaries had promised a showdown.

The next day, November 2, defense lawyer Fitch opened by asking Spicer to revoke his order against the publication of testimony, "as it appeared impossible to curtail the enterprise of the press," with the *Nugget* providing full coverage. Spicer responded by revoking the order. Then the rest of the morning was spent wrangling over the defense's questioning of Spicer's authority. Did a justice of the peace have the authority "to pass on the relevancy or materiality of any evidence offered?" This point of order was finally dropped with Spicer still in charge, and Johnny Behan took the stand.

The dates of Behan's testimony have been confused over the years because he did not sign his deposition until November 13. Actually, he gave his account on November 2, 3, and 4, with the defense reserving the right to cross-examine him further, and thus delaying the filing of the deposition.

Behan basically repeated and elaborated upon his inquest testimony, explaining that on hearing of the trouble, he had told Virgil to disarm the cowboys, only to get the marshal's reply that he "would give them a chance to make a fight." Behan reiterated that he had checked Ike Clanton and Tom McLaury and found them unarmed and that he had instructed the cowboys to remain where they were as he went to meet the Earp party. He had told the advancing men to stop, as he "was down there for the purpose of disarming the Clantons and McLowerys [*sic*]," but they ignored him. He heard one of the Earp party—Wyatt, he thought—say, "You sons of bitches, you have been looking for a fight, and now you can have it." He heard another—Virgil, he believed—say, "Throw up your hands." He watched a nickel-plated pistol in the Earp party pointed at Billy Clanton, saw it fire first, and thought it was fired by Doc Holliday. Just as the shooting began, he heard Billy say, "Don't shoot me. I don't want to fight," and saw Tom McLaury throw open his coat and announce he was not armed. Behan estimated that eight or ten shots had been fired by the Earps and Holliday before he saw a gun in the hands of any of the cowboys.

The defense lawyers attempted to undermine Behan's credibility by questioning how he could have been so ignorant of what was going on that day before hearing news of the impending confrontation in the barbershop. More important, they attempted to extract an admission that when Behan had invited Virgil Earp to have a drink in Hafford's Saloon, the marshal had stated his intention to disarm the cowboys and Behan had argued that they would kill him and offered to go down and disarm them instead. The defense also tried to get Behan to acknowledge that he had told both Charlie Shibell and Wyatt Earp "that it was a dead square fight and that you could not tell who shot first." In addition, lawyers Fitch and Drum attempted to extract from the sheriff admissions that he had coordinated his testimony with Billy Allen and contributed to the prosecution fund. Behan flatly denied each charge.

Yet the cross-examination continued. Hadn't he welshed on his promise to Wyatt Earp to bring him into the sheriff's office after the appointment was won? The sheriff gave his own version of the agreement and his decision not to follow through after the Charleston incident. Hadn't he told "one of the Flys" that "I am about the only witness to that fight"? To this question, Behan replied, "I don't remember. I told him I saw it all. He was trying to get Claiborne out of the house. I told him to let him stay there, as he was not to blame and might get killed."

The defense was not through. Perhaps Behan's attention had been diverted from the Earp party during the crucial opening moments of the fight? Fitch and Drum tried to establish that Holliday's first shot had come from the shotgun, contrary to Behan's testimony. They also used a tactic on Behan which they would employ repeatedly, questioning how he could remain and observe the action with bullets flying hither and yon by asking, "With Allen fleeing into an alley-way, Claiborne or the kid hiding in the photograph gallery, [and]

Ike Clanton running away, why did you hover around there, exposing your person and life?" The question was overruled.

The defense gained one small victory in drawing from Behan an admission that Tom McLaury might indeed have been armed. To the question whether Ike and Tom could have been armed without his knowing it, even after he checked them, the sheriff replied that Tom perhaps could have. However, he provided a flat no to the defense question "Did you see Tom McLaury shoot over the horse's back?"

Now the defense, through its cross-examination of Behan, tried to establish that the Clantons and their associates were malevolent troublemakers. Hadn't Behan heard threats "on the part of the Clantons and McLaurys against the defendants" during the past months? "I never heard any threats at any time," he replied. Well, then, did he know "the reputation of the Clantons in the section of the county in which they live and roam for turbulence?" The prosecution objected, and the objection was sustained. Fitch and Drum tried again: "Have not the disturbances and main difficulties, breaches of the peace and killings in this city and county been in your opinion and knowledge, or either, connected with the Clantons or their confederates?" Again, the prosecution objected, but this time it was overruled. Behan's reply: "I never knew the McLaurys to be in any trouble or rows. Ike Clanton I have seen in one row here [the altercation with Fred Dodge's gambling partner Denny McCann], and Billy Clanton I know nothing about."

On November 4, the defense questioned Behan concerning his visit to Virgil Earp's home on the evening of the shooting. Hadn't he told the wounded marshal that one of the McLaury boys drew his gun in response to Virgil's command, and hadn't he assured Virgil that the marshal "did perfectly right"? Behan denied such a conversation; he had simply explained to Virgil that he had not been trying to throw the Earp party off. He had, he asserted, reassured the marshal of his friendship and had denied trying "to get the vigilance committee to hang" the Earps, as Virgil suspected.

Also on this day, Martha King again took the stand to repeat the brief verbal pact made by one of the Earps and Doc Holliday as they passed Bauer's butcher shop. She still did not or could not identify which of the Earp brothers had said, "Let them have it!"

Up until this testimony of November 4, everyone involved had been simply plowing dutifully along through a messy business. But on the evening of November 3, there had rumbled into town a stage carrying a man whose crusading zeal would fan sympathies for the cowboys and further polarize the community. Will McLaury, a recent widower, had left his young children and Fort Worth law practice in response to the telegrammed news of his brothers' death.

Ironically, in light of the political divisions in Tombstone, McLaury was considered a "radical" Republican in heavily Democratic Fort Worth, had run as a Republican for county attorney, and had only gained some degree of acceptance among the southern Democratic old guard by going into partnership with former Confederate officer S. P. Greene. The *Daily Nugget* of November 5 listed among the arrivals at the Grand Hotel "W. M. McLowry, Texas."

He came as a man wronged, demanding justice. The two brothers buried on the hillside "were very dear to me and would have walked through fire for me," he would write to brother-in-law D. D. Applegate in Iowa. What he discovered in Tombstone only intensified his feelings of loss and desire for vengeance. Frank and Tom "had just sold off their stock and would have started for my place in a day or two and they calculated to have visited their father and sisters in Iowa." Instead, they had become victims of "as cold blooded and foul a murder as has been recorded," he explained to partner Greene in Fort Worth. "My brothers had no quarrel nor interest in any quarrel with these men."

As for motive, McLaury wrote that Billy Clanton had knowledge of Doc Holliday's part in the Benson stage robbery attempt and the Earps' interest in it. Thus, the Clantons and his brothers "had got up facts intending to prosecute . . . Holliday, and the Earps and Holliday had information of it." He was so sure of this that he expected indictments against Holliday "and I think two of the Earps and one [Marshall] Williams for the murder in the attempted stage robbery."

However, McLaury quickly found he would have to fight hard for the outcome he sought. Not only did he learn that sixteen hundred dollars of the money Tom had been carrying was now missing, but he was incensed to discover his brothers' killers walking around freely—at least, the two who could walk. In addition, he reported to Greene that Wyatt and Doc attended court "heavily armed" and were keeping "many" of the citizens in "dread." He made it his first order of business to get the two back into custody and outlined his frustration in doing so to Greene:

> The Dist. Atty. was completely "cowed" and after promising me on the fourth to move the court to commit these men without bail he would not do it and after agreeing in the presence of all our attys. to do so he would not do it and none of our attorneys would do so and would not permit me to do so and said they did not want to see me killed and to prevent me from making this motion refused to support me if I made it.

The fourth was a Friday; on Lyttleton Price's motion, McLaury got himself admitted as associate counsel for the prosecution, then spent the weekend trying to round up prosecution witnesses and find another lawyer who would make the motion to commit Wyatt and Doc without bail. Meanwhile, on Saturday, November 5, James Kehoe and Andy Mehan testified.

Kehoe related that he had been talking with Frank and Tom in front of Bauer's when Behan came up and wanted their weapons. He remembered that Frank at first demurred—"Johnny, as long as the people in Tombstone act so, I will not give up my arms"—then agreed to go with Behan. The men left, with Tom to all appearances unarmed. The Earp party passed, and Kehoe heard two to four shots, then saw Frank running, drawing his gun. Saloon man Mehan simply testified that Tom McLaury had left his pistol, "chambers all loaded," with Mehan between one and two o'clock on the day in question.

Wes Fuller took the stand on Monday, the seventh. He identified himself as a gambler, but his allegiance was with the cowboys; he testified he was hurrying to warn Billy Clanton to get out of town when the confrontation began. Fuller explained he had seen Doc Holliday pocketing a six-shooter at Fourth and Allen and had noticed that Wyatt and Morgan were both armed. Having stopped to talk to a woman named Mattie Webb, whose house bordered Allen, he arrived at the vacant lot to see Billy Clanton with his hands up, protesting he didn't want to fight, as the firing commenced by the Earp party—five to seven shots before Billy Clanton could draw and respond. In fact, he testified, Frank McLaury had not drawn his weapon until he got a little past the middle of the street, after seven or eight shots had been fired.

Fuller identified Doc Holliday and Morgan Earp as the members of the Earp party he thought had fired first. He stated that he saw no arms on Ike or on Tom during the fight, nor did he see any on Tom after he was carried, mortally wounded, into the house at the corner of Third and Fremont.

The defense tried to discount Fuller's testimony in three ways. First, as with Behan, there was the question of how much *any* witness could have observed while trying to preserve his own safety. Fuller admitted that he backed away from the scene and moved about, "as the bullets were flying around there," but testified that he remained facing Fremont and observing the action.

The defense then tried to establish that Fuller had been too drunk on the day of the fight to provide a reliable witness. The gambler acknowledged that he had been drinking over a period of days before the fight, but denied that he had imbibed on that day or that he had suffered a fit of delirium tremens.

Finally, the Earp-Holliday attorneys attacked Fuller's motives with regard to Doc Holliday, asking him if he did not "on the 5th day of November, 1881, about 5 o'clock in the afternoon, in front of the Oriental saloon in Tombstone, say to or in the presence of Wyatt Earp, that you knew nothing in your testimony that would hurt the Earps but that you intended to cinch Holliday, or words of like import or effect?"

Fuller's answer: "I told Wyatt Earp then that I thought Holliday was the cause of the fight—I don't say positively I did not use the words, 'I mean to cinch Holliday,' but I don't think I did."

In the midst of Fuller's testimony, a motion "was made by

attorney for the prosecution that the defendants be remanded to the custody of the Sheriff without bail" because "the proof so far was conclusive of murder." Will McLaury had gained Spicer's assurance that a motion to jail the two uninjured defendants without bond would be granted and told the prosecution attorneys "to do as they pleased." He would make the request himself.

"I did not think they, the defts., would make a move and did not fear them," McLaury wrote of that moment to his law partner. "The fact is I only hoped they would as I would be on my feet and have the first go. And thought I could kill them both before they could get a start." To Applegate he wrote that he made the motion, "then stood where I could send a knife through their hearts if they made a move. . . . [I]t was perhaps good for me they did not—for I was anxious to have an opportunity to send them over the bay."

Not only did the two defendants fail to react violently, but, according to McLaury, "They were as quiet as lambs, only looked a little scared." Wyatt and Doc "sat and trembled and now whenever I go near them I can see it makes them nervous. I think we can hang them."

Spicer promptly ordered Sheriff Behan to take the two into his custody "until the further order of Court, or until they be legally discharged." The lawyers for Wyatt and Doc countered by filing a writ of habeas corpus with Probate Judge and gunfight witness J. H. Lucas, arguing that once the defendants had been out on bail, Spicer "had no power to order them into custody."

On the evening of the seventh, the various attorneys wrangled over the writ, with McLaury pressing to keep his work from being undone. "The petition was discussed—People were afraid to talk," he wrote to Greene. "Our witnesses were running away—No one but the [illegible] and ranchmen dared come forward to give any information unless brought into court by attachment."

Nonetheless, McLaury won the battle; after argument, "the writ was dismissed and Earp and Holliday remanded into the custody of the Sheriff." McLaury wrote to his partner, "Last night after it was known the murderers were in Jail the Hotel was a perfect jam until nearly morning. Everybody wanted to see me and shake my hand." He reported general sympathy for the prosecution among the populace, and now "We are going on with the examination of witnesses before exa[min]ing Court for we fear some of our most important witnesses will be killed by the friends of these brutes."

The Fort Worth attorney admitted that the whole affair "has a tendency to arouse all the devil there is in me," but he was determined to continue pressing. The killers, he reported, "are in jail and in bed but my D[ea]r Capt. this don't bring back my dead brothers. If . . . George wants to know where *Hades* is I can inform him." To his sister in Iowa, McLaury wrote, "I am afraid this will seriously affect the health of my father—I have suffered a great deal this summer—in the loss of my wife, and now my children are being cared for by strangers—This thing nearly made me sick—I was well on the day I recd the news but have not been well since." Nonetheless, McLaury determined to remain until mid-December, as a ruling for the prosecution on Spicer's part would bring the murder charge before the grand jury that was about to convene.

On Tuesday, November 8, Billy Claiborne's testimony only fanned the flames of McLaury's wrath. Claiborne, a former drover for John Slaughter's herds, laconically admitted that he "saw a little shooting" between the four members of the Earp party and Billy Clanton and Frank McLaury, giving an account in line with his previous coroner's inquest testimony.

The Mississippi native, now a slag cart driver and smelter worker for the Neptune Mining Company in the tiny mining community of Hereford, was not sure whether the same Earp party member had said both "You sons of bitches have been looking for a fight" and "Hold up your hands!" Doc Holliday began the firing; questioned as to the dentist's clothing, Claiborne remarked dryly, "I cannot say. I was not watching his clothing. I was watching the six shooter he had in his hand." When Holliday fired, Billy and Ike had their hands up; Tom was holding his coat open. Morgan Earp fired and hit Billy Clanton from close range—less than a foot. Tom was unarmed, both during the shooting and after being brought into the house to die. Ike also was unarmed. He had seen all four members of the Earp party shooting, Morgan at Billy, Doc and Wyatt at Frank, Virgil "first at one of them, then the other."

The defense used the same lines of attack it had with Wes Fuller. Attorneys Fitch and Drum implied that Claiborne could not possibly have seen all he claimed to see—that indeed, he had run, or been shoved, into the photo gallery by Behan at the first shot—and that he had been drinking on the day in question. Claiborne steadfastly maintained that sixteen to eighteen shots had been fired before he reached the safety of the gallery; he did admit to having had "two or three glasses of beer" before the encounter.

In Claiborne's case, the defense also tried to establish that he held a grudge against the Earps. Claiborne had killed James Hickey in early October in Charleston after Hickey reportedly attempted to force him to take a drink. One of the Earp brothers had been involved in his subsequent arrest. Claiborne now stated he had nothing against the brothers, and Spicer sustained the prosecution's objections to this line of questioning as immaterial and irrelevant.

However, the witness was called to answer two other questions attacking his veracity: Had he coordinated his story with Sheriff Behan, and wasn't he a close friend of the McLaurys and Clantons? To the first, Claiborne answered an unequivocal no; to the second, he responded noncommittally, "I liked the boys, not more than I do any other of my acquaintances," acknowledging that he had "stopped at their ranches and stayed all night, once or twice."

As an interesting footnote to Claiborne's testimony, he was questioned as to how he had earned the sobriquet "the Kid." "Well, I came to Arizona when I was small, when Tombstone was first struck," the twenty-one-year-old witness explained. "John Slaughter's men called me the 'Kid,' because I was the smallest one in the outfit." The name apparently no longer fit and caused some dubious looks, however, because Claiborne was further questioned and testified that in the two and a half to three years since he had arrived he had grown "nearly two feet."

On the following day, saloonkeeper J. H. Allman testified briefly, establishing that Ike Clanton's weapons had been behind the bar at the Grand when the confrontation occurred. In fact, Allman recalled, "I heard the shooting and ran into the bar to arm myself, not knowing what was going on, and picked up a new pistol, and the Winchester rifle was there then."

Deputy Sheriff Billy Soule then testified that he had rounded up Billy's and Frank's horses in front of Bauer's after the shooting and had taken them to Dunbar's Livery Stable. He recalled that Billy's horse carried a rifle with a full chamber of shells. For some unexplained reason, Soule had "put five or six cartridges" into the rifle on Frank's horse.

The third witness that Wednesday was the man who had filed the murder complaint, Ike Clanton. His testimony and cross-examination would continue for a number of days. Ike identified himself as a stock raiser and cattle dealer and stated that he had sold approximately seven hundred head of cattle "in connection with the McLaury boys" in the past year, despite the absence of a brand registered in his name in either Cochise or Pima County.

He now reiterated and expanded upon his inquest testimony, outlining his series of run-ins with Doc Holliday and the Earps from the evening before until, preparing to leave town, he reached the vacant lot with his brother and friends. Here Johnny Behan had found him and Tom McLaury unarmed, had allowed Billy to keep his gun since the Clantons were departing, and had tried to convince a reluctant Frank to turn over his weapon. With the approach of the Earps, Behan had ordered the cowboys to stay put. They had done so only to have the Earp party walk up, announce, "You have been looking for a fight," and commence shooting—Doc first at one of the McLaurys, then Morgan at Billy Clanton. Ike repeated that he, Frank, and Billy had had their hands in the air, while Tom's were holding open his coat.

Ike was the one man on the cowboy side who could perhaps provide an explanation for the motives behind the enmity that had exploded on October 26, but he maintained that he had had friendly relations with the Earps up until the late-night lunchroom encounter. The defense worked to show that he had threatened the Earps before, that he was angry over what he perceived as Wyatt's loose talk regarding their arrangement with regard to the Benson stage robbers, and that he had sought a fight with the brothers and Doc Holliday throughout the morning of the twenty-sixth.

Counsel for the defense presented a scenario in which Ike and Frank McLaury rode up in front of Hafford's Saloon "about four weeks ago" and said to William Daly, "We understand they have formed a vigilance committee against us." Daly replied that "there was some talk about the matter but he did not know much about the matter."

"Can you deny but that man in there belongs to the committee?" one of the two allegedly asked, indicating Morgan Earp.

"He does not belong to it."

"We don't believe it. Even if it were so, it don't make any difference, they [the Earps] are in our way anyway, and will have to be got out."

Presented with this conversation under cross-examination, Ike flatly denied its having taken place and commented, "I don't remember of ever riding up to that saloon in company with Frank McLaury."

Both defense and prosecution wanted to get into the matter of the agreement between Wyatt and Ike in some detail, with the defense seeking to prove that Ike had met with Wyatt a number of times on the matter of capturing or killing the Benson stage robbers, then turned on him when news of their secret negotiations leaked out.

Thus, Fitch and Drum asked, "Have you not frequently, you and Frank McLaury, charged Wyatt Earp, Virgil and Morgan Earp, with having given you two away to Marshall Williams and Doc Holliday, in making them confid[ants] in your effort at surrendering Leonard, Head and Crane to justice—your particular friends and associates?"

Although he had mentioned in his inquest testimony that he personally had had a "transaction" with the Earps, Ike insisted that he had declined to assist Wyatt and that he had met with him only once on the matter, not in the presence of his friend. "In regard to Frank McLaury, I don't know whether he ever charged anything of the kind or not," Ike testified, but "as to my part, I had nothing to do with bringing them to justice, consequently I could not charge the Earp brothers with giving me away to anybody."

Instead, Ike contended, he had received numerous confidences from the Earps and Holliday regarding their need to silence Leonard, Head, and Crane. According to his testimony, Holliday had admitted to him that he was the robber who killed Bud Philpot, both Wyatt and Morgan had admitted that they had secretly channeled stage money to Doc and Billy Leonard, and Virgil had told him that he had led the posse away from the three suspected robbers to keep from getting "all of his friends into trouble."

It was certainly convenient that each of the accused had confided their illegal doings to the chief prosecution witness, and the defense could not resist poking fun at Ike's claims, asking, "Did not James Earp, a brother of Virgil, Morgan and Wyatt, also confess to you that he was a murderer and stage robber?" The prosecution objected to the question, and the objection was sustained. Ike was also asked why, if he had this extensive knowledge of such perfidy, he had not shared it before. "Before they told me, I made a sacred promise not to tell it," he explained, "and never would have told it had I not been put on the stand."

He also gave as a second reason his fear of being murdered for knowing too much. However, in response to a question as to whether he was frightened when the Earps approached the vacant lot, he stated, "Well, sir, I cannot say that I was frightened when they first came there, because I had no idea they intended to murder the boys or me. But when I came to see them shooting the boys with their hands up, and knew I was disarmed, and while Wyatt Earp was trying to murder me, I knew I would be killed if I did not get away."

The whole affair of Wyatt's and Ike's secret dealings remained a tangled puzzle, with the Earps continuing to push their version and Ike continuing to adhere to his. In the matter of Ike's threats on the morning of the twenty-sixth, however, there were other witnesses who corroborated the Earps, and Ike developed a convenient case of amnesia about his role in that portion of the drama. Although he admitted to making threats against the Earps in Kelly's Saloon, he was generally vague on his activities of the morning. Fitch and Drum questioned him regarding the upcoming testimony of Oriental barman Ned Boyle, who would state that Ike had made threats

against the Earps that morning. Ike replied, "I don't remember of speaking to Ned Boyle about it. I think I saw him
but don't remember saying anything to him about it. I don't
think I said the Earps had to fight when they came on the
street. There are three of them that I never had an unpleasant
word with in my life, up to that time. I don't remember of
having any pistol in my hand."

Ike's testimony would have carried more weight if he had
been more straightforward about his animosities and intentions on the morning of the twenty-sixth. Meanwhile, as his
examination extended over a week's period, interspersed with
the testimony of others, the other witnesses were helping his
case more than he was. On the tenth, bookkeeper J. H.
Batcher testified to seeing Wyatt Earp buffalo Tom McLaury.
Batcher's testimony worked for the Earp party in that he reported Tom's announcing himself ready to fight if Wyatt was,
but it also worked against them in that Batcher testified that
Tom had first spoken to Wyatt "and said he didn't know what
he had against him, that he had never done anything against
him and was a friend of his."

Butcher Bauer, who said he had known Tom only since
October 11, reinforced this picture of a man drawn reluctantly
into fighting by relating that Tom had had his hands in his
pocket when Wyatt struck him, that he had removed them
and backed away to ward off the blows, and that, in response
to Wyatt's question as to whether he was heeled, Tom had announced, "No, I am not heeled. I have got nothing to do with
anybody."

A third witness to the buffaloing, Thomas Keefe, also
took the stand on the tenth and reported seeing Tom raise his
arms to ward off the blows. However, his testimony about the
aftermath of the gunfight was more important, for he explained that he had picked up Tom, with some assistance from
others, and tended him during his dying moments. Keefe,
who said he did not know Billy Clanton or the McLaurys at
the time of the gunfight and had known Ike Clanton for only
two weeks, swore he had seen no pistol on or around the mortally wounded cowboy. "As soon as Dr. Matthews came, we
searched the body and did not find any arms on him," he explained. "We examined him close enough to see if there were

any arms on him, and there were none on him—we only found money on him."

This sure statement that Tom was unarmed—and the vivid picture Keefe presented of Billy's and Tom's painful last moments—led the defense to attack Keefe as a paid lackey of supporters of the prosecution, most likely of Ike Clanton or of Will McLaury. Concerning Ike, Keefe testified that he had had no business dealings with him and was not "intimate," but had talked with him at Hafford's Corner twenty minutes to half an hour before the shooting. He also admitted talking to Will McLaury, who had sought him out after arriving in town, but the carpenter still denied "receiving either promise or money from Ike or anyone else connected with the prosecution" or "having conversed with anyone outside counsel for the prosecution, prior to giving testimony."

Fitch and Drum then brought in a second discrediting point by questioning Keefe about his own arrest and incarceration in Nevada. "I was arrested and put in jail and honorably acquitted," Keefe responded. "I was in jail for entering my own house, after coming back from Idaho and dispossessing a certain gentleman who was living there." The "gentleman" was living with Keefe's wife in the latter's eight-month absence; by Keefe's account, when he returned, he went home and asked the man to leave and got shot at and put in jail for his troubles.

This story of the wronged husband brought that line of questioning to a close. There was one more point the defense wanted to explore. Keefe had stated he saw a Smith & Wesson revolver lying on the floor by the door of the house at Third and Fremont. Of course, the defense would be interested in establishing this as Tom McLaury's gun. Keefe, however, was mistaken; the gun was brought into court and found to be a Colt, and the next witness, Coroner Matthews, stated that it was Frank McLaury's weapon, which Matthews himself had picked up (with two loads in it) on his way to examine Billy and Tom. Billy Clanton's gun, Matthews explained, had been handed to him the next day by Camillus Fly.

Meanwhile, Ike continued his testimony, laying everything at the feet of the Earps and Holliday. Then, on the fifteenth, the prosecution rested. It was time for the defense to bring in the accused themselves to answer Ike's charges. However, Doc Holliday and Morgan Earp—both volatile, both identified by many as starting the gunfight, both living on the fringes of respectable society and lacking the social standing of Virgil and Wyatt—were not considered good risks. No, Wyatt and Virgil would have to pull the fat out of the fire on this one. The defense would start by putting the coolest Earp of all on the stand. They would start with Wyatt.

CHAPTER 12

"To Save Themselves from Certain Death"

On November 12, 1881, the Fort Worth *Daily Democrat* reported, "The trial of the Earps and Holliday for murder is now going on in Tombstone, and public sentiment, which was at first in their favor, has turned now since the evidence shows that it was the gratification of revenge on their part, rather than desire to vindicate law which led to the shooting." Other newspapers presented vastly different views. One Dodge City paper maintained, "The Earp boys were acting as peace officers, and from all reports were justified in doing what they did." In addition to such widely divergent opinions, newspapers provided a wealth of misinformation; for instance, a Wichita newspaper, still referring to Wyatt "Erp," had Wyatt and his brother "Ike" and a third unnamed brother trying to arrest a "crowd" of drunken cowboys when the gunfight occurred.

In short, bias and unreliability ran through the newspaper reports of the gunfight and hearing. Newspaper editors picked up letters and narratives written by Tombstone citizens or garnered accounts of what happened from Tombstone's own biased journals. Clum's *Epitaph* and Earp supporters provided reports identifying the Clantons and McLaurys as leading outlaws of the region, causing the *Nugget* to complain, "Before the smoke of the pistols had scarcely been blown away, dispatches were sent forth telling of a desperate fight between officers and desperadoes. (And all the Munchausen abilities of tenderfoot correspondents were called into aid to magnify the affair into an event of the age.)"

These exaggerated reports of a lawman-outlaw clash made their way to McLaury relatives in Iowa. On November 9, Will McLaury responded to a brother-in-law's queries by writing, "The men who committed the murder caused the sending out of dispatches in the manner it was done [and] they also called on our acting Governor for troops to protect the city," thus obscuring the characters of those killed:

> Now I find that my Brothers stood as high with these people both in the city and in the country as you did in your county when I knew you there— In fact I find that with the exception of about thirty or forty men here whose business is gambling and stealing among whom are the Earp brothers and one J. H. Holliday, my brothers were universally esteemed as Honorable, Peaceable, and Brave citizens never having been charged nor suspected of having committed any offense.

The Democratic newspaper of his adopted home, Fort Worth, backed McLaury in this matter, telling readers that "the McLaury boys owned a large ranch in San Simeon [*sic*] Valley, and were large cattle raisers and ranchmen, and from the nature of their business ignorant people class them as cowboys and cattle-thieves." The paper also quoted an account by a Tombstone resident who had seen Frank and Billy ride into town and who gave a detailed statement reflecting most of the testimony damaging to the Earps and Holliday.

The Tombstone *Nugget* at first was not overtly partisan. It provided balanced coverage of the hearing and gave a reasoned assessment of the gunfight itself days after it happened: ". . . there were bitter personal feuds existing between individuals on either side. They were all of that class to whom any imputation of not possessing 'staying qualities' in a fight is sufficient to provoke one immediately. It was inevitable that a difficulty would some time occur between some of them. . . ." Nonetheless, in identifying the Earps and Holliday as feudists rather than as law enforcers holding the cowboy hordes at bay, the *Nugget* was regarded as overly sympathetic to the cowboys by *Epitaph* editor Clum and by other strong law-and-order advocates across the West. Clum was succeeding in making the word *cowboy* "synonymous with criminal, not only in Cochise County but elsewhere in the West" and in linking the *Nugget* with this criminal class. In reporting the death of a cowboy at Camp Rice, the San Francisco *Exchange* editorialized snidely, "The Tombstone Nugget should send down a special reporter to weep over the remains. That journal is now recognized in Arizona Territory as the great obituary organ of all slaughtered cowboys."

If strong opinions were held across the West, it was because every frontier community struggled with the issues the gunfight had blasted into the open. To whom should a community give police authority? How should it be administered? By what standards should license be defined and order be imposed? How could the frontier values of independence and self-reliance be balanced with the need for social cooperation and order? Individual answers to these questions were tied up with political and economic viewpoints. Not surprisingly, many westerners of the time agreed with John Madden, who as a young lawyer in Dodge had received the help of Bat Masterson and Wyatt Earp in winning a case against the "Texas men" in a range feud. "God bless old Wyatt Earp and men of his kind," Madden would write many years later to Stuart Lake. "They shot their way to heaven."

It was a view Wyatt Earp would naturally not care to dispute, especially when he took the stand at the Spicer hearing on November 16, 1881. As his testimony began, it became clear that he would not have to deal in court with any questioning of his role, anyway, for he was allowed simply to read a long prepared statement and was not submitted to cross-examination.

The testimony started with the standard questions—name, age, length of residence, business, and profession. To the last, Wyatt answered, "Saloon keeper at present.* Also

---

*City records do not show Wyatt as licensee for any saloon and/or gambling operation, although he clearly had a stake in more than one.

have been deputy sheriff and also a detective." Then the defense handed him a carte blanche: "Give any explanations you may think proper of the circumstances appearing in the testimony against you and state any facts which you think will tend to your exculpation."

"The difficulty which resulted in the death of William Clanton and Frank and Tom McLaury originated last spring," Wyatt began, reading his statement. At this point the prosecution objected to the defendant's "using a manuscript from which to make such statement" and to his "being allowed to make statement without limit as to its relevancy."

Spicer overruled the objection, and Wyatt continued unchallenged with his own catalog of events. He outlined the July 1880 trip to the McLaury ranch to locate the stolen mules and testified that about a month after that incident, Frank and Tom McLaury had tried to "pick a fuss" with him in Charleston, telling him "if I ever followed them up again as close as I did before they would kill me." He also launched a number of unsubstantiated charges against the Clantons and McLaurys and their associates (Frank and Tom had participated in the Skeleton Canyon holdup, John Ringo had shot a man "in cold blood" near Camp Thomas) and forcefully linked them with the stage robbers. "It was generally understood among officers and those who have information about criminals that Ike Clanton was a sort of chief among the Cow Boys; that the Clantons and McLaurys were cattle thieves and generally in the secret of the stage robbery; and that the Clantons' and McLaurys' ranches were meeting places and places of shelter for the gang."

Thus, he explained, he had gone to Ike Clanton, Frank McLaury, and their confederate Joe Hill in hopes of striking a deal to capture the stage robbers and enhance his own standing before the first sheriff's election. Ike had been most amenable, as he was wrangling with Billy Leonard over ownership of a New Mexico ranch. The deal had been sealed with all three, and Joe Hill had been dispatched to lure Leonard, Head, and Crane back into the Tombstone area. But he had reached New Mexico too late; Leonard and Head were dead. Now, Wyatt testified, "Ike Clanton and Frank McLaury claimed that I had given them away to Marshall Williams and

Doc Holliday, and when they came in town they shunned us, and Morgan, Virgil Earp, Doc Holliday and myself began to hear their threats against us."

The situation was only exacerbated, in Wyatt's account, by the Earp brothers' participation in the September arrest of Frank Stilwell and Pete Spencer, a move that led Frank Mc-Laury to threaten Morgan Earp outside the Alhambra with Ike, John Ringo, and two other rustlers looking on. Wyatt testified that he and his brothers also heard of cowboy threats against them from Marshall Williams, William Daly, Ed "Byrries" (probably Ed Byrnes, the Benson gambler of doubtful reputation with whom Morgan Earp associated), "Old Man" Urrides, Charlie Smith, "and three or four others."

As for the events immediately preceding the gunfight, Holliday and Ike had quarreled, while Wyatt himself, Virgil, and Morgan had tried to maintain the peace. Ike had made threats personally to Wyatt before the night was over, and Wyatt had been awakened late the next morning with news of further threats on Ike's part. Wyatt, Virgil, and Morgan had all found Ike at the same time and hauled him into court, where Ike started the threats and accusations rolling again. After responding, Wyatt left the courtroom, only to be immediately threatened by Tom McLaury on the street. When the Earp party received word of further threats, they went to the vacant lot to disarm the cowboys, only to have Frank McLaury and Billy Clanton start to draw on them, while Tom McLaury at least appeared to do so.

> I never fired at Ike Clanton, even after the shooting commenced, because I thought he was unarmed. I believed then and believe now, from the acts I have stated and the threats I have related and the other threats communicated to me by other persons as having been made by Tom McLaury, Frank McLaury and Ike Clanton, that these men last named had formed a conspiracy to murder my brothers, Morgan and Virgil, Doc Holliday and myself. I believe I would have been legally and morally justifiable in shooting any of them on sight. But I did not do so, not attempt to do so. I sought no advantage when I went as deputy marshal to help disarm them and arrest them. I went as a

part of my duty and under the direction of my brother, the marshal. I did not intend to fight unless it became necessary in self-defense and in the performance of official duty. When Billy Clanton and Frank McLaury drew their pistols, I knew it was a fight for life, and I drew and fired in defense of my own life and the lives of my brothers and Doc Holliday.

Wyatt and his attorneys were clearly conscious of the fact that Doc Holliday was a sore liability, for Wyatt took pains in the statement to explain that he was friends with the dentist because the latter had saved his life in Dodge. Wyatt also attacked Ike's account of their secret dealings as "a tissue of lies from beginning to end" and charged that Behan's account of their deal concerning the sheriff's position was "false in every particular."

Finally, he introduced two ringing testimonials to his good character. The first, from five past city officials and two active ones in Wichita, stated that during Wyatt's time in that town he "was a good and efficient officer, and was well known for his honesty, and integrity"; his character "while here was of the best, and . . . no fault was ever found with him as an officer, or as a man." The second was signed by sixty-two leading citizens and firms of Dodge City, everyone from liquor dealers to the local school director and the Presbyterian church pastor. It attested to Wyatt's high social standing while in the cow town and described his law enforcement performance as exemplary: "[H]e was ever vigilant in the discharge of his duties and while kind and courteous to all, he was brave, unflinching, and on all occasions proved himself the right man in the right place."

The prosecution fought having these testimonials added to the court record, but again, the defense won the legal skirmish.

Prosecutors did win a small victory in stopping barman E. F. Boyle's testimony on November 17, the day after Wyatt's presentation. Ned Boyle explained that he had met an armed Ike in front of the telegraph office about 8:30 or 9:00 A.M., but when the defense asked him to relate any threats made by Ike at that time and relayed by Boyle to the Earps, the prosecution objected, and Spicer sustained the objection.

Nor did the defense get anything of value from the other witness of the day, saloonkeeper Robert Hatch. Hatch, who had served as a bondsman for Virgil as city marshal, had watched the brothers and Holliday walk up Fremont, encounter Behan, then meet the cowboys, but he was vague on important defense points. He hadn't seen any hostile demonstration on the part of the cowboys when Virgil announced, "We have come to arrest you," for the Earp party at the time "was standing between me and the Clantons." He had not heard anyone say "son of a bitch," but, then, he wasn't sure he would have. He didn't see anyone fire over a horse's back, as the defense asserted Tom McLaury had.

After the first three or four shots, Hatch testified, he had ducked into Bauer's butcher shop, then emerged as the shooting ended and entered Fly's, where he found Behan and a badly frightened Claiborne. Fitch and Drum tried to establish through Hatch's testimony that Behan and Claiborne had been hiding in Fly's since the opening shots, but since Hatch had not gone into the photographer's until the shooting subsided, this line of reasoning was not particularly fruitful.

Will McLaury's letter to his sister on this date indicates that the defense was hoping for better from Hatch. McLaury explained that "one of their principal witnesses has been on the stand today and they feel bad his evidence is much stronger for us than it is for them. I think the scoundrel feared to act out his role, and I am of the opinion that his fears are not wholly groundless."

McLaury's sister, Margaret Applegate, had apparently taken him to task for leaving his motherless children in order to pursue the charges, for he also wrote that her letter did not "suit my mind or temper," arguing, "My children will be provided for and I don't think a father would be any great advantage to them who would leave it to god to punish men who had murdered their uncles."

Overall, McLaury painted an optimistic picture of the way matters were developing. "I had little support from the people when I came here," he reported, as most were "intimidated," but "I now have the whole camp with the exception of a few gamblers." In fact, he had found "a large number of my Texas friends here who are ready and willing to stand by me and with Winchesters if necessary." He explained, "The only thing now is to keep my friends quiet—there came near being a general killing here last night which had it not been prevented would have closed my business here." Not that McLaury would mind such an outcome; he wrote, "I am trying to punish these men through the courts of the country first if that fails—then we *may* submi[t]." He envisioned the defendants' only hope as escape from jail, but then "their bones will bleach on these mountains." If the image gave him some vengeful satisfaction, he nonetheless expressed great bitterness: "You can ask your preacher and he may be able to locate definitely Heaven—I thought for this two years previous to March last I was having a little taste of it. But I am now able to definitely sufficiently for my purpose locate Hades."

McLaury's bitterness could only intensify, for his assessment of the situation at the hearing was overly optimistic. The defense had suffered only a minor setback with Boyle's blocked testimony and Hatch's less-than-conclusive statement.

After their appearances on the seventeenth, S. B. Chapin, clerk of the city council of Tombstone, made an appearance on the nineteenth to read from the book of city ordinances in a move calculated by the defense to show that the Earps and Holliday had acted within the bounds of law enforcement. Ordinance No. 7, Section 1 stated that an officer could enter any place "open to the public" to "arrest such persons as he may then find engaged in or causing" breaches of the peace. Ordinance No. 9 outlined the regulations for carrying of deadly weapons in town. It basically prohibited concealed weapons and instructed that guns, bowie knives, and dirks be relinquished for deposit while an individual was in town.

The prosecution could have argued that Frank McLaury and Billy Clanton—the only two cowboys clearly armed—had entered town just a short time before the shooting and that the latter, at least, had voiced plans to leave as quickly as possible. If they did, however, the record does not show it. It does show that Price and his fellow prosecution attorneys objected to the entering of the ordinances into the hearing record and found themselves overruled.

Now Fitch and Drum put the injured chief of police, Virgil Earp himself, on the stand. It was all well and good to cite statutes concerning what police officers could do, but the defense needed to show that the mantle of police authority had covered all four members of the Earp party. Thus, Virgil was immediately questioned as to the appointments of his brothers and Holliday.

He testified that on the day of the gunfight Morgan had been acting as special policeman for about a month: "He was sworn in as special policeman and wore a badge with 'Special Police' engraved on it." Wyatt "had been sworn in to act in my place while I was at Tucson [for the Stilwell-Spencer trial], and on my return his saloon was opened* and I appointed him a 'special,' to keep the peace, with power to make arrests, and also called on him on the 26th, to assist me in disarming those parties—Ike Clanton and Billy Clanton, Frank McLaury and Tom McLaury."

As for Doc Holliday, Virgil simply stated, "I called on him on that day for assistance to help disarm the Clantons and McLaurys."

Now the witness was asked to recount the events of the twenty-sixth. He began with his conversation with Ike at about six or seven that morning. Ike had wanted him to carry a challenge to Doc Holliday. Virgil had refused. He had gone home to bed, only to be awakened with news of Ike's further threats. Virgil had gone onto the street and buffaloed Ike, who admitted he would have killed the marshal, given the chance.

In contradiction to some of the other testimonies, Virgil stated that he had heard no quarrel between Wyatt and Ike, either in the courtroom that day or elsewhere; that all four cowboys—or at least three of them—had been in the gunshop loading up on ammunition; that Johnny Behan, anticipating a fight, had refused to go with him to disarm the cowboys and instead decided to try disarming them himself; that Behan had warned the approaching Earp party that the cowboys would murder them if they continued, then announced that he had disarmed them; that the cowboys had "moved in between the two buildings, out of sight of me" as the marshal's party approached; that Frank McLaury and Billy Clanton had responded to his command to throw up their hands by draw-

---

*Which saloon is unclear. See note, p. 279.

ing and cocking their six-shooters; that Billy Clanton's was one of the first two shots fired, Wyatt's probably the other; and that Tom McLaury had shot "once if not twice over the horse's back."

Under questioning, Virgil went into the deal making with Ike Clanton and the threats he said Frank McLaury had made about a month before the gunfight. As for his own part in the altercation of the twenty-sixth, he testified, "I fired four shots—one at Frank McLaury and I believe the other three were at Billy Clanton. I am pretty positive one was at Frank McLaury and three at Billy Clanton."

The defense's ace in the hole, railroad engineer H. F. Sills, began his testimony at the conclusion of Virgil's on the twenty-second. An avowed stranger to all the participants, Sills had arrived on a Wells Fargo wagon with one other passenger only the day before the gunfight. On the afternoon of October 26, he had seen four or five men, two of them clearly armed, standing in front of the O.K. Corral, threatening to kill Virgil Earp—and indeed, "the whole party of the Earps"—on sight. He had made inquiries as to who the Earps were, then found and warned Virgil. Sills explained that he had followed the marshal and party along Fremont and had seen in the vacant lot "the party I had heard making those threats." He had watched as the two groups met and had seen Virgil throw up his right hand with the cane in it, then switch the cane to the left hand and draw his revolver as the shooting started. Sill, alone among the hearing witnesses, supported Wyatt's and Virgil's contention that Wyatt and Billy Clanton had shot first.

Under cross-examination, Sills was required to give detailed personal background. The defense, of course, wanted to enhance his credibility as an objective observer, while the prosecution wanted to establish some link with the Earp faction. Sills explained that he had come to Tombstone during his temporary layoff from his locomotive engineer job with the Atcheson, Topeka, and Santa Fe; he had since entered the local hospital for an extended period. He was closely questioned as to whom he had traveled with and talked to during his stay in Tombstone. He even wound up trying to describe the horses that had pulled the wagon carrying him to town.

The prosecution could not expose a chink in Sills's story

of the unbiased stranger come to town, although interestingly, he acknowledged that "the first word" he spoke of his knowledge of the incident "was to Jim Earp, I believe."

The Earp faction was gaining the upper hand again, if, indeed, these men had ever lost it. Meanwhile, testimony continued on the twenty-third. Sills's cross-examination ended; then saloonkeeper Julius Kelly stated that Ike had entered his establishment on the morning of October 26 and told him about the altercation of the night before and his determination to have it out with "the Earp crowd and Doc Holliday," despite Kelly's warning that "the other side would also fight, if it came to the point." Ned Boyle was also recalled; this time the prosecution protest was overruled when the defense asked him what threats he had heard Ike make on the morning of October 26. "He insisted that he wouldn't go to bed," Boyle noted, "that as soon as the Earps and Doc Holliday showed themselves on the street, the ball opened—that they would have to fight."

The defense lawyers clearly established that Ike had played a large role in precipitating the fight. They also had tried, with less success, to paint him, his brother, and his confederates as leading outlaws. However, if they could not establish criminality, they could at least show the four as potentially dangerous gunmen. Barkeeper Boyle testified that he had never known Frank McLaury, Tom McLaury, or Billy Clanton to be in any difficulties that would involve the law, but he could attest to their reputations as experts with firearms: "The hearsay is that they were the finest in the country." He had known Tom McLaury "about eighteen months" and had heard from a group of men at Pick 'Em Up [a small community south of Tombstone] of Tom's reputation for courage and as "one of the best shots in the country." He had known Frank and Billy about the same length of time and had heard of their reputations for coolness and expertise with firearms as well. Frank's had been related to him by a man now living in Los Angeles; Billy's he had picked up "from the association of men he travelled with."

R. J. Campbell, clerk of the county board of supervisors, testified on the same day and gave a similar assessment: "The reputation of Frank McLaury was a brave and courageous

man and that he was an expert in the use of fire arms. Ike
Clanton is the same. William Clanton, I can't say for him, only
by reputation, that he was an expert in the use of fire arms. I
did not know Tom McLaury only by sight."

Campbell also testified concerning the courtroom scene
when Ike was charged with carrying a concealed weapon on
the morning of October 26, relating the heated discussions
and taunts between Ike and Morgan and Wyatt, including
Ike's words "If you fellows had been a second later, I would
have furnished a coroner's inquest for the town."

Fitch and Drum now felt confident enough to win the release on bail of the two defendants being held. On motion of
counsel for the defense, Wyatt and Doc "were admitted to bail
pending the remainder of the examination in the sum of
$20,000 each." They had already raised more than that after
their initial arrest, but now E. B. Gage and James Vizina
stepped in as sureties. The Earps' and Holliday's support
could not come any higher in Tombstone, as Gage and Vizina
both held important positions in leading mining operations.

On November 26, army surgeon J. B. W. Gardiner took
the stand. Gardiner had witnessed the buffaloing of Tom by
Wyatt. He soon saw Tom enter Everhardy's butcher shop and
quickly reemerge. "I saw no pistol but supposed at the time,
on seeing the right hand pocket of his pants extending out-
wards that he had gotten a pistol."

Gardiner was followed by newly appointed Cochise
County Deputy District Attorney W. S. Williams, who stated
that he had witnessed the talk between the sheriff and Virgil
Earp on the evening of October 26. Williams testified that
Behan had said what he denied saying—that "one of the
McLaury boys" reacted to Virgil's order by drawing his gun.
The witness also indicated that in another conversation he
had heard Behan assure Virgil that the marshal's actions had
been "perfectly right."

Gardiner's companion in front of the Cosmopolitan, Albert Bilicke, was next. Bilicke's father, Cosmopolitan proprietor Chris Bilicke, had filed a mining claim with Wyatt
Earp, and one of the two Bilickes had contributed to Wyatt's
first bail. Now Albert reported seeing Tom McLaury, whom
he knew by sight, enter Everhardy's a short time before the

gunfight and come out with his pants pocket protruding. The prosecution then asked a logical question: "You say in your examination in chief that you only knew Thomas McLaury by sight and had no personal acquaintance with him. How did it happen that you watched him so closely the different places that he went and the exact position of his right-hand pantaloons pocket when he went into the butcher shop and the exact form of a revolver in the same right-hand pocket when he came out?"

Bilicke's reply: "Every good citizen in this city was watching all those cow boys very closely on the day the affray occasioned [sic], and as he was walking down the street my attention was called to this McLaury by a friend, and so it happened that I watched him very closely."

This answer tinged with sanctimony drew sarcasm from the cross-examining attorney. "Do you know every good citizen in Tombstone, or did you on that day?"

"I know not all of them but a great many," Bilicke replied, his complacency apparently unruffled.

"Do you know what the opinions of all good citizens of Tombstone were on that [day] by conversation or conversations with them about watching Thomas McLaury in this city and if so tell us who they were."

Here this line of questioning so clearly showing the gulf in perspectives in Tombstone was dropped.

The next witness was dressmaker Addie Bourland, whose vague testimony concerning the gunfight itself provided support for the Earp version but could only serve to frustrate those seeking any clear picture of events. Her oblique answers to questions raised the possibility that she was being intentionally vague as to the threatening nature of what she had seen. From her window she had noticed the "five men opposite my house leaning against a small house west of Fly's gallery and one man was holding a horse, standing a little out from the house." She had seen the Earps and Holliday approach and reported that the cowboys "came out to meet them from the side of the house."

One of the newcomers, a man wearing a long coat, whom Bourland could later identify as Holliday, walked up to the man with the horse and stuck a pistol in his belly. The gun wielder, she related, then "stepped back two or three feet, and then the firing seemed to be general. That is all I saw." She had noticed no hands in the air and no one falling before moving away from the window with the commencement of shooting. To the question "Were all the parties shooting at each other at the time you were looking at them?" she replied, "It looked to me like it."

It was significant that Bourland could or would not identify which side shot first and thought everyone had commenced firing, but the key point was that she was in a position to see if the cowboys raised their hands and testified she saw no such movement. Justice of the Peace Spicer was so aware of this point, and so concerned by the vagueness of her testimony, that he visited Bourland after she had completed her testimony and gone home, then recalled her to the stand.

The prosecution objected, arguing that the witness had already been examined and cross-examined, but Spicer explained that "he believed she knew more than she had testified to on her examination," and thus he was reintroducing her "for the purpose of further examination without the solicitation of either the prosecution or defense." In doing so, he strengthened the defense's case. To the prosecution question "What conversation did you have with Judge Spicer, if any, with reference to your testimony to be given here since you signed your testimony this morning?" Bourland responded, "He asked me one or two questions in regard to seeing the difficulty and if I saw any men throw up their hands, whether I would have seen it, and I told him I thought I would have seen it." However, she reiterated, she had not.

Fitch and Drum had followed their ace Sills with a strong suit: Gardiner, Williams, Bilicke, Bourland. They also called Probate Judge Lucas, whose testimony about seeing Billy Clanton standing and firing during the gunfight was used to cast doubt on prosecution witnesses' contention that Billy had been hit and gone down early in the struggle.

The prosecution had to do something, and it made one countermove on the twenty-ninth, calling Ernest Storm of Everhardy's butcher shop to refute the testimony of Gardiner and Bilicke. Storm testified that he saw Tom enter the shop with his head bleeding between 2:00 and 3:00 P.M. and stay about five or ten minutes. Tom "had no arms on his person and did not get any in there that I saw."

"Was there any thing said in there about arms for Mc-Laury?"

"No sir."

With this "no sir" on November 29, 1881, the hearing into the charges of murder against Virgil Earp, Wyatt Earp, Morgan Earp, and John Henry Holliday came to an end, and Justice Spicer had to determine whether the evidence weighed heavily enough against the accused to turn the case over to the grand jury.

Spicer's was not an enviable job; he had a mass of contradictory testimony. Naturally, each person who had witnessed one of the events leading up to the shooting or a portion of the gunfight itself had a vantage point and a perspective a little different—or quite different—from that of another witness only a few yards away. Genuine confusion played a part in the gunfight and in the testimonies of those who saw it.

At the same time, lies were told on both sides. Ike Clanton said whatever he could to hang the Earps; the Earps said whatever they could to put their actions in the best possible light. Even researchers who have seen the Earps and Holliday responding to real lawlessness on the part of the Clantons and McLaurys have concluded that Wyatt and Virgil perjured themselves concerning who fired the first shot. If they did so, one can conclude that they were conscious of not being completely in the right, of needing to buttress their story to ensure the support of as many citizens as possible.

Spicer knew that whatever he concluded would anger one faction or another. The justice obliquely acknowledged the situation in his preamble to the decision he handed down on November 30 at 2:00 P.M.: "The great importance of the case, as well as the great interest taken in it by the entire community, demand that I should be full and explicit in my findings and conclusions and should give ample reasons for what I do."

He did not flinch from taking a strong stand in the reasoning that followed: "I cannot resist the conclusion that the defendants were fully justified in committing these homicides—that it is a necessary act, done in the discharge of an official duty."

The justice rejected Ike Clanton's story of the illegal machinations of the Earps and their desire to have Ike out of the way by noting that if this were so, Ike "could have been killed first and easiest." Instead, Spicer viewed the matter as strictly one of law enforcement, pointing out that in his job as chief of police, Virgil Earp was authorized to arrest, "with or without warrant, all persons engaged in any disorderly act, whereby a breach of the peace might be occasioned" and anyone carrying a deadly weapon in town without written permission. Ike Clanton had clearly been armed and threatening the Earp party on the morning of October 26. Ike's threats, the cowboys' movements and actions before the gunfight, and the reports Virgil Earp received from Sills and other citizens all indicated to Spicer a clear threat which Virgil as the police authority had every right to meet.

The justice did raise objection to Virgil's choice of companions to meet the threat. Noting the altercation between Ike and Doc Holliday the evening before, the words passed between Ike and Wyatt in court on the morning of the twenty-sixth, and Wyatt's buffaloing of Tom McLaury shortly thereafter, Spicer concluded that the marshal had committed "an injudicious and censurable act" in selecting the men he did to help him disarm the cowboys. However, he also greatly mitigated this criticism by pointing out the troubled, fearful atmosphere in which the marshal was operating:

> . . . although in this he [Virgil] acted incautiously and without due circumspection, yet when we consider the conditions of affairs incident to a frontier country; the lawlessness and disregard for human life; the existence of a law-defying element in [our] midst; the fear and feeling of insecurity that has [sic] existed; the *supposed* [emphasis mine] prevalence of bad, desperate and reckless men who have been a terror to the country and kept away capital and enterprise; and consider the many threats that have been made against the Earps, I can attach no criminality to his unwise act. In fact, as the result plainly proves, he needed the assistance and support of staunch and true friends, upon whose courage, coolness and fidelity he could depend, in case of an emergency.

As for the gunfight itself, Spicer was equally forceful in his conclusions. "Witnesses of credibility" testified that the Clantons and McLaurys were surrendering; other "witnesses of credibility" testified that Billy Clanton and Frank McLaury were preparing to fight. Spicer adopted the latter view, attaching no importance to who actually shot first. If those in the Earp party did, he reasoned, it was because "they saw at once the dire necessity of giving the first shots, to save themselves from certain death!!!" He cited as evidence Johnny Behan's testimony concering the earlier incident in which Ike Clanton believed the sheriff was coming to arrest him and had armed his friends to resist. He also cited Frank McLaury's refusal to give up his arms unless the Earps and Holliday were disarmed, and he pointed to Sills's and Bourland's testimonies indicating that both sides had fired almost simultaneously. Spicer further noted that Frank and Billy Clanton "made such quick and effective use of their arms as to seriously wound Morgan Earp and Virgil Earp."

He also interpreted the information on the cowboys' wounds as an indication that they had not been surrendering at the time the firing started. First, he rejected the testimony that Billy Clanton had been shot in the stomach at close range as the firing began. He did so on the basis of the fact that there were no powder burns on Billy's clothing and on the basis of Judge Lucas's testimony that Billy was standing and shooting during the gunfight before being hit. (Lucas's actual testimony is limited and ambiguous on this point.) Spicer concluded that Billy had received the wrist wound at the beginning of the fight and that "this wound is such as could not have been received with his hands thrown up." Further, Tom McLaury's side wound "was such as could not have been received with his hands on his coat lapels." As for whether Tom McLaury was armed or not, Spicer concluded that it did not matter if he was one of a party resisting arrest.

Finally, in support of the idea that the gunfight was a fair one rather than a slaughter, Spicer noted that Billy Clanton and Frank McLaury "were standing their ground and fighting back, giving and taking death with unflinching bravery" and thus accepting "the wager of battle."

In short, Spicer found the cowboys resisting legal authority and found no proof of felonious intent on the part of the Earps and Holliday. When the members of the Earp party marched to the vacant lot, "they were going where it was their right and duty to go; and they were doing what it was their right and duty to do; and they were armed, as it was their right and duty to be armed, when approaching men whom they believed to be armed and contemplating resistance." Frank McLaury's insistence that the other party be disarmed before he would surrender his weapon was "a proposition both monstrous and startling" when one considered that he was speaking of the chief of police and his assistants.

There it was—the crux of the matter. The Earps and Holliday—good, bad, or indifferent—*were* the law on that overcast October afternoon, and how could a frontier community survive if, as Spicer interpreted it, the Clantons and McLaurys were flouting that law? Spicer's conclusion simply reinforces John Clum's question "Was the police force of Tombstone to be bullied and cowed?"

In the decision, Spicer attempted to address the criticism he knew was coming. He had, he noted, "given over four weeks of patient attention" to the matter and had arrived at the only judgment which his understanding of the law allowed him to make. Indeed, he was quite clear on the point:

> The evidence taken before me in this case, would not, in my judgment, warrant a conviction of the defendants by a trial jury of any offense whatever. I do not believe that any trial jury that could be got together in this Territory, would, on all the evidence taken before me, with the rule of law applicable thereto given them by the court, find the defendants guilty of any offense.

Perhaps, he acknowledged, the grand jury already in session would see matters differently. If so, "it is quite within the power of that body, if dissatisfied with my decision, to call witnesses before them or use the depositions taken before me" and to "find an indictment against the defendants."

Predictably, the judge's conclusions drew immediate fire from anti-Earp forces, with the *Daily Nugget* sniffing that to many observers, Spicer did not "stand like Caesar's wife 'Not only virtuous but above suspicion.'" The Tucson *Star* was more direct in its criticism; the justice "was guilty of culpable ignorance of his duty or was afraid to perform the same, or acted corruptly in discharging them [*sic*]."

Actually, Spicer's decision has been acknowledged since as a highly competent piece of legal writing, and his basic conclusion—that Virgil Earp and the men he deputized were acting under the authority of the law—was legally sound. Some of his conclusions were far less compelling, arising as they did from an acceptance of the version of events most favorable to the Earps and Holliday and springing from a faulty logic. For example, the nature of Billy Clanton's and Tom McLaury's wounds does not preclude an early attempt to surrender on their part, as the actual moments of injury could not be accurately determined.

Spicer's political and socioeconomic interests were bound up with those of Tombstone's law-and-order businessmen, but he appears to have brought a fair degree of objectivity to the hearings. He did not "exonerate" the Earps and Holliday, as their supporters claimed; he merely acknowledged that they were acting within their rights as designated officers of the law. His biggest lapse involved not his reasoning in the decision but his allowing Wyatt Earp to read a prepared statement and escape cross-examination, that cornerstone of the fair legal process.

In truth, after the hearing and decision, the whys of the gunfight remained as controversial and as elusive as ever. Spicer himself concluded that "With what purpose they [the cowboys] crossed through to Fremont St., will probably never be known." He saw the Earps' and Holliday's purpose in going to the vacant lot as law enforcement, pure and simple. But many still maintained that the cowboys had not been looking for a fight—that the four were not challenging police authority, or, if they were, they were doing so after being goaded into it by misuse of that authority on the part of the Earps and Holliday. Two strong and contradictory scenarios remain and are worth reviewing.

SCENARIO NO. 1: The Clantons and McLaurys were determined to get the Earp brothers and Holliday—because the Earps had been cramping their style, because the cowboys were angry over the secret deal gone sour, and/or because of the string of humiliating incidents that began with Ike's entrance to the lunchroom the night before. Thus, the four were lying in wait for Doc Holliday beside the rooming house.

EVIDENCE: Ike had been making threats all morning. Sills testified he heard the cowboys plotting to kill the Earps, and other citizens found their movements suspicious enough to warn the marshal.

PROBLEMS: Ike would have to be not only stupid but crazy or incredibly drunk to plan to confront Holliday unarmed. Tom McLaury, too, to all appearances was unarmed. Why would men walk into a gunfight without weapons? Also, if the Clantons and McLaurys planned to shoot their adversaries, Breakenridge and other old-timers have argued that they could have pulled the rifles from the scabbards on Billy's and Frank's horses and fired before the Earp party got within gunshot range. Other students of the fight have argued that the Earps and Holliday would already have been in pistol range when the cowboys first spotted them. Either way, if the cowboys intended to fire, why did they wait until the Earps were almost upon them?

SCENARIO NO. 2: The Earps and Holliday were determined to get the cowboys, either because the cowboys knew too much about their criminal activities or because they were simply fed up with the cowboys' threats and itching to put them down.

EVIDENCE: Witnesses not unfriendly to the Earps testified that both Virgil and Wyatt had made statements strongly showing they were ready to shoot it out with Ike and his friends. Martha King had heard one Earp say, "Let them have it," and heard Doc Holliday give his assent. Also, the actions of the Earps and Holliday from the evening lunchroom scene onward can be read as a pattern of intimidation designed to goad the cowboys into a violent response that could be quashed under the guise of police authority.

PROBLEMS: Whether the Earps and Holliday really had a strong enough motivation for *killing* the cowboys is questionable. As enterprising, broad-based businessmen with some social standing, Virgil and Wyatt in particular had much to lose through such an action. Also, as with the cowboys, why did the

Earp party wait to open fire until nine men and two horses were crowded into a small vacant lot?

In order to develop a third scenario more promising than either of the above, it is necessary to look at the underlying charges against each group. Were the Earps and Holliday in on the Benson stage robbery and possibly other stage robberies in the area? From the evidence available, it is highly doubtful that the Earps would be involved in so chancy and illegal an enterprise when they were making money and building reputations by legitimate means. But Doc Holliday is a far more likely candidate. It is hard to see him simply as the victim of a *Nugget* smear campaign, as Earp loyalists claim, when one looks at his friendship with Billy Leonard, his past close association with robber and murderer Josh Webb, his own violent, erratic record and reckless disposition, and Kate's charge implicating him in the stage robbery and killing of Philpot.

As for the Clantons and McLaurys, one must ask whether they had indeed proven a problem to the town in general and to the Earps in particular. The answer is clear in regard to the town; neither the Clantons and McLaurys nor the other men identified as cowboys had directly made themselves a problem to the peace and order of the community, with the exception of Curly Bill's killing of Marshal White in October 1880. Contemporary sources such as the *Nugget,* the *Epitaph,* and Parsons's journal show that only infrequently were the men who lived and worked outside the southeastern Arizona settlements involved in the periodic violence that flared within Tombstone itself. The town's own population, including the drifting opportunists who made it home for a week or a year, consistently provided the fireworks that boosted Tombstone's bloody reputation.

Curiously, even Spicer himself would bear this out in mid-December, commenting in the wake of escalating violence that the Clanton brothers "and men outside the city, living on ranches and engaged in raising cattle or other lawful pursuit, as heartily denounce all such affairs as any man can." Instead, he would contend, "the real evil exists within the limits of our city" among a "rabble" who "would like to be thugs if they had courage" and "would be proud to be called cowboys, if people would give them that distinction."

However, businessmen such as Clum would continue to look outside town for the source of their troubles. In part, they had a reason for doing so, for anyone who participated in rustling continued to contribute to the general political and economic instability of the area. As the correspondence of military and territorial authorities attests, rustlers, and ranchers involved with rustlers, by their activities still discouraged development and complicated relations with Mexico. On the very day that the Clantons and McLaurys met the Earps and Holliday in the vacant lot, General William Tecumseh Sherman had written the United States secretary of war urging that the army be allowed to enter Mexico and make arrests, for "it is notorious that the civil authorities of Arizona on that extensive frontier are utterly powerless to prevent marauders from crossing over into Sonora, and to punish them when they return for Asylum with stolen booty."

So there was some justification for regarding the Clantons and McLaurys, with their rustler associations, as part of a general threat to the region's economic welfare. As for whether the four offered a personal threat to the Earps, it simply depends upon whom one chooses to believe. The Earps and their supporters claimed that the cowboys had been mounting a vendetta for some time, but evidence from other witnesses at the trial only establishes that Ike Clanton—and possibly the others—made threats *after* the harassment and buffaloing by the Earp party. As Ike Clanton said of his statements of the morning of October 26, "I made no worse threats against them than they did against me."

With all of this in mind, one can consider a third scenario. Wyatt Earp wants the county sheriff position. He tries to make a deal with Ike Clanton to capture Leonard, Head, and Crane in order to gain points with Cochise County voters. He may or may not be concerned that Holliday was involved with the three. When the deal falls through, both Wyatt and Ike get nervous. Faced with the fact that Doc Holliday and Marshall Williams know or suspect something about the deal, Ike gets very nervous, and friction develops between him and the irascible Doc. Meanwhile, Wyatt and his brothers are still trying to make points with the law-and-order forces that are smiling beneficently upon them. Here is Ike—foolish, rash, loose-talking

Ike, one of the "cowboys" dreaded by an influential portion of the town's citizenry. The Earps can come down hard on him and impress these people with their tough brand of police work.

Ike responds by becoming more belligerent, which is all well and good for the Earps. They can repeatedly show that they will tolerate no nonsense from southern Democratic rancher-rustlers. For good measure, Wyatt pistol-whips Tom McLaury. Then Frank and Billy hit town. The cowboys huddle. They are angry and confused, divided as to what to do, whether to get the hell out of town or attempt to respond to their adversaries.

Now the Earps really have a chance to show their stuff, and they are egged on by all the nervous and excited citizens running to them with reports on the dreaded cowboys. Anyway, by this time, the Earps are truly hot under the collar at that fool Ike; they would really like to shoot the son of a bitch. But Virgil does have a strong sense of his duty as marshal, and his party heads for the vacant lot with the intention of intimidating any fight out of all four cowboys.

At least, Virgil and Wyatt do. As Wyatt said he had told Ike the evening before, "I would not fight no one if I could get away from it, because there was no money in it." No, they will rough the cowboys up and enhance their own reputations with the local power brokers.

But Morgan Earp, on the way down to the vacant lot, says, "Let them have it," and Doc Holliday says, "All right." These two have no political, social, or economic positions to protect; they are very much men of the moment, especially prone to quick violence and not likely to give a damn about consequences. When Virgil asks for the cowboy weapons, Doc and Morgan are impatient for something more from this confrontation—and perhaps anxious to eliminate men who know how tenuous is their own claim to law enforcement. They aim and fire. Virgil's cry "Hold! I don't mean that!" then becomes a plea to his brother and to Holliday rather than a warning to the cowboys. And Wyatt's testimony that he fired the first shot is given in order to protect his friend and younger brother, troublemakers who would not be dealt with as easily as a respected mining investor, lot owner, and gambling operation proprietor would.*

Or perhaps, in a variation of this scenario, Doc and Morgan were just looking forward to a little intimidation, too. Perhaps when Tom McLaury reached to open his vest to show he was unarmed, the Earp party misread the signal and thought he was about to fire. Then the killing itself was just an accident.

There is a lot to be said for this final view. As noted earlier, gunfights in the West were usually confused, even bumbling affairs made even more confusing when more than two people were involved. Only a few months before the Earps and Holliday met the Clantons and McLaurys in their shootout, a typical gun battle had erupted in El Paso, Texas, when a drunken George Campbell tried to pick a street fight with El Paso Constable Gus Krempkau. Campbell's friend John Hale, also drunk, then ran up and shot Krempkau. El Paso Marshal Dallas Stoudenmire responded by shooting Hale; then both Stoudenmire and the dying constable shot and killed Campbell, despite his cries of "This is not my fight."

In sum, once the first bullet was fired, anything could and did happen. Thus, Doc Holliday may be seen as a catalyst—intentional or not—for "a confrontation that got out of control," with neither side desiring or anticipating "such a bloody spectacle." Nor could any of the surviving participants or their supporters anticipate how much strife and bloodshed yet lay ahead.

---

*See Turner, *The O.K. Corral Inquest*, pp. 172 and 202, for this interpretation.

CHAPTER 13
"Except by Continuous Bloodshed"

Arizona's Acting Governor Gosper was growing exasperated with the whole situation in the southeastern part of the territory. Since he visited Tombstone in September, the enmities he had outlined to United States Secretary of State James G. Blaine had obviously only worsened. Gosper had returned to Tombstone during the Spicer hearing and found that whatever the verdict on the murder charges, there were still far too many bitter rivalries percolating and too many illegal activities in the area as a whole. On November 28, a few days before Spicer's decision, Gosper assessed the difficulties to Arizona Territorial Marshal Crawley Dake in a wholesale indictment of the citizens of the area:

> . . . the underlying cause of all the disturbances of the peace, and the taking of property unlawfully, is the fact that all men of every shade of character in that new and rapidly developed section of mineral wealth, in their mad career after money, have grossly neglected local self-government, until the more lazy and lawless elements of society have undertaken to prey upon the more industrious and honorable class for their subsistence and gains.

Gosper identified two such lawless elements: "Highway Robbers" and "Cattle thieves called 'Cow Boys.'" Both had seized the illegal opportunities such an environment produced and had "no doubt" paid officers of the law to release them or to look the other way.

The acting governor cited among the area's myriad problems the rivalry over the sheriff's job between Johnny Behan and Wyatt Earp, "the latter being in some manner connected with the police force for the city of Tombstone." This rivalry, he wrote, had "extended into a strife to secure influence and aid from all quarters" and had led the two and their friends to "sins of commission and omission greatly at the cost of peace and property." Gosper also noted the enmity between the two Tombstone newspapers and the secret dishonesty of many southeastern Arizona residents in accepting the beef cattle stolen by the cowboys. He felt that Behan should be removed from office, and he suggested that Dake remove his deputies as well.

Virgil Earp still held a deputy marshal appointment. So did another Tombstone man, Les Blackburn, who had been appointed in March. Despite the fact that he was also a deputy sheriff and collector, Blackburn remains a shadowy figure. His name cropped up occasionally in the Tombstone papers—for example, as foreman of a volunteer fire company and as a potential city marshal candidate. Johnny Behan had claimed at the hearing that Blackburn was riding with him on the night he went to Charleston and found Wyatt Earp and Doc Holliday trying to set up a Behan-Clanton confrontation. But the record is generally sketchy on this double-faceted lawman's participation in local affairs.

Gosper clearly wanted someone new, someone who could not only work in harmony with other law enforcement branches but show himself "a man of well known *courage* and *character* of cool sound judgment . . . who, with a suitable posse of men, can first *fully comprehend* the true nature of the situation, and then with proper discretion and courage, go forward with a *firm* and steady hand bringing as rapidly as possible the *leading* spirits of this lawless class to a severe and speedy punishment."

However, Gosper was making this suggestion to a Republican official and former Union soldier firmly in the Earp camp. Crawley Dake was a Canadian native with a receding hairline, a dark, scraggly beard, and hooded eyes. He had worked as a Michigan storekeeper and as a minor government bureaucrat; he had also run for a state representative seat in Michigan and lost. Why such a government functionary in poor health from wounds received during the Civil War should be chosen territorial marshal remains a mystery, but Dake had arrived in Prescott to assume his duties in the summer of 1878, with the Yuma *Arizona Sentinel* noting approvingly, "We augur . . . that the Marshal of Arizona is hereforth to amount to something."

He amounted to about fifty thousand dollars of misappropriated funds. An investigator would soon conclude, "I do not find anyone who thinks him fit for the position he now holds." In December 1881, however, Dake's flagrant channeling of government monies into his personal bank account and his abysmal handling of the duties of his office had not yet been uncovered. On December 3, he provided an indignant response to Gosper's letter, charging that Behan tried to interfere with the Earps but denying that rivalry with county officers "in any way interferes or retards my deputies from bringing to justice outlaws or 'cow boys' so called."

The Earps, he averred, had "rid Tombstone and neighborhood" of the outlaw element and had just been "vindicated" by Spicer in the killing of the three cowboys. Hereafter, Dake asserted, "my deputies will not be interfered with in hunting down stage Robbers, Mail Robbers, Train Robbers, Cattle thieves, and all that class of murdering *banditti* on the border."

He concluded that such dedicated pursuit of villains required money. "I will promptly send on the vouchers for your approval as they accrue and will keep close attention to the expense list, and will be as economical in this matter as I possibly can," wrote the man who would leave office without turning over a single accounting book or paper.

Thus, as 1881 drew toward a tumultuous end, Crawley Dake still wielded great power and made clear that he would continue to place that power at the disposal of the Earps. The brothers certainly had reason to feel optimistic. Not only did they have the backing of the federal marshal, of many of Tombstone's most prominent citizens, and of law-and-order advocates across the West, but they had beaten the murder charge and had little to fear from the grand jury. When that body had convened during the Spicer hearing in November, one judge had objected to "the swearing of certain grand jurors to act as such, because in the cases of Wyatt, Morgan and Virgil Earp and Doc Holliday, there were strong advocates of their actions in cases wherein they would come before the jury."* Earp confidant Marshall Williams himself was one of the jurors. Predictably, on December 16, the body would refuse to find an indictment against the four.

But if the Earps hoped that the continued support of the law-and-order faction and the end of legal proceedings would banish resentments over the October deaths of the three cowboys and allow them to continue in their normal patterns, they were sadly mistaken. Clum and other Earp supporters would see the troubles that erupted in December as the result of a concentrated effort by the "rustlers" to get rid of the brothers and their friends by violent means; others would see the Earps and their supporters as trying to settle scores against those who had dared oppose them and would wish the brothers and their sidekick Holliday out of Tombstone.

John Clum, he of the amateur theatricals and purple pen, would present a dramatic scenario in remembering the weeks following the end of the hearing. Not only was the "rustler-clan" rumored to be planning an attack on the bank, the Wells Fargo office, and the post office, but they had "marked for death" the Earps, Holliday, Spicer, lawyer Fitch, Marshall Williams, "and one or two others whose names I do not now recall. . . . [I]t was whispered that the 'DEATH LIST' had been prepared with most spectacular and dramatic ceremonials, enacted at midnight within the recesses of a deep canyon, during which the names of the 'elect' had been written in blood drawn from the veins of a murderer. Not one of those whose names appeared on this blood red 'DEATH LIST' would be permitted to escape from Tombstone alive."

---

*At this point, the judge anticipated Spicer's recommending grand jury action on the murder charge; there was also the robbery charge pending against Doc Holliday.

Clum could easily have become a writer for the dime novel industry still flourishing on the East Coast. But his basic assertion was valid; anonymous threats were being made against the Earps and their backers. Postmaster Clum now worked in the post office at night with the plank doors and shutters "securely fastened."

At the same time, Tombstone residents unfriendly to the Earps were receiving threats, and by at least one account at the time, the Earps were going around armed, intimidating and threatening the people who had dared to call the October 26 killings "murder." Thus, it might help to catalog what was happening to some of the players in the Tombstone drama in early December 1881.

Will McLaury was still in town awaiting the grand jury verdict. He wrote his sister on December 9 that he would leave after the court adjourned later in the month and noted of Earp champion Clum, "I think the postmaster here is a scoundrel." Billy Claiborne was on trial for murder, the grand jury having indicted him on November 29 in the Charleston killing mentioned during the Spicer hearing. John Ringo was also under grand jury indictment on the August robbing of the poker game charge. Ringo had been in and out of the Grand Hotel during the hearing; on November 30, Deputy Sheriff Neagle arrested him. Both Claiborne and Ringo pleaded not guilty; Ringo, at least, got out on bond. Frank Stilwell had been released from custody on the Bisbee stage robbery charge during the hearing, with the county recorder and the deputy recorder going "on the bond" for him. His trial in Tucson would not begin until late January. Neither Ike Clanton nor Pete Spencer was making the news, but they were still around and mad at the Earps.

After their brush with the legal system, the Earps were carefully staying within the letter of the law. It helped to have powerful friends; for example, Mayor Clum issued gun permits to those he favored. But Doc Holliday found circumspection an impossibility. He still had the robbing-the-mails charge pending in district court. On December 3, he was arrested for firing a pistol and won a quick acquittal.

A week later, Dr. Goodfellow pulled a pistol trigger and demonstrated the state of nervous excitement in Tombstone.

"Doc snuffed light with revolver tonight in his office," Parsons wrote in his journal, "and about 500 people were on hand in a minute. Great excitement. Done for devilment."

Goodfellow could get away with something like that. He lived up to his name, being a highly personable type who skillfully provided needed medical services to everyone from Parsons to Curly Bill Brocius. In 1877, he had arrived in Prescott to become company doctor at a mine, but he quickly switched to contract surgeon work for the United States Army at Fort Lowell. Finally, he had moved to Tombstone and opened a popular private practice.

The variety of work in and around Tombstone fed Goodfellow's wide range of medical interests. A surgical pioneer, he became an expert at treating gunshot wounds and in the late 1880's would produce papers on "the impenetrability of silk to bullets" and "cases of gunshot wounds of the abdomen treated by operation." He also dealt with mining accidents, pressing a somewhat unwilling yet enthralled Parsons into service. In one case, Parsons reported helping "Doc" sort through the "remains of two poor fellows who were blown up on the Barlacomari [sic]." He reported, "Nothing human was recognizable but their boots. Boots—bones and flesh mixed with hair and pieces of clothing presented anything but a cheerful aspect."

Through all his dissections and operations, Goodfellow maintained a wry humor. During a stint as county coroner, he examined a corpse ventilated with bullet holes and noted in his report that he had "performed assessment work" and found the body "rich in lead, but too badly punctured to hold whiskey."

Goodfellow practiced in a handy spot for procuring customers with gunshot wounds—just above the Crystal Palace Saloon at the northwest corner of Fifth and Allen. Parsons, who had moved into the doctor's rooms in November in anticipation of surgery on his battered nose, had noted on November 29, "This is the hardest corner in town . . . shots fired once in a while. Am wondering when a bullet will come through floor or wall." On December 12, just down the street, a pistol shot rang out. "Benson fired at Billy Crayton missing him and the latter used him up badly before they were parted," Parsons reported, adding, "Twice now Benson has done this." On the same day, Parsons reported a Citizens League, or Citizens Safety Committee, meeting.

The growing visibility of this group and the unsettling state of affairs in November and early December had led to greater citizen participation. Thus, Parsons wrote, "Citizen's League meeting tonight—but impossible to do anything. Great crowd and much noise. I tried to pass motion but was cried down. We'll have to make a close[d] corporation affair of it. Only way."

The leaders of this group remained solidly behind the Earps, but not all vigilantes or potential vigilantes did. Area residents continued to be divided over whether the Earps were part of the problem or the solution. In other words, different factions disagreed over who should be the target of vigilantism: the cowboys, Behan, the Earps and Holliday, or any combination of the three. Remember that Behan had testified Virgil Earp was worried over a vigilante committee coming to *get* the Earps after the shooting.

Perhaps the sheriff was lying. But others, too, indicated that citizens organized against the Earps and Holliday as well as for them. One pioneer would state that "a few days after [the gunfight], I was one of three men appointed by a Citizens Committee to inform Wyatt Earp and his bunch that 'no more of this killing stuff must be pulled off inside the town limits,' and that if the Earp gang, or the cowboy gang either, killed innocent decent men in their warfare, the Committee would take a hand and they would have no court trial either." John Pleasant Gray recalled that "many of the better citizens" of Tombstone soon began to have second thoughts about "giving the Earps the upper hand of authority."

John Clum, however, was adamant in his support. He was also leaving town for the holidays, going to visit his parents, who were caring for his young son in Washington, D.C. He also may well have been lobbying for another political appointment. There were rumors he was interested in the governorship, and the *Arizona Enterprise* had reported a petition circulating for his reappointment to the San Carlos Indian agent position. The San Francisco *Stock Exchange* commented sarcastically on Clum's aspirations in a paragraph picked up by the *Daily Nugget:* "How many public teats does Mr. Clum want to pull at once? He is already Postmaster at Tombstone, and Mayor of the city. He has been an Indian agent once, and didn't impoverish himself at it by any means. He would like to have gone to Congress as a delegate, and wouldn't now mind changing places with Fremont. The truth is, Clum is a chronic office-hunter."

Whatever his motivation, Clum planned to set off on the evening stage on December 14. He would recall that as he boarded the stage at 8:00 P.M., he mentioned to a member of the *Epitaph* staff that "my greatest probable danger was that, if the rustlers knew I was going, they would pull off a sham stage-robbery, during which they would make it convenient to properly perforate my anatomy with a few of their spare bullets, and thus definitely blot me out of the picture." George Parsons, bidding good-bye to another passenger, simply remarked that "it was about time for [the] stage to be jumped again."

The Concord coach rolled out of Tombstone carrying five passengers, all riding inside, with Clum alone occupying the middle seat in case he needed to make a "hasty exit." Driver Jimmie Harrington guided the six-horse team along the route to Contention and Benson, passing Malcolm's Well, a single dwelling and water station about four miles out of Tombstone. A man identified only as "Whistling Dick" was following the stage in an empty bullion cart to be loaded in Benson. Scarcely had the two conveyances passed the lights of Malcolm's Well when they descended into a gully and were met with a command to halt. Gunfire erupted from the darkness—fifteen to twenty shots fired from both sides of the road.

Harrington tried to brake, but the horses were spooked and careened onward, outdistancing the attackers. The other passengers had flattened themselves on the floor of the rocking carriage; Clum, by his account, at least, remained upright with six-shooters at the ready for a possible second attack. Suddenly, someone called from the road ahead, the horses plunged to a halt, and Clum jumped out, six-guns ready. But the speaker was only Whistling Dick, whose team had outbolted the stage horses, passing them in the confusion.

Everyone got out and assessed the damage. One of the lead stage horses had been shot in the neck and was bleeding to death; Whistling Dick had received a minor bullet wound in the leg. The two lead horses were cut from the team, Dick's wound was wrapped with handkerchiefs, and the party prepared to continue its journey.

At this point, Clum decided to walk, for, as he later recalled, he was convinced that he was the target of the attack and was endangering the other passengers. He was not missed; the driver thought he had reentered the coach, and the other riders concluded he had moved to the top with Harrington. The stage and bullion wagon continued without incident the twenty miles to Benson.

Clum's critics would have fun with the mayor's claim that the attack was directed at him and with his sudden disappearance, attributing it to stark fear. The *Daily Nugget* would report caustically the next day, "The prevailing opinion is that he is still running."

Clum would present matters differently, casting himself as a persecuted champion of the good and true and as a brave wanderer through the desolate vastness of the Arizona landscape. He admitted to some initial nervousness over the possibility of being overtaken by the rustlers, but he soon had other considerations, as in the darkness he stumbled across first one, then another "yawning prospector's shaft." Writing for a later generation, Clum pulled out all the stops:

> And so it happened that at midnight I stood in the midst of the wide open spaces of the Arizona desert, pondering the fate that had saved me from the bullets of would-be assassins, only to lead me to this lonely spot with its yawning pitfalls, set like death-traps in my very pathway, where a misstep in the darkness might mean a plunge into a living tomb, there, with broken limbs and bruised body to endure a lingering death through days and nights of most excruciating mental and physical sufferings. Assuredly, a weird and thrilling chapter in my frontier experiences, with its kaleidoscopic changes, was being unfolded in most dramatic fashion during the passing hours of that memorable December night.

Clum avoided the "yawning pitfalls" of prospectors' shafts and made it to the Grand Central Quartz Mill on the San Pedro, where he caught a couple of hours of sleep and borrowed a horse to take him the remaining distance to the railway station in Benson. In a scene straight out of a Saturday western, he depicted himself near Contention coming across "the camp of the rustlers," those very shadowy beings who were out to get John P. Clum, and stealing by their sleeping forms undetected.

Meanwhile, back in Tombstone, the arrival of another stage with news of the assault led to formation of a search party composed of Johnny Behan, Clum's business partner, Charles Reppy, and three other men. While the others went first to Malcolm's Well, Behan and Reppy headed for Contention, where the stage had stopped, and interviewed the passengers there at about 4:00 or 5:00 A.M. The stage went on to Benson, and the searchers gradually made their way to the Grand Central Quartz Mill, where Clum had obtained his horse. He was riding along, enjoying a multihued sunrise, and got into Benson only a short time after the stage, reaching the railroad town about 8:00 A.M. Here he ate breakfast, saw and talked with driver Harrington, and caught the train for the East.

A correspondent who claimed to be on the eastbound train provided a skewering account of Clum and fellow traveler J. C. Tiffany, San Carlos Indian agent:

> Clum jumped on the train I was on, looking paler than ever before . . . and was the most scared man I have ever seen for some time. Passing Deming, he crawled under a seat tramp fashion, to keep the cowboys from raising his hair in case they happened to pass through the cars. He is on his way to Washington to put in a bid for the Gubernatorial chair of Arizona, or any other office he could lay his hands on. With Clum was "Colonel" Tiffany—one wants the governership and one wants to boss the Indians.

Actually, Tiffany had been doing such a poor job of bossing the Indians that he would soon be fortunate to be allowed to resign without punishment. The agent had found a variety of ways to defraud the government, including putting his own brand on government cattle, feeding them with government grain, and using salaried employees from the reservation to tend them. Clum had been by far the better agent, but if he sought an Arizona appointment in Washington, he did not receive it.

He *did* return to Tombstone after his eastern visit, and he returned still insisting that the "rustler-clan" had laid elaborate plots to eliminate him and had almost succeeded. In his absence, the *Epitaph*, too, identified the stage assault as an attack against the mayor and went to hyperbolic lengths, calling the incident "the greatest outrage ever perpetrated upon the traveling public of Arizona and . . . an event calculated to do more harm to the business interests of Tombstone than all other causes operating against us put together." The paper asked for "the general government to step in and declare military law, and to keep a sufficient force here to maintain peace and order . . . or else all good men will abandon the place."

Clum critics felt that the newspaper was magnifying the situation—and its editor's significance—by identifying him as the target of the nighttime holdup men. The editor and his friends could and did argue that he *had* been a target of threats and that everyone knew such nighttime stages carried nothing worth stealing. Clum himself would later claim in a letter to Stuart Lake that two passengers heard one of the assailants say, "Be sure and get the old bald-headed son of a b----." He also would state that the evidence that horses had often been staked near the holdup spot showed the rustlers had been patiently waiting for him night after night.

However, some were suspicious enough to see the whole thing as a ploy of the pro-Earp forces, with or without Clum's knowledge, in order to drum up sympathy for the mayor and convince a doubtful public of a real cowboy threat. There are other possible explanations for the incident as well. The attack may have been a random one or an attempt simply to scare the unabashedly partisan mayor and give warning to the Earps. It also may have been a real robbery attempt, with someone—cowboys, town dwellers, or drifters—erroneously expecting the stage to be carrying something of value or hoping at least to relieve the passengers of their valuables.

Whatever the circumstances, this latest flash of violence

added to Tombstone's woes. Acting Governor Gosper wrote to the secretary of the interior pleading that the repeal of the Posse Comitatus Act be urged upon Congress so that cavalry troops could be dispatched to maintain order in Tombstone. In the silver town itself, ill feelings continued unchecked. County Commissioner Milt Joyce, no longer managing the Oriental, made the mistake of laughingly commenting to Virgil Earp in a Tombstone saloon that he had been expecting something like the stage attempt ever since the Earps and Holliday had been released. One of the Earps "immediately struck Joyce with his open hand in the face," backed up by "four or five of Earp's warmest partisans, all heavily armed." Joyce backed out of the door, telling them they would have to shoot him in the front, not by their "favorite method" in the back.

As a sequel to this, on December 17, an armed Joyce confronted Wyatt and Doc in the Alhambra, asking "if they wanted to fight as bad as they did the night before." Johnny Behan, who, according to Deputy Breakenridge, was close friends with Joyce, nonetheless did his job, slipping up behind the aggressor, clutching him around the waist, and bodily carrying him out the door. This move cooled relations between the two Democratic county officeholders; Joyce was fined fifteen dollars for carrying weapons. Meanwhile, George Parsons was confiding to his journal the tensions in town, identifying the killing of Billy Clanton and the McLaurys as the continuing catalyst and indicating that the law-and-order forces were even trying to drive Behan out. "Bad state of things in town," Parsons wrote. "I fear another bad out-break any day. Threatening letters have been sent certain parties with orders to leave town among them sheriff and others well known."

The law-and-order faction itself remained under fire, with a letter received by Wells Spicer appearing in the December 18 *Epitaph* at Spicer's direction.

> TO WELLS SPICER:—Sir, if you take my advice you will take your departure for a more genial clime, as I don't think this One Healthy for you much longer. As you are liable to get a hole through your coat at any moment. If such sons of Bitches as you are allowed to dispense Justice in this Territory, the Sooner you Depart from us the better

for yourself And the community at large you may make light of this But it is only a matter of time you will get it sooner or later So with those few gentle hints I Will Conclude for the first and last time.

At least one researcher has speculated that this letter appeared to be written by an educated man trying to appear uneducated and has pointed to Will McLaury. Ex-Justice James Reilly would hint that Spicer himself concocted the letter. It was signed simply "A MINER," and Spicer's stinging reply followed in the *Epitaph* pages. The justice complained of "similar threats" against him, as well as "the daring attempt to murder Mayor Clum" and the abuse he himself endured. Since the decision, he wrote, "I have been reviled and slandered beyond measure," the target of "every vile epithet that a foul mouth could utter."

Spicer contended that no one had improperly approached him in the interest of the Earps and Holliday in the course of the hearing but that prosecution supporters had even tried to buy his friends. At the same time, as noted earlier, he remained oddly careful to absolve the Clantons from any participation in these activities, instead pointing to an element that "exists within the limits of our city," men who desired the power of an urban "thug" or the distinction of a "cowboy" but deserved neither. Rather, Spicer declared, this group were "low-bred, arrant cowards." In a play upon Ike Clanton's statement to the Earps that "Fight is my racket," Spicer issued his own challenge to any detractors threatening him: "[They] know that 'fight is not my racket'—if it was they would not dare to do it.

"In conclusion, I will say that I will be here just where they can find me should they want me. . . ."

This public broadside, and the continuing dissension in Tombstone, brought ex-Justice Reilly rocketing into the war of words. On December 21, the *Daily Nugget* printed his exasperated assessment of the situation. Reilly complained that the *Epitaph* had given full play to the menacing warning addressed to Spicer but treated as "all fun" the threats made by pro-Earp forces, those "communicated by words, letters and postal cards" to Milt Joyce, to "Messr. Leslie" (perhaps Buckskin

Frank, taking sides after all), and to "many others who have denounced the killing of the McLaurys."

The way Reilly saw it, Mayor Clum, the Earps, and other law-and-order types had mounted "a systematic attempt to inaugurate a state of terrorism in Tombstone" even before the infamous gunfight in an effort "to inculcate the idea that all good citizens of Tombstone were in danger of being assassinated" by cowboys. As for the problems with the stagecoach robberies, Reilly asserted, "I am convinced that seven of every ten of the stage robberies committed in Arizona for the last fifteen years have been put up and engineered by the trusted agents of the post office, of Wells Fargo & Co's agents and agents of the stage companies."

Nonetheless, the townspeople who believed the cowboy threat to be real had revived the Citizens League as a vigilante group against such men as the Clantons and McLaurys. Many in this league, Reilly acknowledged, were good men, but the league itself was "unlawful, foolish, and dangerous," for only under "despotic governments" could such extralegal organizations "for the redress of public wrongs" be justified. In this case, he argued, members were responding to "imaginary assassins" and magnifying evils "at most only temporary, and incident to all countries alike, and capable of redress by the ordinary methods ballot-box and jury-box." In doing so, they provided a power base for the likes of the Earps and Holliday, who, he insisted, were far from deserving of it. ". . . [I]s it, or is it not true, that the Earps and Holliday, while undergoing examination, threatened that when they got out they would make those men who called the killing of the McLaurys a murder, 'take it all back' and that since they got out they have gone around town armed, abusing and picking quarrels with men of that opinion and have threatened many persons, telling them they had better leave[?]"

An admission that this was indeed true, Reilly argued, meant three things. First, the Earps and Holliday "are not good men, and do not, themselves, believe that they were justified in that homicide, for if good men are unfortunate enough to be compelled to kill, they regret it: they are sorrowful, modest, and ask only to be allowed to live down the prejudice excited against them by good conduct and submis-

sion to the laws. They do not, by threats, assaults and braggadocio, attempt to bulldoze a whole community into giving
countenance to their acts."

Second, Reilly contended, the four had exhibited no respect for the law, for public opinion, for their own lives, or for
the lives of others, and were thus dangerous to the community. And third, their misguided supporters were aiding and
abetting these menaces, incurring "the danger of encouraging
and assisting real assassinations." The most obvious example
of this was that Clum had provided the Earps and their
friends with gun permits "while all others are subject to fine
and imprisonment if they carry arms." Further, the Earps
maintained a "thug's den, where they keep their implements
of terror."

The latter contention brought a mild rebuke in the pages
of the *Epitaph* the next day, with bartender E. F. Boyle, whose
testimony had helped the Earps, taking issue with the "thug's
den" remark and testifying in print that Wyatt "is one of the
partners of the firm I am working for, and a more liberal and
kind-hearted man I never met." (Boyle was apparently referring to Wyatt's interest in the Oriental gambling operation
and perhaps in the Oriental itself, since Joyce was no longer in
charge.) The three oldest Earps continued in their roles as
businessmen and were often linked with other prominent
townsmen. In mid-December, Wyatt, James, and Virgil had
joined Holliday's lawyer T. J. Drum in leasing a right-of-way
through a mining claim to the Tombstone Water, Mill and
Lumber Company, and about the same time Wyatt Earp "et
al." transferred mining property to an assignee of Spicer's.

The Earps may or may not have consciously begun selling
out at this point. They were certainly being shown the door by
some. On December 23, the *Daily Nugget* commented, "It is
reported that the Earps have received intelligence of a lively
mining camp in San Bernardino County, California, and that
they contemplate making it the scene of their future operations. Should the report prove true, it would be rather rough
on the aforesaid mining camp."

Such barbed attempts at a send-off were of less conse-
quence, however, than was an alleged incident in Glenn Boyer's
I Married Wyatt Earp. One evening Jim Earp answered the door at

Virgil Earp's home to find a veiled woman who claimed to have the wrong address and disappeared. Wyatt Earp suspected the visitor to be a man dressed as a female and there to kill him, Virgil, or Morgan, only to be disappointed when Jim opened the door. Thus, by this account, the unsettling incident led them to move with their families into the relative safety of the Cosmopolitan Hotel.

The three older Earp brothers and most of their family members did move into the Cosmopolitan sometime in December, though accounts differ as to when and the *Daily Nugget* log of hotel arrivals gives no clue. Josie Marcus moved into a local boardinghouse about the same time. The long-suffering Mattie apparently stayed on in the home she had shared with Wyatt; she did not check into the Cosmopolitan until February 21, 1882.

Christmas came, with its temporary cessation of daily cares and tensions. "Xmas day and a charming one," Parsons confided to his journal. "District court room tastefully decorated and appropriate services rendered." Others celebrated the holiday differently. Johnny Behan, perhaps decked out in the two diamond studs and gold quartz scarf pin his deputies had just given him, was in Tucson racing his prize horse, Nellie. The patrons of the Crystal Palace Saloon, directly under Goodfellow's office, where Parsons was still living, apparently celebrated in their own style. Parsons concluded his Christmas entry, "Terrible time below tonight. A circus till early morning which seemed to terminate in a free fight. Expecting a bullet to come up every minute for awhile but was spared."

The Crystal Palace was one of the saloons that managed to stay popular by making every night a holiday, but the various watering holes and entertainment halls were about to be eclipsed by the Bird Cage Variety Theater, which former variety performer Billy Hutchinson opened that Christmas week in Tombstone near the corner of Sixth and Allen. It was certainly worth a visit, as an early description shows: "The building has one and a half stories, two main rooms—a saloon and a theatre section. Balconies, divided into boxes, run down the length of both sides. Percentage girls distribute drinks to these suspended boxes singing as they serve—hence the name Bird

Cage. Stage lighting is accomplished by a gas system. Scenery and backdrops are built and painted by the actors as they need them."

Hutchinson booked everyone from jig dancers to a strong woman named Mrs. De Granville, "the woman with the iron jaw." Eddie Foy would perform at the Bird Cage and comment that it "should have been named the coffin, for it was built in the shape of one." But just as Tombstone's name didn't deter anyone from landing in town, the Bird Cage's shape didn't seem to keep anyone away. Oh, it never quite became the place for respectable families out for a night's entertainment, as Hutchinson had hoped it would, but it certainly turned into a hot spot for the rest of the populace, with plenty of drinking before and during the show, and dancing and more drinking after it.

Even the dead came back to life just to enjoy the show, if one believes the legends that have Russian Bill Tettenborn, hanged in New Mexico in November, occupying a box right beside the stage night after night. The legends that have both the Earps and the remaining cowboys frequenting the place are probably exaggerated; Breakenridge reported the Earps primarily congregated with their friends at Bob Hatch's saloon, while the cowboys when they visited town spent most of their time in the Grand Hotel across the street. But the Bird Cage was the kind of place which attracted just about anyone out for a good time, and men with the bitterest personal enmities were likely to share the pleasure of a show.

As the Bird Cage swung into operation, times were getting worse for the Earps. On Wednesday, December 28, about 11:30 P.M., Virgil Earp left the Oriental Saloon on the northeast corner of Fifth and Allen, starting up the street for his room at the Cosmopolitan. Barely had he gotten into the thoroughfare, however, before a fusillade erupted from an unfinished two-story building across the street to the south. Virgil was struck by buckshot in the left arm and on the left side. Sixteen stray shots tattooed the side and awnings of the Crystal Palace, while three flew through the saloon's windows into an opposite wall and a fourth barely missed George Parsons as he prepared for bed in Goodfellow's office above the establishment. Parsons heard "four shots fired in quick succes-

sion from very heavily charged guns, making a terrible noise."
The *Epitaph* reported five rapid shots from three double-barreled shotguns.

Virgil, his left arm shattered, turned around, went back
into the Oriental, and told Wyatt he was hurt. The *Epitaph*
reported that three men "ran past the ice house on Tough
Nut street and sung [*sic*] out to the man in attendance who
had his door open at the time, 'Lock your door.' The same
three men were seen by a miner a few minutes later making
down into the gulch below the Vizina hoisting works." Parsons
complained, "Cries of 'There they go,' 'Head them off' were
heard but the cowardly apathetic guardians of the peace were
not inclined to risk themselves and the other brave men all
more or less armed did nothing."

Virgil was escorted to his room, where both Dr. Matthews
and Dr. Goodfellow attended him. Parsons was sent to the
hospital for medical supplies and found the hotel so well
guarded on his return "that I had hard trouble to get to
Earp's room. He was easy. Told him I was sorry for him. 'It's
hell, isn't it!' said he. His wife was troubled, 'Never mind, I've
got one arm left to hug you with,' he said."

Virgil's side wound was not serious, but he had suffered
"a longitudinal fracture of the bone between the shoulder and
elbow." Parsons was getting into the spirit of Goodfellow's
medical practice, noting in his journal on the twenty-ninth
that Virgil's elbow joint had had to be removed, "and we've
got that and some of the chattered [*sic*] bone in room."

Meanwhile, as crowds gathered to examine the buckshot
and bullet holes, there was naturally speculation as to who was
responsible for this latest violence. Parsons wrote, "It is surmised that Ike Clanton 'Curly Bill' and McLaury did the
shooting."

Actually, Will McLaury had left town bound for Fort
Worth two days earlier, though that certainly does not preclude his involvement. He had made it clear in his letters during the hearing the extent of his desire for vengeance, and
there would be later hints that he tried to orchestrate a revenge. By one account, his son related that Will had paid Ike
Clanton a thousand dollars for the very purpose of tracking
and killing Virgil's brother Wyatt.

As for Ike Clanton, he was a most logical suspect. Wyatt would later point a finger at Ike and at Frank Stilwell, writing that "Virgil saw Stilwell go into the vacant building just as he was coming out of the Oriental. . . . We found Ike Clanton's hat, that he dropped in getting away from the rear end of the building." Fred Dodge would identify another Clanton associate, Johnny Barnes, as one of the gunmen.

A completely different vengeance motive was provided in the pages of the *Rocky Mountain News* by an unidentified Tombstone "mining man," who related that he had observed a gang including at least one of the Earp brothers work the top-and-bottom game on a sucker in a Tombstone saloon, with a "marshal" appearing on cue in a common embellishment on the scam. Many western towns hypocritically outlawed gambling while encouraging it; thus, the "marshal" could threaten to arrest the sucker for gambling and accept his story of being conned only when the tricksters had made good their getaway. The anonymous source linked the shooting of Virgil to the sucker's revenge.

Whatever vengeance the assailants were extracting, they had effectively knocked the eldest of the "fighting Earps" out of commission, giving him a crippled arm for life.

Meanwhile, another election was heating up in Tombstone, and this time the town would split more clearly than ever along pro- and anti-Earp lines. On January 1, 1882, the *Daily Nugget,* supporting the People's Independent Ticket of John Carr for mayor and Behan deputy Dave Neagle for city marshal, warned of a rumor concerning the opposing candidates. L. W. Blinn was running for mayor; James Flynn, who had been appointed acting city marshal with Virgil's suspension, was now trying to remain in the job. If Blinn and Flynn were elected, the *Nugget* warned, the plan was that Flynn would soon resign, allowing Blinn to appoint one of the Earps. Thus, the paper concluded, "There is little doubt that a vote for Flynn is equivalent [to] a vote for a new lease of power for the Earps." The same issue contained the withdrawals of two other candidates for city marshal, citing as reason the need to support Neagle in order to defeat the machinations of "outgoing municipal officials."

On top of all this, the paper printed a second scorching

letter from James Reilly. The former justice charged the *Epitaph* since the Benson stage robbery in March with devoting "all its power, as well as that of the Associated Press, whose agency it has, to give to the world the opinion that none but fighting citizens could live in peace in Tombstone, and for this purpose it has continually praised the Earps." He charged that Bud Philpot's murder was "a well concocted scheme, put up by the men who knew all about Wells Fargo & Company's business, to rob the stage and kill Robert Paul." He also charged both Virgil and Wyatt with holding in their pockets warrants against friends rather than serving them and with helping a swindler escape. Reilly accused outgoing Mayor Clum of favoritism and mismanagement and called Tombstone "the unwilling asylum of four or more men whose lives must be a burden to them and who cannot hope to live in it except by continuous bloodshed."

January 3 was election day, and the *Nugget* did not relax its attack. "Doc Holliday and the Earps are solid for Blinn and Flynn," the paper proclaimed. "So is the Daily Strangler [Epitaph]. The election will to-day decide whether Tombstone is to be dominated for another year by the Earps and their strikers. Every vote against the People's Independent Ticket is a vote for the Earps."

The People's Independent Ticket won, with Dave Neagle becoming the new city marshal in a setback for the law-and-order businessmen and the Earp coterie. Parsons glumly noted, "My ticket Blinn, Flinn, Eccleston etc. beaten by the ring and other crowd." But even members of the opposing camp could appreciate Neagle's election, for despite his background as Behan's deputy, he was a nonpartisan "Square Man" respected by both factions.

As for the *Daily Nugget,* it crowed gleefully, "It is rumored the Earps will take a Holliday" and headlined its election story EXEUNT EARPS!

But they weren't gone yet. And they weren't completely out of power. Hearing of Virgil's injuries, Crawley Dake had telegraphed a deputy United States marshal appointment to Wyatt—and Wyatt, armed with a badge once more, was planning his moves.

CHAPTER 14

"We Didn't Get Out When the Gettin' Was Good"

Despite the enmities boiling just below the surface, Tombstone seemed to be flourishing with the new year 1882. Eager boosters put the town's population at up to fourteen thousand, although the census that year would show less than six thousand. The Boston *Post* joked, "Tombstone, Arizona, is growing so rapidly that they soon expect to be big enough to change its name to Sarcophagus." "Rather a grave subject to jest on," the *Daily Nugget* would respond.

Of course, boosters had to confront the pesky matter of the "man for breakfast" reputation of Tombstone in particular and the western frontier in general. In the seat of Cochise County, recent events seemed to confirm the existence of a wild and woolly West, but westerners themselves were quick to note the differences between myth and reality and to mock easterners' apparent inability to separate the two. For example, the *Daily Nugget* the preceding August had wryly taken note of the reputation of Leadville, Colorado, as "a tolerably healthy place to live in now," explaining that with the town's two lockups and four policemen, a newcomer could "go from the depot to the hotel without being shot at—that is, if he runs like a race horse."

Now, in the wake of the shooting of Virgil Earp, a New York newspaper judged Tombstone "well named":

> Few people there die in their beds. Between the cowboys and other desperadoes the uncertainty of life is constantly exemplified. A man with good luck and extraordinary vitality may manage to keep out of the tomb long enough to become a citizen, but such instances are rare. Not long since Deputy United States Marshal Earp was found with nineteen bullets in his body and he is alive yet. He seems to be the right sort of man for the place.

The Tucson *Daily Star* could not resist facetious comment. "Pshaw! This is not half, nor a twentieth part," it commented. "The marshal had fifty-seven bullets extracted and it is believed there is about a peck yet in his body." All citizens—men, women, and children—went armed, the *Star* reported, more than four fifths of them walking about with one or more bullets in their bodies, and every house was equipped with portholes from which to shoot at cowboys. Indeed, the level of violence made Tombstone "a great place for suicides; if a fellow wants to die with his boots on he just steps out in the street and yells out, 'You're another,' and immediately he is pumped through from all sides with a shower of bullets."

Furthermore, the *Star* concluded, "it is no uncommon occurrence to see twenty men dumped out of a club room in the morning and pitched down some mining shaft where the ore has petered out. This is but a faint picture of the situation. Our New York exchange had better try and get the facts."

In Tombstone, citizens would rather point to the signs of progress which were everywhere. Businesses were now illuminated with gas rather than oil, and the city boasted a brand-new fire engine that could shoot three streams of water at once over the Grand Hotel. Men with money continued to visit the community on Goose Flats and to invest in mining operations in the area as the established mines continued to yield impressive amounts of ore. That vital artery of commerce the railroad was drawing nearer, pushing southward from Benson to Contention only eight miles northwest of Tombstone and from Contention on down to Mexico.

But there were signs that Ed Schieffelin's mecca of mining opportunity was beginning to lose some of its appeal. In early January, ex-Governor and Tombstone investor A.P.K. Safford arrived in town, reportedly closing out his Arizona interests in favor of a Florida project. And the news that out-of-work Comstock miners were heading for Tombstone looking for jobs would soon prompt the *Daily Nugget* to cite overpopulation and high unemployment in Tombstone in advising, "Don't come, boys."

Most of Tombstone's residents either didn't see such warning signs or chose to ignore them. The town still throbbed with vitality, a strong sense of possibilities yet to be realized. Besides, civilization was taking root in the dry and rocky desert soil as Tombstone continued its transition from rollicking mining camp to established community. The big investors chose to build their grand mansions and raise their families elsewhere, but the city located atop the Tough Nut mine now boasted a proper culture, with literary clubs and debating societies and church socials. Efforts to bring religion to Tombstone had proven uneven at best, but in January 1882 the Methodists, Presbyterians, Catholics, and Episcopalians were all organized and active, with church buildings partially completed for the latter two groups. The Episcopal building effort had faltered, but that month the arrival of Episcopal minister Endicott Peabody would cause an upsurge in religious interest and ensure completion of the project.

"Cotty" was a member of the Salem, Massachusetts, Peabody clan that traced its roots to the Puritans and wielded such clout in Salem that it was said one was either a "Peabody, or nobody." Son of a prominent banker, Endicott Peabody had received his education in England, worked in his grandfather's Boston investment banking firm, and then entered the Episcopal Theological School in Cambridge, Massachusetts. While there, he received a letter from Grafton Abbott, a former Massachusetts resident living in Tombstone, who complained that the Arizona mining camp was "the rottenest place you ever saw" and needed an Episcopal minister.

The youthful, handsome Peabody—later famous as founder and headmaster of the Groton School near Boston—answered the call. He arrived in late January and brought "muscular Christianity"—a celebration of strength, vigor, and manliness as Christian virtues—to Tombstone. He would demonstrate that he was not above partaking of a glass of claret or a good cigar and would charm almost everyone. Parsons, who had grumbled over the poor preaching and inconsistent efforts of other ministers in Tombstone, would quickly conclude, "He's a sensible, manly fellow and I like him very much. Is quite an athlete and of magnificent build weighing nearly 200 lbs, muscles hard as iron." The *Daily Nugget* would comment, "Talk about muscular Christianity. We overheard a miner yesterday say, upon having the Episcopal minister pointed out to him, 'Well, if that lad's argument was a hammer, and religion a drill, he'd knock a hole in the hanging wall of skepticism that Bob Ingersoll could crawl through.'"

Parsons would even plan a sparring match between Peabody and the local Methodist minister, who may have been a bit bemused at the form which religious rivalries were suddenly taking. But then, by the time Peabody arrived, the spirit of contention would be so strong in Tombstone that no kind of rivalry seemed out of place.

Hardly had the city elections been peacefully concluded before back-to-back stage robberies fueled Tombstone tensions. The first occurred on Friday, January 6, as R. A. Waite guided the Sandy Bob stage along the Tombstone-to-Hereford-to-Bisbee route. The coach carried passengers and pay for Bisbee miners—sixty-five hundred dollars, primarily in cash. Guard Charles Bartholomew first observed men riding in the distance between Tombstone and Hereford, apparently pacing the stage. In midafternoon, after the coach had stopped at Hereford, three men tried to halt it, and Bartholomew fired at them. A running gunfight ensued, with the robbers wounding a horse and thus bringing the stage to a stop.

The bandits did not approach, but sent a note by a wood hauler stating that the travelers could proceed unharmed if they would throw out the Wells Fargo box. Bartholomew rejected the idea, but his fellow travelers did not. Finally, the guard and the passengers followed orders to remove themselves to a distance of about two hundred yards, while driver Waite remained. Two of the highwaymen then rode up wearing masks, helped themselves to the money and a stage horse, and departed.

The next day, two black-masked bandits held up the Benson stage, relieving the passengers of three pistols and seventy-five dollars. This was a relatively minor haul, but a major embarrassment for Wells Fargo, as chief company detective James Hume was on the stage en route to Tombstone to try to get to the bottom of the robbery problem. Two of the pistols stolen were his.

Hume immediately announced a five-hundred-dollar reward and "one-fourth of the treasure recovered for the arrest and conviction of each of the parties concerned" in the larger Bisbee stage haul. According to Fred Dodge, Hume privately sent Dodge, Wyatt and Morgan Earp, and an Earp ally named Charlie Smith to Charleston to find the men who had relieved him of his pistols. He then confused matters by going to Charleston himself and drinking with two of the suspects in J. B. Ayers's bar as his four assistants tried to collect evidence.

If Wyatt and Morgan were doing a little private detective work, they were unable to quash further hints that the Earps themselves were involved in the crimes being investigated. Hard on the heels of James Reilly's accusations and the EX-EUNT EARPS! headline, the *Daily Nugget* noted pointedly, "Who robbed the Bisbee stage? Six thousand dollars is a good stake to leave the country on, and we suggest they leave." Meanwhile, Wells Fargo closed its office at Bisbee, "owing to their recent heavy losses on that route."

The company retained its office at Tombstone, but not with Marshall Williams at the helm. His replacement would discover that the former agent had departed owing at least two thousand dollars to his employer and having accumulated thirty thousand dollars in other liabilities. And soon the *Daily Nugget* would report, "Marshall Williams is in Brooklyn. He dresses in the height of fashion and to all appearances is well supplied with money. There are more ways than one of making a raise."

Williams had turned out to be something of an embarrassment to the law-and-order crowd. Wyatt Earp, on the other hand, despite the continuing climate of suspicion, still enjoyed its support and apparently still felt he could both make a reputation as the answer to the county's crime problems and extract retribution for the wounding of Virgil. His actions would soon be directed to these ends. However, in early January, Wyatt experienced a setback in another line when Milt Joyce, reassuming control of the Oriental from Lou Rickabaugh, shut Wyatt out of that saloon's gambling operation. "Wyatt Earp has sold his interest in the Oriental Saloon [gambling concession] to Rickabaugh & Clark," the *Daily Nugget* reported on January 8. A few days later, the paper announced, "The Oriental saloon was reopened last evening under the auspices of M. E. Joyce, who is to be congratulated upon bringing the Oriental back to its old-time popularity."

There were always other saloons. By one account, Wyatt simply moved his former Oriental gambling operation to the Bank Exchange Saloon. He was pressing his luck and the Earp family luck, however, in the face of a continuing backlash of anti-Earp feeling—from the cowboys, according to pro-Earp sources, and from a good portion of the county residents, according to others. During this period, Allie was "fed up with Tombstone." She spent her time stuck in a Cosmopolitan hotel room nursing her bedridden Virgil, whose recovery was agonizingly slow. The couple sensed the negative mood in town but delayed leaving until after Virgil's health improved. As Allie later recalled, "We didn't get out when the gettin' was good, and now I didn't know when we'd ever get away."

Sometime during this period, Frank Stilwell, still awaiting trial for the first Bisbee stage robbery, decided to shoot Doc Holliday. Billy Breakenridge was patrolling the streets one night when he "ran up against a gun-barrel" held by Stilwell, who said "a certain party had boasted that he was going to get him that night, and that he would not do it if he saw him first." Breakenridge convinced the ex-deputy to go home, using the curious argument that "it was too late for him to kill anyone that night" and the more logical one that "he was in enough trouble already." Soon Breakenridge met Doc Holliday on the street, and "It flashed through my mind that I had inadvertently saved Holliday's life that night."

Neither Wyatt nor Doc seemed in any hurry to depart such a threatening climate. From the time of Virgil's ambush onward, "the Earp party consisted of from five to eight men, and they were always together heavily armed," with Wyatt at the head using his deputy United States marshal appointment to designate them a posse.

These were not the Earps' respectable-citizen backers, but men such as Holliday, solitary wanderers rumored to be handy with a gun. They were also shadowy figures with colorful monikers and enticing legends. Turkey Creek Jack Johnson had supposedly chosen a graveyard outside Deadwood as the site for a gun duel, had hired the gravediggers, and, having made these preparations, had plugged his two opponents. Texas Jack Vermillion was reputedly a native of Virginia who had come to Tombstone from Dodge, who lived in a cave in the Dragoon Mountains, and who may or may not have been the Texas Jack reported to have killed a man in the vicinity of Flagstaff in October 1881. Sherman McMasters, the bewhiskered Earp confederate who had been linked with rustler associate Pony Diehl, was still wanted on the charge of stealing a valuable saddle horse from Contention mine manager E. B. Gage.

Wyatt Earp was about to use these men in an attempt to round up outside city limits the "cowboys" he considered most responsible for the climate of suspicion and violence directed at the Earps. However, one of his potential targets was ready to force the issue in town. On the afternoon of January 17, John Ringo confronted Doc Holliday and Wyatt on a Tombstone street in an incident that has become encrusted with legend as the Big Showdown between champions of the two warring factions. Parsons presented the scene in bare but vivid outline: "Much blood in the air this afternoon. Ringo and Doc Holliday came nearly having it with pistols. . . . Bad time expected with the cowboy leader and D H. I passed both not knowing blood was up. One with hand in breast pocket and the other probably ready. Earps just beyond. Crowded street and looked like another battle. Police vigilant for once and both disarmed." By various accounts, Ringo had challenged either Doc Holliday or Wyatt Earp to settle the feud in a one-on-one gunfight. John Pleasant Gray painted such a scene in his memoirs:

Ringo on horseback was riding out of town when he saw
three of the Earps together in front of the Crystal Palace
Saloon. Ringo rode up and dismounted near them and
called out to Wyatt that they had just as well have it out
there and then. Ringo pulled from his neck his big, red
silk handkerchief, flipped it in the air towards Wyatt, told
him to take the other end and say when. Of course Wyatt
Earp was too wise to be caught in such a trap. . . .

Billy Breakenridge would recall a similar incident in
which Ringo told Wyatt Earp that he wanted to settle the feud
in a gun duel with Doc Holliday. When word reached the
sheriff's office, Behan sent Breakenridge out and the deputy
found the challenger pacing the street alone and fuming,
complaining that "he was trying to end the feud, but the others were not game to meet him man to man and face to face,
that they would rather wait for a chance to shoot him in the
back." Breakenridge brought Ringo in, and Behan relieved
him of his guns, but when Ringo complained to the deputy
that he wouldn't stand a chance against the Earps as he left
town, Breakenridge quietly opened the drawer containing the
weapons and left. Naturally, he later found both Ringo and
the guns gone.

The Gray and Breakenridge accounts may describe other
related encounters or may be variations on the one legendary
confrontation. Police court records show that in the January 17
incident, Ringo, Holliday, and Wyatt Earp were all charged with
carrying concealed weapons. The charge against Wyatt was dismissed because of his United States deputy marshal appointment, while Holliday and Ringo were fined thirty dollars each.

Meanwhile, Territorial Marshal Crawley Dake was collecting money, ostensibly to outfit Wyatt Earp's posse. Dake appeared at the Wells Fargo offices in San Francisco in January,
complaining that he "was powerless to do good as U.S.
Marshal for want of funds, & if the Company would advance
him $3000.00 he would use it in quieting the disturbances &
return the amount as soon as the vouchers could be approved
at Washington and the money could be gotten in return."
Wells Fargo officials gave him the $3,000. On January 20, he
deposited $2,985 with Hudson & Company for Wyatt's use in
tracking down stage robbers.

This money would be the subject of much dispute in the years to come. The irresponsible Dake would later claim that he had expended $8,000 to $12,000 in combating "Cow Boy Raids," with most of this money going to Wyatt Earp. Wyatt himself would state that Dake had provided him with the $2,985 in the Hudson & Company account, minus $340 which Dake had spent while drunk, and that Wyatt used the remaining $2,645 in outfitting and maintaining his posse: Morgan and Warren Earp, Doc Holliday, Sherman McMasters, Turkey Creek Jack Johnson, Texas Jack Vermillion, Charlie Smith, and two others.

However, a special examiner would later find that Wyatt drew only $536.65 of the amount, with Dake himself drawing out the rest by February 7. And posse member Charlie Smith would later testify that to his knowledge Wyatt received only about $500 from Dake. "He states it is his belief that Earp never got more than $500.00 from Dake & that his opportunity for knowing is good, since he was continually with Earp during the time of the disturbance," the special examiner would report. Furthermore, in the one meeting between Dake and Wyatt which Smith witnessed, Dake borrowed $100 from the posse leader.

The confusion was only heightened by the existence of a citizens' fund raised by law-and-order businessmen and placed, at least in part, at Wyatt's disposal. The examiner found Smith satisfied "that Earp got most of the money to defray the expense of his men from a fund raised by the Citizens of Cochise Co." Lawyer and Citizens Safety Committee member William Herring of Tombstone would also identify a citizens' fund held by George Parsons's friend Milton B. Clapp and would state that Wells Fargo contributed to this fund, with all or most of the money collected "placed at the disposal of Earp." Herring would reject the idea that Dake had contributed any significant sum, "for the citizens had gotten tired of waiting on the authorities & had taken the matter in their own hands."

Whatever the origins of the money, Charlie Smith estimated costs of the Earp posse at twenty-five hundred dollars "for the entire time of their service including everything." From this amount, Wyatt furnished each of his nine posse members with "horse, bridle, saddle, carbine, six-shooter & rations," plus five dollars a day pay over a thirty-day period.

It was a pretty frugal undertaking, if the estimates of Dake's Tucson deputy, J. W. Evans, are any indication. In September 1881, Evans had calculated that he would need thirty thousand dollars to field a posse, reasoning that "Good men could not be had for less than $10 per day and expenses, with everything furnished; a good horse at $100, horse trappings for $25, plus a carbine and two pistols." But, then, Evans was apparently an apt pupil in the Crawley Dake school of inflated numbers.

The day after Dake deposited the money in the Hudson & Company account, Parsons confided to his journal, "Something brewing in town. Trouble ahead." Two days later, Wyatt Earp would ride out of town with his posse, carrying "warrants for the arrest of divers persons charged with criminal offenses." Ike Clanton, brother Phineas, and Pony Diehl, charged with the murder attempt against Virgil, were at the top of the list.

At the time Wyatt rode out, John Ringo was back in town, having been brought in by Billy Breakenridge to await a review of his bond in the case of the August poker game robbery for which he had been indicted by the grand jury. Soon after Wyatt Earp departed Tombstone, however, John Ringo rode out, too. Breakenridge later asserted that Ringo's lawyer had erroneously reported the bond approved by Judge Stilwell, making Ringo think he was free to go.

He was not, and for once, James Earp stepped into the drama, immediately going before Stilwell and swearing out an affidavit against the rustler. By leaving before his bond was approved, Ringo had become "an escaped prisoner from the jurisdiction of the Court of the First Judicial District," and further, Ringo's intent was to "obstruct the execution" of warrants carried by Wyatt Earp.

Ringo was rearrested the next day. Breakenridge would later claim that Judge Stilwell secretly gave Wyatt's posse a warrant for the arrest, but that Ringo confounded them by quietly returning and appearing just as Behan was about to be called to account in court for letting the prisoner go. There is more to the matter than that, though, for a second posse had entered the field; it was led by a man named J. H. Jackson who had no legal authority anyone could determine but was given a warrant for Ringo, apparently a duplicate of one carried by Wyatt. "Was routed out of bed night before last to help get a horse for posse which left about 4 A.M. for Charleston to rearrest Ringo. Jack headed them and they had quite an experience but no shooting," Parsons wrote on January 25. By one account, Jackson found Ringo at Charleston and got his promise to come in, with Ringo following the posse by about an hour and twenty minutes. By January 25, he was lodged in the county jail, his bond judged insufficient after all.

Meanwhile, Wyatt Earp had drawn to him thirty to forty more men—some of them reportedly Henry Clay Hooker's ranch employees—and ransacked Charleston, scouring the community for cowboys in a middle-of-the-night door-to-door search that netted only a Mexican carrying Pete Spencer's revolver, recognizable to one of the posse members. Crawley Dake was in Tombstone to provide the law enforcement clout necessary for Wyatt's actions, and Mayor John Carr signed a notice in the *Epitaph* to "the citizens of Tombstone" informing them that Judge Stilwell had provided Wyatt with the warrants he carried and requesting "the public within the city to abstain from any interference with said warrants."

Nonetheless, a man named Ben Maynard came into town angry enough to challenge the Earps. Indications are that he was no friend of the Earp faction anyway; on the same day John Ringo and Doc Holliday had nearly come to shooting on the street, Maynard and Earp associate Lou Rickabaugh had "tried to kick each other's lungs out." Now Maynard asserted that the Earp posse had accosted him between Tombstone and Charleston and forced him to go with them on their cowboy hunt. The *Daily Nugget* also reported that the group had harassed a deputy sheriff from the Huachucas en route to Tombstone, calling him a "cattle-thieving son of a b---h." The irate Maynard went with Mayor Carr before the district judge, trying to get a warrant against the Earp party, but it was denied.

At about the same time, Johnny Behan got a telegram from Charleston complaining that "Doc Holliday, the Earps, and about forty or fifty more of the filth of Tombstone" had turned the town upside down and begging the sheriff, "Please come here and take them where they belong."

At least, that's what the *Daily Nugget* said when it published the telegram. Earp supporters over the years have considered the missive a fake. The impact of the Earp force's visit, however, is attested to by George Parsons, who would meet the posse leaving Charleston as he traveled to a mill location on January 30. Parsons recorded Charleston looking "almost like a deserted village and as though having undergone a siege." The Las Vegas *Optic* reported:

> Doc Holliday and the Earp boys are at it again in Arizona, and are acting a great deal worse than they ever dared to carry on in Las Vegas. The other day these frontier terrors got acquainted with Uncle Sam and gained his affections sufficiently to secure the appointment to positions called United States Marshals. Under this coat of authority, they swooped down on a little camp called Charleston and raised the awfullest din the poor people had ever listened to.

Throughout the whole episode, the *Daily Nugget* remained critical of the "pestiferous posse" and mildly critical of Dake for empowering such a body considering the enmities that already existed. It even printed a speculation attributed to Mayor Carr that the posse was organized to "absorb" the several thousand dollars deposited in Dake's hands.

Meanwhile, yet another posse took the field. "The large number of armed men leaving town the past few days has completely exhausted the supply of rifle scabbards usually kept by Patton, the harnessmaker," the *Daily Nugget* reported.

Posse No. 3 was guided by Pete Spencer and led by Charley Bartholomew. This may well have been the Charles Bartholomew who had ridden guard on the Bisbee stage a few weeks earlier, but one cannot be too sure. Another Charles Bartholomew, a mining man, would announce through the newspaper that he was tired of being confused with his namesake, and further, "he has not in the past, nor does he propose to in the future, engage in hunting for cowboys, because, he says, he has not lost any."

The posse that Charley Bartholomew led was a protective

one, raised in response to messages from Ike and Phin Clanton "that they would surrender to either the city or county officials," but not—for fear of being killed—to Federal Deputy Marshal Wyatt Earp. When Wyatt brought his posse back to town on January 30, Ike, Phin, and Pony Diehl were already appearing in court on the attempted murder charge, to their surprise. The warrants had been kept secret, and the Clantons and Diehl had been led to believe the charge was a robbing the mails one related to the stagecoach robberies.

On the same day, Johnny Behan was brought up on a charge of perjury "in swearing to certain bills presented to the board of supervisors." Behan's counsel argued for a change of venue, on suspicion of prejudice since the court "had ignored the sheriff of the county in placing [arrest] warrants" in other, unauthorized hands. The judge denied a change of venue, but dismissed the case.

Meanwhile, City Marshal Dave Neagle was serving a warrant on one of the Earp party as it returned from Charleston and settled into a camp near Pick 'Em Up. Sherman McMasters had to appear in court on the horse-stealing charge. Neagle brought him in, soon followed "by the Earps, Doc Holliday and other members of the posse." McMasters was booked, and bail set at a thousand dollars.

In the midst of all this trouble and litigation, Acting Governor Gosper again made a hurried appearance in Tombstone. He apparently threw up his hands at the whole mess and beat a hasty retreat.

On January 31 Judge Stilwell heard the charges against Phineas Clanton and Pony Diehl. "No evidence being adduced to warrant their being held to answer, the two were discharged." Ike, too, quickly won dismissal and release.

Crawley Dake remained in Tombstone. On February 1, the *Daily Nugget* published a notice from "MANY CITIZENS" announcing a public meeting at 7:00 P.M. at the courthouse "to confer with the United States Marshal of this Territory in regard to the selection of a deputy or deputies for this section." Dake would bow to anti-Earp pressure enough to make J. H. Jackson his "regular" deputy, but without rescinding Wyatt Earp's appointment.

Dake left on February 3. So did the "honorably acquitted"

Clantons and their friends. On the fourth, Morgan's common-law wife, Louisa, still using the name Louisa Houston, wrote to her sister, "It is quite impossible to tell you all the trouble and anxiosity [sic]" in which the Earp family found itself. Of their residence at the Cosmopolitan, she wrote that it was "very disagreeable to be so unsettled." She also noted that her husband's brothers would open "any letter that is not directed to me at this name [Louisa Houston]."

Ike Clanton was back in Tombstone on the seventh, and on the ninth, he went to Justice of the Peace J. B. Smith in Contention and again filed charges against the Earps and Doc Holliday for the murder of Billy Clanton and the McLaurys. "To Any Sheriff, Constable, Marshal or Policeman in the Territory of Arizona, Greetings," read Smith's order commanding those addressed "to arrest the above named Wyatt Earp, Morgan Earp, Virgil Earp and J. H. Holliday and bring them forthwith before me at my office on Main Street in the Village of Contention, in the County of Cochise, Territory of Arizona."

The Earps' lawyer, Tom Fitch, was touring the East with his wife. This time around, the defendants hired Citizens Safety Committee member William Herring. Ike retained J. S. Robinson and Ben Goodrich as counsel, and a legal battle royal began. Behan took Wyatt, Morgan, and Doc into custody, with Virgil again escaping arrest because of his second, more serious injury, which still kept him confined to his hotel room.

On February 11, the defendants filed a petition for a writ of habeas corpus, asserting that they were "illegally restrained of their liberty by John Behan, sheriff of the County of Cochise" on the order of Smith, "an alleged justice of the peace." No district court judge was present to consider the petition, and County Commissioner T. J. Drum was automatically disqualified because of his previous representation of Holliday concerning the charge. So the three applied to Probate Judge Lucas, arguing on two grounds: that the charge had already been examined and rejected, by both Spicer and the grand jury, and that Smith did not possess the legal authority to order an arrest. The Epitaph editorialized on the first point, "If it is a fact that this warrant has been allowed to issue without new evidence to warrant it, the code of rights that protects all alike has been violently infringed."

However, when the defendants went before Lucas on the morning of February 13, the second issue—whether Smith had the power to have the defendants incarcerated—took precedence, and Lucas decided he did. Wyatt, Virgil, and Doc found themselves remanded to Behan's custody. On the same day, Wyatt and Mattie, as husband and wife, mortgaged their Tombstone dwelling for $365, agreeing to pay 2 percent interest per month. (A week later Mattie would check into the Cosmopolitan under the name Earp, but using as address Cedar Rapids, Iowa, where she had originally come from.)

The accused, accompanied by their own protective posse, were taken to Contention on the fourteenth to appear before Smith. Parsons recorded the day's events with foreboding:

> Quite a posse went out. Many of Earp's friends armed to the teeth. They came back later in the day, the good people below beseeching them to leave and try case here. A bad time is expected again in town at any time. Earps on one side of the street with their friends and Ike Clanton and Ringo with theirs on the other side—watching each other. Blood will surely come. Hope no innocents will be killed.

The Earps and Holliday might engage in glaring matches, but they were still in Behan's custody. As Parsons indicated, Smith had simply adjourned the trial to Tombstone for the next day. Ike Clanton wrote exultantly to Guadalupe Canyon massacre survivor Billy Byers, now in Leavenworth, Kansas, "I have got the Earps all in Jail and am not going to unhitch. I have got them on the hip and am going to throw them good."

On February 15, the three appeared before Smith again, and he once more adjourned the examination "to a future day." The defendants immediately filed a second writ of habeas corpus with Lucas, complaining that the Contention justice had failed to show them "the complaint and depositions upon which said warrant had been alleged and issued," so that they still had not been informed by Smith of "the offence with which they are charged." Furthermore, they argued, they were not being held "under a formal decree of any court in this territory, or upon any judgement executed thereunder against your petitioners."

Ike Clanton attempted to keep his adversaries "on the hip" by filing another set of murder charges on the same day, this time with Lucas, but he was fighting a losing battle. The Earps and Holliday had now gone before Smith and been remanded to Behan's custody without Smith's making the necessary order of commitment. Thus, Lucas now ruled, their continuing imprisonment was unlawful.

In addition, he now took into account the defense's argument that the accused had already been examined and released in a lengthy proceeding. "The facts of a former examination of the parties for the same offense, by a Committing Magistrate, occupying weeks, and then discharged, and the sitting of a grand jury in this County since the alleged offense, are so notorious, that I feel justified in taking judicial notice thereof," Lucas wrote in his decision. "Whether Petitioners are guilty or not, it is apparent to any reasonable being, that an examination at this time could serve no good purpose." The probate judge noted that another examination would merely duplicate the Spicer hearing, "unless new evidence be discovered or circumstances occur subsequent to the first examination, sufficient to appeal to the discretion of the Magistrate." Thus, Lucas refused a second examination and ordered the three defendants discharged.

The three legal attempts to hang the Earps and Holliday had come to nothing. Wyatt immediately picked up his posse and was off again, as the *Daily Nugget* reported on February 18:

> Wyatt and Morgan Earp, Doc Holliday, "Texas Jack," -----
> Smith, McMasters and one or two others left the city yesterday afternoon for ---- where, no one apparently knows, but when in the vicinity of Waterville they separated, four of the party going in the direction of San Simon valley, to arrest, it is claimed, Pony Dehl [sic] and one or two other well known characters, and the remainder to Charleston.

The paper concluded, "It is supposed they are acting in the capacity of U.S. Deputy Marshals, their resignations not having been accepted or their appointment revoked by U.S. Marshal Dake, as was generally supposed some time ago."

The Earps had been provided with a legal reason to go after Pony Diehl because stage guard Bartholomew had on February 12 charged Diehl, Charles Hawes, and Al Tiebot or Thibolet with the January robbery of the Bisbee stage. A rumor reached Tombstone that a telegraphic alert had resulted in the three's quick apprehension in Cisco, Texas, but the news had proven to be false, and the men were still at large.

The Earp party would reportedly move toward the Mexican border, and a Prescott *Miner* account, with information probably provided by Dake himself, would assert that Dake, "trusting to Congress for reimbursement," had a posse on the border "trying to capture certain outlaws who committed outrages last fall in southern Arizona." The *Daily Nugget,* identifying the posse as Wyatt's, would complain that when the entourage headed for the border, Dake had "telegraphed to certain parties in this place that he knew nothing of their movements but supposed they desired to serve some old warrants, and further, that John H. Jackson was his deputy at this place." Dake's waffling concerning Wyatt's official status in light of the marshal's own financial mismanagement became clear in a Prescott *Democrat* item: "We are informed by Marshal Dake that the resignation of the Earps . . . has not yet been accepted, owing to the fact that their accounts have not yet been straightened up. As soon as that is done they will step down and out."

The whole messy situation continued to attract the attention of territorial officials—and national ones. President Chester Arthur had already in December asked Congress for an amendment to the Posse Comitatus Act so that the army could act as a potent force to deal with depredators on the border, but Congress had not responded. On February 2, in hopes of reviving the posse comitatus issue, Arthur had also forwarded to the United States Congress Gosper's letters to Dake and to the secretary of the interior outlining the problems of lawlessness in southeastern Arizona. And on February 6, he had finally appointed a new governor, a fervent territorial booster and mining man named F. A. Tritle.

On top of all the other troubles, numerous Apaches once again erupted out of their reservation confines, inciting fears and further uncertainties in Cochise County in March. Bound for Mexico, they raided Henry Clay Hooker's ranch in the Sulphur Spring Valley, driving off two hundred horses, then holed up temporarily in the Dragoon Mountains. In Arizona's southeastern communities, rumors multiplied—including a report that the renegades were going to sack Tombstone. General George Crook, an unusually fair and respected veteran of Indian battles, was called upon to meet the latest crisis and would spend many months trying to effect a peace.

Tombstonians made plans for armed defense of their community and went on about their business as best they could. As Wyatt and Morgan ranged about the territory and followed their standard pursuits in town, Virgil Earp remained confined to his room in the Cosmopolitan. Finally, on March 15, he ventured onto the street, his first appearance since the shooting. If he wore a pained expression, it was not necessarily from his bullet wounds. Shot in October, he had lost the city marshalship; shot again in December, he had lost the federal marshalship. In addition to these disheartening events, since the second shooting, former City Policeman T. J. Cornelison had been released from seven months in jail on a theft charge involving the rifling of a lady's trunk and had announced to anyone who would listen that the arresting officer, Virgil, had given him a choice of arrest or a hundred-dollar bribe.

No, the future for Virgil Earp in Tombstone looked cloudy at best. It did for Morgan Earp, too. The younger brother was ready to leave, according to Waters's account, telling Allie Earp on Saturday, March 18, that he wished Virgil would get better, since "I'd like to get away from here. Tonight!" He did, but not in the way he wished.

The weather on the eighteenth was harsh and gloomy. "Very disagreeable day," Parsons wrote. "Rainy and windy . . . . Stormy and disagreeable night." The Earps and their friends attended the theater in the evening, then retired to Robert Hatch's saloon and billiard parlor beside the Alhambra on Allen, where Morgan and proprietor Hatch engaged in a game of billiards.

There were rumors that someone was out to get the Earps again. Briggs Goodrich would testify that Wyatt had suspected a threat the night before, telling him, "I think they were after us last night. Do you know anything about it?"

Goodrich had responded in the negative but stated his opinion that the Earps "were liable to get it in the neck at any time."

"I don't notice anybody particularly in town now—any of the [cowboy] crowd," Wyatt mused.

"I think I see some strangers here that I think are after you," Goodrich replied.

Goodrich also claimed that John Ringo and Frank Stilwell had disassociated themselves from any attempts on the Earps, with Goodrich passing on Ringo's remarks to Wyatt: "John Ringo wanted me to say to you, that if any fight came up between you all, that he wanted you to understand that he would have nothing to do with it, that he was going to look out for himself, and anybody else could do the same." Stilwell he characterized as afraid the Earps would blame him for any violence. "He said there were some boys in town who would toe the mark, and the worst of it was the Earps would think he was in it, as they did not like him." Goodrich offered to "tell them the same for him as I had for John Ringo," but Stilwell insisted "he would rather die than let them know that he cared a damn what they thought." Goodrich advised him to stay off the streets at night and maintain a good alibi.

Earp confederate Dan Tipton would also testify that the Earps possessed a foreknowledge of danger that evening. Tipton had accompanied the Earps to the theater and to Hatch's. He would state they had been warned "to look out, as some of them would catch it that night," and that he personally had been warned repeatedly, "by businessmen especially."

At ten-fifty, Morgan and Hatch were into their second game, with Hatch about to make a play. The room they occupied had a rear door with four panes, the two below painted, the two above clear and providing a view of the billiard room. Morgan stood with his back to this exit as Wyatt, Sherman McMasters, Tipton, and a few other men watched the game. Suddenly a shot came crashing through one of the upper panes, striking Morgan. The bullet "entered the right side of the abdomen, passing through the spinal column, completely shattering it, emerging on the left side, passing the length of the room and lodging in the thigh of George A. B. Berry, who was standing by the stove." A second bullet followed, hitting above Wyatt Earp's head.

Hatch, McMasters, and others ran into the alley within seconds of the shooting, but the gunman or gunmen escaped in the darkness. Wyatt, McMasters, and Tipton hurried to Morgan, while three doctors, including Goodfellow and Matthews, were called to the scene. Goodfellow found the youngest of the "fighting Earps" lying on the floor of the saloon:

> He was in a state of collapse resulting from a gunshot, or pistol wound, entering the body just to the left of the spinal column in the region of the left kidney emerging on the right side of the body in the region of the gall bladder. It certainly injured the great vessels of the body causing hemorrhage which, undoubtedly, causes death. It also injured the spinal column. It passed through the left kidney and also through the loin.

Morgan was moved to a couch in the cardroom and lived less than an hour, spending his last minutes surrounded by family and friends. Wife Louisa is missing from accounts of Morgan's death, and Warren was visiting the Earp parents in Colton at the time. But Virgil and Allie came, as did James and Bessie. The *Epitaph* reported Morgan dying gamely, whispering to "his brother," and only complaining when someone tried to set him on his feet, remarking, "Don't, I can't stand it. This is the last game of pool I'll ever play." In Glenn Boyer's account, Morgan confided, "They got me, Wyatt. Don't let them get you!" and then asked him to tell their parents goodbye. Allie remembered his last words as "It won't be long. Are my legs stretched out straight and my boots off?"

And then he died. The Earp women, who had found him affable and "good-hearted," cried. Boyer's *I Married Wyatt Earp* has Doc Holliday going on a rampage, with Josie recalling that he went around town armed, busting open the doors of private residences, hunting for the men he considered responsible, Johnny Behan and Will McLaury. Meanwhile, Wyatt Earp looked at his dead brother, the one intimates called his favorite, and decided that he was tired of all the political and legal maneuvering. From here on out, he would have no regard for any law but his own.

CHAPTER 15
Trail of Blood

As news of Morgan Earp's murder spread, Frank Stilwell quickly became the prime suspect in the crime, just as he had reportedly feared. And a hastily formed coroner's inquest jury soon heard an unlikely witness implicate Stilwell and four other men in the killing. Marietta Spencer, Pete Spencer's Mexican wife, was not finding marriage idyllic. Pete disappeared and reappeared at odd hours, ordered her around, and verbally and physically abused her and her mother, Mrs. Francisco Castro. Castro had filed assault charges against him, and Marietta was ready to talk.

She told the inquest jury that on the day before the murder, she, her mother, Spencer, and an Indian who went by the name of Charlie were standing in front of the Spencer house when Morgan Earp walked by. "Spence nudged the Indian and said, 'That's him; that's him,'" she reported. The Indian then moved down the street "so as to get ahead of him and get a good look at him."

The next night, the evening of the shooting, Pete was away from home. Indian Charlie appeared at the Spencer house with Frank Stilwell about midnight. They both carried pistols and carbines. Soon Pete himself arrived, along with a

German named Freis and another man. Marietta knew only that this fifth man lived "in the house of Manuel Acusto." The three newcomers carried rifles, and they met with Stilwell and Indian Charlie in the front room of the Spencer house, talking in low and excited tones. Marietta had arisen from bed to receive them and found her husband, Freis, and the unknown man white and "all of a tremble," with Spencer's teeth chattering.

The next morning, Marietta and her husband had a quarrel "during which he struck me and my mother and during which he threatened to shoot me, when my mother told him he would have to shoot her too." Spencer still threatened to kill his wife and light out for Sonora, leaving her dead body behind, "if I said a word about something I knew about."

That morning when Marietta heard the news of Morgan Earp's death, she immediately concluded that her husband and his confederates had killed him, with Pete, Freis, and the third man going from the scene to get their horses outside town while Stilwell and Indian Charlie came on to the house.

Marietta gave her testimony on March 21, explaining that her husband had departed the day before, apparently for Sonora. By the time Marietta testified, however, Wyatt Earp and friends had already taken revenge on Frank Stilwell, and Pete Spencer was seeking the safety of Behan's jail.

Stilwell had been seen in Tucson early on the morning after the shooting; by one account, he had checked into a Tucson hotel at 5:00 A.M. Some questioned how he could have participated in the murder and traveled the seventy miles so quickly. However, even Earp detractors considered Stilwell a likely perpetrator, and the Earps and friends did not need Marietta's testimony before they pegged the ex-deputy as a prime suspect. In Tombstone, they readied for the removal of Morgan's body to the Earp parents' home in Colton, California, for burial. Virgil, his arm still in a sling, and Allie would accompany the corpse to its destination, while Wyatt, Warren (who had immediately come from Colton at news of Morgan's death), Doc, Sherman McMasters, and Turkey Creek Jack Johnson would travel with them as far as Tucson.

On the twentieth, the Earp entourage boarded the new passenger line at Contention, after journeying by horse and buggy from Tombstone. Another train traveler later recalled, "McMasters said that they would leave the train at Benson but afterwards [they] changed their minds and came to Tucson to see Virgil Earp and his wife on their way to California." As they journeyed westward, McMasters, sporting two belts of cartridges, "particularly inquired as to the arrival and departure of trains at Tucson depot."

McMasters may have been getting jittery and thinking about breaking off from the crowd. Two underlying motivations for the decision to travel on to Tucson have been advanced, and neither one has anything to do with simply seeing Virgil and Allie off. Virgil himself would state in a newspaper interview two months later that his brothers had gotten dispatches from Tucson "saying that Stilwell and a party of friends were watching all the railroad trains passing that way, and were going through them in search of all Earps and their friends, carrying short shotguns under their overcoats and promising to kill on sight."

In other words, in this version, Wyatt and friends accompanied Virgil and Allie to Tucson in the face of a clear and organized threat awaiting them from their enemies. Although nothing would come out at the inquest into the death of Frank Stilwell to substantiate this claim, certainly, after Virgil's wounding and Morgan's killing, the Earps had much reason to be wary. In all probability, they proceeded to Tucson in part to ensure Virgil's safe departure from the territory. But there are also indications that they arrived in hopes of settling the score with one or more of their enemies. A special report to the *Epitaph* stated that Ike Clanton, in Tucson, had "received several dispatches from Tombstone warning him to look out— that a party was coming down to put him out of the way, which put him on his guard."

After the train rolled into Tucson in the early evening, David Gibson, at the depot with checks for passengers' baggage, fell into conversation with a newsboy who had disembarked.

"I guess there will be hell here tonight," the newsboy commented. When Gibson inquired why, the boy responded that "the Earps and Holliday were aboard and were going to stop here as they had told him that the man who killed Morgan Earp was in Tucson."

Crawley Dake's Tucson deputy, J. W. Evans, was standing at the depot when the train arrived and saw Doc Holliday get off "with a shotgun in each hand," go to the railroad office, and return without the guns. The train stopped long enough for passengers to disembark and enjoy an evening meal nearby; during this interval, Evans saw Doc "several times" and at one point heard him instruct "a small man who was standing near him" to get the guns from the office.

While the train was stopped, Evans also encountered Wyatt Earp at Porter's Hotel. As they talked, Virgil Earp, having finished eating, emerged from the hotel and shook hands with Evans. Then Virgil and Allie reboarded the train, with Wyatt and other members of the party assisting them. Evans would testify that the party had no guns with them at this point, in direct contradiction to the testimony of other witnesses.

For example, engineer S. A. Batman. He "saw a man with a Winchester rifle walking up and down by the side of the train and was told by some one that the man in question was one of the Earps guarding a party that were going through to California; shortly afterwards saw a man and lady come out of the hotel, the man carrying one arm in a sling; two men carrying Winchester rifles walked behind them. They got on the cars, the one outside still looking everywhere."

David Gibson would testify that on the heels of his conversation with the newsboy, he saw Doc, Wyatt, "another Earp" [Warren], and a short man whom the newsboy identified as McMasters walk from Porter's Hotel toward the depot. The two Earps carried short Wells Fargo shotguns; Holliday was also armed, although Gibson didn't think McMasters was.

As [the four] reached the end of the sleeper one of them stepped up on the platform and passed to the opposite side and then looked up and down the train. Returning all four of them walked toward the rear end of the sleeper when they faced about and walked about towards the engine at the head of the train. The newsboy pointed out the wounded Earp [Virgil] who was sitting in the bar [of the train] with two ladies in front of him. The conductor's bell then rang and two shots were fired towards the head of the train, instantly followed by about five more, [Gibson]

could plainly see the flashes of the guns, but could not see
the Earps or the other man [McMasters].

Frank Stilwell had come to the depot, ostensibly to meet a
deputy from Charleston to testify at his trial for the Bisbee
stage robbery, perhaps to get a shot at the Earps. Either way,
he was dead, and Ike Clanton had narrowly missed joining
him on the tracks. According to Ike's later testimony, he had
arrived at the depot at Stilwell's request and was sitting on the
hotel porch when Stilwell found him and pulled him behind
the building to inform him that the Earps and Holliday had
arrived on the train. Soon Ike saw Doc, Wyatt, Warren, Sherman McMasters, and Turkey Creek Jack Johnson emerge
from the hotel and walk toward the train.

One newspaper report would explain that when the Earp
party appeared, Stilwell "advised Clanton to leave at once saying they wanted to kill him." Presumably, the ambiguous
"him" was Clanton, and Stilwell was either confident that he
had covered his tracks in Morgan's murder or blissfully innocent of the suspicions against him. Whatever the circumstances, Ike started toward his room—one imagines toward
any other place on earth besides the vicinity of the Earps—but
"the deceased walked down the track between the cars and the
hotel." Ike paused at a livery stable and waited for Stilwell to
catch up, a suspicious action that suggests Stilwell planned to
shoot and run. A dispatch to the *Epitaph* cited this as one of
three possible reasons for Stilwell's actions: "Some say that he
was decoyed to the spot where he fell, as he possessed strong
evidence against certain stage robbers. Others think he was
trying to get away from the Earp party and was overtaken,
while it was thought by some he went down the track to shoot
one or more of the Earp party as the train was moving out."

The fireman on the departing locomotive, James Miller,
noticed a man running along the track on the east side of the
engine and crossing in front of it, then saw "four armed men
pass on the west side of the engine and down to the left of the
coaches standing on the side track." Shortly thereafter, he
heard "five or six shots fired in rapid succession" and saw one
man in the act of shooting. As the train pulled out, he could
see the other three men as well, all with guns in their hands.

Locomotive engineer R. E. Mellis gave basically the same account.

Neither of these workers saw a weapon on Stilwell, although he was carrying a pistol. A number of witnesses reported impressions similar to those of the fireman and the engineer, although details varied widely. Alman J. Hinckey saw the gun flashes and "some six or ten men standing on the south side of the track near where the body was found" as the train pulled out about seven-fifteen. Engineer Batman saw one of the Earp party walking along the track and soon heard two shots, then five or six others, as well as "some cheering in the direction in which the shots were fired." A. McCann, who saw the four men go to the head of the train and heard six to ten shots, also reported cheering. John Magee saw one of the Earps, armed with a Winchester, briefly enter the train, then step to the ground, speaking "low but excitedly to a stranger." The two moved toward the engine, and Magee heard "seven or eight shots in quick succession."

Virgil Earp would claim that his brother had extracted a confession from Stilwell before killing him. Wyatt Earp himself, talking to a reporter in 1896, would assert, "Even at the depot I was forced to fight Ike Clanton and four or five of his friends who had followed us to do murder. One of them, named Frank Stilwell, who was believed to be Morgan's murderer, was killed by my gun going off when he grasped it."

In biographer Stuart Lake's heroic saga, the lone Wyatt Earp spots crouching figures and the glint of rifle barrels, then chases one of the figures, ignoring the rifle shots directed his way by his prey. Finally, the man stops at his order, and Wyatt recognizes Stilwell. The latter tries to draw his gun but, like other ne'er-do-wells who have the temerity to go up against the great Wyatt Earp, instead stands paralyzed in mid-draw. Wyatt moves closer, and Stilwell lunges. As the two struggle, Wyatt forces the gun into a position just under Stilwell's heart. The desperate Stilwell calls, oddly enough, "Morg! Morg!" and Wyatt shoots him, bringing Doc Holliday running from a nearby restaurant.

One problem with such stories is the nature and number of Stilwell's wounds. A doctor would find that a ball had passed from one armpit to another, piercing the lungs. Another had penetrated the upper left arm, and yet another the right leg. A buckshot charge, fired at close range, had passed through the abdomen, liver, and stomach, while another buckshot charge had fractured the left leg. Stilwell's gun remained unfired, and he was not only dead but "shot right through."

Yet nobody apparently took the trouble to find and report the body until the next morning, despite clear signs of a killing. One can perhaps understand Ike Clanton's self-preserving reluctance to go down and investigate when Stilwell failed to catch up with him, but the depot was crawling with people. The Earp party had attracted attention by its guarded posture and display of artillery. The newsboy had arrived talking about a confrontation, and fireman Miller had heard someone say before leaving "that there would be murder done there." Various witnesses had seen the running victim, the pursuing killers, and the flash of the guns. Yet W. J. Dougherty, who lived "within about 150 feet of where the body was found," heard the shots, saw a flash, and "thinks he saw the upper part of a man's body," but didn't bother to investigate, according to his testimony. And Deputy Evans would testify that he was walking "up town," turned around at the sound of the shots, and tried to find out what had happened, only to be satisfied by the explanation that "it was done by some Mexicans below the depot."

A somewhat more satisfactory explanation was later provided by Kate Elder, who remembered that those who heard the shots thought they were in celebration of the fact that Tucson streets were being lit with gas for the first time that evening. But some may have initially approached the shooting site only to be warned away by the shootists themselves. Hinckey testified that when he saw the "flashes of guns and some six or ten men standing on the south side of the track near where the body was found," he was "with several others, all of whom were challenged." This may be an oblique reference to what the Tucson *Star* reported: "Several railroad hands, just after the shooting, chanced to approach going to their duties, and were warned back by the crowd of shooters."

Meanwhile, the train disappeared into the evening darkness. A watchman at the depot was "almost certain" that one man, about five feet eight inches tall with a black hat and dark whiskers, remained on board, armed with two rifles. Despite his absence from other accounts and the reference to "dark whiskers," this may well have been Jim Earp, for two Earps were mentioned as remaining on board in one news dispatch, and James himself would tell an interviewer in Los Angeles a week later that he, wife Bessie, and the widowed Lou Earp had accompanied the body to Colton. Lou may well have been one of the two ladies sitting in front of Virgil whom David Gibson mentioned; Bessie, however, would not be reported as leaving Tombstone until March 24.

According to legend, as the train departed the depot, Wyatt ran to the window where Virgil sat, and called, "It's all right, Virg! It's all right! One for Morg!" Allie Earp's account in the Waters narrative is less dramatic. In it, she and Virgil heard the shooting, and Virgil grabbed for his six-shooter, which Allie had placed within reach on the window. However, she had also placed her coat and a baking powder can filled with salve for his back wound on top of the weapon; when he grabbed for the gun, the salve can tipped over, creating a mess.

The couple was well out of a much bigger mess. Wyatt wasn't. Five minutes after the shooting, a man approaching the Tucson depot passed "four men dressed in dark clothes and carrying guns." Wyatt and friends were heading back to Tombstone.

They walked to Papago Station just east of Tucson and flagged a train to take them back to Contention, where they either caught a stage or picked up their buggy and horses. By early evening on March 21, they were again lodged in the Cosmopolitan Hotel, this time making preparations to get out of town for good.

Meanwhile, a telegram from Pima County Justice of the Peace Charles Myers had come in informing Johnny Behan that the returnees were wanted for the killing of Stilwell. The manager of the telegraph office, friendly to the Earps, showed the newly arrived message to Wyatt as he rode into town and agreed to hold it long enough for the Earp party to proceed with their arrangements for leaving town. The telegram was not given to Johnny Behan until about 8:00 P.M.

Billy Breakenridge would remember what happened next:

> Behan told Deputy Sheriff Dave Neagle and me to get our shotguns and come back as soon as possible, as he had to arrest the Earps again. We had not gone a block on our way after our weapons when they came out of the hotel. Behan met them on the sidewalk as they were getting on their horses and tried to arrest them alone. . . . There were six of them, Wyatt Earp, Doc Holliday, Sherman McMasters, Johnson, who was a mysterious man called "The Unknown," Tipton, and Texas Jack. Behan was unarmed.
>
> They drew their guns on him, and told him they had seen him once too often and rode out of town as fast as they could go.

Both the anti-Earp *Nugget* and the pro-Earp *Epitaph* reported basically the same scenario, although the *Epitaph,* citing eyewitnesses, argued that the Earp party had not leveled its guns at the sheriff—or technically resisted arrest, since Behan himself failed to mention a warrant.

> Sheriff Behan was standing in the office of the Cosmopolitan hotel when Wyatt Earp and the others comprising the party came into the office from the rear entrance, each one having a rifle in his hands, in the ordinary manner of carrying a gun, and passed through the room to the street. As Wyatt advanced to the front and approached Sheriff Behan, the sheriff said to him, "Wyatt, I want to see you." Wyatt replied, "You can't see me; you have seen me once too often," or words to that effect. He passed out into the street and turned around and said, "I will see Paul," and then the party passed on down the street.

Wyatt Earp himself would write to his biographer Stuart Lake in 1928 that when Behan and deputies came to arrest him, "I just laughed at them and told them to just run away." Lake would heighten the odds in this encounter, having Wyatt confront Behan and Deputy Neagle as eight "heavily armed" deputies waited outside. He would also follow the lead of John

Clum's "It All Happened in Tombstone" in reporting the exchange between Wyatt and Behan to show off better the tough threat of Wyatt Earp, western hero. To Johnny's "Wyatt, I want to see you," Clum had him retorting, "Johnny, you may see me once too often," while in Lake's version he said, "Behan, if you're not careful, you'll see me once too often." Bat Masterson, writing an adulatory sketch in 1907, had Wyatt announcing, "You will see me once too often," then adding, "And remember, I'm going to get that hound you are protecting in jail [Pete Spencer, who had just turned himself in] when I come back, if I have to tear the jail down to do it."

Then Wyatt Earp rode out of Tombstone. The *Epitaph* added a seventh man, Charlie Smith, to his party, although Breakenridge would recall that Harelip Smith had been sent on ahead in a light wagon carrying baggage and equipment to a camp about eight miles north of Tombstone. Warren Earp had apparently disappeared from the picture, though he would reappear as a member of the roving band.

The morning after the Earp party's departure, Johnny Behan gathered a posse and rode out in pursuit. Parsons wrote, "Sheriff went out with a posse supposably [*sic*] to arrest the Earp party, but they will never do it. The cowboy element is backing him strongly." Indeed, this group excited quite a bit of controversy, for even Breakenridge acknowledged it was composed "mostly of rustlers and cowboys" and included John Ringo and Ike and Phin Clanton. Breakenridge would argue that Behan chose such clear adversaries of the Earps both in order to avoid Earp sympathizers and in order to capitalize on the enmity between the pursuers and the pursued; the cowboys, he reasoned, could be counted on to stay and fight if and when the Earp party resisted arrest.

By this time, Marietta Spencer's testimony at the coroner's inquest had resulted in the naming of five men wanted in the murder of Morgan Earp: Frank Stilwell, Pete Spencer, "a party by the name of Freis, and two Indian half breeds, one whose name is Charlie." Stilwell was already dead, and Spencer was in custody. The prisoner was placed in jail armed, in case the Earp party tried to take him. Indian Charlie would also enjoy the relative safety of jail, being brought in by "Deputy Bell" from Charleston on the twenty-third.

Meanwhile, as Behan's posse rode out to hunt them, Wyatt Earp and his men were at Pete Spencer's wood camp in the South Pass of the Dragoon Mountains killing a Mexican named Florentino Cruz. Cruz has been the object of much confusion over the years; Lake and others would identify him as Indian Charlie. But Cruz was either the unknown fifth man, erroneously referred to as an Indian, or an innocent woodchopper who happened to be in the wrong place at the wrong time.

Five men were at the camp on the morning of March 22: Cruz, teamster Theodore Judah, Pete Spencer's half brother Samuel Williams, Mexican laborer Simon Acosto, and another Mexican or "half-breed." In addition, two Mexican woodchoppers were camped about fifty yards away. Between 11:00 A.M. and 12:00 noon, Williams mounted his horse and left camp to look for some straying mules; Cruz soon followed on foot for the same purpose. Theodore Judah would tell a coroner's jury what happened next: "He [Cruz] had been gone but a few minutes, while I was lying in the shade waiting for them to come back, when I looked up and saw Wyatt Earp coming over the hill on horseback, followed by five men. They were Warren Earp, Sherman McMasters, Doc Holliday, Texas Jack [Vermillion] and a party whom I have heard was named Johnson."

These men stopped at the camp of the two Mexicans and questioned them as to where the road went, then began talking among themselves. Judah called out, asking if they had seen any mules, and Sherman McMasters replied that he had noticed some nearby. The whole group then rode up to Judah, with Wyatt asking where Pete Spencer and a "half-breed" named Hank were. Judah replied that he had left Spencer in Tombstone that morning and that the other man was not at the camp. Wyatt wanted to know how many *were* at the camp. "I told him exactly how many there were, and what they were doing, and mentioned that two of the men were out in the hills in search of some strayed animals. He asked me when Pete Spencer would be out in the camp again. He also asked me my name and wanted to know if I was not a friend of Pete

Spencer's and also of Frank Stilwell, to which question I answered that I was."

Judah's was either a very brave answer or a very dumb one, but the Earp party made no hostile moves toward him. Instead, they wheeled their horses and "passed out of my sight toward the main road leading to Tombstone." Judah grabbed the Mexican laborer Acosto, and they started up a hill in hopes of watching the Earp party's movements. But the two "had not gone twenty feet," Judah would report, before they heard shooting—nine to eleven shots in rapid succession, then a final one about eight seconds later.

Judah would testify that he did not see the actual killing; by the time he spotted Wyatt and confederates across the road on top of another hill, all he observed was that "two or three got off of their horses and were there two or three minutes" before coming down the hill "very leisurely."

Judah's companion, Acosto, however, claimed that as the shooting commenced, he ran up the hill and saw the Earp party on horseback chasing and firing at Cruz. "When I saw Florentino he was running away," Acosto would testify. "The pursuing party spread out, some on each side, and others immediately following." Acosto disagreed with Judah on the number of men in the Earp group, insisting that there were eight rather than six.

Epimania Vegas, cutting wood on top of a nearby hill, agreed with Acosto on the number and also provided an eyewitness account of the shooting: "There were eight men doing the firing. I saw the man that was shot running and jumping from side to side. I saw him fall. They were about from 1,000 to 2,000 yards from me. After doing the shooting they passed close to me on the main road. They saw me, but did not speak to me."

Cruz was found lying "face downwards, with his right arm resting under his head, and his coat . . . placed over his legs." This gave rise to the anti-Earp story that Cruz had been peacefully taking a siesta when Wyatt and friends rode up and began pumping bullets into him. Equally at odds with the testimonies, however, is the story as propagated by Lake that Cruz gave an extensive confession to the party, then was forced into a one-on-one shoot-out by Wyatt, who handicapped himself by counting to three and letting Cruz draw first.

George Goodfellow examined the body and found evidence of four hits—the first shot penetrating the right temple and entering the brain, the second producing "a slight flesh wound in the right shoulder," the third slamming into Cruz's right side and exiting "to the right of the spine," and the fourth striking the left thigh and exiting "about seven or eight inches above the point of entry." Both the first and third wounds he judged "sufficient to cause death." The fourth he conjectured had been received after Cruz died, as there was an "absence of blood around the wound."

Faced with the wood camp workers' testimonies and Goodfellow's report, the coroner's jury would render the verdict that Cruz had come to his death "from the effects of gunshot wounds, inflicted by Wyatt Earp, Warren Earp, J. H. Holliday, Sherman McMasters, Texas Jack, Johnson, and two men whose names are unknown to the jury."

Wyatt Earp still had his backers. On hearing of the shooting on March 23, Parsons wrote in his journal, "More killing by Earp party. Hope they'll keep it up. Paul is here—but will not take a hand. . . . If the truth were known he would be glad to see the Earp party get away with all of these murderous outfits."

Indeed, Pima County Republican Sheriff Paul was disturbed by Johnny Behan's use of cowboys and rustlers to try to apprehend the Earps. This distaste for Behan's methods—and probably for Behan himself—has been interpreted then and now as showing that Bob Paul, respected even by southern Democrats for his honesty and bravery, was 100 percent behind Wyatt and friends. However, a interview with Paul appearing in the *Rocky Mountain News* two months later would reveal that Paul understood the complexities of the situation and held—or had come to—a decidedly dark view of the Earps' activities, classing them with those of the cowboys. He would be asked if Doc Holliday was a member of the Earp "gang." He answered: "He was, and in fact was one of the leaders. The so-called Earp gang, or faction if you please, was composed entirely of gamblers who preyed upon the cowboys, and at the same time in order to keep up a show of having a legitimate calling, was organized into a sort of vigilance committee, and some of them, including Holliday, had United States Marshal's commissions."

Asked if Holliday could be considered a desperate man, Paul would expose some of his own ambivalences born of the knowledge that it took tough men to administer any type of law on the frontier: "Not by any means. He was always decently peaceable, though his powers when engaged in following his ostensible calling, futhering the ends of justice, made him a terror to the criminal class of Arizona."

Two members of the Earp crowd, Charlie Smith and Dan Tipton, attempted to reenter Tombstone on the twenty-third. These two may have been the extra members of the Earp party whom Acosto and Vegas reported seeing at the wood camp, or they may simply have maintained camp for Wyatt and the others. At any rate, when the two appeared, Behan arrested them on charges stemming from the Earp party's defiant leave-taking on the evening of the twenty-first. Tipton and Smith, he claimed, had at that time both resisted arrest and obstructed by threats, intimidation, firearms, and force the seizure of those members of the Earp party wanted for Stilwell's murder. "Much excitement," reported Parsons. "False charges."

Meanwhile, the two members of the Earp clan remaining in Tombstone—Jim's wife, Bessie, and the unfortunate Mattie—were preparing to leave. Both the *Nugget* and the *Epitaph* on the twenty-fourth would report the departure of the two remaining wives, with the *Epitaph* providing a courteous send-off: "Mrs. James Earp and Mrs. Wyatt Earp left today for Colton, California, the residence of their husbands' parents. These ladies have the sympathy of all who know them, and for that matter, the entire community. Their trials for the last six months have been of the most severe nature." Mattie's hardest trial had come in the form of Josie Marcus, who probably left Tombstone about the same time Mattie did. Josie would return home to San Francisco, and both the common-law wife and the mistress would wait for Wyatt in California.

The object of their affections, having ranged eastward to Spencer's wood camp, was now roaming to the west of Tombstone in the vicinity of the Whetstone Mountains across the

San Pedro and just north of the Babocomari. On the afternoon of the twenty-fourth, he and his men rode toward a
spring, although sources differ as to which spring it was. Some
place the Earp party at Iron Springs, a popular watering hole
for desert wayfarers between the Whetstones and the Mustang
Mountains farther west; others locate them at Mescal Spring
on the eastern side of the Whetstones. At one of these two
sites, they encountered a band of cowboys, and a battle of
sorts took place. The particulars of that battle, and the results,
were hotly disputed in the Tombstone papers at the time and
in the accounts of old-timers later on.

The first rumors filtering into Tombstone had four of the
Earp party killed in the confrontation, but such accounts were
quickly discredited. Another report, that the cowboys were
members of Behan's posse, was immediately denied by Behan
himself. A third report, that Curly Bill Brocius was the lone
fatality, would prove harder to dismiss. The *Epitaph* published
an account moving the whole incident to a site south of Tombstone in an apparent attempt to throw the Behan posse off.

The paper claimed that an informant had witnessed near
a spring eight miles south of town "one of the most desperate
fights between the six men of the Earp party and nine fierce
cowboys, led by the daring and notorious Curly Bill, that ever
took place between opposing forces on Arizona soil." According to this heavily penned narrative, the Earp party had dismounted at Burleigh Spring when the cowboys suddenly arose
nearby and unleashed a fusillade. Miraculously, none of the
six intended victims was hit, but "like a thunderbolt shot from
the hand of Jove," the members of the Earp band "charged
upon their assailants like the light brigade at Balaklova," getting within "easy reach," returning the fire, and felling one of
the attackers. The other assailants, having only fatally wounded
an opponent's horse, rode toward Charleston "as if the King of
Terrors was at their heels in hot pursuit."

Wyatt Earp and his coterie then "remained at the spring
for some time refreshing themselves and their animals" before
heading south toward Sonora. When the Earps left, the informant claimed to have ridden to the scene of the battle and
found the dead cowboy, "who, from the description given was
none other than Curly Bill." The *Epitaph* concluded, "Since

the above information was obtained it has been learned that during the night the friends of Curly Bill went out with a wagon and took the body back to Charleston where the whole affair has been kept a profound secret so far as the general public is concerned."

Wyatt's own account, given to a reporter in 1896, agreed in some particulars with the *Epitaph* narrative and differed in others. Wyatt related that he and his friends planned to camp at the spring, but as they arrived, "nine cowboys sprang up from the bank where the spring was and began firing at us." Wyatt dismounted to return the fire, expecting his friends to follow suit, "but they retreated." Curly Bill stood "trying to pump some lead into me with a Winchester," but "I fired both barrels of my gun into him, blowing him all to pieces." Wyatt's narrative of what happened next provides a surprisingly comic picture of the legendary "lion of Tombstone":

> . . . I retreated, keeping behind my horse. He was a high-strung beast, and the firing frightened him so that whenever I tried to get my Winchester from the saddle he would rear up and keep it out of my reach. When I had backed out about a hundred yards I started to mount. Now, it was a hot day, and I had loosened my cartridge belt two or three holes. When I tried to get astride I found that it had fallen down over my thighs, keeping my legs together. While I was perched up thus, trying to pull my belt higher with one hand, the horn of the saddle was shot off. However, I got away all right, and just then my men rallied. But I did not care to go back at the rustlers, and we sought out another water hole for camp. The skirt of my overcoat was shot to pieces on both sides, but not a bullet had touched me.

The *Daily Nugget* reported only four cowboys at the spring when the confrontation took place, firing erupting from both parties almost simultaneously, and the Earp party retreating and leaving the cowboys in possession of the water hole. This narrative provided additional details based upon an interview the paper claimed to have had with an informant from Tombstone whom the Earp party had planned to meet at the spring.

The informant had arrived at the spring late and found himself "confronted by three cowboys with drawn weapons, who ordered him to dismount, and demanded the cause of his presence there." He told them he was looking for a stray horse, and the cowboys immediately "abandoned their hostile attitude and invited the stranger to camp there and prepare his dinner." He did so. The cowboys soon departed, and so did the informant, who then ran into Wyatt Earp only a short distance away and learned the details of the encounter:

> One shot from the cowboys passed through the clothing of McMasters, just grazing his side; another killed Texas Jack's horse; a third knocked the pommel off Wyatt Earp's saddle; while another cut the straps of the field-glass carried by McMasters. The volley fired by the Earp party apparently did not take effect. The latter then started to retreat, Texas Jack jumping up behind one of the party.

At this point, Wyatt had reportedly explained, a cowboy he believed to be Curly Bill jumped from behind a rock, and Wyatt "turned in his saddle and fired," felling Brocius. The Earp party then retreated behind a nearby hill and watched as a wagon was brought to the spring and the body was loaded upon it. They had also watched, unable to call out, as the *Nugget* informant approached the three remaining cowboys.

So far, so good. A fight had occurred, and one participant had apparently been killed. Then the *Epitaph* came out with another scenario along with an update on its earlier one, under the heading TWO VERSIONS OF THE FIGHT: YOU PAYS YOUR MONEY AND YOU TAKES YOUR CHOICE. In this alternate version, two men out hunting stray mules stumbled across four cowboys, who first drew their guns, then invited the newcomers to their campfire.

> [The cowboys] said that they were camped at the spring, when they saw the Earp party ride down, and not knowing how they stood with them they thought that they would give them a shot just for luck, so they blazed away and shot off the pommel of Wyatt Earp's saddle and killed the horse that Texas Jack was riding. They said that not one of

the Earp party charged upon them but Wyatt, the balance all running away. Wyatt dismounted and fired his gun at them but without effect. Texas Jack is said to have jumped up behind one of the other boys a la Mexicans, and off they went as rapidly as they could.

Billy Breakenridge published much the same account in *Helldorado*, although he had Wyatt firing the first shot. According to Breakenridge, cowboy Alex Arnold and two others were camped at the spring, and that day had been joined by Pink Truly, who brought Arnold supplies. Arnold and Truly were accused of a Charleston store robbery; Arnold was standing trial, but Truly was hiding out. When they saw the Earp party approach, the four quickly "took refuge behind an embankment, and all but Wyatt of the Earp party turned and rode away. Wyatt, however, rode up rather close to them and dismounted, and with the bridle rein over his arm stepped in front of his horse, raised his rifle and fired at them." The cowboys returned the fire, shooting the horn from Wyatt's saddle and killing Texas Jack's horse as the group made its retreat. Curly Bill was not present, having departed for Mexico two months earlier. This account, Breakenridge asserted, was provided by Truly and Arnold themselves. The two also insisted that Wyatt's white shirt had made a fine target, that he had staggered as if hit, and that he apparently was wearing a bulletproof vest.

By contrast, Earp supporter Fred Dodge would later claim that one of the cowboys in the fight, Johnny Barnes, had told him that Curly indeed breathed his last at the spring that day, while Barnes himself was injured seriously enough to die of his wounds eventually. In this version, the cowboys "opened up on the Earp party just as Wyatt Earp swung off his horse to the ground and they thought they had hit Wyatt but it was the horn of his saddle that was struck." Then "Wyatt throwed down on Curly Bill right across his horse and killed him," with Curly's companions burying the cowboy at the Patterson ranch on the Babocomari.

More important than the actual details of the fight, however, were the roles of the participants. The Earp party maintained that it was acting as a duly constituted posse trying to serve warrants on stage-robbing cowboys and killing one such notorious miscreant in the process. Within two months of the incident, Doc Holliday would assert to a newspaper reporter that eight rustlers, "all outlaws, for each of whom a big reward has been offered," had attacked the Earp party, with Wyatt killing Curly Bill. Despite the fact that no stage robbery charge against Curly Bill has ever been uncovered, Wyatt, too, would claim in his 1896 interview that Bill was "a stage robber whom I had been after for eight months, and for whom I had a warrant in my pocket." The Earp party's insistence that they were acting as the law at this point met with increasing incredulity among many citizens of southeastern Arizona.

Bob Paul remained in Tombstone waiting for news of the Earp party's whereabouts. "He has assurances from friends of the Earps that the desired information will be imparted to him within a day or two," the *Daily Nugget* explained on March 25. Meanwhile, Dan Tipton and Charlie Smith had their case heard in a Tombstone court, with former Earp lawyer William Herring arguing for dismissal of the charges of resisting and obstructing an officer. Behan, he successfully contended, had needed a warrant in hand, not a telegraphed message, for the charge to be binding.

Smith apparently left that evening to rejoin Wyatt and friends, while Tipton stayed temporarily in Tombstone. The whole town, like it or not, was caught up in the drama between Johnny Behan and Wyatt Earp. Shots rang out repeatedly on the night of the twenty-fifth, leading to speculation that the Earps were signaling their backers in town. Parsons was not privy to the secret code, but he certainly remained a backer, applauding the apparent killing of Curly Bill and complaining about Behan and the Democratic county ring: "Sheriff Behan has turned all of the cowboys loose against the Earps and with this lawless element is trying to do his worst. . . . Feeling is growing here against the ring. Sheriff etc and it would not surprise me to know of a necktie party some fine morning. Things seem to be coming to this pass."

That very night, trouble came from another direction. M. R. Peel, civil engineer of the Tombstone Mill and Mining operation, was shot to death, for no discernible motive, in his Charleston office. He was "the last one I would think to meet such a tragic death," Parsons reported. According to one newspaper account, two masked men with Winchester rifles had simply walked in on Peel, the mill superintendent, and a third man and fired at Peel and the superintendent, piercing the former through the heart. Parsons speculated that the incident could be a cowboy response to the Tombstone Mill and Mining Company's stance against lawlessness, while Billy Breakenridge would consider the killing of the inoffensive, well-liked Peel an accident, a case of itchy trigger fingers during a botched robbery attempt.

This was a matter for the county sheriff, but Johnny Behan was still out chasing Wyatt Earp. Meanwhile, the Tucson *Daily Star* published thumbnail sketches of the major players in the Earp-cowboy feud. The deceased Billy Clanton and brothers Ike and Phin were characterized as "fine specimens of the cattle man." James Earp was a professional saloon man, "the most agreeable one of the family," popular and unlikely to be a target for assassination. The departed Morgan Earp was called the handsomest and most hotheaded of the brothers, while poor Virgil Earp, who had carried the most responsibility and nearly gotten shot to pieces, was described as having "a sinister expression" and being "a bold, daring man, not to be trifled with."

The *Star* depicted Wyatt as "the brain of the outfit," his judgment "generally law with the rest" and his appearance more refined. Doc Holliday was "a consumptive-looking man," one "generally known as a desperado of the first order."

Wyatt's and Doc's whereabouts remained unknown, with rumors of their activities and movements buzzing through Tombstone's dusty streets. Bob Paul returned to Tucson, complaining about Behan's judgment in selecting a posse and expressing confidence that "the Earps will come to Tucson and surrender to the authorities." Johnny Behan came into town with his controversial posse; then they all rode out again. And on Monday, March 27, Governor Tritle arrived in Tombstone to investigate the "sad state of affairs here."

As a prominent mining man in partnership with William Murray, who had offered Virgil Earp a vigilante force of twenty-five on the day of the gunfight, Tritle was naturally aligned with Tombstone's law-and-order forces and stayed during his visit with Citizens Safety Committee member Milton B. Clapp. The new chief executive quickly reached the conclusion that a force of rangers was needed to quell lawless activities in southeastern Arizona and to deal with hostile Indian activities. Even if the Army could be used as a posse comitatus, he reasoned, it would not be able to respond quickly enough to crises. Thus, Tritle wrote to President Arthur from Tombstone asking for an appropriation of $150,000 for his ranger plan.

On the same day that Tritle arrived, Parsons wrote in his journal, "Report that the Earps have left the country was current today and seems to gain general credence. Supposed they left by way of Willcox." The next day, the *Daily Nugget* carried a fuller report, with a sarcastic coda:

> There are fresh rumors almost every hour of the day. . . . D. G. Tipton, well known as one of their friends, was called out of bed at about 4 o'clock and left on the 5 o'clock stage, and arrived at Willcox on the morning train. He immediately obtained a horse and started at a rapid rate to overtake the party, evidently knowing their destination. Possibly they may be going to deliver themselves up to Sheriff Paul—by way of New York, Colorado, or Montana.

Deputy Breakenridge had not gone with Behan in pursuit of the Earps. The sheriff had first wanted him to go, then decided that he should stay in the office and that John Ringo should borrow Breakenridge's rifle and horse. Behan then reversed himself again, calling on the deputy to accompany the posse, but Breakenridge balked on being told he would have to obtain another horse and rifle rather than get his own back from Ringo.

Thus, he was the official who set out to get the two men suspected in the Peel killing, Billy "the Kid" Grounds and Zwing Hunt, when news came that they were at the Chandler milk ranch. Chandler himself was in Tombstone and had received word that the two were waiting at the ranch for seventy-five dollars which they claimed he owed them. When Chandler received the message, he informed the sheriff's office.

Former Texas cowhand Hunt and his companion Grounds had a warrant outstanding for them in a cattle-rustling case. Breakenridge took the warrant, a jail guard named Allen, and two men he identified simply as miners, Jack Young and John Gillespie, and set out for the ranch. When they reached the site shortly before daybreak, the plan was to station Young and Gillespie at the back of the adobe ranch dwelling and Allen and Breakenridge at the front, wait for the wanted men to emerge to look for their horses, and demand their surrender. According to Breakenridge, however, Gillespie, who was hoping to capture the sheriff's job at the next election, made a bold move that cost him his life. As Breakenridge and Allen moved close to the house from the front, still under the cover of darkness, they heard Gillespie knock at the back door and announce himself as the law. The two rustlers opened the door and shot him dead.

A teamster named Bull Lewis, also staying at the ranch, immediately came running out yelling, "Don't shoot, I am innocent." He and Breakenridge were the only ones present who would escape injury. A shot from inside the house hit jail guard Allen in the neck and briefly knocked him out. Breakenridge dragged him behind a dry creek bank, then jumped behind a tree as another bullet came whizzing out, striking the tree. "As the person who fired it stepped to the door to fire the second shot, I fired one barrel of my shotgun, loaded with buckshot, into the opening. Just as I fired I remembered an old adage always to aim low in the dark, and I pulled down thinking I would hit him in the stomach. But I hit him in the head and heard him strike the floor."

Breakenridge had fatally wounded Billy Grounds. Meanwhile, Allen came to, and Zwing Hunt came wandering around the side of the house, calling for Grounds. Both Allen and Breakenridge fired at Hunt and were satisfied he was hit. Breakenridge then rushed to help miner Young, who had also been hit in the melee.

Of the two rustlers, Billy Grounds wasn't going anywhere; he lay in the doorway of the ranch house with a face full of buckshot. Hunt, however, disappeared. Breakenridge tracked him to the nearby creek, where he found him hiding in the bear grass, wounded in the chest. Meanwhile, jailer Allen had sent the teamster to Tombstone for an ambulance and a doctor. When the doctor and a number of Tombstone's curious and concerned arrived, they found Gillespie dead, Hunt and Grounds seriously wounded, and Young and Allen nursing less serious wounds. Breakenridge and Allen had brought Hunt into the house to try to make him comfortable; when they carried him out to the ambulance through the narrow door, they inadvertently "squeezed his shoulders together and the blood spurted from his lung," an accidental treatment that Breakenridge felt probably saved Hunt's life.

George Parsons wrote on the thirtieth, "Hats in office today with bullet holes through them" and a large buckshot from Breakenridge's gun "lodged in the 'kids' silk handkerchief not going through it." (It was from George Goodfellow's examination of Grounds that the doctor's paper on the impenetrability of silk to bullets arose.) Grounds died on the thirtieth, and Goodfellow decided to dissect the head but couldn't get the weak-stomached Breakenridge to hold the light for him.

The Chandler Ranch shoot-out only highlighted the need for new measures to control the level of lawlessness in southeastern Arizona, and Tritle was not the only one advocating a ranger force. In the wake of this latest violence, *Arizona Daily Star* editor L. C. Hughes came out strongly in favor of such a band:

> The officials of Cochise County with all the available strength which they can muster seem to avail nothing in putting down the blood thirsty class infesting that county. Ex-city and United States officials [the Earps] have taken to the hills as so many Apaches. A lot of loose, marauding thieves are scouring the country killing good, industrious citizens for plunder. The officials are out in every direction, but nothing is accomplished.

Hughes cited "the outlawry of the Earps," the deaths of Peel and others, and the Chandler Ranch fiasco as "causing the people to understand the frightful condition of affairs" in southeastern Arizona.

Tombstone was feeling as jittery as a miner sitting on a

load of black powder. "Calky times very," wrote Parsons, citing the number of recent murders. "A hanging bee anticipated tonight—but not carried out. Cow-boy raid on town expected tonight."

Some Tombstonians continued to reject the idea of a cowboy threat, while others remained convinced it was quite real. Men such as Parsons had looked to the three "fighting Earps" as an answer to this threat. But Morgan was dead, Virgil was crippled and removed to California, and Wyatt was—well, Wyatt was kicking the dust of Tombstone from his heels and headed for a more favorable clime about the time the cowboy troubles settled down for good, leaving indefinitely open to debate whether he had been part of the problem or part of the solution.

CHAPTER 16
Men on the Run

After the shoot-out at the springs, Wyatt Earp and party—Warren Earp, Doc Holliday, Sherman McMasters, Texas Jack Vermillion, and Turkey Creek Jack Johnson—had returned to the Tombstone vicinity, camping about six miles north of town and picking up confederate Charlie Smith, newly cleared of the resisting arrest charges in Tombstone.

Smith was most likely the "ONE OF THEM" whose account of the Earp party's movements appeared in the *Epitaph* on April 5. The writer explained that he had joined his companions on Saturday evening, March 25. The next day the group had traveled with three prospectors to a railroad stop called Summit Station, in Dragoon Pass, east of Benson and northeast of Tombstone. Here "we had dinner and awaited the arrival of the passenger train from the west, expecting a friendly messenger." Afterward on that same day, Sunday, March 26, the group traveled to "Henderson's ranch."*

Cochise County Deputy Sheriff Frank Hereford was visiting this ranch and, when the Earp party was spotted approaching, hid in the granary at the request of the ranch

---

*Billy Breakenridge would identify the location as "the McKittrick ranch."

owner, who had an ill wife and did not want any trouble. Billy Breakenridge would claim that Hereford, peering from the granary, observed "a bullet hole through each side of the front" of Wyatt's coat and heard one of the other men tell its wearer, "The steel saved you this time."

It certainly would have been prudent for Wyatt to wear a bulletproof vest, and Kate Elder in her memoirs would mention his donning a "steel shirt" only a short time after the Iron Springs/Mescal Spring incident. But Wyatt himself would hotly deny the idea. He would later write to biographer Lake, "I never wore a steel vest, and never had such a thing in my possession, another one of his [Breakenridge's] damn lies." In another instance, Wyatt would also ridicule the idea by pointing out how hot the desert got and how uncomfortable such protection would be.

The Earp party dined at the ranch, then camped "on good grass one mile north"; they had agreed to eat and move on for the same reason the deputy agreed to hide. "ONE OF THEM" would later relate that the group learned of Hereford's presence during their stay at the ranch: "Here we were informed that a gentlemanly deputy sheriff of Cochise County, Mr. Frank Hereford (for whom we have the greatest respect as a gentleman and an officer) was at the ranch at the time of our arrival and departure, and have since learned the reason for not presenting himself was fears for his safety, which we assure him were groundless."

Meanwhile, Johnny Behan's posse, including *Nugget* editor and Undersheriff Harry Woods, was in Tombstone, readying for a second attempt to bring Wyatt and most of his companions in on the Stilwell murder charge. They rode out early on the morning of Monday, March 27, and picked up the Earp party's trail to Summit Station. Behan and confederates were afraid the men they hunted had boarded the train, but they found the party's tracks crossing the rail and proceeding northward, toward Henry Clay Hooker's Sierra Bonita ranch. By some accounts, Behan also received a wire from Deputy Hereford identifying Hooker's as the Earp party's next destination.

Wyatt Earp and his men reached Hooker's on Monday afternoon and found a ready welcome. The rancher, whose northern Sulphur Spring Valley location lay uncomfortably close to the cowboy haunts in the San Simon Valley, remained one of the law-and-order faction's most powerful allies outside Tombstone. He had suffered from the depredations of cowboys and Indians alike and favored a tough approach toward rustlers.

Hooker was pretty tough himself. He certainly had staying power. A New Hampshire native whose forebears included a line of prominent New England ministers, Hooker had started his own western adventure in 1853 with a California store, then had driven cattle to the Nevada mining camps. Wiped out by fire in 1866, he had responded by purchasing 150 turkeys at $1.50 each and herding them overland to Carson City, Nevada, where he sold them at $5 a head. In 1866, he had arrived in Arizona Territory to provide beef to the scattered forts and reservations. Ranching was still virtually impossible because of the frontier isolation and frequent Indian raids; cattle to fill contracts had to be brought in from California, Texas, and Mexico. Gradually, however, Hooker carved out an impressive ranching operation in the Sulphur Spring Valley, experimenting successfully with a variety of livestock. He employed many workers and was known for his hospitality to travelers. He also was a person with decided views, one who had "no use whatever for scrubs of either the human or brute kind."

Now Hooker provided the Earp party with food and possibly with horses. An *Epitaph* correspondent at the ranch reported that Wyatt and friends arrived asking for both, and the *Nugget* noted that provisions and fresh horses had been provided. "ONE OF THEM," however, would argue in the *Epitaph* of April 5 that Hooker had not provided them with fresh mounts, that "we are riding the same horses we left Tombstone on, with the exception of Texas Jack's horse, which was killed in the fight with Curly Bill and posse [*sic*], which we replaced by hiring a horse on the San Pedro river."

A rumor also circulated at the time that Hooker, head of the Cattlemen's Association, paid a thousand-dollar reward to Wyatt Earp for the killing of Curly Bill. Over the years this story became garbled into pro- and anti-Earp versions; Lake would have Wyatt valiantly turning down such "blood-money," while James Hancock would insist that Wyatt and entourage, in hopes of getting the reward, had brought with them a sack containing a head covered with black, curly hair. In Hancock's version, presented with the head, Hooker simply "gave them the laugh and sent them on their way."

However, again, "ONE OF THEM" provided a denial at the time: "No reward has been asked for or tendered." Wyatt and friends did not stay at Hooker's long. They left about 7:00 P.M. without saying where they were going.

Behan's posse did not reach Hooker's until about 7:00 A.M. the next day, Tuesday, March 28. The sheriff determined that Dan Tipton had joined the Earp party here, but overall, this stop provided little information and much unpleasantness. When Hooker saw John Ringo and other known rustlers riding in as part of the posse, he was not inclined to be very hospitable.

The *Nugget* and the *Epitaph* naturally would present different versions of the Behan posse's visit to the ranch. The *Nugget* gave a scenario in which the duly appointed officers of the law were hampered by an irascible, fugitive-aiding rancher:

> The proprietor of the ranch utterly refused to impart any information concerning the direction taken by his whilom guests of the day before; said he didn't know and wouldn't tell if he did know, and concluding [sic] by saying, "Damn the officers and damn the law." He furnished the posse with food for themselves and animals, for which he received liberal compensation—but positively refused to supply them with fresh horses.

On the other hand, the *Epitaph* published a fuller description of the visit, one that highlighted the disreputableness of the Behan group. In this account, provided by an anonymous correspondent at the Sierra Bonita ranch, Hooker responded to their requests for information on the Earp party's whereabouts as he had in the *Nugget*'s narrative—by stating that he did not know and would not tell if he did know.

"You must be upholding murderers and outlaws, then," announced Behan.

"No, sir, I am not; I know the Earps and know you; and I know they have always treated me like gentlemen, damn such laws, and damn you, and damn your posse; they are a set of horsethieves and outlaws."

At this, one of the posse members cried out, "Damn the son of a b----, he knows where they are, and let us make him tell."

Hooker's hostler responded by grabbing a Winchester and aiming it at the speaker. "You can't come here into a gentleman's yard and call him a son of a b----! Now you skin it back! Skin it back! If you are looking for a fight, and come here to talk that way you can get it before you find the Earps; you can get it right here."

At this point, Hooker turned to Behan and repeated his opinion: "These are a pretty set of fellows you have got with you; a set of horse thieves and cut-throats." Both Behan and Undersheriff Woods responded by disclaiming the other posse members as associates; "they are only here on this occasion with us."

"Well, if they are not your associates," Hooker replied, "I will set an extra table for you and set them by themselves."

He did so. After breakfast, Behan reportedly approached the hostler and from his own shirt pulled a diamond stud, presumably one of those presented to him by his deputies a few months earlier. The sheriff then handed it to the man, telling him it cost a hundred dollars and instructing him not to say "anything about what occurred here." Behan also announced to Hooker, "If I can catch the Earp party it will help me at the next election."

Whatever the particulars of this stop at the Hooker ranch, it was certainly frustrating to all concerned. Shortly after breakfast, the Behan posse rode out—Behan and Woods heading for Fort Grant to procure Indian scouts, the rest of the group scouting around the mountains north and west of the ranch.

The posse came very close to its quarry, according to the ubiquitous "ONE OF THEM," who reported the Earp party camping with a freighter in the vicinity of Eureka Springs, a few miles northwest of Fort Grant, on the morning of the twenty-eighth. "Our stay was long enough to notice the movements of Sheriff Behan and his posse of honest ranchers," the Earp confederate noted sarcastically. In fact, "had they possessed the trailing abilities of the average Arizona ranchman, we might have had trouble, which we are not seeking. Neither are we avoiding these honest ranchers as we thoroughly understand their designs."

One might well ask what the Earp party's own designs were at this point. Wyatt Earp's adherents at the time depicted him as a fugitive only because of an unjust legal machinery, a man earnestly desiring to do the right (i.e., lawful) thing, but forced to hide out and assess his chances of receiving any kind of justice. His detractors saw him as a troublemaker whose machinations had caught up with him, forcing him to show his true colors by eluding the legal process. The first group continued to believe he would turn himself in to the proper authorities; the second group either hoped he was gone—and good riddance—or wanted him prosecuted.

Behan kept on trying to serve the Stilwell warrants. He met with no luck at Fort Grant. The *Nugget* reported that the commander there received the sheriff and undersheriff "with great cordiality" but told them the Apache scouts had only recently been discharged. The *Epitaph* countered with another version; when Behan told the commander that Hooker had refused to help, the commander replied, "Well, if he did you can't get any scouts here." Behan and Woods gathered up their posse and camped on the night of the twenty-eighth at Eureka Springs, near the spot where the Earp party had been only that morning. Yet the sheriff quickly decided "that the fugitives had not effected their escape in that direction." The posse returned to Hooker's ranch.

Now Hooker told them that "the Earp party was much the better armed" anyway, and would win in a fight. He also may have informed them this time around where to find Wyatt and friends. In 1896, Wyatt would recall, "Sheriff Behan trailed us with a big posse composed of rustlers, but it was only a bluff, for when I left word for him where he could find us and waited for him to come, he failed to appear." Stories have Wyatt waiting variously on "Reilly hill" and "Hooker's Butte," with Behan either purposely avoiding an encounter or studying the matter from the bottom of the butte and wisely deciding against an assault.

The posse scouted the mountains to the south of Hooker's, then returned to Tombstone empty-handed on Thursday afternoon, March 30. Nobody knew whether or when the Earp party would resurface, and the two newspapers, at least, were not about to give the events of the last two weeks a rest. On March 31, the *Nugget* published its account of the Behan posse's activities and a criticism of rancher Hooker.

> Under-Sheriff Woods speaks in the highest terms of the treatment of the posse by the citizens of Cochise and Graham counties, with the single exception [of] . . . Mr. H. C. Hooker, of the Sierra Bonita ranch, a man whom, from [the] large property interests he has in the county, would naturally be supposed to be in favor of upholding the constituted authorities and the preservation of law and order.

This statement drew a rebuttal on April 2 from an anonymous "JUSTICE," who argued that Hooker had "suffered, probably, beyond anyone else, from the raids of hostile Indians and marauding cowboys" and had paid protection money only to be "annoyed, persecuted, and prosecuted." Further, "JUSTICE" pointed out, no one had a greater stake in the fortunes of Graham County than did Hooker, "and therefore no one there has a greater desire for the rigid enforcement of law and order and the prompt punishment of criminals." The rancher's damning words to the county officers, then, were "but the terse way of strongly putting in language a feeling and sentiment which is prevalent in the minds of many citizens and large taxpayers."

The controversy over Hooker's actions, however, was eclipsed by the debate over whether Curly Bill Brocius was really dead. Despite his star status as an outlaw, Curly Bill had remained a rather mysterious boogeyman to many residents of Tombstone ever since the killing of Marshal Fred White a year and a half earlier. His demise had even been rumored two months before Wyatt Earp claimed to have blown him in half at the mountain spring, for the February 21, 1882, *Daily*

Nugget had noted, "The reported death of 'Curly Bill' is, we are informed by reliable parties, without foundation."

Now the *Nugget* offered a thousand dollars to anyone who could prove Curly Bill dead, and the *Epitaph* responded on April 3 with a promise of two thousand dollars to any deserving charity if Curly would present himself. Neither reward was ever claimed, and there were rumors of Curly Bill sightings for years. If Wyatt Earp indeed killed the rustler leader, it is clear that many contemporaries didn't want to give him the satisfaction by acknowledging it. Old-timer James Hancock would write that Curly Bill departed Arizona for Mexico soon after the Galeyville shooting incident of May 1881, and rancher Melvin Jones had him leaving the territory that summer as well. But neither account fits with Parsons's journal notations showing the cowboy at the McLaury ranch in October.

Billy Breakenridge would advance two accounts, one given him by "a reliable merchant and rancher living at Safford," the other by "a Tombstone resident." In the first, Bill appeared at the rancher's home just two weeks after his supposed death at the spring and announced "that he was leaving the country and going to Wyoming where he was going to get work and try to lead a decent life, as he was tired of being on the dodge all the time." In the second, the Tombstonian related that Bill paid a brief visit to the town ten years after all the excitement with the Earps.

Wyatt Earp apparently dissected somebody with a shotgun at Iron Springs or Mescal Spring. It seems reasonable to assume the victim was the genuine Curly Bill Brocius, but if not, another cowboy served the purpose just as well. For Curly Bill was, to many Arizona townspeople, less a man than a symbol of an alien, dissolute, and threatening way of life. In this view, the Curly Bills impeded civilization's march as much as did the Indians.

The crux of the matter was not simply lawlessness. The *Daily Nugget* would try to tarnish Earp support in this regard by alleging on April 7 that Turkey Creek Jack Johnson, still riding with Wyatt, was actually a desperado with a twenty-five-hundred-dollar price on his head. But whether he was or not didn't really matter very much. No, the key factor was whether one aligned oneself with the more respectable business interests in town, with the proponents of civilization and progress. The Earps and, by extension, their friends had done so. Now, Tombstone realized, that alliance was ended. Wyatt Earp and friends were heading for New Mexico, and the mining investors and bank clerks who had backed them would have to deal with lawlessness and with political and economic differences without the buffer provided by the "fighting Earps."

So some mourned the news that Wyatt Earp really appeared to be gone, and others breathed sighs of relief, either loudly or quietly. As noted earlier, John Pleasant Gray would contend that "many of the better citizens" of Tombstone had tired of the Earp brand of law enforcement and were trying to figure how to "put them out" anyway. In his view, "The Earps ruled as they saw fit for quite a while and things happened in the name of the law which were very injurious to the welfare and good name of Tombstone. All this ended only with the exit of the Earps when they finally knew the game was up."

The Earp band, eight men strong, pushed northeastward toward Silver City, New Mexico, the Grant County boomtown on the edge of the Gila wilderness. The most direct route was through the San Simon Valley and over mountains to the territorial line, then across a long, unbroken stretch of desert. On Saturday evening, April 8, the men had arrived, "well mounted and armed to the teeth," in the New Mexico town and were making arrangements to get to the Atchison, Topeka, and Santa Fe rail line vertically bisecting the state to the east.

They maintained a low profile during their brief stay in Silver City, spending the night in a private home and giving aliases to the suspicious proprietor of the Elephant Corral, where they stabled their horses. He became even more suspicious on the morning of the ninth, when they offered him six of their steeds for a bargain price. The corral proprietor refused, but a man eager to open a livery stable came up with the money. The two horses that remained unsold were simply left in another man's care, and the entourage boarded the stage to Fort Cummings with many Silver City residents unaware of their overnight guests and the notoriety attached to them.

For by now, the Tombstone troubles and the Earps' part in them were standard fodder for western journals. On April 11, the San Francisco *Daily Exchange* published a tongue-in-cheek account.

> It was rumored that the Earp brothers would arrive in Oakland, and the Light Cavalry was immediately put under arms. That gallant and well-trained body resolved that if the two Earps came to Oakland and showed the least disposition to attack them, every man would bite the dust before those redoubtable bandits were allowed the run the town.
>
> Fortunately, the men who were mistaken for the Earps proved to be the Earl brothers, on their way to this city. The joyful news spread like wildfire. . . . Everything is quiet in Oakland now.

As the press spread the dubious fame of the "fighting Earps" and Doc Holliday, Wyatt's party pushed onward. From Fort Cummings, they could proceed a short distance to Rincon and pick up a train bound either southward to El Paso or northward to Albuquerque, Las Vegas, and the Colorado border. They went north, stopping briefly in Albuquerque. On April 18, the Albuquerque *Journal* would complain, "At no time in their lives, did the Earp desperadoes call at the Journal office. They seem to have consorted with the sandy sorehead on the sundown sheet [apparently the editor of a rival paper] while they remained in hiding in this city." From Albuquerque, the fugitives proceeded on the rail line toward Trinidad, Colorado, where they could definitely relax; Wyatt's old friend Bat Masterson was there serving a stint as city marshal.

Back in Tombstone, Johnny Behan was still determined to serve warrants on most of the party. The case against Pete Spencer and the German Freis or Freeze, now identified as "Fritz Bode," in the killing of Morgan Earp had been dropped because of lack of evidence; Spencer had successfully objected to the calling of his wife as a prosecution witness. Curly Bill still had not shown up to collect the reward for charity, nor had his body surfaced. John Clum sold the *Epitaph*—to a Democrat—and readied for a move to a post office job in

Washington, D.C. The rustlers did not overrun the town—either because Wyatt Earp had intimidated them into submission before leaving the territory or because they had never really been a substantial threat to it to begin with. Many Tombstonians still considered nervously what might happen next, anticipating some climactic battle between Wyatt Earp and the cowboys. But the city council, at least, attempted to put a good face on things, inviting the traveling General William Tecumseh Sherman and his staff "to visit the city of Tombstone and partake of its Freedom."

Another visitor, Governor Tritle, returned that month of April 1881. The situation in Tombstone had developed into a major embarrassment to the territory, with press reports not only using Tombstone's problems for facetious humor but seriously reflecting the sense of anarchy and confusion that reigned in the wake of the recent series of events. Tritle felt he had to try to implement his militia idea, as a response both to any outlawry still existing and to possible Indian raids. He designated J. H. Jackson head of a posse that would become a militia company when it reached thirty members.

The executive remained unable to offer any government money for this venture, instead advising citizens to fund it themselves until he could obtain an appropriation. He also felt hamstrung concerning a measure Gosper had considered desirable, removing Behan from the sheriff's job. On March 31, Tritle had written to President Arthur asking for congressional approval "to summarily remove from office any county officer that he found to be corrupt, inefficient, and incompetent."

Meanwhile, the Earps' Republican friend territorial Federal Marshal Dake was coming under fire for the same reasons cited by Tritle in wanting authority to remove a county official. The United States Department of Justice had sent S. R. Martin to investigate Dake's performance, and on April 19, Martin reported to a superior, "I do not find anyone who thinks him fit for the position he now holds." Martin explained that the United States collector of internal revenue had complained he could not get his writs served, and the United States district attorney had charged that no federal court had convened since the preceding September "for the reason that the Marshal refuses to summon a jury—giving as a reason that he had no money to pay their fees." Furthermore, Martin reported, Dake "retains upon his force as Deputy, one of the Earp boys of Tombstone who is now an outlaw and with others are [*sic*] hiding in the mountains awaiting the time for a big fight in Tombstone."

President Arthur was still trying to address the various troubles in southeastern Arizona by pressing Congress for the amendment to the Posse Comitatus Act so that the military could be used to quell outlawry. On April 26, he proposed this change, including recommendations for such a measure from Governor Tritle and General Sherman, to Congress. As a result, a bill was actually prepared in the House, but it was soon tabled and died. In the Senate, a committee rejected any change, concluding that "the existing provisions for imposing martial law were adequate to meet the specific problem."

Arthur had received such dire reports for so long that he felt he had to do something, and he took the Senate committee at its word. On May 3, he issued a proclamation threatening the residents of southeastern Arizona with martial law. He announced himself convinced that "it has become impracticable to enforce by the ordinary course of judicial proceedings the laws of the United States" within Arizona Territory and asserted that it was his presidential duty under the law "to use the military forces for the purpose of enforcing . . . the laws," when necessary. Thus, he commanded any "insurgents" to "disperse and retire peaceably to their respective abodes" and instructed the territory's citizens to stop "aiding, countenancing, abetting or taking part in any . . . unlawful proceedings." If they did not by twelve o'clock noon on May 15, martial law would be imposed.

The proclamation was displayed in the post offices of Arizona and elicited responses ranging from mild puzzlement to consternation. John Pleasant Gray, who doubted that there were more than a hundred rustlers and didn't see them as much of a threat, would recall, "To the good citizens of Arizona it was rather an amusing document, as it stated a condition referring to 'lawless element wandering over the country in large bands,' commanding them to 'immediately disperse and go their respective ways to peaceful occupations.'" The new editor of the *Epitaph,* taking umbrage at Arthur's depiction of southeastern Arizona citizenry, got up an indignation meeting on May 10, but, as another newspaper facetiously reported, it "fell flat as a cold mashed potato."

Arthur's move actually had an antecedent in President Rutherford Hayes's declaration of a state of insurrection in Lincoln County, New Mexico, in October 1878. The Lincoln County Range Wars had spiraled into bloody anarchy as a result of political and economic tensions similar to those that had flared in Tombstone. In New Mexico, however, more people were directly involved on a grander, even more convoluted scale. An influential Republican ring in Santa Fe controlled the political and economic life of the county until challenged by cattleman John Chisum and by a number of owners of small ranches and farms. Gradually, the fight centered on the mercantile monopoly awarded by the Republican ring and a rival mercantile attempt by rancher John Tunstall and lawyer Alexander McSween. Questions of landownership entered the picture, too, making switches in allegiances common. As the ring tightened its hold on the courts and on law enforcement, a series of bloody encounters ensued, with both Tunstall and McSween killed. Meanwhile, various hard cases flocked to one side or the other, and the attention of President Hayes and the hard work of the new territorial governor, Lew Wallace, only partially stemmed the violence.

In southeastern Arizona, while political and economic tensions were just as great, the number of actual players was limited, and affairs were settling down even before Arthur made his proclamation. There would still be sporadic, one-on-one violence in and out of the communities, but extreme factional strife virtually ended with the Earp coterie's departure. Rustling and robbing activities diminished, too. While Earp supporters would see this as a result of Wyatt's intimidation of outlaws, there are many other possible factors as well: the glare of public attention; a natural falling away of free-ranging rustlers and robbers in the face of the growing structures of civilization; quarreling among the outlaws themselves; greater solidarity among the ranks of the cattlemen in response to rustling threats. On May 21, the Tucson *Citizen* would remark, "Outlaws remain but are quiet and crime which has run riot in Cochise County for two years has made way for peace and quiet."

However, the controversy generated by the Earp-cowboy rivalry was not at an end. For on May 15, Doc Holliday was arrested in Denver for the murder of Frank Stilwell.

There were rumors that Wyatt had been sighted back at Hooker's ranch as late as the first week in May, but actually, the Earp party had arrived in Trinidad about that time. On reaching Colorado, they quickly disbanded. By one account, Johnson, McMasters, Tipton, and Vermillion simply headed back across the New Mexico line, while by another, McMasters and Johnson lit out for Utah, and Texas Jack for Denver, with Tipton remaining in Trinidad. Charlie Smith is not mentioned in the fragmentary references to these secondary members of the party at this point, an indication that he had already pulled out.

That left Wyatt and Warren Earp and Doc Holliday. In Trinidad, Wyatt and Doc had a falling-out. Kate Elder later alleged it was because of Wyatt's steel shirt. The two, she reported, were "in some sort of a deal," and Wyatt was donning the garment when Doc announced, "You should take the same chances I take, I'm out." Doc himself would soon allude to "a little misunderstanding" between himself and the Earps.

Whatever the reasons for the split, Doc had certainly proven a tremendous liability to the Earp brothers, as witnessed by his prickly personality, his propensity for barroom violence, his friendship with Billy Leonard, his volatile relationship with Kate Elder, his suspected participation in—or perhaps simply knowledge of—the Benson stage robbery attempt, his goading of Ike Clanton on the night before the gunfight, and his apparent firing of the first shot in the fight. However close the two men were, Wyatt had to breathe a sigh of some relief on parting.

Accompanied by Bat Masterson and at least one other gambler, Doc left the southern Colorado community first, heading for gambling opportunities to the north in Pueblo and Denver. Wyatt and Warren remained briefly in Trinidad, enjoying an easy popularity. The Trinidad *Daily News* had called the whole Earp party "'way up' boys—gentlemen of the first water," and with Masterson as their champion, Wyatt and

Warren could breathe fairly easily. But they knew they could still expect trouble from Arizona authorities, and wisely, they chose to head out to remote Gunnison, across the Continental Divide. Here Wyatt began operating a faro bank.

Meanwhile, the big city of Denver drew Doc Holliday. Situated on the eastern side of the Rocky Mountains at a spot where the South Platte River and Cherry Creek met, the town founded on an 1858 gold strike had burgeoned into one of the premier cities of the West. Not only did it boast three railroads and a steady trade supplying Colorado's silver mining camps, but the community had become the state capital in 1881, and boosterism brought in a steady tourist trade as well. Denver had multistory brick buildings, electric lights, hundreds of telephones, and elegant restaurants, hotels, and gaming houses.

If Doc Holliday reached the city coughing and hacking with his tuberculosis, that was all right, too, for in addition to everything else, the high, dry air of Denver was considered most salubrious for health seekers with respiratory problems. In other words, Doc wasn't the only tuberculosis sufferer wandering the streets. But he was the only one wanted in Arizona on the Stilwell murder charge.

About 8:30 P.M. on Monday, May 16, Doc was walking along Fifteenth Street under the arc of an electric light when a man brandishing two six-shooters, stepped from the shadows, ordered him to throw up his hands, and hustled him into the nearby sheriff's office. A reporter for the Denver *Tribune* happened into the office and stayed to observe. He found Holliday to be "a thin, spare man, with a blond mustache and a piercing eye," a man of "meek appearance and quiet demeanor"; his captor was "a young, thick set man, with a short-cropped reddish mustache." The latter gave his name as Perry Mallan, or Mallen, and his position variously as deputy sheriff in Los Angeles, California, and as law enforcement officer from Arizona.

Mallan had a list of crimes for which he was arresting Doc. In addition to the Stilwell murder charge, Mallan cited the alleged murder of Curly Bill, the killing of "a ranchman named Clanton near Tombstone" (apparently a reference to Billy Clanton), the "attempted murder of his brother" (appar-

ently Ike), "the murder of a railroad conductor on the Southern Pacific road," and "half a dozen other crimes." Among
them was the alleged killing of Mallan's own partner, Harry
White, seven years earlier; the heavyset young man with the
red mustache clearly had vengeance in mind. He also connected Doc with the "notorious" tinhorn gamblers and confidence men of Benson, Arizona, with whom the deceased
Morgan Earp had been linked as well.

The deputies in the Denver sheriff's office knew a sticky
situation when they saw one. They immediately started trying
to arrange for a hack to take Holliday to the Arapahoe County
jail until the charges could be sorted out. Meanwhile, Mallan
fingered his gun and threatened to do to Holliday what Holliday had done to his partner.

A glacially cool Doc and an excited Mallan stood on either
side of a desk as a deputy telephoned "frantically" for a hack.
Mallan clutched a revolver.

"Oh you can drop that," said Doc. "Nobody is going to try
to get [it] away from you. I have no weapons." The statement
was followed by "hot words" between the two as a number of
"rough looking men" filed into the room, giving the *Tribune*
reporter the sense that "a murder or lynching" might be im-
minent.

"No, you won't get away from me again," announced Mallan, who had peacefully introduced himself to Doc in Pueblo
only a short time before. "You killed my partner, you bloodthirsty coward, and I would have taken you in Pueblo if the
men I had with me had stood by me."

Holliday appealed to the sheriff and to the mysterious
crowd, but "It was evident that the whole spirit of the Sheriff was
with Mallan, and as he still grasped his revolver he held the
winning hand." Doc tried to argue that his captor was not
the Arizona law officer he claimed to be, but the deputies at the
office wanted to hear none of it. When the hack arrived, they
loaded the prisoner into it. The *Tribune* reporter identified
himself to Doc and asked to ride along, a request the prisoner
eagerly granted. However, the fugitive from Arizona justice
declined to reveal much until he could confer with Bat Masterson and with a lawyer: "He refused to say who Mallan was, only
reiterating that he was no officer of Cochise County, Arizona.

He said that Mallan came to him in Tom Kemp's variety theater, Pueblo, a few days ago and claimed to be his friend, telling him that the Stilwells were on his track to kill him and that he wanted to warn him."

It is quite possible that Frank Stilwell's brother, the well-known Indian Territory scout Comanche Jack, had his own vengeance plans. According to some sources, he actually rode with Behan's rustler posse. However, although Stilwell may have visited Tombstone more than once, the *Daily Nugget* indicated a later arrival, for on April 23, the paper showed "Jack Stillwell [*sic*], Indian Territory" checking in at the Grand Hotel.

If Stilwell was after Doc Holliday and friends, that was understandable enough. But Mallan was a mystery man. Doc Holliday seemed to know who he was, but nobody else did. A few years later, Doc himself would indicate that he only found out afterward that Mallan was an associate and perhaps even a brother of John Tyler, the racketeer who had clashed with Doc in the Oriental. At the time of the arrest, the *Tribune* suggested that he might be "Sim [*sic*] Clanton," another Clanton brother eager to draw Holliday back into the clutches of the Arizona cowboys.

The *Tribune* was initially sympathetic to Doc, as was the Denver *Republican;* the city's *Rocky Mountain News* championed Mallan's viewpoint. Doc Holliday for a time became the hottest news story in Denver.

The *Tribune* reporter who accompanied Doc to the county jail did not realize who this neatly dressed, peaceable-seeming J. H. Holliday really was until they got to the lockup and the reporter heard him addressed as "Doc." As Doc Holliday had become a familiar name to western newspaper readers, the reporter then knew that his instincts had served him well.

Clearly, part of Doc's appeal as a major news story was the aura of the wild and woolly West which surrounded him. The *Tribune* account partook of the romantic myth of the West in laying out the night's events. Mallan's dramatic arrest of Holliday, the reporter asserted, "reads more like the story of a mining camp than a tale of Denver in her metropolitan splendor and all the circumstances are tinged with the romance of a past and bygone day."

This angle was only enhanced by the appearance of Bat Masterson, whom the reporter encountered upon leaving the jail. True, the *Tribune* got the name wrong, calling the Trinidad marshal "Bob Masterson." But it had his violent, romantic reputation down pat: "[He is] known as the 'man who smiles.' The New York *Sun* once wrote him up for this characteristic. He is said to have killed twenty-one men in the discharge of his duty each time so politely and with such a pleasant smile on his face that it was almost a pleasure to die at his hands."

Masterson still didn't much care for Doc Holliday. He would later write, "While I assisted him substantially on several occasions, it was not because I liked him any too well, but on account of my friendship with Wyatt Earp who did." Doc was lucky that Bat so valued the friendship with Wyatt, for now the personable gambler-lawman did assist the prisoner substantially.

First, Bat countered Doc's desperado image, telling the *Tribune* "that Holliday was a responsible man, a Deputy United States Marshal, and for a time Deputy Marshal of Tombstone, and that the cowboys only wanted to assassinate him as they had Virg and Morgan Earp." Second, in the early morning hours of Tuesday, May 17, he obtained a writ of habeas corpus to ensure Doc's safety until Doc was brought before the court in Denver. And third, he engineered a charge against Doc in Pueblo in hopes of legally moving him to a more favorable environment.

The Pueblo *Chieftain* came out solidly behind the gambling dentist on May 17, speaking approvingly of the fact that he "made no effort to conceal his identity, and when questioned as to his doings in Arizona, said he had nothing to fear from that quarter, as he had received full pardon from the governor for his bloody work, in consideration of the effective services he had rendered the authorities." The paper reported Holliday insisting "he had left Arizona for the single purpose of being at peace with everyone around him, and he hoped his enemies would allow him that privilege."

Then there was Doc's pleasing appearance and manner. He was such a well-dressed, gentlemanly person, "rather tall," lean and arrow-straight, with "large, sharp, and piercing" blue eyes and an air of "considerable culture." Perry Mallan—or whoever he was—by contrast, the paper depicted as "a small man, with reddish face and beard, with small, ferretty [*sic*] eyes, and not an inviting cast of features." Besides, Mallan had told too many people too many different stories about himself and his official status, and he owed money to several men in Pueblo.

Thus, the Pueblo paper championed Doc, and the Pueblo city marshal agreed to go to Denver to arrest him on a charge of operating a confidence game in which he allegedly relieved a "sucker" of $150. By such a move, Bat Masterson and Doc's other allies hoped to beat any extradition attempts. Bat would later in an interesting slip identify the Pueblo charge as highway robbery but leave no doubt as to its purpose; it was, he noted, "a subterfuge on my part to prevent him from being taken out of the state by the Arizona authorities."

Word had reached southeastern Arizona of Doc's capture. According to the *Epitaph*, Denver's sheriff had wired both Behan and Paul that he had Doc *and* the Earps in jail, a statement that would lead to much confusion. Wyatt and Warren, of course, were in Gunnison 150 miles from Denver, and when Gunnison City Marshal S. Beyers wired Paul and Behan wanting to know whether he should arrest the brothers, Paul quickly wired yes. Behan apparently considered the telegram bogus; the *Epitaph* speculated that the inquirer was "a fraud and a delusion," as the Earps were in jail in Denver.

Wherever the Earps and Holliday were, Johnny Behan wanted to go get them and bring them back to Cochise County, while Bob Paul wanted to return them to Pima County on the Stilwell charge. The newspapers predictably took sides. The Tucson *Daily Citizen* argued that Pima County was the place for the Earps and Holliday to have their day in court, and Bob Paul was the man for the job of bringing them in. Behan had "notoriously failed to arrest important criminals in his own county" and had allowed the escape of "at least a half dozen" prisoners. But when Governor Tritle selected Paul to carry the extradition requests, a Tombstone dispatch complained that Paul was "notorious for his friendship for the Earps," that it was "common opinion" he had "connived at their escape from the Territory," and that Behan should have gotten the nod, as he "worked the case up and offered a reward out of his own pocket."

Paul had to go to Prescott and pick up the necessary requisition forms. Meanwhile, Pueblo's marshal tried to serve his warrant against Doc as the defendant was being brought into Denver court. The Denver sheriff did not take kindly to this ploy, sending the marshal "through the door in the most approved one-two-three-bounce-'em style." The sheriff then angrily cleared the courtroom of the gamblers and confidence men who had come to cheer Holliday on, returned the prisoner to jail, and complained to the *Rocky Mountain News* that "the [attempted] arrest by the Pueblo parties is a put up job to secure Holliday's release."

The *Tribune* now sounded a less partisan note than it had heretofore: "It is evident that if anything like a fair opportunity was presented, a break would be made by Holliday's friends to rescue him from the Sheriff. The latter has good reason to fight all efforts to release Holliday. He has received stacks of telegrams from the California and Arizona officers to hold Holliday at all hazards, and by fair means or foul. This he intends to do." An Arizona officer was expected in "a couple of days," with Holliday's return to "the scene of his alleged crimes" an apparent inevitability.

By May 22, Bob Paul had arrived, carrying warrants for Doc, Wyatt, Warren, Sherman McMasters, and "John Johnson." He quickly found himself frustrated on two points. First, he had hoped that the Earps would be in jail in Denver by now, too, but he found only Holliday. Second, Paul had to await further requisition papers before Colorado Governor Frederick Pitkin would consider the prisoner's extradition.

The *Rocky Mountain News* carried an interview with Paul on the twenty-second. The reporter found the Arizona sheriff a large man, about two hundred pounds, with a "frank, open countenance" and a "pleasant air of refinement." Paul attributed the troubles in Tombstone to a "deadly feud" between the Earps and the cowboys. Asked what the sentiment of the people of Arizona was regarding the Earp party and the murder of Stilwell, Paul found the question difficult to answer. "The feeling is, however, very strong," he explained, "especially among the more respectable citizens who have been terrorized for years by the cowboys and the Earp gang and justice will no doubt be meted out to Holliday and his partners."

On the same day, the Denver *Republican* carried an interview with Holliday himself. He was described as a man of about 150 pounds, with a thin face, "hair sprinkled heavily with gray," and hands "small, and soft like a woman's." In addition, the paper reported, he had a "soft voice and modest manners." Yet appearances were deceiving, for he had been "the terror of the lawless element in Arizona, and with the Earpps [*sic*] was the only man brave enough to face the bloodthirsty crowd, which has made the name of Arizona a stench in the nostrils of decent men."

In other words, Doc had a ready audience for his version of events, which included an assertion that *he* was the one who had arrested Curly Bill Brocius for the murder of Tombstone Marshal Fred White. Doc neatly sidestepped the question of his role in the Stilwell murder—"I do not know that I am in any way responsible for his death." He *did* know, however, that Stilwell was one of Morgan's killers and a stage robber, the latter "from the fact that he gave the money to a friend of mine to keep." He explained that the "wild and reckless" cowboys in the Tombstone area had gradually been replaced by "a gang of murderers, stage robbers and thieves," rustlers who had been part of a Fort Griffin, Texas, outlaw band. These men, Holliday asserted, ran things in southeastern Arizona with the aid of Johnny Behan.

Much of Doc's recorded conversation centered on Behan, "a deadly enemy of mine, who would give any money to have me killed." Doc pronounced himself "almost certain" that the Cochise County sheriff was behind Morgan's assassination, as Behan "was afraid of and hated Morgan Earpp [*sic*], who had quarrelled with and insulted him several times." Relations between the speaker and Behan had been no better. "I have known [Behan] a long time. He first ran against me when I was running a faro bank, when he started a quarrel in my house, and I stopped him and refused to let him play any more. . . . In the quarrel I told him in the presence of a crowd that he was gambling with money which I had given his woman. . . . He always hated me after that, and would spend money to have me killed."

The allusion to Behan's woman is interesting; Josie Marcus is the only person mentioned filling that role in various source materials on Tombstone. Whether Doc was referring to this woman who had since become Wyatt's lover, speaking of another amorous interest, or just engaging in false sexual braggadocio, he pronounced himself so sure of the sheriff's deadly intentions that extradition could mean only one thing: "If I am taken back to Arizona, that is the last of Holliday." Bob Paul was "a good man" but would not be able to protect him; Tombstone's "respectable element" would stand by him, but they were "intimidated and unorganized."

What about the Earps? Holliday admitted that he had parted with Wyatt and Warren over a "misunderstanding," but insisted that they would still help him if they were not wanted themselves.

As for Perry Mallan, Doc labeled him a "crank" who had first approached him in Pueblo. In this account, Mallan announced that Doc had saved his life in Santa Fe, a place Doc politely told him he had never been. Mallan ignored this information and warned him that Frank Stilwell's brother had arrived on the train threatening to shoot Doc on sight. That done, Mallan threatened to kill Doc himself if the latter revealed the source of this intelligence. "I told him I wasn't travelling around the country giving people away, and he left me," Doc commented dryly. He saw Mallan once more in Pueblo, in a saloon, then did not encounter him again until that evening under the Denver streetlight.

Mallan buttressed Doc's charge that he was a crank by apparently switching stories at every turn. At one point, he claimed to have been with Curly Bill at the Arizona water hole when the gun battle with the Earp party erupted. He admitted that the story of Doc's killing of a partner seven years earlier was a fabrication, and he told the *Rocky Mountain News* that Behan had offered five hundred dollars, the Cochise County commissioners a thousand, for Doc's return. Mallan still had produced no proof of official law enforcement status. He was either a bounty hunter or a crackpot or both.

Bat Masterson, still working to prevent extradition, naturally took advantage of Mallan's questionable character, calling him a fraud and cowboy cohort who sought to force Doc back to Arizona to be killed. Mallan countered by charging that

Masterson was wanted for a Utah killing. Meanwhile, Doc had a hearing and was discharged, with the judge citing lack of evidence. Paul quickly had him rearrested with the Stilwell murder warrant he had brought, but Doc's three lawyers, "all sporting men in his favor," were contesting the warrant. "Holliday's friends are doing everything in their power to get him off," Paul wrote on May 26, the day the extradition request was formally presented to Governor Pitkin. Paul reported, "There is more feeling over the Holliday affair here than there is in Tucson, and all in his favor."

Paul was hoping to go to Gunnison and get Wyatt and Warren if the governor approved extradition for Doc. "The United States Marshal came from Gunnison yesterday," Paul wrote in his May 26 letter. "He says some of the party were there, but they kept hidden while he was there. He says they have a great many friends there."

On May 29, Governor Pitkin refused extradition, giving as reasons the Pueblo charge and faulty legal phrasing in the paper work from Arizona. Partisan politics may have been at work; Pitkin was a Republican. Bat Masterson later stated that he had secured an audience with Pitkin and convinced him to make such a move; a Denver *Tribune* reporter claimed to have had the decisive talk with Pitkin at Bat's request.

Either way, Bob Paul had to return home empty-handed, and Doc could now breathe easily—or at least try to, considering the state of his lungs. He returned to Pueblo and posted bond for the fraudulent charge which had served its purpose so well. "He has no fears of the outcome," the *Chieftain* reported. Doc would simply get a continuance and let the charge remain pending until his death.

All the Denver arrest had done was to heighten the gunfighting dentist's glamorous notoriety. For example, the Cincinnati *Enquirer* ran a biographical sketch of Holliday in which, the *Chieftain* noted, "It was made to appear that he has in his time killed over fifty men, and that Jesse James is a saint compared to him." Back in Doc's hometown of Valdosta, Georgia, the Valdosta *Times* loyally reported that father H. B. Holliday had received the assurances of Tombstone citizens and of the Spicer decision "entirely exonerating John from the charge of willful murder" in the shoot-out with the Clan-

tons and McLaurys, but "of the subsequent murders and outrages which are charged to 'Doc' Holliday his father knows
nothing. We can but hope the charges are ill founded."

Doc remained in Pueblo, Wyatt and Warren in Gunnison.
Virgil stayed in the family home in Colton, California, still adjusting to his crippling wounds. The Earps had sold off many
of their business interests in Tombstone but retained others,
and Virgil was having trouble adjusting to the fact that his
business efforts, as well as his law enforcement ones, had been
consumed in an unholy mess that spelled an end to his days
there. As late as May 22, he was writing to a friend, Prescott
City Marshal James Dodson, that he planned to return to
Tombstone soon. He insisted to Dodson that the Earps had
only been doing their duty as law enforcers in the late troubles
and that they would still surrender if they could expect bail.
Prescott was "the only place that seems like home," he wrote
plaintively, but it was Tombstone which drew him.

A few days later, Virgil traveled to San Francisco to check
into the possibility of an operation to increase the use of his
injured arm. A San Francisco *Daily Examiner* reporter, half expecting to see wild desperado in light of all the conflicting
press reports, met the train and provided a vivid picture of
the eldest of the "fighting Earps":

> Virgil Earp is not a ruffian in appearance. He was found
> in a sleeping car, smoking a cigar. His face, voice, and
> manner were prepossessing. He is close to six feet in
> height, of medium build, chestnut hair, sandy mustache,
> light eyebrows, quiet, blue eyes and frank expression. He
> wore a wide-brimmed, slate-colored slouch hat, pants of
> brown and white stripe, and a blue diagonal coat and vest,
> both the latter with bullet holes in them, bearing testimony
> of a recent fight when he was shot in the back, the bullet
> coming out at the front of the vest. His left arm was car-
> ried in a sling, also a memento of the last fight.

Virgil's account of the situation in Tombstone in significant ways echoed the one provided by Acting Governor Gosper the previous fall. Gosper had complained Tombstone area
citizens were so intent on making money quickly that they

failed to practice and support local self-government. Now Virgil noted, "Most of the business men there stay simply to make money enough to live somewhere else comfortably and, of course, the greatest object with them is to have as much money as possible spent in the town and to get as much of it as they can, careless of the means of dispensation or the results of rough manners."

In particular, he charged the saloonkeepers as being dependent upon, and thus friendly to, a lawless element. All in all, he described the situation as a grim and lonely one for a lawman: "An officer doing his duty must rely almost entirely upon his own conscience for encouragement. The sympathy of the respectable portion of the community may be with him, but it is not openly expressed."

Virgil gave an account of events in line with his previous Spicer hearing testimony, adding in regard to Morgan's murder that Frank Stilwell had confessed and named his co-conspirators at the time Wyatt and friends killed him on the train track. The former marshal professed the Earps ready to turn themselves in to Arizona authorities in six months when court reconvened.

News of this interview and of Virgil's letter to Dodson in Prescott made its way to Tombstone, where the Democrat-owned *Epitaph* reacted with sarcasm. To Virgil's claim that Stilwell had confessed and named his cohorts, the paper responded, "Without any desire to irritate Mr. Earp, we nevertheless cannot help expressing astonishment that a man with two pounds of buckshot in his stomach, four bullets in his heart, and his head mutilated by lead beyond recognition, could have had either time or inclination to make any statement whatever." As for Virgil's plan to return to Tombstone, the paper reacted with understandable incredulity: "Extremely doubtful."

Actually, although the Earps had delayed in Tombstone long enough to lose Morgan to an assassin, they *had* gotten out when the getting was good from an economic standpoint. In April, the Tombstone Mill and Mining Company had stopped paying dividends, and at the same time a gush of water into the Grand Central mine stopped progress on that operation. Tombstone, which had had so much trouble obtaining enough water for a city's needs, would now ironically be plagued with the problem of flooding in the mines.

Life was in many ways as unstable as ever. Indian troubles flared up again in April, with George Parsons calling the newest outbreak "probably the worst we've ever had." The situation calmed in early May, but by late that month the Apaches were threatening again. And when a water closet in Tombstone's Tivoli Saloon caught fire, the business district experienced its second big fire, more devastating than the first, with one death and losses estimated at as much as half a million dollars' worth.

By May 30, Parsons, who as a partner in the firm of Parsons and Redfern had achieved his goal to become a mining man, expressed disgust with Tombstone and its citizens as he prepared to leave on a trip. "Bad state of things," he wrote. "People don't care here. Never saw such apathy. Am glad to leave the cursed place and be with those who have some little spunk and energy left."

Tombstone was beginning a slow slide into near oblivion. The Bird Cage Theater still reverberated each night with laughter and shouts, men still talked excitedly about the potential of various mining locations, and citizens noted with pleasure that it looked as if the community were finally going to get a railroad branch. But the sense of unlimited possibility which had fueled the town's early growth was missing, and all roads no longer led to Tombstone. There were other, more exciting, places to be.

John Ringo hung around awhile and provided the coda to the Earp-cowboy troubles in southeastern Arizona. For on Friday, July 14, he was found sitting on a rock between the spreading branches of interlaced black and white scrub oaks in West Turkey Creek Canyon in the Chiricahua Mountains, a bullet hole "large enough to admit two fingers about half way between the right eye and ear" and an equally large hole on top of his head where the bullet had exited. In addition, a small part of his scalp was missing, "as if cut out by a knife." The circumstances of his death were to add a final mysterious controversy to the story of the Earp-cowboy conflicts in Tombstone.

CHAPTER 17
And Die in the West

Wood hauler John Yoast was guiding his team along the road to Morse's Mill in West Turkey Creek Canyon, also known as Morse's Canyon, on the afternoon of July 14 when he noticed a man seated on a stone about twenty yards from the road and close to the creek, his back against the limbs of two intertwined scrub oak trees. The man was clad in a blue shirt, a vest, pants, and a light hat. Yoast passed by, assuming the fellow to be asleep, but he glanced back to see his dog "smelling of the man's face and snorting." The wood hauler alighted from his wagon and found John Ringo dead, a bullet hole through his head. Yoast had known Ringo both in Texas and in the territory, so he could immediately identify the body.

Despite the canyon's remoteness from any town or railroad station, the wood hauler had discovered Ringo beside a well-traveled thoroughfare and in a spot reportedly favored by teamsters for their noon break on the way to the mill. Only a quarter mile away sat the ranch house of B. F. Smith, and when Yoast "gave the alarm," eleven men assembled within about fifteen minutes.

They found Ringo facing west, his head "inclined to the

right," his right hand clenching his .45 caliber Colt revolver, which contained five cartridges. Ringo's Winchester rifle was propped against the tree near at hand. He wore both rifle and revolver cartridge belts, the latter, mysteriously, buckled on upside down. Also curious was the fact that the cowboy's boots were missing. On his feet he wore torn-up strips of undershirt; their condition showed that he had not traveled far with the makeshift foot coverings. His horse was nowhere to be found. B. F. Smith's son would later discover the thousand-pound bay, still saddled, about two miles away.

Ringo had been dead about twenty-four hours. On inquiry, it was learned that two women had passed by the seated figure the previous afternoon but thought, like Yoast, that he was merely sleeping. The occupants of the Smith ranch house also reported hearing a shot about 3:00 P.M. on the day preceding.

The men who had converged in response to Yoast's alarm buried Ringo's body beside the creek, close to the spot where it had been found, and made their report to the coroner and sheriff in Tombstone. Unfortunately, neither their official statement nor the coroner's report made clear whether one of the five rounds, or a possible sixth round, had been fired. However, one of the men of the burial party, Robert Boller, later said the pistol contained one empty shell, and the Tucson *Star* also reported one chamber emptied.

The death looked like a suicide, but there were many puzzling aspects. Why were the feet bound in cloth? Why was the cartridge belt upside down? Why were no powder burns around the wound mentioned in the official reports, as there should have been if Ringo had been shot at close range? Why did a part of the scalp, "including a small portion of the forehead & part of the hair," appear to have been cut out? And would John Ringo have been likely to kill himself? The odd circumstances of the death and the variety of possible answers to these questions gave rise to two theories: suicide and murder.

Ringo himself had fueled both theories by his character and statements. "Many people who were intimately acquainted with him in life have serious doubts that he took his own life," reported the *Epitaph*, "while an equally large number say that he frequently threatened to commit suicide and that event was expected at any time." Ringo was "subject to frequent fits of melancholy" and possessing "an abnormal fear of being killed." He had recently told the *Epitaph* writer "he was as certain of being killed, as he was of being living then. He said he might run along for a couple of years more, and may not last two days."

If Ringo had indeed been murdered, one suspect was Frank Leslie. Billy King, a bartender who arrived in Tombstone in 1882, later told a story of an argument between Leslie and a drunken Ringo. Ringo rode out of town only to be found dead that very day by some cowhands who followed his riderless horse, and everyone suspected Leslie, who "rode into the back gate of the O.K. Corral" about the time the body was discovered. His horse was "white with lather," and he claimed "he had been giving the critter a hard run to take some of the ginger out of him." There are a number of problems with King's story. For example, Ringo supposedly taunted Leslie concerning a killing that actually happened months later. In addition, King's account does not match with the newspaper particulars and testimony of the men who found the body at all.

However, there are indications that the Oriental bartender did court the notoriety of being the well-known rustler's killer. Both Robert Boller and Breakenridge would report that Leslie claimed to have dispatched Ringo, "to curry favor with the Earp sympathizers," according to Breakenridge. Yet neither of these old-timers believed the claim. Boller, who had helped bury the body, considered the death a clear case of suicide. Breakenridge, too, favored the suicide theory: "We all know that Leslie would not care to tackle him even when he was drunk." John Pleasant Gray was more favorable to Leslie in his assessment. Gray considered the deed murder, but "Buckskin Frank had never shown any evidence during his career which could make one think he could be guilty of such a cowardly deed."

Other names were mentioned, including that of Lou Cooley, a worker and "perhaps a hired gunman" for Henry Clay Hooker. Fred Dodge would identify the killer as Johnny O'Rourke, or Johnny-Behind-the-Deuce, the young gambler who had shot mining engineer W. P. Schneider and narrowly missed lynching at the hands of a mob. O'Rourke had escaped from jail a full fifteen months earlier; now, according to Dodge, the fugitive was camping out in the Chiricahua area, and there was bad blood between O'Rourke and Ringo. O'Rourke, "afraid" of the rustler leader, grabbed a chance to dispatch him. Dodge claimed that he and Leslie found O'Rourke's deserted hideout shortly after the murder. He also claimed that Pony Diehl, Ringo's "bosom friend," killed O'Rourke in retaliation a few days later.

Dodge told all this to Wyatt Earp's biographer Lake, and Lake wrote it up as fact. Few researchers have found this version at all convincing, and some have seen it simply as a cover-up for the real killer: Wyatt himself.

Wyatt claimed to interviewers in his later years that he had returned to Arizona and shot Ringo. Three possible motives have been advanced for his alleged action. Josie Marcus Earp, who became Wyatt's wife by common law, if not by a marriage ceremony, would adopt for her husband the noblest of intentions. Boyer has her calling Wyatt "a bulldog" who "conceived it as his responsibility to put an end to the organized activities of the rustler gang. This meant getting the leadership." Other commentators would see Wyatt as a man still bent on vengeance or simply as a bounty hunter. Whatever his motive or motives, Wyatt Earp still remains a prime suspect to some researchers.

After Wyatt's death, Boyer had Josie provide the most elaborate account of his killing of Ringo, using as the basis snatches of conversations she supposedly overheard. In this version, Wells Fargo secretly wanted John Ringo dead—apparently as a simple blow against lawlessness in Cochise County, for Ringo had not been directly linked to any stage robberies. Anyway, Buckskin Frank Leslie, Billy Breakenridge, and Johnny O'Rourke were all acting as Wells Fargo informants paid to report to Fred Dodge on Ringo's movements. (So much for Dodge's supposedly successful undercover career in Tombstone.) Meanwhile, Wyatt and Doc filtered back into Arizona, using beards for disguise. They congregated with Charlie Smith and four other confederates at the Hooker ranch, then took to the mountains on the intelligence from Breakenridge via Dodge that Ringo was in the Chiricahuas.

They found him in a canyon, shirtless and bootless, making coffee over a small fire. He sensed their presence, grabbed his pistol, and ran into the woods. As it grew dark, he wrapped his feet in the pieces of his undershirt, planning to escape under cover of night, but the light material revealed his position. As he moved away from cover, Wyatt fired a rifle shot and Ringo dropped soundlessly.

According to *I Married Wyatt Earp,* the "posse" had hoped to hang Ringo, but he had not cooperated. Now they moved his body to the spreading oaks by the road in order to avoid another debate like the one that had followed Wyatt's killing of Curly Bill Brocius.

There are obvious problems with this version of the story as well, including the nature of the bullet wound and the fact that Ringo was found with shirt and vest on. In addition, the whole idea of such a large secret operation strains credibility, as does the idea that Wyatt Earp and Doc Holliday would chance a return to Arizona simply for the purpose of getting John Ringo. It has been speculated that Wyatt could get to the Chiricahuas from Gunnison in approximately one week, one day by train and six by horse.* But Wyatt was, according to newspaper accounts, still in Gunnison in mid-July, and Doc Holliday has variously been reported in court in Pueblo on the larceny charge on July 11, July 14, and July 18.

Perhaps the best comment on the whole idea that Wyatt killed Ringo has been made by Ringo biographer Jack Burrows: "I think Wyatt Earp was quite capable of trying to do just that; I do not think he did it." Instead, Burrows accepts the suicide theory.

But even within this theory there are two lines of thought. The first holds that Ringo, waking disoriented and panicky from a drunken spree, spent a grueling period in the desert horseless and waterless, then in desperation took his own life. Billy Breakenridge claimed to have met Ringo in the South Pass of the Dragoon Mountains "shortly after noon" the day he was killed. The rustler, on his way to Galeyville, was plastered, "reeling in the saddle."† That evening, a still-drunken

---

*This possibility was put forth by John Gilchriese in a January 26, 1964, Tucson *Daily Star* article on Ringo's death.

†Josie Marcus Earp had access to this account and apparently used it in asserting Breakenridge had informed Dodge of the cowboy's whereabouts.

Ringo hung his boots over his saddle and bedded down for the night, but his horse wandered away searching for water. Breakenridge concluded, "When Ringo awoke, he must have been crazed for water and started out afoot. He was within sound of running water when he became crazed with thirst and killed himself."

However, newspaper reports of the time, while confirming that Ringo had been on an extended spree and apparently lost his horse, effectively undercut this "crazed with thirst" notion. The *Weekly Epitaph* reported that Ringo had been drinking in Tombstone on July 12, that he had then gone to Galeyville, "where he kept on drinking heavily." He apparently had moved from there to West Turkey Creek Canyon; people in the Chiricahuas generally believed "that his horse wandered off somewhere, and he started off on foot to search for him; that his boots began to hurt him, and he pulled them off and made moccasins of his undershirt." Yet Ringo could not have been tormented by thirst, for "He was about 200 feet from water [when found], and was acquainted with every inch of the country, so that it was almost impossible for him to lose himself." Indeed, the *Epitaph* announced, "The circumstances of the case hardly leave any room for doubt as to his self destruction."

The coroner saw the situation that way, too, and Boller insisted, "There is no question in the minds of any of the five [*sic*] who found him but what [he] committed suicide." Biographer Burrows presents a well-reasoned case for a fairly lucid Ringo doing away with himself, citing in particular both the fact that "the upward angle of the path of the bullet clearly supports self-infliction" and the apparently suicidal character of Ringo himself, with alcohol acting as "a serious depressant." Burrows identifies the two most puzzling aspects of the death as the missing piece of scalp and the cartridge belt buckled on upside down, speculating that the first was the work of a wild rodent or large bird, the second perhaps the result of mild disorientation.

Tombstonians had a lot to talk about after Ringo's mysterious death. The Tucson *Star* reported, "He was known in this section as 'King of the Cowboys,' and was fearless in the extreme." The *Weekly Epitaph* treated him almost as a favorite son, while acknowledging that he had enemies as well as friends:

> There were few men in Cochise county, or Southeastern Arizona better known. He was recognized by friends and foes, as a recklessly brave man, who would go any distance, or undergo any hardship to serve a friend or punish an enemy. While undoubtedly reckless, he was far from being a desperado and we know of no murder being laid to his charge. Friends and foes are unanimous in the opinion that he was a strictly honorable man in all his dealings and that his word was as good as his bond.

The account went on to call him "a fine specimen of physical manhood," concluding, "Many friends will mourn him, and many others will take secret delight in learning of his death."

Despite the interest in Ringo's demise, such strange and violent occurrences were again eclipsed by the latest signs of progress. The railroad drew tantalizingly close that midsummer of 1882, the grading finished up to within two and a half miles of Tombstone. The town was recovering satisfactorily from its second big fire and finally developing a more than adequate water supply by tapping into a large reservoir in the Huachuca Mountains. That strapping example of muscular Christianity Endicott Peabody was returning to the East, but not before seeing the Tombstone Episcopal Church building through to completion. Johnny Behan had weathered the storms of criticism from the law-and-order faction and remained sheriff, but that fall a Republican named Ward was elected in his place—and Buckskin Frank Leslie killed Spicer hearing witness Billy "the Kid" Claiborne outside the Oriental Saloon.

Claiborne had beaten the murder rap pending against him during the gunfight hearing the year before. In February, the jury in his trial for the Charleston killing of "Hicks" had hung at eight for conviction and four for acquittal. A second jury in May had acquitted him. Perhaps this acquittal fueled Claiborne's braggadocio, for according to Breakenridge, the young cowboy challenged Endicott Peabody.

Breakenridge had the dates wrong, placing the incident in the summer of 1881, before Peabody even arrived in Tombstone. More likely, if Claiborne did threaten the minister, it was in the summer of 1882, shortly before Peabody went East. According to Breakenridge, Peabody rode down to Charleston and preached a sermon on "the evil of the cattle-stealing rustlers and the drinking and carousing cowboys." Claiborne was not present, but took offense and sent word that if Peabody returned to preach a similar sermon, he would be on hand—to make the preacher dance. Peabody responded by announcing that he planned to return in two weeks and present a sermon which he thought appropriate; if Claiborne wished, he could come and listen. Then, if the cowboy believed he could make Peabody dance, he was welcome to try. That, apparently, was the end of that.

Now Claiborne went after Leslie—and went too far. According to Leslie, the Kid walked into the Oriental and began verbally abusing him, resisted Leslie's attempts to calm him, and finally announced, "That's all right, Leslie, I'll get even on you." Claiborne was soon on the streets with a gun, repelling passersby's attempts to keep him out of trouble. Leslie, who remained in the saloon, related what happened next:

> In a short time a man came in and said there was a man waiting outside to shoot me, but I didn't pay much attention to it. A few minutes later another man came in looking quite white and said Claiborne was waiting outside with a rifle to shoot Frank Leslie. I then went out, and as I stepped on the sidewalk saw about a foot of a rifle barrel protruding from the end of the fruit stand. I stepped out in the street and saw it was Claiborne, and said, "Billy, don't shoot, I don't want you to kill me, nor do I want to have to shoot you." Almost before I finished he raised the gun and shot, and I returned the fire from my pistol, aiming at his breast.

Leslie's shot slammed through Claiborne's midsection. The wound was fatal, and Claiborne knew it. He announced, "My backbone is all shot out," and to Leslie he said, "Don't shoot again, I am killed." Leslie complied, waiting for the law with gun in hand. When an officer arrived, the bartender warned him to be careful with the fully cocked weapon, uncocked it, and went peacefully with the lawman.

Claiborne lived through an initial doctor's examination, but not much longer. The physician, G. C. Willis, testified that the victim had a gunshot wound on the left side "and an opening in the back close to his spinal column, probably the wound of exit." As Willis checked the latter injury, the Kid denounced Leslie as "a murdering son of a b- to shoot a man in the back." However, the doctor remarked, "I think he received the wound in the front."

Some people didn't share Willis's opinion. Saloon man Billy King, multiplying the number of shots, would write, "Everyone on the inside knew that Frank had put those five shots into Billy's back." Breakenridge probably came closer to a true account by relating that Leslie "came out of a side door behind the Kid and spoke to him, and as the Kid turned Leslie shot and killed him." Aside from the doctor's statement, testimony at the inquest was vague on this point, but witness Otto Johnson's account makes Breakenridge's version a distinct possibility: "[Leslie] walked to the side door on Fifth Street, opened the door, stood there a minute and looked around. He closed the door and walked on the sidewalk. The next thing I heard the shots fired."

If Leslie approached his would-be assailant from the back or side, the scene simply echoes some of Wild Bill Hickok's ruses and shows Leslie acting in the tradition of western gunfighters, who didn't shilly-shally around with points of honor when it was important to get a drop on a man.

Leslie won dismissal of the charges and stuck around as Tombstone began to sag. In 1883, mine production started to taper off, and more people were leaving. Johnny Behan successfully fought a charge of collecting taxes after expiration of his term of office by showing that he had acted under legal authority; then he came up with a position as assistant warden of "the Hell Hole," Yuma Penitentiary. Billy Breakenridge kept working for the new sheriff but soon decided to try ranching in the Sulphur Spring Valley instead. George Goodfellow, fascinated by everything Tombstone had to offer, from gila monsters to gunshot wounds, remained in town, lending his enthusiasm and expertise to a number of projects. As soon as Tombstone got its adequate water supply, he even established a municipal swimming pool.

But city improvements or no, early 1884 brought new troubles for Tombstone. Mineowners tried to cut their workers' daily wages from four dollars to three, and the miners responded on May 1 by initiating a strike. On May 10, a Tucson bank failed; its branch in Tombstone had held many of the miners' savings, and this new economic disaster only fed the anger and unrest in the town. By the time the strike ended, numerous miners—and inevitably, the business people who made money from the miners—had moved on, and many of the mines remained closed.

Tombstone was already a shadow of its boomtown 1879–1882 self; ironically, shortly before the miners' strike, the town had had its only lynching, and only as a result of playing host to a mob from Bisbee. In December 1883, five gunmen bent on robbery had burst into a Bisbee store filled with Christmas shoppers and clumsily fired into the crowd, killing a woman and three men. The posse that responded to what became known as the Bisbee Christmas Massacre found it was being fed misinformation by one of its own members, John Heath. When other posse members grilled him, Heath admitted planning the robbery and named the men who had carried it out. The five were captured, given the death penalty, and executed, but Heath, who had not directly participated in the carnage, drew only twenty years. Bisbee residents were not particularly happy with this sentence and in late February whisked Heath from the county jail in Tombstone and hanged him from a telegraph pole. Dr. Goodfellow examined the body and provided a wryly ambiguous report: "We the undersigned find that J. Heath came to his death from emphysema of the lungs—a disease common to high altitudes—which might have been caused by strangulation, self-inflicted or otherwise."

Tombstone itself was growing pretty sedate by this time, although bodies still turned up in the desert and stock was still rustled now and again. Bob Hatch of Campbell and Hatch's Saloon and Billiard Parlor became the elected county sheriff in 1885. That year Johnny Behan, now superintendent of the

Yuma Prison, got a vote of confidence for a law enforcement position, too, when the *Southwestern Stockman* endorsed him for marshal of Arizona Territory and proclaimed, "To him more than any man in Arizona is it due today that the stockmen may enjoy their ranges and possessions in peace." Behan didn't get the job. Meanwhile, a federal investigator was still trying to sort out ex-Marshal Dake's financial finaglings.

Two members of Behan's infamous 1882 posse, Ike and Phin Clanton, continued to range through eastern Arizona and western New Mexico. In 1882, they were in the vicinity of Springerville, Apache County, where they bet one hundred cattle that their mare could win a horse race. The mare lost, and Phin tried to welsh on the bet, but the owner of the winning horse faced him down and got the cattle. In 1886, the Clantons were at their ranch in Animas Valley, New Mexico, by some accounts operating as heads of a ranch-jumping gang of ne'er-do-wells, including a man named Renfro. The Clantons invited a neighboring ranch owner named Ellinger to their dwelling, and Renfro began abusing the guest over a ranch claim. Renfro picked up a six-shooter and strode toward Ellinger. Ike Clanton jumped in between the two, but "Renfro suddenly threw his pistol around Ike and shot Ellinger in the breast." The rancher, the Tombstone *Prospector* reported, "lived several days in great agony, suffering a thousand deaths, and died on or about the 10th of November last [1886]."

The Clantons made news again in June 1887, when they were caught rustling cattle on Eagle Creek, not far from Fort Grant. Phin halted at correspondence school detective J. V. Brighton's command to stop. Ike didn't, and Brighton shot him dead.

Phin wound up in the Yuma Hell Hole, eventually drawing a pardon. He was not the only former Tombstone area resident to surface on the wrong side of the bars at Yuma. Pete Spencer, too, served time there for assault. And Frank Leslie, his luck run out with the shooting of two more people, spent the early 1890's inside the prison walls.

Not surprisingly, Leslie's crime involved a woman. May Killeen Leslie had divorced him in 1887, charging him with adultery with a prostitute, physical violence, drunkenness, and failure to provide for her. Rumor also had it that Leslie had stood his wife up against a bedroom wall and outlined her silhouette with bullet holes, an incident she may understandably have considered unsanctioned by their wedding vows.

The prostitute mentioned in the divorce papers may well have been Molly Bradshaw, for by 1889 Leslie was living with Molly on Milt Joyce's Seven-Up ranch east of town in the Swisshelm Mountains. Business at the Oriental had dwindled, perhaps in part because of the bartender's reputation for shooting more than flies and in part because of Tombstone's continuing economic woes, including the dropping price of silver. Joyce had departed for the greener pastures of San Francisco and left Leslie in charge of the Seven-Up. The shootist brought Molly there after her husband and pimp, E. L. Bradshaw, had conveniently turned up dead in a Tombstone alley one morning, and the couple settled down to a life of nonmarital bliss.

However, Leslie was extremely jealous and increasingly prone to drunken rages. On July 11, the proprietor of a neighboring ranch, William Reynolds, rode into town with the news that Leslie had the previous evening shot "a woman supposed to be his wife" and a man named James Neal, a hired hand at the ranch. Reynolds, who had hidden the wounded Neal at his own ranch during the night, reported Leslie "still on the fight and acting like a crazy man" as Reynolds had departed for Tombstone to find a surgeon.

Doc Goodfellow immediately rode out. He reached the ranch the evening of the eleventh and found Molly dead where she had fallen. James Neal was nursing "wounds in the arm and body." A reporter found him reposing in a spring wagon on the afternoon of the twelfth and drew a narrative of events from him. Leslie and Molly had been drinking and arguing incessantly, with Leslie repeatedly striking the woman and threatening to go kill neighbor Reynolds. (The implication is that Leslie considered his fellow rancher a rival or potential rival for Molly's affections.) In fact, Leslie left for Reynolds's home, but returned the evening of the tenth complaining that the neighbor would not fight.

When Leslie returned, Molly and Neal were seated on the porch together, apparently further fueling the former bartender's jealousies. He began quarreling with Molly again, downed a drink, and announced, "I'll put a stop to all this." Entering the house, he emerged with a pistol and fired at the woman. As Neal sat shocked, Leslie turned to him, put the gun "close to his chest," and fired.

"Don't be afraid, it's nothing," said Leslie, and Neal briefly believed the gunman "was only fooling." Then Neal felt the blood on his body and saw Molly run and fall. He ran, too—to Reynolds's. The next morning, Leslie appeared there as well. He had apparently transferred all of his jealous rage to the ranch hand, for he announced he had come to find him and finish the job. Leslie was finally persuaded that his prey was not there and departed.

Armed with this information, Cochise County deputies set out to arrest Buckskin Frank. They were acting under the direction of Bob Hatch's successor, the formidable and renowned cattleman John Slaughter, who had accepted the sheriff's job in 1887. Slaughter shared Wyatt Earp's brand of tough ruthlessness, but he usually acted quietly and alone. When, for example, he went on the trail of a stolen animal, he would eventually return with the animal, and nobody considered it wise to inquire as to the whereabouts of the thief. His law enforcement philosophy was perhaps best expressed in the admonition he reputedly gave his deputies: "Shoot first and yell 'throw up your hands,' afterwards."

However, such a scenario did not occur when the deputies dispatched to pick up Frank Leslie met their quarry coming along the road to Tombstone. He peacefully surrendered to them, and they turned around and took him to the sheriff's office.

Bartender Billy King later claimed to be one of the men deputized and related that Leslie, unaware that Neal had surfaced and told his story, announced to the officers that the hired man had killed Molly, and Leslie thus had had to kill Neal. The deputies wisely remained silent concerning their knowledge of the affair, informing Leslie of the charges already pending against him only after they had safely conducted him to the county jail.

King's story is appealing, but his name was not listed among those sent to bring the shootist in, and the newspaper simply reported Leslie surrendering to the deputies. This time he drew life in the Yuma Penitentiary, arriving there in 1890, shortly before John Behan's prison superintendency ended. Leslie quickly became involved in a prison break plan, thwarted when Behan got wind of it. After that, Leslie was the exemplary inmate, working as the prison druggist—dispensing medicinal compounds rather than drinks—and winning a parole from the governor in 1896.

A conviction for killing his lover and a jail term had not diminished Leslie's appeal for the ladies—at least not for one. A divorcée who had begun corresponding with the convict after reading an 1893 San Francisco *Chronicle* interview with him was waiting upon his release, and the two were wed on December 1, 1896. The *Chronicle* wrote of the bride, "Mrs. Stowell has been and still is drawing $40 monthly alimony from her husband. The husband is now tired of paying her and has sent a detective here to investigate."

Fragmentary tales of Buckskin Frank's later years abound. Breakenridge, who became a special officer for the Southern Pacific Company, claimed to have secured a freighting job for Leslie into Mexico as part of a Southern Pacific geological survey. King remembered the former bartender appearing in Tombstone "gray and broken down" and relating that he had a job guiding insect collectors into Sonora. Leslie was rumored to turn up here and there in the West, an increasingly pathetic figure. For the frontier West—that landscape of wide-open towns dominated by bars, gambling halls, and whorehouses, and populated by restless, risk-taking young men looking for the quickest way to make money—was fast disappearing, and there wasn't much call for a shootist anymore.

Doc Holliday had fallen on hard times, too, up in Colorado, but he had escaped the civilized, industrialized West by dying a few months after Ike Clanton took a bullet on Eagle Creek. Doc didn't go, however, before tangling again with one—and maybe two—old enemies from Tombstone days.

The first encounter took place in Leadville, Colorado, in August 1884. Leadville had boomed about the same time as Tombstone and, like Tombstone, was experiencing a decline. But Leadville remained the premier silver camp of the West, still a way-up town with plenty of possibilities. Doc had spent most of his time there since successfully fighting the Arizona extradition request. At first, things had gone well. Doc brought with him a reputation as a dangerous man, but he stayed out of trouble and dealt faro at the Monarch Saloon. Then he got fired and was unable to find any other work. Bitter over the firing, Doc made threats against the Monarch Saloon. To add to his woes, he was sick with pneumonia a good bit of the time, and Johnny Tyler, with whom he had clashed in Tombstone in 1880, was now living in Leadville. The old enmities were renewed, with factions developing around each man.

Spicer hearing prosecution witness Billy Allen, now a bartender at the Monarch, was a member of Tyler's faction, and Doc was foolish or desperate enough to borrow five dollars from the former cowboy champion. When Allen began demanding repayment, Doc couldn't come up with the money. The borrower would testify that Allen then issued an ultimatum: "I walked into the Monarch before this trouble, and was coming out, when Allen came out, with an apron on, with his hand under his apron. He said, 'Holliday, I'll give you till Tuesday to pay this money and if you don't pay it, I'll lick you, you son-of-a-b-.' I said my jewelry is in soak and as soon as I get the money, I'll give it to you." Two other witnesses reported that Allen had threatened Doc with a deadline and physical violence as well, one stating that Allen had promised to knock his debtor down and "kick his d-d brains out" if the Tuesday noon time limit was not met. Allen also told a Leadville officer that Holliday was illegally carrying a gun; Doc got a warning and shelved the weapon because he was unable to pay the fine should he be caught with it.

Tuesday arrived, and the noon deadline came and went. Holliday would testify that he heard Allen had a gun and was looking for him; fine or no fine, Doc went and got his weapon. The bartender at Hyman's Saloon saw Holliday come in that afternoon and heard him say "he had heard Allen was going to do him up, and that he did not intend to be murdered."

About 5:00 P.M., Billy Allen approached Hyman's, looking for Doc. The Tyler faction contended that Allen "had no ill feeling toward Holliday, and apprehended no danger, and intended to have no difficulty," though some of them claimed they had warned him not to go. A local law officer would testify that he told Billy not to enter because word was that Doc was gunning for him. Allen entered anyway, telling friends "he would not have any trouble." As soon as Allen entered Hyman's, Holliday, standing behind a cigar case, pulled his cut-off single action Colt and fired.

> The first shot missed Allen and went through the glass at the top of the folding doors and lodged in the upper part of the door frame. When the first shot was fired, Allen turned to get out, but stumbled and fell, and just as he fell, Holliday reached over the cigar case and fired the second time, the ball entering Allen's right arm from the rear about half way between the shoulder and the elbow and passing out in the front.

The bartender grabbed Holliday after the second shot, and he was quickly taken into custody. As he was led away, Doc asked for protection—"that is," said the *Daily Herald,* "not to let anyone shoot him in the back." Meanwhile, Allen stumbled out of the saloon and was conveyed by hack to his room, where the arm wound was sewn up.

Allen prosecuted, refusing any out-of-court settlement. Doc's friends said that the defendant had been targeted for harassment and even death by the Tyler faction. Doc himself, on examination, contended that Allen's threats had driven him to the shooting: "I saw Allen come in with his hand in his pocket, and . . . I fired the shot, and he fell on the floor, and [I] fired the second shot; I knew that I would be a child in his hands if he got hold of me; I weigh 122 pounds; I think Allen weighs 170 pounds; I have had the pneumonia three or four times; I don't think I was able to protect myself against him."

Doc was released on eight thousand dollars' bail and finally acquitted in March 1885. But he was asked to leave Leadville. The Allen shooting had only added to his notoriety.

The Valdosta *Times,* Doc's hometown Georgia paper, picked up a New York *Sun* article on Doc datelined Silverton, Colorado, in June 1886. The article is fascinating in that it purports to be a transcript of Holliday addressing a crowd who had been listening to old-timers' tales about him. "When any of you fellows have been hunted from one end of the country to the other, as I have been, you'll understand what a bad man's reputation is built on," the article quoted Holliday saying. "I've had credit for more killings than I ever dreamed of."

At the same time that this well-known shootist debunked the myths, however, he also fed them. In Tombstone, he explained, he operated a gambling house, but customers dissatisfied with their losing record "put up a job" to kill him. He told them "that sort of thing couldn't go on in a well-regulated community, and then, just to restore order, I gave it to a couple of them." The speaker cast himself in the role of heroic lawman, his every action taken for the public good: "The claim that I make is that some few of us pioneers are entitled to credit for what we have done. We have been the fore-runners of government. . . . If it hadn't been for me and a few like me there never would have been any government in some of these towns. When I have done any shooting it has always been with this in view."

This particular forerunner of government was picked up for vagrancy in Denver in August 1886, with the Denver *Tribune-Republican* reporting that Doc had been living in the city whenever "the police did not drive him out of town." The paper reported, "His only means of living was gambling in its worst form and confidence work. Three weeks ago he left town on a penalty of being arrested, but returned a few days ago, the police say, in company with a score of other confidence men, thieves, and sure-thing workers."

Gone were the days when Denver celebrated a gambler-gunman from Arizona. Doc drifted back into Leadville, where he was reportedly the target of two mysterious shots in the dark. Johnny Tyler, still residing in Leadville, seemed a likely suspect. According to an unauthenticated letter from Doc in Glenn Boyer's *An Illustrated Life of Doc Holliday*, Doc and old crony Wyatt tracked Tyler and a companion to Glenwood Springs, then up the canyon of the Colorado River. The trackers quietly crept up on the camp of the two men and killed them as they arose. The second man turned out to be Perry Mallan, the would-be lawman who had captured Doc in Denver in '82. The letter alleges that Doc and Wyatt buried the two underneath a rock pile: "Probably nobody would find them anyhow, but why take chances? I found that out in Ariz. We should've drug Stilwell's dead ass out of the R.R. yard and buried him in the desert."

With the tuberculosis eroding his slender frame at a faster rate, Doc knew he didn't have long to live. He was thirty-five years old, but "emaciated and bent," his hair going completely silver. He stayed in Glenwood Springs, a hot-springs health spa, living in a hotel and paying a busboy to bring him liquor. In September 1887 he became virtually bedridden; in late October, he entered a two-week period of delirium, and on November 7, he ceased to talk at all.

On November 8 at 10:00 A.M., John Henry Holliday died. He reportedly opened his mouth twice that morning—first to ask for a glass of whiskey, then, after drinking it, to announce to the world, "This is funny." Researchers have logically speculated that Doc was commenting on the fact that he, the risk-taking gunfighter, was dying in bed. Considering his wryly profane outlook on life, however, the statement can be taken as a general comment on life and death as well.

Doc was buried in Glenwood Springs. The local paper gave him a nice write-up, reporting that the event occurred "in the presence of many friends" and commenting favorably on the "fortitude and patience" he had exhibited in his last months. It also noted, "He only had one correspondent among his relatives—a cousin, a Sister of Charity, in Atlanta, Georgia."

The story of this relative is almost too romantic to be true. According to family sources, Doc and his cousin Mattie Holliday, close since childhood, had corresponded throughout his western adventures, with Mattie entering the Sisters of Mercy order at St. Vincent's Academy in Savannah in 1883. Here and in Atlanta she was Mary Melanie, who her sister nuns later claimed was the model for Margaret Mitchell's character of Melanie in *Gone with the Wind*. It is tempting to consider Sister Melanie the gambling dentist's long-lost love, the pure figure hovering over his alcoholic reveries, but family members discounted this romantic connection. Nonetheless, the two maintained a long correspondence, and "Sister Melanie told her family that had she herself not destroyed some of

Doc's correspondence, the world would have known a different man from the one of Western fame."

Doc's real-life lover, Big Nose Kate Elder, spent most of her time in Arizona after her Tombstone days with Doc. She bounced about the territory, working variously as a cook, boardinghouse operator, and housekeeper, and marrying once but leaving her husband.

The Earp women stayed with their men—all, that is, except the discarded Mattie Blaylock. She wound up in Pinal, Arizona, another mining town just west of the San Carlos Indian Reservation. Here in the harsh, dusty desert she drank, sold her body, and took laudanum to sleep. She told one of her acquaintances, a laborer named T. J. Flannery, that "Earp had wrecked her life by deserting her and she didn't want to live." On July 3, 1888, Flannery found her dead, the whiskey and laudanum bottles near her bed emptied. The verdict was suicide. Newspapers referred to her as "a frail denizen of Pinal" who had topped off a drinking bout with an overdose of laudanum.

Wyatt Earp's liaison with Josie Marcus was to prove far more long-lasting. They lived in Colorado for a while, moving about among the various towns and mining camps. Wyatt also made a solo return trip to Dodge in 1883 to participate in what became known as the Dodge City War, a controversy centering on old friend Luke Short.

Short had bought an interest in Dodge's Long Branch Saloon with W. H. Harris and had increased its popularity. In doing so, he drew disgruntled opposition both from jealous rival saloonkeepers and from a town reform group wanting to clean up Dodge's image and attract more settlers. There are various accounts as to how the trouble started; by one, city police arrested a female "singer" at the Long Branch for soliciting. Bat Masterson later charged that the saloon-owning Dodge mayor got an ordinance passed banning music in the saloons and gambling houses, failed to honor it himself, and had Short's band arrested when the Long Branch proprietor reassembled it. Whatever the circumstances, Short, too, was quickly arrested, escorted to the train station, and placed on a train with the understanding that he was not to return.

Short went to Kansas City and rallied some of his old

friends, including Bat, who came from Denver. The ousted saloon owner also went to Topeka and complained to the governor and the press. When the governor failed to respond, Short's friends devised their own plan, as Bat Masterson recalled: "Wyatt was selected to land in Dodge first. With him, but unknown to the Dodge authorities, were several desperate men. Several more dropped into town unobserved by the enemy. It finally became whispered about that Wyatt Earp had a strong force already domiciled in town in the interest of Luke Short."

Dodge officials wired to the governor asking for a militia force in the face of this gunfighter threat, but as he had with Short, the governor refused to intervene. Masterson reported that Wyatt negotiated with the mayor and council, and Luke Short was allowed to return and resume operation of the saloon. Short, partner Harris, Bat and Wyatt, and a few of their friends gathered for a picture, later wryly titled "The Dodge City Peace Commission." Then Bat and Wyatt headed back to one of Wyatt's points of escape from Arizona, Silver City, New Mexico, where new silver deposits had just been discovered. Along the way, they stopped and visited Wyatt's elder half brother, Newton, now marshal of Garden City, Kansas.

Wyatt just kept moving—often with Bat, sometimes with brother Jim, occasionally with other gamblers on the western gambling circuit, frequently with Josie. He paid a brief visit to Fort Worth in 1884. For Will McLaury, still practicing law in the Texas cow town, Wyatt's presence was galling, recalling to mind that his own Arizona attempt to get justice for his brothers was "very unfortunate—as to my health—and badly injured me as to money matters—and none of the results have been satisfactory—The only result is the Death of Morgan and crippling of Virgil Earp and death of McMasters." (McMasters's death was not substantiated; in fact, Wyatt asserted that McMasters did not die until 1898, while in the United States Army in the Philippines.)

Wyatt got his own bit of revenge while on the gambling circuit in Globe, Arizona, at least according to Glenn Boyer, who had Josie relating that Wyatt happened upon Johnny Behan on the street and decked him. The couple followed the Coeur d'Alene gold rush in 1884; depending on which source one reads, Wyatt and brother Jim either tried to jump a number of claims or simply "tested in court the validity of several claims previously filed by proxy." Meanwhile, Virgil and Allie settled in Colton, where Virgil established his own private detective agency and in 1887 became the town's first elected marshal.

Eventually, Wyatt and Josie settled in San Diego, where he operated a saloon, engaged in real estate speculation, and raised and raced Thoroughbred horses. An interviewer in 1888 noted that he "Has Killed over a dozen stage robbers, murderers and cattle thieves" and "To him more than any other man is due the credit for driving out the banditti" of Arizona Territory. The interviewer provided a vivid thumbnail sketch with maudlin flourishes: "He is tall, slim, florid complexion, blue eyes, large nose, as quick as a cat. Socially he would be taken for a minister. He has a heart as big as an ox and feelings as tender as a child's. Is worth $30,000, owns property in San Diego, Tombstone . . . has about $6000 or $7000 cash."

By 1896, Wyatt and Josie were living the high life in San Francisco, staying at the hotel of colorful mining and real estate speculator Lucky Baldwin and following the races. They had left their disturbing beginnings in Tombstone far behind them, with Josie acknowledged as Mrs. Wyatt Earp and with the San Francisco *Examiner* publishing Wyatt's sanitized, heroic tales of the old days in its pages in August of the year. The Stilwell murder charge was still pending, as were a few debts Wyatt had incurred in Tombstone, but who was going to bother with all that now, fifteen years later?

Then Wyatt accepted a one-shot job that would bring his past under considerable critical scrutiny. In November 1896 San Francisco buzzed with talk of the big fight scheduled for December 2 at Mechanic's Pavilion. Thirty-four-year-old Bob Fitzsimmons would battle twenty-three-year-old Tom Sharkey for a ten-thousand-dollar prize and a title bout with world heavyweight champion Gentleman Jim Corbett. Fitzsimmons, a bull-like, unrelenting fighter with a wicked punch, was considered the favorite, but Sharkey had a dynamic left hook and the ability to take punches and keep on coming.

The promoters needed a referee, but this turned out to be a difficult matter. Fitzsimmons's manager had heard rumors that the fight might be fixed in Sharkey's favor, and he rejected any referees the promoters suggested. The promoters, afraid that Fitzsimmons would back out, scrambled madly and on the day of the fight came up with a compromise candidate, Wyatt Earp.

When Wyatt entered the arena, the crowd at first greeted him warmly, then reacted angrily when it realized that he, an "utterly inexperienced referee," was going to officiate. Wyatt promised a fair fight, then took off his frock coat, exposing his .45 and leading the fans to respond negatively again, with one shouting that Earp was a "two-gun man." But a San Francisco police captain attending announced, "Wyatt Earp's word is good with me!" The crowd settled down, and the fight began.

It was a brutal slugfest, "more a street brawl than a prizefight," and the inexperienced Wyatt apparently tried his best to control it. In the third round, Fitzsimmons landed a blow below Sharkey's belt, but Sharkey told Wyatt he wasn't badly hurt and asked him not to stop the fight. In the eighth, as the fighters came together in a clinch, Fitzsimmons landed another low blow, apparently unintentionally and hidden from the view of most of the audience. Sharkey fell, out cold, and Wyatt declared him the winner because of the low-blow foul.

Fitzsimmons's manager and the many prominent San Franciscans who had lost money by the decision were livid. They argued that Sharkey had repeatedly fouled without being reprimanded by Wyatt, and they questioned whether the final, hidden foul had actually been committed.

Wyatt insisted that it had, and that he had only done "what was right and honorable and feeling." He asserted, "No man until now has ever questioned my honor." A team of six doctors "approved by all concerned parties" confirmed that Sharkey had received a foul blow, and Sharkey later claimed that Fitzsimmons had apologized for the low hit. But Fitzsimmons backers considered the decision proof that the fight had been fixed.

The upshot of all this for Wyatt was that he received a fifty-dollar fine for carrying a concealed weapon, had old debts suddenly called in—including one incurred with Marshall Williams in Tombstone in 1881—and was roasted in the press. The San Francisco *Chronicle* reported with glee the legal entanglements of the "Tombstone Terror," painting a picture of Wyatt as a swaggering, publicity-loving character who was getting his just deserts.

The picture was not accurate. Human nature being what it is, Wyatt Earp did enjoy good publicity. He didn't enjoy any other kind, and he quit the big city in disgust, deciding to go back to prospecting in the desert.

Mining had become almost completely industrialized at this point, but many still clung to the shimmering dream of independently finding mineral riches. Only a few months after the Fitzsimmons-Sharkey fight, old Ed Schieffelin was buried with pick, shovel, and canteen, as he had specified, back at the site of his first camp in the Tombstone hills, just outside the town founded on his dream. He had prospected to the last, dying in the doorway of his cabin twenty miles east of Canyonville, Oregon. A short time earlier, he had written a friend, "I am getting restless here in Oregon and wish to go somewhere that has wealth, for the digging of it. . . . I like the excitement of being right up against the earth, trying to coax her gold away and scatter it."

Fittingly, Schieffelin's death was quickly followed by "a prospector's dream come true," the last great American gold rush—to the Alaskan frontier. Americans fastened onto the news of gold on Alaska's beaches with the fervor of the forty-niners a half century earlier. The "virulence of interest" became almost "a kind of gesture toward the vanished frontier . . . [and] into this progressive, respectable and somewhat unexciting period was thrust news that promised one last adventure." Wyatt Earp would go. So would John Clum. But the Alaska adventure would be all too brief; Earp and Clum and many of their friends and enemies from Tombstone days would live to inhabit a different world and to reinvent in memory the one in which they had been young. For the West as they knew it—that gambler's paradise of tremendous uncertainty and tremendous excitement—died before they did.

Epilogue
"It Must Be a Nice Clean Story"

The year 1900. Americans are still making their way westward, with the center of United States population now calculated to be a spot in south-central Indiana. However, massive changes are occurring in American life as the country becomes more settled. Increasing numbers of people move to the cities, east and west, to work in the big industry and big business that have been replacing small-scale individual enterprise and agrarian life. About eight thousand motorcars have made their appearance on the nation's roads, and Americans are enjoying general economic prosperity. Life has become more circumscribed for most westerners; Carry Nation is busy destroying Kansas saloon furnishings in the name of temperance, and Civilization, with all of its comforts and restrictions, has taken root on the prairies of the Midwest, in the hills, mountains, and deserts of the Southwest, in the rich valleys of the Pacific Coast.

In other words, the days of the rough, raw, near-boundless frontier have virtually ended. America has not lost its appetite for a mythic frontier—if anything, that appetite has grown with the fading of the real one—but many of the men who made their living by roaming the West engaging in quintessential frontier occupations—prospector, gambler, hired gunman, cattle puncher, saloonkeeper, boomtown business-man-on-a-shoestring—will find the transition a hard one.

Two former Tombstone players, Virgil Earp and Johnny Behan, made that transition fairly well, only to die before the century was well under way. His arm still crippled from the December 1881 attack, Virgil Earp continued in law enforce-ment, ranched, and prospected. Eventually he moved with his Allie back to Prescott, Arizona, the town he had wistfully called "the only place that seems like home." Here in Sep-tember 1900 he received the highest honor of his career: nomination for sheriff of Yavapai County at the County Re-publican Convention. Standing to speak before the assembled delegates who had given him this vote of confidence, he pre-sented himself as the ultimate frontier hero. In Dodge City, he related, the businessmen and property owners told him they would have to leave town if he didn't take the city marshal's job, so he did. (No record of Virgil as an officer in Dodge has been uncovered.) In Tombstone, leading citizens such as E. B. Gage told him the mines would have to be shut down if he didn't take the marshal's job there.

Despite the hyperbole, there was no question that Virgil had performed conscientiously as a frontier lawman, and busi-nessman Gage himself backed him up, stating, "I know per-sonally that whatever Virgil Earp did in Tombstone was at the request of the best men in Cochise County." However, the candidate soon dropped out of the race, with poor health given as the reason. He was serving as deputy sheriff of Esmeralda County, Nevada, when he died of pneumonia in October 1905.

Johnny Behan, too, managed to continue working suc-cessfully within the government and law enforcement system, although rumors of graft and administrative ineptitude fol-lowed in his wake. After running the state penitentiary, he became an inspector of customs, served in the Spanish-Amer-ican War, became a member of the American brigade sent to China's Boxer Rebellion, and finally worked as the code clerk for the Arizona legislature. He died of "hardening of the ar-teries and acute Brights disease" at St. Mary's Hospital, Tuc-son, on June 7, 1912. In 1885, in talking with a federal investigator concerning the 1882 troubles with the Earps and the cowboys, Behan had insisted that as Cochise County sheriff "he himself had done more to quell the disturbance than anyone else." An honor guard consisting of members of the Arizona Pioneer Society attended him to his grave.

As the pioneer generation died away, Americans still liked to read about the rough frontier past—and particularly about the exploits of the shootists. Bat Masterson made the transition from frontier gambler to twentieth-century sporting man by writing about his friends and acquaintances—Wyatt Earp, Doc Holliday, Luke Short, Bill Tilghman, Ben Thompson, and Buffalo Bill Cody. With the gambling profession increasingly falling into disrepute, Bat had been asked to leave Denver in 1902. He had moved to that most eastern and urban of cities New York, where he picked up a deputy United States marshal appointment for the southern district of the city from President Teddy Roosevelt. Then, in 1907, he produced a series of articles on "Famous Gunfighters of the West" for *Human Life* magazine.

The pieces were no pat glorification of the characters of the shootists; here we have Luke Short selling whiskey to the Indians and secretly killing a few that dared get uppity with him, Doc Holliday spreading his tuberculosis germs and his "mean disposition" around the West. However, Bat's sketches did celebrate the dangerous lives of the gunmen, and their nerve and skill.

He was particularly deferential toward Wyatt Earp, behaving throughout their relationship much like a loyal, supportive younger brother. Bat, too, rewrote history to his friend's advantage. The Clantons and McLaurys, he told *Human Life* readers, were desperadoes wanted "dead or alive," yet repeatedly eluding or successfully resisting United States troops sent out to bring them in. The four sent Virgil word "that on a certain day they would be in town prepared to give him and his brothers a battle to the death." Sure enough, the four rode into Tombstone on the appointed day. They fired first, but "nearly every shot fired by the Earp party went straight home to the mark," with the McLaurys and Billy Clanton "hit by no less than half a dozen bullets each."

Bat's articles led to a job as a newspaperman, and by 1921

he was sports editor of the New York *Morning Telegraph*. Meanwhile, America's silent film industry was growing; since the landmark 1903 film *The Great Train Robbery*, westerns had developed into a major genre. On October 9, 1921, western film star William S. Hart, calling himself a "mere player," published in the *Morning Telegraph* a tribute to "those great gunmen who molded a new country for us to live in and enjoy peace and prosperity"—Hickok, Short, Holliday, Thompson. And, he noted, "we have today in American two of these men with us in the flesh," Bat Masterson and Wyatt Earp. Hart urged readers not to forget these living heroes, "for no history of the West can be written without their wonderful deeds being recorded."

Sixteen days later, Bat Masterson collapsed at his *Morning Telegraph* sports desk, dead of a heart attack at sixty-seven.

His old buffalo-hunting companion, Wyatt Earp, lived on in a world which increasingly celebrated his past but in which he had no vital present. Wyatt had thriven during the Alaska gold rush, setting up gambling and saloon operations that netted him a fine profit. But after that last great frontier experience, where to go and what to do had become a problem. He roved between California, Arizona, and Nevada, prospecting in the last during its mining boom in the first years of the twentieth century. Eventually, he and Josie established a pattern of prospecting in the desert during the winter and living in Los Angeles during the warmer months.

The years brought with them problems stemming from Wyatt's notoriety, as demonstrated by a Tucson *Daily Citizen* article in May 1900:

> Wyat [*sic*] Earp, the well known gunfighter who made his reputation in Tombstone in its wild and wooley [*sic*] days, was knocked out in San Francisco, a few days ago by Tom Mulqueen, a well known horseman. Earp attempted to do the horseman, but the latter put it all over him and knocked him glassy-eyed in the first round. It is thought that Earp will try his gun the next time, but Mulqueen has been there before and the Tombstoner may head the funeral.

Earp researchers have disputed this story, charging that Mulqueen instead backed down when facing the man he had bragged about being able to best. Certainly the aging Wyatt's reputation made him a target for challenges and hearsay.

He also suffered legal and financial humiliations. In 1911, Wyatt was picked up in Los Angeles on a charge of conspiracy with two others "to fleece J. Y. Peterson out of $25,000.00 on an alleged bunco game." He already had a vagrancy charge standing. He continued to escape annually with Josie to the desert, to the small community of Vidal across the state from Los Angeles and beside the Colorado River on the Arizona line. He and Josie had a mine in the area, the Happy Days, but it did not provide much in the way of income.

Living in Los Angeles for much of the year placed Wyatt near the heart of the movie industry. According to different sources, he had either approached western moviemakers, trying to sell his stories and services, or they had approached him and pumped him for information without providing any recompense. However the connection occurred, he did find a staunch friend in film star William S. Hart, and Hart's papers contain a sad plea for a fifty-dollar loan from the former shootist. The movie actor also tried to help Wyatt get his "autobiography" published in the mid-1920's.

The manuscript had been produced by Wyatt's friend John Flood. It was awful, an overwrought Victorian paean to manliness and virtue with the Wyatt Earp character moving, pristine, magnificent, and wooden, through one vague, improbable scenario after another. It took more than five pages of sentimental verbiage for the hero even to enter the world and nestle into his mother's loving arms under the light of his father's proud gaze.

Wyatt must have participated in and approved of this misguided attempt to tell his story; in 1926 he rejected writer Walter Noble Burns's plan to write a book on him by citing Flood's effort and the continuing attempts to market it. Perhaps he thought such excess was the only antidote to the negative stories that surfaced concerning his exploits. In 1925, he had written a Scribner's author politely protesting an embarrassing and untrue story placing him in Dawson, Alaska. "Notoriety has been the bane of my life," he noted at that time.

Flood never found a publisher. Walter Noble Burns did,

purportedly telling Wyatt the book was to be about Doc Holliday and thus enlisting his aid. Burns produced a distorted, rip-roaring, and highly readable broad chronicle, *Tombstone,* in 1927, with a daring Wyatt one of the principal players.

Then Billy Breakenridge's book, *Helldorado: Bringing the Law to the Mesquite,* hit the bookstands in 1928. Breakenridge was by now a well-loved Arizona old-timer, and his account of the wild early days of Tombstone drew national attention. The former deputy did not castigate the Earps and Holliday, but neither did he provide a very flattering picture of them. Breakenridge made clear that he found the shootists too quick on the trigger, and he remained loyal to Johnny Behan, whose method of law enforcement he found both more effective and more humane.

Wyatt Earp was incensed. Breakenridge, working as a private investigator in an estate litigation case, had visited Wyatt in 1925 and received his assistance. Now the former deputy had opened up all the controversies of the past, clearly indicating that Wyatt held an ambiguous, and perhaps downright troublesome, place in frontier affairs. About this time, Wyatt agreed to work with another would-be biographer, Stuart Lake. To Lake, he wrote that *Helldorado* was "all a pack of lies and me, me, me." Coming from a man who had apparently given his blessing to Flood's glorification of Wyatt Earp, frontier hero, the charge sounds suspiciously like sour grapes. Meanwhile, Josie Marcus Earp, the former traveling actress who had lived with Behan, then bested Mattie Blaylock in a contest for Wyatt's affections, was admonishing the biographer to provide a moral little tale. "Several of our friends Mr. Lake tell us it will go big," she wrote, "but it must be a nice clean story."

Lake would produce a volume in which imaginative recreations and outright fabrications were skillfully interwoven with well-researched fact, an account that was all Wyatt, Wyatt, Wyatt. How much Wyatt himself had to do with this work has been a subject of some confusion, with many writers attributing all of the claims in Lake's 1932 product, *Wyatt Earp, Frontier Marshal,* directly to his subject. Evidence indicates that Lake had only limited contact with Wyatt, and then found him less than garrulous. The two visited and exchanged a few letters, but the biographer would later write to Burton Rascoe, "As a matter of cold fact, Wyatt never 'dictated' a word to me. . . . He was delightfully laconic, or exasperatingly so."

However, Lake's imaginative, myth-ridden manuscript may nonetheless be considered simply a continuation of Wyatt Earp's own claims to newspaper reporters and to Flood. (Lake, assessing the poor quality of Flood's manuscript, claimed to have only skimmed it.) How much Wyatt sought to present himself as a western hero and how much he simply gave his interviewers what they wanted to hear remains open to debate today. By the time Lake got to him, the former frontiersman was nearing death.

He was the last of the Earp brothers. Morgan, of course, had died almost half a century earlier in a Tombstone billiard room. Youngest brother Warren had returned to Arizona in the 1890's, working for Henry Clay Hooker and as a bartender in Willcox, only to take a bullet through the heart in a barroom confrontation in 1900. Attempts to link the incident to the earlier troubles in Tombstone have been unsuccessful; Warren was killed by one Johnny Boyett, with whom he had been at odds for some time. Despite the fact that the youngest Earp carried only a half-opened pocketknife when he was shot, Boyett won a dismissal of his case. The judge ruled that an indictment on the evidence available was unlikely.

Five years later, Virgil had died in Nevada. Older brothers Newton and James proved more long-lived, with James driving a hack in San Bernardino, California, for years and dying in Los Angeles in 1926. Newton passed away in 1928 in Sacramento.

Wyatt had remained close to James through the years. Now he had only a few of his old friends with whom to talk over the early days. Chief among them was John Clum, who in 1910 had retired from the postal service and gone on the lecture circuit, giving "America Picturesque" talks designed to promote tourism for the Southern Pacific Railroad. His 1916–17 lecture advertisement grandiosely promised, "America Picturesque Will Make You a Better Member of Your Family, A Better Citizen, A BETTER AMERICAN." The former Tombstone mayor had also settled in the Los Angeles area. He visited with his old ally, watching Wyatt's health decline, and was with him on the last evening of his life, January 12, 1929. Wyatt died the next morning of chronic cystitis. His funeral drew quite a crowd, including Clum and another Los Angeles resident, former city chamber of commerce director George Parsons. Actors Hart and Tom Mix were present for the occasion, too. "OLD WESTERNERS" PAY WYATT EARP LAST TRIBUTE, read the Los Angeles *Evening Herald.*

Clum published his version of events in Tombstone in the pages of the *Arizona Historical Review* later that year, lauding Wyatt as "quite my ideal of the strong, manly, serious and capable peace officer." Meanwhile, Lake proceeded on the book that would ensure his subject's lasting fame as a noble law bringer, a man who "shot [his] way to Heaven." He found a number of old-timers ready to agree with this view, including Parsons, who wrote Lake that Wyatt "never killed a man who did not richly deserve it." Other old-timers such as John Pleasant Gray and James Hancock provided their own reminiscences refuting this view and reflecting the divisions that had existed in Tombstone when the Earps lived there.

But whether one saw Wyatt Earp and his friends as heroes or villains, the story of Tombstone during its boom days provided fine fodder for the dramatic imaginations of those fascinated by the idea of a Wild West. The tale also became the lifeblood of Tombstone itself.

Despite its status as Cochise County seat, Tombstone almost died in the early years of the twentieth century. By 1914, all mine production in the area had ground to a halt. Then in 1929, in a final, near-fatal blow, the county seat was moved to Bisbee. Tombstone had only one asset left: its colorful past. Billy Breakenridge's *Helldorado* had generated interest in that past only the year before, so in October 1929, nine months after Wyatt Earp's death, "The Town Too Tough to Die" mounted its first Helldorado celebration. Tombstone's citizens, fighting for their economic survival, presented all the stuff of myth: stagecoach robberies; Indian attacks; a reenactment of the gunfight on the vacant lot, now part of the O.K. Corral. John Clum returned for the occasion. A nephew of the slain McLaurys also attended and complained that the men playing his uncles were too poorly dressed.

Tombstone today is a tourist town. The Helldorado celebration continues every October, as well as a "Rendezvous of Gunfighters" each Labor Day weekend. At any time of the year, one can find vacationers treading the board sidewalks of Allen Street, touring the Bird Cage Theater, circling the life-size figures of the gunfight participants in the vacant lot, downing ice cream in a parlor garishly decorated with imitation stained glass images of Wyatt Earp and Doc Holliday. If you talk to the people who run the stores and run the town, you will find opinion concerning the famous gunfight as deeply divided as ever. The cowboys still have their champions in Tombstone, as do the Earps and Holliday.

The town's citizens live daily with the myths, but we all live with the myths of the frontier West, many of which are grounded in historical reality. The West of the nineteenth century *did* offer great freedom and frequent opportunities to re-make oneself. These opportunities were accompanied by very real dangers—from knowing whom to trust in a fluid society to knowing how to set a black powder charge so that it didn't blow one into the beyond. Men seized the opportunities and the dangers, often with explosive results.

The men who took these chances were not necessarily "good" or "bad" men, and the idea of the West as setting for a simple ongoing morality play between good and evil is perhaps the shakiest myth of all. Naturally, good and evil, by any human standards, did exist. Everyone could recognize that randomly stealing a horse from an old man alone in the desert and shooting the owner in the head, as Sandy King reportedly did, was a wicked act that bespoke a bad character. But for finer distinctions between good and bad to work, there must be some general agreement as to what constitutes one or the other.

In the confused political, economic, and social climate of the frontier, men could not agree on right and wrong or on degrees of right and wrong. A person was judged "good" because his economic interests were aligned with one's own; he was "bad" because his interests conflicted, or because his allegiances lay with a different political party or geographical group.

The significance of the "gunfight at the O.K. Corral," then, does not lie in its existence as a morality play between "good" lawmen and "bad" cowboys or between "bad" lawmen and "good" cowboys. Rather, the gun battle, the personalities involved in it and the events surrounding it are significant for what they tell us about the real complexities of the western frontier experience. The story of the troubles in boomtown Tombstone reminds us that the whys and wherefores of living and dying have never been as simple as we might wish them to be—particularly in the crucible that was the American frontier West.

Notes

CHAPTER 1: Trails to Tombstone

18. "Inform McLearry [*sic*]": October 27, 1881, Will McLaury Letters, New-York Historical Society.
18. "There's a lot": February 21, 1882.
19. "the effects of": *Daily Nugget,* October 30, 1881.
19. "The verdict reassures": "GLAD TO KNOW," October 30, 1881.
19. "apprehensive and": Entry of October 27, 1881, George Parsons, *The Private Journal of George Whitwell Parsons* (Phoenix: Works Projects Administration, 1939).
20. "the expansive": Don Harrison Doyle, "Social Theory and New Communities in Nineteenth-Century America," *Western Historical Quarterly,* vol. 8, no. 2 (April 1977), p. 165.
20. "considerable trickery": Entry of March 11, 1880, *Private Journal.*
21. "He was about": Quoted in Odie B. Faulk, *Tombstone: Myth and Reality* (New York: Oxford University Press, 1972), p. 33.
23. "While standing": Quoted in William Breakenridge, *Helldorado: Bringing the Law to the Mesquite* (Boston and New York: Houghton Mifflin Company, 1928), p. 90.
24. "The best thing": Faulk, *Tombstone,* p. 38.

24. "Ed, you lucky": Ibid., p. 35.

24. "get Mexico to": Quoted in Robert Wooster, "'A Difficult and Forlorn Country': The Military Looks at the American Southwest, 1850–1890," *Arizona and the West,* vol. 28 (Winter 1986), pp. 345, 350.

25. "all roads led": John Pleasant Gray, "When All Roads Led to Tombstone," typescript in Arizona Historical Society Collection, Tucson.

25. "You soon got": Ibid., pp. 48–50.

27. "wiry, determined-looking": *Tucson Daily Star,* March 26, 1882, Carl Hayden Biographical Files, Arizona State Historical Society.

28. "I was to take": Melvin W. Jones Typescript, Reminiscences, Arizona Historical Society, pp. 1–3.

29. "The McGarey [*sic*]": Richard J. Hinton, *The Handbook to Arizona: Its Resources, History, Towns, Mines, Ruins and Scenery* (Tucson: Arizona Silhouettes, 1954 reprint), p. 234.

29. "decidedly uninteresting": Ibid., p. 231.

29. "The landscape": Ibid.

30. "about to pull": Quoted in A. W. Bork and Glenn G. Boyer, "The O.K. Corral Fight at Tombstone: A Footnote by Kate Elder," *Arizona and the West,* vol. 19, no. 1 (Spring 1977), p. 76.

31. "Five brothers, all": Frank Waters, *The Earp Brothers of Tombstone: The Story of Mrs. Virgil Earp* (Lincoln: University of Nebraska Press, 1976 ed.), p. 27.

31. "knew only two": Glenn G. Boyer, ed., *I Married Wyatt Earp: The Recollections of Josephine Sarah Marcus Earp* (Tucson: University of Arizona Press, 1976), p. 130.

33. "quite my ideal": John P. Clum, "It All Happened in Tombstone," *Arizona Historical Quarterly,* vol. 2, no. 3 (October 1929), p. 50.

33. *"absolutely nothing":* Letter of December 4, 1931, in James C. Hancock Papers, Arizona Historical Society.

34. "in the neighborhood": William Barclay Masterson, *Famous Gunfighters of the Western Frontier* (Houston: Frontier Press of Texas, 1957), p. 56.

34. "no braver": Ibid., p. 54.

34. "after being up": Letter of November 11, 1928, David Leahy to John Madden, Stuart Nathaniel Lake Collection, Huntington Library, San Marino, California.

34. "These boys fear": Quoted in Alford E. Turner, ed., *The Earps Talk* (College Station, Texas: Creative Publishing Company, 1982 ed.), p. 17.

34. "offered some": Letter of November 11, 1928, Lake Collection.
35. "Erp [*sic*] was": Quoted in Waters, *Earp Brothers*, p. 39.
35. "Damon did not": Quoted in Robert K. DeArment, *Bat Masterson, the Man and the Legend* (Norman: University of Oklahoma Press, 1979), p. 227.
35. "deeply anxious about": Obituary quoted in Albert S. Pendleton, Jr., and Susan McKey Thomas, *In Search of the Hollidays* (Valdosta, Ga.: Little River Press, 1973), p. 11.
36. "relieved the monotony": January 2, 1875, quoted ibid.
36. "carved up": Masterson, *Famous Gunfighters*, p. 39.
36. "Where satisfaction is": Quoted in Turner, *Earps Talk*, p. 18.
36. "Keep your baby": Waters, *Earp Brothers*, p. 43.
36. "incessantly coughed it": Masterson, *Famous Gunfighters*, p. 40.
37. "At the report": Quoted in Jack Burrows, *John Ringo: The Gunfighter Who Never Was* (Tucson: University of Arizona Press, 1987), p. 113.
40. "a nice young": Fred Dodge, quoted in Boyer, ed., *I Married*, p. 59, note 16.
40. "the mainstay of": Gray, "When All Roads," p. 32.
40. "technically there never": Odie B. Faulk, *Arizona: A Short History* (Norman: University of Oklahoma Press, 1974 ed.), p. 174.

CHAPTER 2: "A Big Camp This with a Big Future"

41. "an even break": Gray, "When All Roads," pp. 68–71.
42. "millions on millions": Dan DeQuille, quoted in T. H. Watkins, *Gold and Silver in the West: The Illustrated History of an American Dream* (New York: Bonanza Books, 1971), p. 189.
42. "spit bath": Quoted in Faulk, *Tombstone*, p. 80.
42. "a clear sky": Gray, "When All Roads," p. 46.
42. "You never heard": Ibid., pp. 45–46.
42. "never fails": *Daily Nugget,* December 15, 1880.
43. "had no intention": Allie Earp, quoted in Waters, *Earp Brothers,* p. 91.
44. "If hell is": Quoted in Mark Wyman, "Industrial Revolution in the West: Hard-Rock Miners and the New Technology," *Western Historical Quarterly,* vol. 5, no. 1 (January 1974), p. 39.
44. "It looked all": Quoted in Watkins, *Gold and Silver,* p. 97.
44. "It was like": Waters, *Earp Brothers,* p. 92.
45. "There are no": Faulk, *Tombstone,* p. 83.
46. "Chicken Fricassee": Menu quoted in Carolyn Niethammer,

"Frontier Restaurants: The West Wasn't Won on Beans Alone," *True West,* vol. 31, no. 5 (May 1984), p. 47.

46. "hanging in front": Ibid., p. 45.

46. "could be heard": Gray, "When All Roads," p. 14.

46. "In an instant": Quoted in Wyman, "Industrial Revolution," p. 43.

47. "Dead men were": Quoted in Watkins, *Gold and Silver,* p. 210.

47. "I can hardly": Ibid., p. 22.

47. "two dance houses": Quoted in Faulk, *Tombstone,* p. 115.

47. "Aurora of a": Quoted in Roger D. McGrath, *Gunfighters, Highwaymen and Vigilantes: Violence on the Frontier* (Berkeley: University of California Press, 1987), p. 11.

47. "Every house": Elliott West, "The Saloon in Territorial Arizona," *Journal of the West,* vol. 13, no. 3 (1974), p. 61. West's study provides the basis for my discussion of saloons and drinking in the West.

48. "heat, dust, and drudgery": Ibid.

48. "what companionship": Ibid., p. 64.

48. "high in value": Ibid., p. 61.

48. "Well do you": Ibid., p. 62.

48. "Feel tip-top": Ibid., p. 66.

48. "Oh, Moon": Quoted in C. L. Sonnichsen, *Billy King's Tombstone: The Private Life of an Arizona Boom Town* (Tucson: University of Arizona Press, 1972), p. 180.

48. "Nowhere else": Quoted in McGrath, *Gunfighters,* p. 12.

49. "a masculine": Anne M. Butler, *Daughters of Joy, Sisters of Misery: Prostitutes in the American West, 1865–90* (Urbana and Chicago: University of Illinois Press, 1987), p. 2. Butler's study provides the basis for my discussion of prostitution in the West.

49. "a population": Ibid., p. 61.

49. "Elderly gentlemen": Quoted in Ben T. Traywick, *The Chronicles of Tombstone* (Tombstone: Red Marie's Bookstore, 1986), p. 64.

49. "The Call of": September 24, 1880.

49. "far from manifesting": T. M. Thompson, quoted in Ed Bartholomew, *Wyatt Earp, 1879 to 1882, the Man & the Myth* (Toyahvale, Texas: Frontier Book Company, 1964), p. 44.

50. "with bets placed": James C. Hancock, "Comment on an Article in the Saturday Evening Post," Hancock Papers.

50. "More difficult": Entry of March 18, 1880, *Private Journal.*

51. "I have seen": Entry of July 16, 1880, ibid.

51. "About the first": Entry of March 14, 1880, ibid.

51. "Forty young": Quoted in Butler, *Daughters,* p. 53.

51. "Rather curious": Entry of May 6, 1880, *Private Journal.*

51. "Got horrible": Entry of September 17, 1881, ibid.

52. "More brawls": Quoted in Stanley W. Zamonski and Teddy Keller, *The '59ers: Roaring Denver in the Gold Rush Days* (Frederick, Colo.: Platte 'N Press, 1983 ed.), p. 36.

52. "occurred with": McGrath, *Gunfighters*, p. 185.

52. "Several more": Entry of April 6, 1880, *Private Journal*.

52. "I was never": Entry of March 11, 1880, ibid.

53. "Very lively": Entry of February 18, 1880, ibid.

53. "Times prosperous": Entry of March 23, 1880, ibid.

53. "We now have": Quoted in Faulk, *Arizona*, p. 156.

53. "He was a": Bisbee *Brewery Gulch Gazette*, September 12, 1935.

54. "Johnny wasn't": Quoted in Ben Jaastad, typescript account of Oakes's life, Oakes File, Arizona Historical Society.

54. "Johnny would": Quoted in Woodworth Clum, *Apache Agent: The Story of John P. Clum* (Boston: Houghton Mifflin, 1936), pp. 259–60.

54. "Hon. John H. Behan": Quoted in Pat Jahns, *The Frontier World of Doc Holliday: Faro Dealer from Dallas to Deadwood* (Lincoln: University of Nebraska Press, 1979 ed.), p. 156.

55. "I have just": Letter of April 26, 1880, John P. Clum Papers, University of Arizona Special Collections, Tucson.

55. "Tombstone is a": Quoted in Traywick, *Chronicles*, p. 86.

55. "This is a": Entry of April 17, 1880, *Private Journal*.

57. "absence of a": Doyle, "Social Theory," p. 154.

58. "Frame shanties": Quoted in Watkins, *Gold and Silver*, pp. 74–75.

59. "a man whose": Quoted in Bob Palmquist, "Tombstone's Dogberry," *True West*, vol. 34, no. 4 (April 1987), p. 22.

60. "There is another": Carolyn Lake, ed., *Under Cover for Wells Fargo: The Unvarnished Recollections of Fred Dodge* (Boston: Houghton Mifflin Co., 1969), p. 9. Hereafter referred to as Dodge, *Under Cover*.

61. "constructed of walnut": Lonnie Underhill, *Tombstone, Arizona 1880 Business & Professional Directory* (Tucson: Roan Horse Press, 1982), p. 24.

61. "being furnished": Ibid.

61. "a can opener": Gray, "When All Roads," p. 14.

61. "Hardware, Tinsmiths": Underhill, *1880 Directory*.

62. "a very treacherous": Breakenridge, *Helldorado*, p. 116.

63. "Look out, Frank": Testimony in Douglas D. Martin, *Tombstone's Epitaph* (Albuquerque: University of New Mexico Press, 1951), p. 81.

63. "I saw I was": Ibid.

63. "I took one": Ibid., p. 84.
64. "Take that, you": Ibid.
64. "I saw Killeen's": Ibid., p. 85.
64. "shot him": Ibid., p. 82.

CHAPTER 3: The Shootists

66. "I have traveled": Bob Wright, *Dodge City, the Cowboy Capital, and the Great Southwest* (n.p. 1913), p. 74.
67. "every time I fired": Quoted in Elliott West, "Wicked Dodge City," *American History Illustrated,* vol. 17, no. 4 (June 1982), p. 24.
67. "pawed the earth": DeArment, *Bat Masterson,* p. 16.
67. "With razor-sharp": Ibid., p. 17.
68. "a chunk of": Ibid., p. 22.
68. "The noise of": Ibid.
71. "a high respect": Gary L. Roberts, "The West's Gunmen: II, Recent Historiography of Those Controversial Heroes," *The American West,* vol. 8 (March 1971), p. 62.
71. "was said to": Joseph Rosa, *The Gunfighter: Man or Myth?* (Norman: University of Oklahoma Press, 1969), p. 162.
72. "to kill when": Ibid., p. 207.
72. "I have known": Quoted ibid., p. 116.
72. "Both were known": Milt Hinkle, "The Earp and Masterson I Knew," *True West,* vol. 9, no. 2 (December 1961), p. 26.
73. "almost invariably": Letter of October 29, 1928, to Lake, Lake Collection.
73. "hit a can": Quoted in Rosa, *The Gunfighter,* p. 186.
73. "I happen to": Quoted ibid., p. 186.
73. "was not hitting": Bill O'Neal, *Encyclopedia of Western Gunfighters* (Norman: University of Oklahoma Press, 1979), p. 2.
74. "policeman Erp [*sic*]": Quoted in Burrows, *John Ringo,* p. 192.
74. "I found one": Letter to editor of Tombstone *Daily Prospector,* April 13, 1922.
74. "Geo. and I": Ibid.
75. "Don't shoot": Quoted in Rosa, *The Gunfighter,* p. 144.
75. "too much for": Ibid., pp. 114–15.
75. "It is not nearly": Quoted in Wright, *Dodge City,* p. 145.
75. "All right": Ibid., p. 150.
76. "until, as I": Quoted in DeArment, *Bat Masterson,* p. 31.
76. "We are the": Quoted in Watkins, *Gold and Silver,* p. 240.
76. "an overwhelming": McGrath, *Gunfighters,* p. 101.

76. "the line between": Richard White, "Outlaw Gangs of the Middle Border: American Social Bandits," *Western Historical Quarterly*, vol. 12, no. 4 (October 1981), p. 388.

76. "nearly dash[ing]": Watkins, *Gold and Silver*, pp. 240, 245.

77. "Why, the son": Breakenridge, *Helldorado*, p. 86.

77. "the greatest cattle": Wright, *Dodge City*, p. 257.

77. "Point men": Andy Adams, *The Log of a Cowboy: A Narrative of the Old Trail Days* (Lincoln: University of Nebraska Press, 1964), p. 28.

78. "A stampede": Ibid., p. 41.

79. "It is but": Quoted in Peter Lyon, *The Wild, Wild West* ([New York?: 1960?] reprinted from *American Heritage* [August 1960]).

80. "citizen": Rosa, *The Gunfighter*, p. 155.

80. "Wyatt knocked him": Masterson, *Famous Gunfighters*, p. 57.

81. "Earp then pushed": Quoted in Turner, *Earps Talk*, p. 16.

81. "by the scruff": Stuart N. Lake, *Wyatt Earp: Frontier Marshal* (Boston and New York: Houghton Mifflin, 1955 ed.), p. 132.

81. "covered by two": Quote from Franklin Reynolds in Waters, *Earp Brothers*, pp. 38–39.

82. "an efficient officer": Quoted ibid., p. 40.

82. "The undertaker's": Rosa, *The Gunfighter*, p. 140.

82. "one of the most": Ford County *Globe*, quoted in Turner, *Earps Talk*, p. 15.

83. "To Wyatt S. Earp": Waters, *Earp Brothers*, p. 41.

84. "Dave would not": Wright, *Dodge City*, p. 216.

84. "You are all": Ibid., p. 217.

84. "up to some": Quoted in Waters, *Earp Brothers*, p. 38.

84. "Wherever skill": Sonnichsen, *Billy King's*, p. 130.

85. "Singular as it": March 5, 1882.

85. "dexterity and intuition": Sonnichsen, *Billy King's*, p. 59.

85. "There were several": Breakenridge, *Helldorado*, p. 103.

85. "I have no": Quoted in DeArment, *Bat Masterson*, p. 86.

85. "large enough": Newspaper account quoted ibid., pp. 104–5.

86. "that extended": Ibid., p. 110.

86. "for his endeavors": Quoted in Turner, *Earps Talk*, p. 15.

86. "Everyone dropped": Quoted in DeArment, *Bat Masterson*, pp. 114–15.

87. "saw a man": "How Wyatt Earp Routed a Gang of Outlaws," San Francisco *Examiner*, August 2, 1896.

87. "great excitement": Quoted in DeArment, *Bat Masterson*, p. 167.

89. "a sort of": Masterson, *Famous Gunfighters*, p. 41.

89. "The 'finest work'": Quoted in DeArment, *Bat Masterson*, p. 174.

CHAPTER 4: "A Pretty Hard Reputation"

91. "came to my": Quoted in Turner, *Earps Talk*, p. 60.
91. "made some kind": [Pat Hayhurst], Summary/Transcript of Document 94, Spicer Hearing Summary [hereafter referred to as SHS], Arizona Department of Library, Archives and Public Records, Phoenix, p. 136.
91. "It is known": Turner, *Earps Talk*, p. 59.
91. "a coward": Ibid., p. 60.
92. "rough and mountainous": Frank C. Lockwood, *Pioneer Days in Arizona* (N.Y.: Macmillan Co., 1932), p. 282.
92. "some thirty or forty": Breakenridge, *Helldorado*, pp. 104–106.
93. "had no compunction": Ibid.
93. "social bandits": White, "Outlaw Gangs," pp. 387, 393, 403. White's study provides the basis for my discussion of social banditry.
93. "brave, daring": Ibid.
93. "I learned": Breakenridge, *Helldorado*, p. 132.
93. "[Even the toughest]": Gray, "When All Roads," p. 100.
93. "never molested": Hancock, rebuttal to Walter Noble Burns, Hancock Papers, p. 7.
94. "I will say": Quoted in Sonnichsen, *Billy King's*, p. 189.
94. "were very kind": Robert Boller, "Reminiscences of Robert M. Boller as told to Mrs. Geo. F. Kitt, Arizona Historical Society Collection, Tucson, p. 1.
94. "Your livestock": Gray, "When All Roads," p. 99.
94. "One night": Boller reminiscences, p. 2
94. "they were unfortunate": Breakenridge, *Helldorado*, p. 110.
94. "you will have": Ibid., p. 144.
95. "These boys were": Gray, "When All Roads," p. 9.
95. "the fellow who": Ibid., p. 99.
96. "intimate friend": *Daily Epitaph*, July 25, 1880.
96. "He's a first": Quoted in McGrath, *Gunfighters*, p. 214.
97. "with the majesty": *Epitaph*, quoted in Palmquist, "Tombstone's Dogberry," p. 23.
97. "cut the gordian": Ibid.
98. "Your honor": Faulk, *Tombstone*, p. 194.
98. "We deem you": Palmquist, "Tombstone's Dogberry," p. 24.
99. "show[ing] her": Waters, *Earp Brothers*, p. 95.
99. "My shoes were": Ibid., p. 34.
99. "as fine": Ibid., p. 95.
100. "The Messrs Earp": *Daily Epitaph*, October 23, 1880.
101. "a shiftless": Quoted in Bartholomew, *Wyatt Earp, 1879–1882*, p. 10.

102. "[Holliday] walked": October 12, 1880.
102. "Republicans haven't": Entry of September 11, 1880, *Private Journal.*
103. "Our town is": Entry of July 30, 1880, ibid.
103. "Seems from his": Entry of August 9, 1880, ibid.
103. "fully six": Breakenridge, *Helldorado,* p. 101.
103. "a typical": Jones typescript, p. 7.
104. "A lot of Texas": Martin, *Tombstone's Epitaph,* p. 170.
104. "four inches below": *Daily Nugget,* October 31, 1880.
105. "Look out": Letter to Lake, September 30, 1929, Lake Collection.
105. "Wyatt said": Dodge, *Under Cover,* p. 10.
105. "[Curly Bill] was": Breakenridge, *Helldorado,* p. 132.
106. "done [*sic*] the actual": Hancock's rebuttal to Burns, pp. 7–8.
106. "just about any": Lloyd Hamill, quoted in Bartholomew, *Wyatt Earp, 1879 to 1882,* p. 49.
106. "our chief outlaw": Entry of April 1, 1881, *Private Journal.*
106. "fought among themselves": Untitled, unpublished article by O. H. Simpson, Lake Collection.
107. "Suppose we go": Quoted in *Daily Nugget,* October 31, 1880.
107. "If you get": Quoted in Burrows, *John Ringo,* p. 45.
107. "forever trying": Jones typescript, pp. 7–8.
108. "voted all": James Hancock, letter to *Arizona Republican,* April 1, 1927, Hancock Papers.
108. "one hundred": Gray, "When All Roads," p. 31.
108. "hundreds of non-citizens": Jay J. Wagoner, *Arizona Territory 1863–1912: A Political History* (Tucson: University of Arizona Press, 1970), p. 79.
108. "We believe in": Ibid., p. 83.
109. "Tombstone is": Entry of August 9, 1880, *Private Journal.*
109. "Vigilantes will": Entry of October 31, 1880, ibid.
109. "Peculiar organizations": Entry of February 8, 1881, ibid.
109. "emerged as": Butler, *Daughters,* p. 99.
110. "held court": Faulk, *Arizona,* p. 176.
110. "It appears to": Martin, *Tombstone's Epitaph,* p. 140.
110. "Quite a number": Ibid., p. 141.
111. "Our Justice": *Weekly Nugget,* October 2, 1879.
111. "Will be a": Entry of October 28, 1880, *Private Journal.*

CHAPTER 5: Games of Chance

112. ". . . there is": *Weekly Nugget,* October 2, 1879.

113. "Determined men": Entry of November 6, 1880, *Private Journal.*
113. "crouching under": Prescott *Journal-Miner,* October 27, 1905, Earp Family Papers, Arizona Historical Society.
114. "well qualified": November 12, 1880.
114. "I have the": Tucson *Citizen* clipping, February 10, 1984, Notebook No. 151, Arizona Historical Society.
115. "A fine record": November 29, 1880.
115. "a force of": entry of December 4, 1880, *Private Journal.*
116. "There is a great": Clum Papers.
116. "hurried to the spot": Faulk, *Arizona,* p. 94.
116. "the promising Metropolis": Ibid.
116. "I have never": Quoted in Butler, *Daughters,* p. 54.
116. "I never felt": December 5, 1880, letter in Clum Papers.
117. "Very, very sad": Entry of December 18, 1880, *Private Journal.*
117. "fast mare": *Daily Nugget,* December 5, 1880.
118. "was always": Waters, *Earp Brothers,* p. 112.
118. "that bloodthirsty": Quoted in Wagoner, *Arizona Territory,* p. 176.
118. "as the sheriff": Breakenridge, *Helldorado,* pp. 101–102.
118. "A two-gun man": Ibid.
118. "had heard": "How Wyatt Earp," San Francisco *Examiner,* August 2, 1896.
119. "continued in the": Turner, *Earps Talk,* p. 123.
119. "You telegraph": Lake, *Wyatt Earp,* pp. 251–52.
119. "He said": SHS, p. 36.
120. "one man dashed": SHS, p. 47.
120. "took more pride": Gray, "When All Roads," p. 97.
120. "In those early": Mabel W. Moffitt Reminiscences, Arizona Historical Society, Tucson, p. 10.
121. "shot out": Bartholomew, *Wyatt Earp, 1879 to 1882,* pp. 82–83.
121. "when he stole": Ibid.
121. "the punishment for": Butler, *Daughters,* p. 111.
121. "The title is": Quoted in Breakenridge, *Helldorado,* p. 160.
121. "a few days": SHS, p. 47.
121. "a hell of": Ibid.
122. "I thought you": Jan. 17, 1881, quoted in Martin, *Tombstone's Epitaph,* p. 58.
122. "true to his": Ibid.
123. "When Johnny": Hancock's rebuttal to Burns, pp. 6–7.
123. "The officers": Entry of January 14, 1881, *Private Journal.*
124. "only about": Waters, *Earp Brothers,* p. 114.
124. "was jammed": Quoted in Bartholomew, *Wyatt Earp, 1879 to 1882,* p. 112.

124. "a strong": Ibid.

124. "Moving down": Ibid.

124. "No one who": Ibid.

124. "backed his horse": Letter of November 6, 1928, Lake Collection.

124. "One man": Lake, *Wyatt Earp,* p. 250.

125. "This man should": Entry of January 14, 1881, *Private Journal.*

125. "an overwhelming": McGrath, *Gunfighters,* p. 101.

125. "Trouble in town": Entry of February 12, 1881, *Private Journal.*

126. "strong and well organized": Henry P. Walker, "Retire Peaceably to Your Homes: Arizona Faces Martial Law, 1882," *Journal of Arizona History,* vol. 10, no. 1 (Spring 1969), pp. 10–11.

126. "stealing and running": Ibid., p. 4.

126. "calicos, jewelry": Jacob R. Marcus, ed., "An Arizona Pioneer: Memoirs of Sam Aaron," *American Jewish Archives,* vol. 10 (October 1958), p. 102.

126. "camped among": Burrows, *John Ringo,* p. 22.

127. "had lost no": Ibid.

127. "would not hold": Marcus, "An Arizona Pioneer," p. 103.

127. "the most": Boyer, *I Married,* p. 66.

128. "I doubt": Ibid.

128. "quiet and pleasant": Ibid., p. 68.

128. "little strutter": Ibid.

128. "blowhard": Ibid.

128. "big, loutish": Ibid.

128. "not a very": unattributed quote in Waters, *Earp Brothers,* p. 89.

128. "a regular": Entry of March 1, 1881, *Private Journal.*

128. "We didn't": Waters, *Earp Brothers,* p. 93.

128. "came to": West, "The Saloon," p. 70.

128. "not a single": Ibid.

129. "magnificent diamonds": Hancock, "Comment on an Article in the Saturday Evening Post," Hancock Papers, pp. 4–5.

130. "a small band": DeArment, *Bat Masterson,* p. 194.

130. "fine-looking gentleman": Ibid.

130. "by common consent": Ibid.

130. "was what the": Santa Fe newspaper account quoted in Bartholomew, *Wyatt Earp, 1879 to 1882,* p. 120.

131. "stuck the muzzle": Bat Masterson, quoted in Rosa, *The Gunfighter,* p. 141.

131. "I seized hat": Entry of February 25, 1881, *Private Journal.*

131. "earnest attention": Quoted in Turner, *Earps Talk,* p. 110.

131. "from the front": Richard Patterson, "Highway Robbery!," *True West,* vol. 33, no. 12 (December 1986), p. 21.

132. "lay on the": Ibid., p. 22.
133. "ever ready": Quoted in W. Turrentine Jackson, "Wells Fargo: Symbol of the Wild West?," *Western Historical Quarterly,* vol. 3, no. 2 (April 1972), p. 185.
133. "fired from": Patterson, "Highway," p. 24.

CHAPTER 6: "A Most Terrible Affair"

135. "cramps in": Dodge, *Under Cover,* p. 23.
135. "stepped into": *Epitaph,* March 16, 1881, quoted in Boyer, *I Married,* p. 32.
135. "and a shot": Ibid.
135. "almost through": Entry of March 16, 1881, *Private Journal.*
136. "Sure Enough": Dodge, *Under Cover,* p. 23.
136. "the scene of": *Epitaph,* March 16, 1881, quoted in Boyer, *I Married,* p. 32.
136. "Abbott finally": Entry of March 16, 1881, *Private Journal.*
136. "shadow[ing] several": Ibid.
137. "the hunters": Bork and Boyer, "A Footnote," p. 78.
137. "the worst outlaws": Jones typescript, pp. 7–8.
137. "The Erbs [*sic*]": Sam Aaron, in Marcus, "An Arizona Pioneer," p. 103.
137. "were at head": Quoted in Waters, *Earp Brothers,* p. 134.
137. "the whole thing": Gray, "When All Roads," pp. 54–55.
137. "Nearly all": Quoted in Waters, *Earp Brothers,* p. 135.
138. "not agreeable": Entry of March 24, 1881, *Private Journal.*
138. "We can assure": Quoted in Bartholomew, *Wyatt Earp, 1879 to 1882,* p. 14.
139. "a man much": Gray, "When All Roads," p. 163.
139. "and then spent": Ibid.
139. "good friends": Lake, *Wyatt Earp,* p. 264.
140. "was a full": Letter of September 18, 1930, to Lake, Lake Collection.
140. "never could": Waters, *Earp Brothers,* p. 43.
140. "a fine set": Bork and Boyer, "A Footnote," p. 83.
140. "a sense of": Boyer, *I Married,* p. 62.
140. "seemed to be": Masterson, *Famous Gunfighters,* p. 36.
140. "never played": Letter from Dodge to Lake, published in Dodge, *Under Cover,* p. 246.
140. "mean disposition": Quoted in Rosa, *The Gunfighter,* p. 116.
140. "generally known": *Arizona Daily Star,* March 26, 1882.

140. "not a whit": Quoted in Bartholomew, *Wyatt Earp, 1879 to 1882,* p. 10.
140. "He started": Quoted in Breakenridge, *Helldorado,* p. 124.
141. ". . . we heard": Quoted in Waters, *Earp Brothers,* p. 134.
141. "consensus of opinion": Ibid.
141. "It's that sneakin'": Ibid., p. 109.
141. "Then it happened": Ibid.
142. "He held it,": Bork and Boyer, "A Footnote," p. 77.
143. "If you are": Ibid.
143. "I safely say": SHS, p. 146.
143. "broken old": Lake, *Wyatt Earp,* p. 260.
143. "the trailer": Waters, *Earp Brothers,* p. 131.
143. "life of the": Breakenridge, *Helldorado,* p. 123.
144. "[King] escaped": Quoted in Boyer, *I Married,* p. 34.
144. "a certain person": Quoted in Bartholomew, *Wyatt Earp, 1879 to 1882,* p. 131.
144. "King the stage": Entry of March 28, 1881, *Private Journal.*
145. "it is quite": Jahns, *Doc Holliday,* p. 171.
145. "Our horses": Breakenridge, *Helldorado,* pp. 122–23.
146. "I was lolling": Entry of April 1, 1881, *Private Journal.*
146. "Virgil told me": SHS, p. 115.
148. "Town filling up": Entry of March 30, 1881, *Private Journal.*
148. "ownership of": Watkins, *Gold and Silver,* p. 248.
149. "has often resulted": Gray, "When All Roads," p. 26.
149. "was perpetually": Faulk, *Tombstone,* p. 71.
150. "The bullet": Breakenridge, *Helldorado,* pp. 165–68.
150. "every one thought": Typescript in Hancock Papers.
150. "that they did": Breakenridge, *Helldorado,* pp. 165–68.
150. "A great many": Quoted ibid.
151. "I told them": SHS, p. 137.
151. "that if I": Ibid., p. 145.
151. "help put up": Ibid., p. 105.
151. "He said that": Ibid., pp. 105–106.
152. "I then told": Ibid., p. 106.
152. "Clanton said": Ibid., p. 137.
152. "I am going": Ibid., p. 154.
152. "Here are three": Ibid., p. 155.
152. "Jesus Christ": Ibid.
153. "between two": Ibid., p. 137.
153. "The Hazlett boys": Quoted in Bartholomew, *Wyatt Earp, 1879 to 1882,* p. 165.
153. "Mr. Hazlett": Ibid.
153. "some hours": Lake, *Wyatt Earp,* p. 272.

CHAPTER 7: Fire, Flood, and Friction

155. "Probably the new": June 9, 1881.
155. "Though lost": Quoted in Bartholomew, *Wyatt Earp, 1879 to 1882,* p. 154.
156. "his action": Minutes of the Tombstone Common Council, Vol. I, 1880–1882, Special Collections, University of Arizona, Tucson.
156. "It looks": June 14, 1881.
156. "seems to be": June 22, 1881.
157. "In less than": June 23, 1881, story, quoted in Martin, *Tombstone's Epitaph,* p. 121.
157. "instructing tax": Minutes of the Tombstone Common Council, Vol. I, 1880–1882.
157. "a great column": Clum, "It All Happened," p. 49.
157. "did not save": Martin, *Tombstone's Epitaph,* p. 122.
158. "While locking": Ibid.
158. "The flames were": Entry of June 22, *Private Journal.*
158. "the great elements": Martin, *Tombstone's Epitaph,* p. 122.
158. "the worst wound": Entry of June 22, *Private Journal.*
158. "the charred": Martin, *Tombstone's Epitaph,* p. 122.
159. "little round Tents": Dodge, *Under Cover,* p. 35.
159. "to prevent": Minutes of the Tombstone Common Council, Vol. I, 1880–1882.
159. "pompous little dandy": Boyer, *I Married,* p. 30.
159. "He did me": Ibid.
160. "He tore it": Waters, *Earp Brothers,* p. 111.
160. "cowboy swain": Ibid., p. 123.
160. "I always thought": Ibid.
162. "there was not": *Daily Nugget,* July 10, 1881.
162. "Commissioner of Deeds": Underhill, *1880 Business & Professional Directory.*
162. "the Choicest": Quoted in Bartholomew, *Wyatt Earp, 1879 to 1882,* pp. 100–101.
163. "Let Judge Spicer": Quoted in Gary L. Roberts, "The Wells Spicer Decision: 1881," *Montana, the Magazine of Western History,* vol. 20 (Winter 1970), p. 65.
163. "You send": Lake, *Wyatt Earp,* p. 265.
163. "a good chance": Gray, "When All Roads," pp. 54–55.
164. "I did not": Ibid., pp. 35–36.
164. "on Leslie's": Ibid.
164. "Tell Jim": Quoted ibid.
164. "I heard later": Ibid.

164. "by the prompt": Entry of July 11, 1881, *Private Journal.*

164. "the city": *Daily Nugget,* August 2, 1881.

166. "[Frémont's] action": Wagoner, *Arizona Territory,* p. 189.

166. "augmented by": Walker, "Retire Peaceably," pp. 2, 12.

166. "The south-eastern": Ibid., p. 14.

167. "if he had": Gray, "When All Roads," pp. 67–68.

167. "even the other": Ibid.

167. "the regulation": Bartholomew, *Wyatt Earp, 1879 to 1882,* p. 63.

167. "His demeanor": Quoted ibid., p. 179.

168. "were satisfied": Breakenridge, *Helldorado,* p. 135.

168. "Some of the": August 11, 1881, in John Ringo Ephemera File, Arizona Historical Society.

168. "Thus you see": Quoted in Bartholomew, *Wyatt Earp, 1879 to 1882,* p. 190.

168. "He was a": Boller reminiscences, p. 3.

168. "you would not": "Reminiscences of a Stranger," July 29, 1927, in Ringo File.

168. "I had rather": Ibid.

168. "All of Franklin[s']": Quoted in Burrows, *John Ringo,* p. 75.

169. "slam[med] his gun": Ibid.

169. "the people are": Quoted in Martin, *Tombstone's Epitaph,* p. 144.

169. "Now isn't it": Ibid.

169. "Cowboys don't": *Daily Epitaph,* August 16, 1881.

170. "No one knows": Typescript in Hancock Papers.

170. "the d-st lot": Quoted in Walker, "Retire Peaceably," p. 7.

172. "When they first": Arizona *Weekly Star,* September 1, 1881, transcribed in Arizona Historical Society files.

172. "When I saw": Ibid.

172. "Byers certainly": Ibid.

173. "nobly responded": Gray, "When All Roads," p. 64.

173. "The only thing": Ibid., p. 65.

173. "completely out": Ibid.

173. "was too far": Ibid., p. 66.

173. "This killing": Entry of August 17, 1881, *Private Journal.*

174. "[L]ittle did": Gray, "When All Roads," p. 61.

174. "gave me but": Letter of September 20, 1881, Cowboy Depredations File, Special Collections, University of Arizona, Tucson.

175. "every merchant": Quoted in Walker, "Retire Peaceably," p. 13.

175. "[Behan] represented": Letter of September 20, 1881, Cowboy Depradations File.

CHAPTER 8: "I Expect to Record Several Killings"

178. "May be you": Quoted in McDaniels's testimony, as reported in *Daily Nugget,* October 22, 1881.

178. "act[ing] like": Boyer, *I Married*, p. 68.
178. "Stilwell at that": *Daily Nugget*, October 22, 1881.
179. "one like": Dodge, *Under Cover*, p. 14.
179. "as said mine": *Daily Nugget*, October 7, 1880.
179. "one of the": Jones typescript, p. 8.
180. "the hardest": Quoted in Bartholomew, *Wyatt Earp, 1879 to 1882*, p. 211.
180. "had anything": Dodge, *Under Cover*, p. 245.
180. "always friendly": SHS, p. 138.
180. ". . . Frank McLaury": Ibid.
181. "I understand": Ibid., p. 153.
182. "he was sorry": Breakenridge, *Helldorado*, pp. 140–41.
183. "no desire": Quoted in Martin, *Tombstone's Epitaph*, p. 175.
183. "That kind": Quoted in James L. Haley, *Apaches: A History and Cultural Portrait* (Garden City, N.Y.: Doubleday Co., 1981), pp. 335–36.
184. "what result": Entry of September 5, 1881, *Private Journal*.
184. "exceptionally stupid": Haley, *Apaches*, p. 343.
184. "quietly killed": Ibid., p. 344.
185. "20 odd": Entry of October 5–7, 1881, *Private Journal*.
185. "A terrible": Ibid.
185. "some distance": Ibid.
185. "They treated": Gray, "When All Roads," p. 9.
186. "At McL's was": Entry of October 5–7, 1881, *Private Journal*.
186. "The best of": Letter of November 6, 1928, Lake Collection.
186. "not a bad": Entry of October 5–7, 1881, *Private Journal*.
186. "'CB' was polite": Ibid.
187. "bugles blowing": Ibid.
187. "The army horses": Breakenridge, *Helldorado*, p. 164.
187. "badly fagged": Gray, "When All Roads," p. 115.
187. "It was the old": Ibid.
187. "One cavalry troop": Ibid., p. 157.
188. "national theater": Wooster, "A Difficult," p. 345. Wooster's study provides the basis for my discussion of the army situation in the Southwest.
188. "had no intention": Boyer, *I Married*, p. 86.
189. "as an expert": *Epitaph*, October 24, 1881, quoted in Turner, *Earps Talk*, p. 97.
189. "along the line": Letter in Cowboy Depredations File.
189. "A notorious": Ibid.
189. "mere rumor": Quoted in Walker, "Retire Peaceably," p. 14.
190. "a rustler": Entry of October 1, 1881, *Private Journal*.
190. "on the Charleston": Entry of October 4, 1881, ibid.

190. "The cowboy is": Entry of October 5, 1881, ibid.
191. "I know of": Gray, "When All Roads," pp. 112–13.
191. "To this!": Quoted in *Daily Nugget,* November 11, 1881.
192. "Here's seeing": Quoted in Rita Hill, *Then and Now Here and Around Shakespeare* (Privately printed, 1963), p. 38.
192. "What did": Ibid.
192. "We have been": Quoted in *Daily Nugget,* October 25, 1881.
192. "some citizens": Ibid.

CHAPTER 9: "Let the Ball Open"

195. "bucking at": Bork and Boyer, "A Footnote," p. 79.
195. "Doc, we want": Ibid.
196. "his hand in": SHS, p. 99.
196. "You son of a bitch": Ibid.
196. "Yes, you": Ibid.
196. "while Jim was there": Ibid., p. 100.
196. "I walked off": Ibid.
196. "a damned liar": Ibid., p. 139.
197. "arrested him": September 10, 1881.
198. "He told me": SHS, p. 139.
198. "I will be": Ibid.
198. "I told him": Ibid.
199. "another gentleman": Ibid., p. 100.
199. "I thought he": Ibid.
199. "The damned son": Ibid., p. 148.
200. "Why didn't you": Waters, *Earp Brothers,* p. 155.
200. "His pistol was": SHS, p. 84.
200. "I asked Clanton": Ibid., p. 81.
200. "There is liable": Ibid., p. 151.
201. "I said": SHS, p. 60.
201. "Ike Clanton was": Bork and Boyer, "A Footnote," pp. 79–80.
201. "If God will": Ibid.
201. "He has got": SHS, p. 151.
201. "arrest and": Ibid.
201. "What does all": SHS, p. 140.
201. "Ike Clanton is": Ibid.
202. "What does that": Clum, "It All Happened," p. 47.
202. "I saw": Pat Hayhurst Summary/Transcript of Document 45, Coroner's Inquest Summary [hereafter referred to as CI], Arizona Department of Library, Archives, and Public Records, p. 5.

202. "I asked him": SHS, p. 148.
203. "walked up": Ibid., p. 140.
203. "two or three": Ibid., p. 82.
203. "You cattle thieving": Ibid.
203. "an ordinary": Ibid., p. 83.
203. "You damned dirty": Ibid., p. 141.
204. "I will get": Ibid., p. 140.
204. "he would not": Ibid.
204. "You fellows": *Daily Epitaph,* October 27, 1881.
204. "if I would": SHS, p. 100.
204. "I saw Virgil": Ibid., pp. 100–101.
204. "and costs": Recorder's Court Proceedings, from collection of Ben T. Traywick, Tombstone.
205. "Anywhere I can": SHS, p. 149.
205. "both Mr. Earp": Ibid., p. 68.
205. "Are you heeled": Ibid.
205. "opened his eyes": *Daily Nugget,* November 11, 1881.
205. "about that time": SHS, p. 62.
206. "speak rather loud": *Daily Nugget,* November 10, 1881.
206. "I saw Mr. Earp": SHS, p. 63.
206. "If you want": Ibid., p. 141.
206. "I could kill": Ibid., p. 68.
206. "staggered and": Ibid., p. 63.
206. "about 1": Ibid., p. 70.
206. "between one": Ibid., p. 55.
207. "When he went": Ibid., p. 89.
207. "sorry to see": Ibid., p. 90.
207. "bleeding on": Ibid., p. 92.
207. "Doc Holliday went": Ibid., p. 23.
208. "Doc Holliday met": CI, p. 11.
208. "deliberately misleading": Alford E. Turner, *The O.K. Corral Inquest* (College Station, Texas: Creative Publishing Company, 1981), p. 60, note 2.
208. "about to take": SHS, p. 23.
208. "After I told": Ibid.
208. "I want to": CI, p. 21.
209. "I went in": SHS, pp. 113–14.
209. "with his hand": CI, p. 13.
209. "with his head": SHS, p. 41.
209. "For God's sake": Ibid., p. 150.
209. "a dozen": Ibid., p. 158.
209. "took hold of": Ibid., p. 141.
210. "What is the trouble?": CI, p. 13.

210. "to go to some": Claiborne's testimony in *Daily Nugget,* October 19, 1881. [SHS says "mother's horse," but Clanton's mother had died in 1866.]
210. "the corral man": CI, p. 10.
210. "about one": Ibid., p. 1.
210. "a heavy": Behan's testimony, *Daily Nugget,* November 4, 1881.
210. "[I] asked him": SHS, p. 29.
211. "What is the": CI, p. 13.
211. "and see if": SHS, p. 149.
211. "I have been": Ibid., p. 152.
211. "as long as": Ibid.
211. "Billy Clanton": CI, p. 6.
212. "that he should": Ibid.
212. "three or four": SHS, p. 79.
212. "Some one of": Ibid., p. 76.
212. "After seeing": Ibid., p. 25.
212. "There was a": *Daily Nugget,* November 6, 1881.
213. "Frank, I want": SHS, p. 52.
213. "there was likely": CI, p. 2; SHS, p. 30.
213. "tall man": CI, p. 15.
213. "quite a number": Ibid.
214. "How come": SHS, p. 99.
214. "down there": Ibid., p. 124.
214. "on our road": *Daily Nugget,* November 10, 1881.
215. "Why, they are": SHS, p. 152.
215. "Then I called": Ibid.
215. "When this": CI, p. 13.
215. "a running fight": SHS, p. 142.
215. "I did not": Ibid., p. 159.
215. "punishing recoil": Turner, *Earps Talk,* p. 190.
215. "pushed down": Wesley Fuller's testimony, ibid., p. 57.
215. "he was not": Ibid., p. 30.
216. "put his hand": CI, p. 16.
216. "I won't have": Ibid.
216. "I put my arm": SHS, p. 30.
216. "Johnny, I have no": CI, p. 10.
216. "might have": SHS, p. 40.
216. "he would leave": CI, p. 10.
216. "Wait here": SHS, p. 30.
216. "I have to": *Daily Nugget,* October 29, 1881.
217. "At the time": SHS, p. 5.
217. "You need not": CI, p. 6.

CHAPTER 10: "I Am Shot Right Through"

218. "I was there": CI, pp. 2, 4.
219. "Gentlemen, I am": SHS, p. 31.
219. "did not use": Ibid., p. 23.
219. "You are an": Ibid., p. 52.
219. "and told them": Ibid., p. 95.
219. "For God's sake": Ibid., p. 142.
219. "I have disarmed": Ibid.
219. "an old pistol": Ibid., p. 69.
219. "an extra long": Turner, *O.K. Corral Inquest,* p. 125.
220. "There they come!": CI, p. 16.
220. "leisurely": *Daily Nugget,* November 6, 1881.
220. "as any gentleman": Ibid.
220. "And what frightened": CI, p. 16.
221. "when they got": Ibid., p. 2.
221. "You sons of bitches": Ibid.
221. "They both said": Ibid., p. 21.
221. "the Earp": SHS, p. 23.
221. "by which party": p. 7.
222. "Throw up": Ibid., p. 7.
222. "We are going": Ibid., p. 3.
222. "I have come": SHS, p. 143.
222. "We have come": Ibid., p. 72.
222. "Boys, throw up": Ibid., p. 150.
222. "I then thought": CI, p. 7.
222. "I have got": CI, p. 3.
222. "I haven't got": SHS, p. 121.
222. "You sons of bitches": CI, p. 11.
222. "Don't shoot": SHS, p. 31.
222. "I do not": Ibid., p. 24.
223. "Hold, I don't": Ibid., p. 143.
223. "Frank McLaury and": Ibid., p. 150.
223. "Hold on, I": Ibid.
223. "threw his six-shooter": Ibid.
223. "Let them": CI, p. 16.
223. "I heard two": SHS, p. 52.
224. "There was not": CI, p. 19.
224. "The first two": SHS, p. 143.
224. "kind of past": Ibid., p. 150.
224. "by that time": Ibid., p. 76.
224. "I never drew": Ibid., p. 143.
225. "Then the shooting": Ibid., p. 121.

225. "had the impression": CI, p. 9.
225. "a man with": SHS, p. 86.
226. "I saw Frank": Ibid., p. 52.
226. "How do you know": Ibid., p. 96.
226. "fell up against": SHS, p. 121.
226. "in a crouched": *Daily Nugget,* November 8, 1881.
226. "Billy Clanton had": CI, p. 8.
226. "staggered backward": Ibid., p. 22.
226. "I saw Thomas": SHS, p. 24.
226. "followed the movement": Ibid., p. 150.
227. "in quick": Ibid., p. 91.
227. "After the first": Ibid., p. 32.
227. "one right after": Ibid., p. 127.
228. "I suppose there": Ibid., p. 33.
228. "I never saw him": Ibid., p. 143.
228. "caught me": *Daily Nugget,* November 9, 1881.
229. "shoved his pistol": SHS, p. 97.
229. "after about four": Ibid., p. 143.
229. "at the back": Ibid., p. 33.
229. "As I jumped": Ibid., pp. 97–98.
229. "one shot fired": CI, p. 7.
230. "got up immediately": SHS, p. 76.
230. "This is none": Ibid., p. 72.
230. "standing near": Ibid.
230. "two or three": CI, p. 7.
230. "I am shot": SHS, p. 73.
231. "lying on the": CI, p. 3.
231. "I saw from": SHS, p. 91.
231. "one hand to": Ibid., p. 32.
231. "The first man": Ibid., p. 33.
232. "several men in": CI, p. 18.
232. "I have got": CI, p. 7.
232. "You are a good": SHS, p. 72.
232. "You have got": CI, p. 7.
232. "I am shot": Ibid.
232. "His body seemed": SHS, p. 91.
232. "place a pistol": CI, p. 18.
233. "made an unwise": Clum, "It All Happened," p. 54.
233. "bent down": SHS, p. 124.
233. "and stood with": Ibid., p. 72.
233. "I looked then": Ibid., p. 32.
233. "was not exactly": Ibid., p. 121.
233. "Take that pistol": Ibid., p. 73.

233. "Take that pistol": *Daily Nugget,* October 29, 1881.
233. "I said to": SHS, p. 73.
234. "rolling around": SHS, p. 57.
234. "Let's pick this": SHS, p. 63.
234. "We brought [Tom]": Ibid.
234. "I pulled his": Ibid., p. 24.
234. "about four or": Ibid., p. 122.
234. "there were no": SHS, p. 64.
234. "halloing so with": Ibid., p. 63.
234. "Look and see": Ibid., p. 57.
234. "about the thickness": Ibid., p. 65.
234. "was turning": Ibid., p. 63.
235. "Go away and": Ibid., p. 33.
235. "Drive the crowd": Ibid., p. 63.
235. "The son of a bitch": CI, p. 14.
235. "I looked towards": Ibid., p. 17.
236. "at Judge Lucas'": SHS, p. 33.
236. "being guarded": San Francisco *Daily Examiner,* October 27, 1881.
236. "one wound": *Daily Nugget,* November 1, 1881.
236. "laid the palm": Ibid.
236. "underneath the twelfth": SHS, p. 21.
236. "feeling the": Ibid., p. 64.
236. "From the body": Quoted in Faulk, *Tombstone,* pp. 152–53.
236. "jubilant vigilantes": Boyer, *I Married,* p. 93.
237. "a surging": Wyatt S. Earp, *Wyatt Earp: His Autobiography* (Privately printed, 1981), p. 240.
237. "How do you": Ibid., p. 241.
237. "[He] sat on": Bork and Boyer, "A Footnote," p. 80.
237. "as Cool and": Dodge, *Under Cover,* p. 27.
237. "Wyatt Earp said": SHS, p. 48.
238. "I will have": CI, p. 8.
238. "There is no": Ibid., p. 17.
238. "more forceably": Dodge, *Under Cover,* p. 27.
238. "if he was God": Ibid., p. 235.
238. "it was only": Waters, *Earp Brothers,* p. 159.
238. "the three": SHS, p. 54.
239. "Sheriff Behan": Ibid., pp. 53–54.
239. "You better go": Ibid., p. 46.
239. "In the conversation": Ibid.
239. "setting up": *Daily Nugget,* November 9, 1881.
240. "My cowboy": Entry of October 27, 1881, *Private Journal.*

CHAPTER 11: "I Think We Can Hang Them"

254. "was wild over": Quoted in Waters, *Earp Brothers,* p. 164.
254. "This is nothing": Ibid.
254. "many shrewd guesses": Fort Worth *Democrat,* November 12, 1881.
254. "to have": Lockwood, *Pioneer Days,* p. 284.
254. "It has been": Jones typescript, p. 8.
254. "The showdown is": Boller reminiscences, p. 2.
254. "nobody ever did": Hancock's rebuttal to Burns, p. 3.
255. "the better class": quoted in Bartholomew, *Wyatt Earp, 1879 to 1882,* p. 280.
255. "Was the police": Clum, "It All Happened," p. 48.
256. "A funeral": Boyer, *I Married,* p. 97.
256. "red fezzes": Mabel Barbee Lee, *Cripple Creek Days* (Lincoln: University of Nebraska Press, 1984 ed.), p. 82.
256. "He done": CI, p. 17.
258. "GLAD TO KNOW": Oct. 30, 1881.
258. "Some of the": Letter of November 29, 1881, Executive Document No. 58, United States House of Representatives, 47th Congress, 1st Session, p. 4.
259. "resting easily": *Daily Nugget,* October 28, 1881.
259. "and it will": October 30, 1881.
259. "denied bail": Ibid.
260. "hardly knew": Sonnichsen, *Billy King's,* p. 162.
261. "knew all": SHS, pp. 22–23.
261. "the best": Ibid., p. 27.
261. "I have never": Ibid.
262. "as it appeared": *Daily Nugget,* November 3, 1881.
262. "to pass on": Ibid.
262. "would give": SHS, p. 29.
262. "was down": Ibid., p. 31.
262. "You sons of bitches": Ibid.
263. "that it was": Ibid., p. 35.
263. "one of the": Ibid., p. 37.
263. "With Allen": Ibid., p. 39.
264. "Did you see": Ibid., p. 41.
264. "on the part": Ibid., p. 42.
264. "Have not the": Ibid.
264. "I never knew": Ibid.
264. "did perfectly": Ibid., p. 46.
264. "to get the": Ibid.
265. "were very dear": Letter of November 9, 1881, McLaury Letters.

265. "had just sold": Ibid.
265. "as cold blooded": Letter of November 8, 1881, from Will McLaury to S. P. Greene, McLaury Letters.
265. "had got up": Letter of November 9, 1881, McLaury Letters.
266. "heavily armed": Letter of November 8, 1881, McLaury Letters.
266. "The Dist. Atty.": Ibid.
266. "Johnny, as long": SHS, p. 68.
266. "chambers all": Ibid., p. 55.
267. "as the bullets": Ibid., p. 58.
267. "on the 5th": Ibid., p. 59.
267. "was made": *Daily Nugget,* November 8, 1881.
268. "to do as": Letter of November 8, 1881, McLaury Letters.
268. "I did not": Ibid.
268. "then stood": Letter of November 9, 1881, ibid.
268. "They were as": Letter of November 8 to Greene, ibid.
268. "sat and trembled": Letter of November 9, ibid.
268. "until the further": Turner, *O.K. Corral Inquest,* p. 227.
268. "had no power": Probate Court Proceedings, *Daily Nugget,* November 8, 1881.
268. "The petition": Letter of November 8, 1881, to Greene, McLaury Letters.
268. "the writ": *Daily Nugget,* November 8, 1881.
268. "Last night": Letter of November 8 to Greene, McLaury Letters.
269. "has a tendency": Ibid.
269. "I am afraid": Letter of November 8 to sister, McLaury Letters.
269. "saw a little": SHS, p. 120.
269. "I cannot say": Ibid., p. 126.
270. "first at one": Ibid., p. 122.
270. "two or three": Ibid., p. 131.
270. "I liked": Ibid., p. 129.
270. "Well, I came": Ibid., p. 132.
271. "I heard the": Ibid., p. 61.
271. "put five": Ibid., p. 22.
271. "in connection": Ibid., p. 110.
272. "about four": Ibid., p. 103.
272. "I don't remember": Ibid., p. 103.
272. "Have you not": Ibid., p. 108.
272. "In regard to": Ibid.
273. "Did not James": Ibid., p. 118.
273. "Before they": Ibid., p. 111.
273. "Well, sir": Ibid., p. 112.
274. "I don't remember": Ibid., p. 111.

274. "and said": Ibid., p. 62.
274. "No, I am": Ibid., p. 68.
274. "As soon as": Ibid., p. 64.
275. "receiving either": Ibid., pp. 64–65.
275. "I was arrested": Ibid., p. 66.

CHAPTER 12: "To Save Themselves from Certain Death"

277. "The trial of": Fort Worth *Daily Democrat*, November 12, 1881.
277. "The Earp boys": Quoted in Bartholomew, *Wyatt Earp, 1879 to 1882*, p. 245.
277. "Erp": Ibid.
278. "Before the smoke": Quoted in Waters, *Earp Brothers*, p. 163.
278. "The men who": Letter of November 9, 1881, McLaury Letters.
278. "Now I find": Ibid.
278. "the McLaury boys": Fort Worth *Daily Democrat*, November 12, 1881.
278. ". . . there were bitter": *Daily Nugget*, October 30, 1881.
279. "synonymous with": John M. Myers, quoted in Boyer, *I Married*, p. 45.
279. "The Tombstone Nugget": November 2, 1881, quoted ibid., pp. 45–46.
279. "God bless old": Madden to Lake, November 6 [no year], Lake Collection.
279. "Saloon keeper": SHS, p. 135.
280. "Give any explanations": Ibid.
280. "The difficulty": Ibid.
280. "using a manuscript": Ibid.
280. "pick a fuss": Ibid., p. 136.
280. "It was generally": Ibid.
280. "Ike Clanton and": Ibid., p. 138.
281. "Byrries": Ibid., p. 138.
281. "I never fired": Ibid., pp. 143–44.
282. "a tissue": Ibid., p. 144.
282. "was a good": Ibid., p. 134.
282. "[H]e was ever": Ibid., p. 133.
283. "was standing": *Daily Nugget*, November 17, 1881.
283. "one of their": Letter of November 17, McLaury Letters.
283. "suit my mind": Ibid.
283. "I had little": Ibid.
284. "You can ask": Ibid.
284. "open to the": Turner, *O.K. Corral Inquest*, p. 181.

285. "He was sworn": SHS, p. 147.
285. "I called on": Ibid., p. 148.
285. "moved in": Ibid., p. 150.
286. "I fired four": Ibid., p. 159.
286. "the whole party": Ibid., p. 76.
287. "the first word": Ibid., p. 80.
287. "the Earp crowd": Ibid., p. 81.
287. "He insisted": Ibid., p. 84.
287. "The hearsay": Ibid.
287. "one of the best": Ibid., p. 85.
287. "The reputation": Ibid., p. 82.
288. "If you fellows": Ibid., p. 83.
288. "were admitted": *Daily Nugget,* November 24, 1881.
288. "I saw no": SHS, p. 90.
288. "one of the": Ibid., p. 53.
289. "You say in": Ibid., p. 89.
289. "Every good": Ibid.
289. "Do you know": Ibid.
289. "I know not": Ibid.
289. "Do you know": Ibid.
289. "five men opposite": Ibid., p. 85.
290. "he believed": Ibid., p. 87.
290. "What conversation": Ibid., p. 88.
291. "had no arms": Ibid., p. 92.
291. "The great importance": Ibid., p. 160.
291. "I cannot resist": Ibid., pp. 165–66.
292. "could have been": Ibid., p. 164.
292. "with or without": Ibid., p. 160.
292. "an injudicious": Ibid., p. 161.
292. ". . . although in this": Ibid.
293. "they saw": Ibid., p. 165.
293. "made such": Ibid., p. 163.
293. "this wound is": Ibid., p. 164.
293. "were standing": Ibid., p. 165.
294. "they were going": Ibid., pp. 162–63.
294. "given over four": Ibid., p. 166.
294. "The evidence": Ibid.
294. "stand like Caesar's": December 1, 1881.
295. "was guilty of": Quoted in Roberts, "Spicer Decision," p. 72.
295. "With what": SHS, p. 162.
297. "and men outside": Letter in *Epitaph,* December 18, 1881.
298. "it is notorious": Quoted in Walker, "Retire Peaceably," p. 15.
298. "I made no": CI, p. 11.

300. "This is not": Quoted in Rosa, *The Gunfighter,* p. 50.
300. "a confrontation": Traywick, *Chronicles,* p. 151.

CHAPTER 13: "Except by Continuous Bloodshed"

301. ". . . the underlying": Letter of November 28, 1881, House Executive Document 58.
302. "the latter": Ibid.
302. "a man of": Ibid.
303. "We augur": Quoted in G. L. Seligmann, Jr., "Crawley P. Dake," *Arizoniana: The Journal of Arizona History,* vol. 2, no. 1 (Spring 1961), p. 13.
303. "I do not find": Letter from S. R. Martin to Benjamin Harris Brewster, Department of Justice, April 19, 1882, Cowboy Depredations File.
303. "in any way": Dake to Gosper, December 3, 1881, ibid.
304. "the swearing": *Daily Nugget,* November 22, 1881.
304. "rustler-clan": Clum, "It All Happened," p. 56.
305. "securely fastened": Ibid., p. 57.
305. "I think the": McLaury Letters.
306. "the impenetrability": Traywick, *Chronicles,* p. 95.
306. "remains of two": Entry of January 15, 1882, *Private Journal.*
306. "performed assessment": Faulk, *Tombstone,* p. 95.
307. "a few days": Quoted in Waters, *Earp Brothers,* p. 164.
307. "many of the": Gray, "When All Roads," p. 9.
308. "How many public": Quoted in Waters, *Earp Brothers,* p. 181.
308. "my greatest": Clum, "It All Happened," p. 57.
308. "it was about": Entry of December 14, 1881, *Private Journal.*
309. "yawning prospector's": Clum, "It All Happened," p. 59.
309. "And so it": Ibid., p. 60.
310. "Clum jumped": Quoted in Bartholomew, *Wyatt Earp, 1879 to 1882,* p. 277.
311. "the greatest outrage": December 16, 1881, quoted in Clum, "It All Happened," p. 70.
311. "Be sure and": Letter of August 12, 1929, Lake Collection.
312. "immediately struck": *Daily Nugget,* December 16, 1881.
312. "if they wanted": Breakenridge, *Helldorado,* pp. 154–55.
312. "Bad state": Entry of December 17, 1881, *Private Journal.*
312. "TO WELLS SPICER": Reproduced in Roberts, "Spicer Decision," p. 73.
313. "similar threats": Ibid.
313. "exists within": Ibid.

313. "[They] know": Ibid.
316. "The building has": Quoted in Traywick, *Chronicles,* p. 163.
317. "should have": Faulk, *Tombstone,* p. 119.
317. "four shots fired": Entry of December 28, 1881, *Private Journal.*
318. "ran past the": Quoted in Martin, *Tombstone's Epitaph,* p. 205.
318. "Cries of": Entry of December 28, 1881, *Private Journal.*
318. "that I had": Ibid.
318. "a longitudinal": *Epitaph,* December 29, 1881, quoted in Martin, *Tombstone's Epitaph,* p. 205.
319. "Virgil saw Stilwell": Undated handwritten information provided by Wyatt Earp to Lake, Lake Collection.
320. "My ticket": Entry of January 3, 1882, *Private Journal.*
320. "Square Man": Dodge, *Under Cover,* p. 39.
320. "It is rumored": January 4, 1882.

CHAPTER 14: "We Didn't Get Out When the Gettin' Was Good"

321. "Tombstone, Arizona": Quoted in *Daily Nugget,* March 5, 1882.
321. "a tolerably healthy": August 29, 1881.
322. "Few people": Reprinted in Tucson *Daily Star,* January 27, 1882, and quoted in Jahns, *Doc Holliday,* pp. 224–25.
322. "Pshaw! This": Ibid.
323. "Don't come, boys": March 4, 1882.
323. "Peabody, or nobody": Quoted in Frank Kintrea, "'Old Peabo' and the School," *American Heritage,* vol. 31, no. 6 (October/November 1980), p. 100.
323. "the rottenest place": Quoted in Faulk, *Tombstone,* p. 106.
324. "He's a sensible": Entry of March 5, 1882, *Private Journal.*
324. "Talk about": February 18, 1882.
325. "one-fourth of": *Daily Nugget,* January 8, 1882.
325. "Who robbed": January 8, 1882.
325. "owing to": *Daily Nugget,* January 11, 1882.
325. "Marshall Williams": March 9, 1882.
326. "The Oriental saloon": January 11, 1882.
326. "fed up with": Waters, *Earp Brothers,* p. 191.
326. "We didn't get": Ibid.
326. "ran up against": Breakenridge, *Helldorado,* p. 156.
326. "it was too": Ibid.
327. "the Earp party": Ibid., p. 155.
327. "Much blood": Entry of January 17, 1882, *Private Journal.*
328. "Ringo on horseback": Gray, "When All Roads," p. 34.
328. "he was trying": Breakenridge, *Helldorado,* pp. 157–58.

328. "was powerless": Letter from Wells Fargo detective John Thacker, Exhibit G, 1885 investigation into charges against Dake, Cowboy Depredations File.

329. "He states it": Letter from Leigh Chalmers to Attorney General A. H. Garland, August 13, 1885, ibid.

329. "that Earp got": Ibid.

329. "placed at the": Ibid.

329. "for the entire": Ibid.

330. "horse, bridle": Ibid.

330. "Good men could": Walker, "Retire Peaceably," p. 6.

330. "Something brewing in": January 21, 1882.

330. "warrants for the": *Epitaph*, January 24, 1882, quoted in Jahns, *Doc Holliday*, p. 223.

330. "an escaped prisoner": Affidavit of January 23, 1882, Arizona Historical Society Files.

331. "the public": *Epitaph*, January 24, 1882, quoted in Jahns, *Doc Holliday*, p. 223.

331. "tried to kick": Entry of January 17, 1882, *Private Journal.*

331. "Doc Holliday, the": Printed in *Daily Nugget*, January 27, 1882.

332. "Doc Holliday and": Quoted in Bartholomew, *Wyatt Earp, 1879 to 1882*, p. 291.

332. "pestiferous posse": *Daily Nugget*, January 27, 1882.

332. "The large number": January 16, 1882.

332. "he has not": *Daily Nugget*, January 31, 1882.

333. "that they would": *Daily Nugget*, January 27, 1882.

333. "in swearing to": *Daily Nugget*, January 31, 1882.

333. "by the Earps": Ibid.

333. "No evidence": *Daily Nugget*, February 1, 1882.

334. "It is quite": Quoted in Glenn G. Boyer, "Morgan Earp— Brother in the Shadow," *Old West* (Winter 1983), p. 20.

334. "To Any Sheriff": SHS, p. 5.

334. "illegally restrained": Ibid., p. 11.

334. "If it is": February 11, 1882, quoted in Jahns, *Doc Holliday*, p. 225.

335. "I have got": February 14, 1882, Byers Papers, Arizona Historical Society.

335. "the complaint": Petition for Writ of Habeas Corpus, SHS, p. 16.

336. "The facts of": Lucas Decision, ibid., p. 8.

337. "trusting to": Quoted in *Daily Nugget*, February 28, 1882.

337. "telegraphed to": Ibid.

337. "We are informed": Quoted ibid.

338. "I'd like": Waters, *Earp Brothers*, p. 192.

339. "I think they": Inquest summary in *Epitaph,* March 23, 1882.
339. "to look out": Ibid.
339. "entered the right": Martin, *Tombstone's Epitaph,* p. 207.
340. "He was in": *Epitaph,* March 23, 1882.
340. "Don't, I can't": Martin, *Tombstone's Epitaph,* p. 208.
340. "They got me": Boyer, *I Married,* p. 103.
340. "It won't be": Waters, *Earp Brothers,* p. 193.

CHAPTER 15: Trail of Blood

342. "Spence nudged": Testimony reproduced in Martin, *Tombstone's Epitaph,* pp. 211–12.
343. "during which he": Ibid.
344. "McMasters said": Typescript Summary of Stilwell Inquest Testimony, pp. 3–4, Traywick Collection.
344. "saying that Stilwell": Interview of May 27, 1882, San Francisco *Daily Examiner.*
344. "received several": Martin, *Tombstone's Epitaph,* p. 210.
344. "I guess there": Summary of Stilwell Inquest Testimony, p. 2.
345. "with a shotgun": Ibid.
345. "saw a man": Ibid., p. 5.
345. "As [the four] reached": Ibid., p. 3.
346. "advised Clanton": Martin, *Tombstone's Epitaph,* pp. 209–10.
346. "the deceased walked": Summary of Stilwell Inquest Testimony, p. 5.
346. "Some say": Martin, *Tombstone's Epitaph,* pp. 209–10.
346. "four armed men": Summary of Stilwell Inquest Testimony, pp. 6–7.
347. "some six": Ibid., p. 1.
347. "some cheering": Ibid., p. 5.
347. "low but excitedly": Ibid., p. 6.
347. "Even at the": "How Wyatt Earp," San Francisco *Examiner,* August 2, 1896.
347. "Morg!": Lake, *Wyatt Earp,* pp. 325–26.
348. "that there would": Summary of Stilwell Inquest Testimony, p. 7.
348. "within about": Ibid., p. 3.
348. "it was done": Ibid., p. 2.
348. "flashes of guns": Ibid., p. 1.
348. "Several railroad": Quoted in Bartholomew, *Wyatt Earp, 1879 to 1882,* p. 309.
348. "almost certain": Summary of Stilwell Inquest Testimony, p. 4.

349. "It's all right": Lake, *Wyatt Earp,* pp. 325–26.

349. "four men": Summary of Stilwell Inquest Testimony, p. 3.

350. "Behan told": Breakenridge, *Helldorado,* pp. 173–74.

350. "Sheriff Behan was": *Epitaph,* March 22, 1882, quoted in Jahns, *Doc Holliday,* p. 232.

350. "I just laughed": March 6, 1928, letter, Lake Collection.

351. "Wyatt, I want": Clum, "It All Happened," p. 64.

351. "Behan, if you're": Lake, *Wyatt Earp,* p. 330.

351. "You will see": Masterson, *Famous Gunfighters,* p. 64.

351. "Sheriff went out": March 22, 1882.

351. "mostly of": Breakenridge, *Helldorado,* pp. 178–79.

351. "a party": *Epitaph,* March 23, 1882.

352. "He [Cruz] had been": Inquest testimony in *Daily Nugget,* March 25, 1882.

352. "I told him": Ibid.

353. "When I saw": Inquest testimony, ibid., March 26, 1882.

353. "There were eight": Ibid.

353. "face downwards": Inquest testimony, ibid., March 25, 1882.

354. "a slight flesh": Ibid.

354. "from the effects": Ibid.

354. "He was, and": "Holliday's HOPE. It is Vanishing into Very Thin Air," Denver *Rocky Mountain News,* May 22, 1882.

355. "Not by any": Ibid.

355. "Much excitement": Entry of March 23, 1882, *Private Journal.*

355. "Mrs. James": Quoted in Jahns, *Doc Holliday,* p. 234.

356. "one of the most": *Epitaph,* March 27, 1882.

357. "nine cowboys": "How Wyatt Earp," San Francisco *Examiner,* August 2, 1896.

357. ". . . I retreated": Ibid.

358. "confronted by three": *Daily Nugget,* March 26, 1882.

358. "One shot": Ibid.

358. "[The cowboys] said": *Epitaph,* March 27, 1882.

359. "took refuge behind": Breakenridge, *Helldorado,* pp. 175–77.

359. "opened up on": Dodge, *Under Cover,* pp. 234–35.

360. "all outlaws": Denver *Republican* interview, May 22, 1882.

360. "a stage robber": "How Wyatt Earp," San Francisco *Examiner,* August 2, 1896.

360. "Sheriff Behan has": Entry of March 25, 1882, *Private Journal.*

360. "the last one": Entry of March 26, 1882, ibid.

361. "fine specimens": Tucson *Daily Star,* March 26, 1882, Hayden File, Arizona Historical Society.

361. "the Earps will": *Epitaph,* March 27, 1882, quoted in Jahns, *Doc Holliday,* p. 235.

361. "sad state": Entry of March 27, 1882, *Private Journal.*
362. "Report that": Ibid.
362. "There are fresh": March 28, 1882.
363. "Don't shoot": Quoted in Breakenridge, *Helldorado,* p. 183.
363. "As the person": Ibid.
364. "squeezed his shoulders": Ibid., p. 185.
364. "The officials of": *Arizona Daily Star,* March 30, 1882, quoted in Wagoner, *Arizona Territory,* p. 198.
365. "Calky times": Entry of March 30, 1882, *Private Journal.*

CHAPTER 16: Men on the Run

366. "we had dinner": April 5, 1882, *Epitaph* story in transcript of April 14, 1882, *Epitaph* information summary [hereafter referred to as EIS], Earp Family Papers, Arizona Historical Society.
367. "a bullet": Breakenridge, *Helldorado,* pp. 175–77.
367. "steel shirt": Bork and Boyer, "A Footnote," p. 81.
367. "I never wore": Letter of March 6, 1928, Lake Collection.
367. "on good grass": *Epitaph,* April 5, 1882, EIS.
367. "Here we were": Ibid.
368. "no use": Gertrude Hill, "Henry Clay Hooker: King of the Sierra Bonita," *Arizoniana,* vol. 2, no. 4 (Winter 1961), p. 12.
368. "we are riding": *Epitaph,* April 5, 1882, EIS.
368. "blood-money": Lake, *Wyatt Earp,* p. 347.
369. "gave them": Quoted in Waters, *Earp Brothers,* p. 199.
369. "No reward": *Epitaph,* April 5, 1882, EIS.
369. "The proprietor": Quoted ibid.
369. "You must be": Ibid.
370. "Our stay": Ibid.
371. "with great cordiality": Quoted in EIS, p. 3.
371. "Well, if he": *Epitaph,* April 5, 1882, EIS.
371. "that the fugitives": *Nugget,* March 31, 1882, ibid.
371. "the Earp party": Ibid.
371. "Sheriff Behan": "How Wyatt Earp," San Francisco *Examiner,* August 2, 1896.
372. "Under-Sheriff Woods": *Nugget,* March 31, 1882, EIS.
372. "suffered, probably": Ibid.
373. "a reliable": Breakenridge, *Helldorado,* p. 177.
374. "many of the": Gray, "When All Roads," p. 9.
374. "well mounted": Undated Silver City *New Southwest* newspaper story, quoted in Bartholomew, *Wyatt Earp, 1879 to 1882,* p. 324.

375. "It was rumored": Quoted in Waters, *Earp Brothers*, p. 202.

375. "At no time": Albuquerque *Journal*, April 18, 1882.

376. "to visit": April 1, 1882, Minutes of the Tombstone Common Council, Vol. I, 1880–1882.

376. "to summarily": Wagoner, *Arizona Territory*, p. 198.

376. "I do not": Letter of April 19, 1882, Cowboy Depredations File.

377. "the existing": Walker, "Retire Peaceably," p. 17.

377. "it has become": Quoted ibid, p. 1.

377. "To the good": Gray, "When All Roads," pp. 97–98.

378. "fell flat": Unidentified, undated newspaper report in Frederick Tritle Scrapbook 7, AHS.

378. "Outlaws remain": Quoted in Walker, "Retire Peaceably," p. 18.

379. "in some sort": Bork and Boyer, "A Footnote," p. 81.

379. "'way up' boys": Quoted in DeArment, *Bat Masterson*, p. 225.

380. "a thin, spare": Denver *Tribune*, May 16, 1882, quoted in Jahns, *Doc Holliday*, pp. 240–42.

381. "Oh you can": Ibid., p. 242.

381. "He refused to": Ibid., p. 244.

383. "[He is] known": Ibid., p. 245.

383. "While I assisted": Quoted in DeArment, *Bat Masterson*, p. 226.

383. "that Holliday": Denver *Tribune*, May 16, 1882, quoted in Jahns, *Doc Holliday*, p. 245.

383. "made no effort": Pueblo *Chieftain*, May 17, 1882, ibid., p. 247.

384. "a subterfuge": Quoted in DeArment, *Bat Masterson*, p. 228.

384. "a fraud and": Undated *Epitaph*, quoted in Jahns, *Doc Holliday*, p. 257.

384. "notoriously failed": *Daily Citizen*, May 17, 1882, Tritle Scrapbook 7.

384. "notorious for his": Undated, unidentified newspaper dispatch, ibid.

385. "through the door": *Tribune*, May 19, 1882, quoted in Jahns, *Doc Holliday*, p. 248.

385. "the [attempted]": *Rocky Mountain News*, May 19, 1882, quoted in DeArment, *Bat Masterson*, pp. 228–29.

385. "It is evident": *Tribune*, May 19, 1882, quoted in Jahns, *Doc Holliday*, p. 248.

385. "frank, open": *Rocky Mountain News*, May 22, 1882.

386. "hair sprinkled": Denver *Republican*, May 22, 1882.

386. "I do not": Ibid.

386. "I have known": Ibid.

388. "all sporting men": May 26, 1882, Paul letter in unidentified newspaper clipping, Tritle Scrapbook 7.

388. "Holliday's friends": Ibid.

388. "He has no": Quoted in Jahns, *Doc Holliday,* p. 255.
388. "It was made": Pueblo *Chieftain,* June 1, 1882, quoted ibid, pp. 255–56.
388. "entirely exonerating": Valdosta *Times,* June 24, 1882, quoted in Pendleton and Thomas, *In Search.*
389. "the only place": Letter of May 22, 1882, in Prescott *Weekly Courier,* May 27, 1882.
389. "Virgil Earp is": San Francisco *Daily Examiner,* May 27, 1882.
390. "Most of the business": Ibid.
390. "Without any": *Epitaph,* June 3, 1882.
391. "probably the": Entry of April 26, 1882, *Private Journal.*
391. "Bad state": Entry of May 30, 1882, ibid.
391. "large enough": Transcript of July 22, 1882, *Weekly Epitaph* story, John Ringo Ephemera File.

CHAPTER 17: And Die in the West

392. "smelling of": Transcript of July 22, 1882, *Weekly Epitaph* story, Ringo File.
392. "inclined to": Ibid.
393. "including a": Ibid.
393. "Many people who": Ibid.
394. "rode into": Sonnichsen, *Billy King's,* pp. 30–32.
394. "to curry favor": Breakenridge, *Helldorado,* pp. 187–89.
394. "We all know": Ibid.
394. "Buckskin Frank": Gray, "When All Roads," p. 35.
394. "perhaps a hired": Burrows, *John Ringo,* p. 186.
395. "a bulldog": Boyer, *I Married,* p. 107.
396. "I think Wyatt": Burrows, *John Ringo,* p. 170.
396. "shortly after noon": Breakenridge, *Helldorado,* pp. 187–89.
397. "where he kept": Transcript of July 22, 1882, *Weekly Epitaph* story, Ringo File.
397. "There is no": Boller reminiscences, p. 3.
397. "the upward": Burrows, *John Ringo,* pp. 195–96.
397. "He was known": Quoted ibid., p. 78.
398. "There were few": Transcript of July 22, 1882, *Weekly Epitaph* story, Ringo File.
399. "the evil of": Breakenridge, *Helldorado,* p. 128.
399. "That's all right": Martin, *Tombstone's Epitaph,* p. 89.
399. "In a short": Ibid.
399. "My backbone": Ibid., p. 91.
400. "and an opening": Ibid.

400. "Everyone on the": Sonnichsen, *Billy King's,* p. 30.

400. "came out of": Breakenridge, *Helldorado,* pp. 116–17.

400. "[Leslie] walked": Martin, *Tombstone's Epitaph,* p. 92.

401. "We the undersigned": Faulk, *Tombstone,* p. 159.

402. "To him": Quoted in March 20, 1885, Prescott *Weekly Courier* story, Hayden Files.

402. "Renfro suddenly": Tombstone *Prospector,* September 14, 1887, quoted in Turner, *Earps Talk,* p. 61.

403. "a woman": *Epitaph,* July 11, 1882, in Martin, *Tombstone's Epitaph,* p. 93.

404. "I'll put a": Ibid., p. 94.

404. "Shoot first": Traywick, *Chronicles,* p. 172.

405. "Mrs. Stowell": Quoted in Martin, *Tombstone's Epitaph,* p. 95.

405. "gray and": Sonnichsen, *Billy King's,* p. 45.

406. "I walked": Leadville *Daily Herald,* August 26, 1884, quoted in Jahns, *Doc Holliday,* p. 271.

406. "kick his": Ibid., p. 270.

406. "he had heard": Ibid.

406. "had no ill": Ibid., p. 269.

407. "The first shot": Ibid., p. 268.

407. "I saw Allen": Ibid., pp. 271–72.

408. "When any of": Quoted in Pendleton and Thomas, *In Search,* p. 47.

408. "the police": Quoted in Jahns, *Doc Holliday,* p. 280.

409. "Probably nobody": Letter reproduced in Glenn G. Boyer, *An Illustrated Life of Doc Holliday* (Glenwood Springs, Colo.: The Reminder Publishing Co., 1966).

409. "emaciated and bent": Obituary quoted in Jahns, *Doc Holliday,* pp. 284–85.

409. "This is funny": Traywick, *Chronicles,* p. 81.

409. "in the presence": Jahns, *Doc Holliday,* pp. 284–85.

409. "Sister Melanie": Pendleton and Thomas, *In Search,* p. 68.

410. "Earp had": Inquest testimony quoted in Waters, *Earp Brothers,* p. 212.

410. "a frail denizen": Waters, *Earp Brothers,* p. 212.

411. "Wyatt was": Masterson, *Famous Gunfighters,* p. 17.

411. "very unfortunate": Letter of April 13, 1884, McLaury Letters.

412. "tested in court": Boyer, *I Married,* p. 126, note 4.

412. "Has Killed": "Earp Brothers Dictations given Bancroft book agents," Bancroft Library.

413. "utterly inexperienced": Peter F. Stevens, "Wyatt Earp's Word Is Good with Me!," *American West,* vol. 35, no. 2 (February

1988), p. 46.

413. "more a street": Ibid.

413. "what was": Quoted in Turner, *Earps Talk*, p. 158.

414. "I am getting": Quoted in Faulk, *Tombstone*, p. 187.

414. "a prospector's": Watkins, *Gold and Silver*, pp. 155–56.

414. "virulence of": Ibid., p. 147.

EPILOGUE: "It Must Be a Nice Clean Story"

416. "the only place": Letter of May 22, 1882, in *Prescott Weekly Courier*, May 27, 1882.

416. "I know": Phoenix *Republican*, September 26, 1900, quoted in Turner, *Earps Talk*, p. 81.

416. "hardening of": Tucson *Star* obituary, June 8, 1912, in Hayden Files.

417. "he himself": Leigh Chalmers, investigating misappropriations of Crawley Dake, to Attorney General A. H. Garland, August 13, 1885, Cowboy Depredations File.

417. "mean disposition": Quoted in Rosa, *The Gunfighter*, p. 116.

417. "dead or alive": Masterson, *Famous Gunfighters*, p. 61.

418. "mere player": New York *Morning Telegraph*, October 9, 1921, quoted in DeArment, *Bat Masterson*, p. 396.

418. "Wyat [sic] Earp": Tucson *Daily Citizen*, May 22, 1900, Wyatt Earp File, Arizona Historical Society.

419. "to fleece": Arizona *Daily Star*, July 26, 1911, ibid.

419. "Notoriety has": May 21, 1925, letter, Lake Collection.

420. "all a pack": Letter of March 9, 1928, to Lake, ibid.

420. "Several of our": Letter of September 19, 1928, ibid.

421. "As a matter": Letter of January 9, 1941, ibid.

421. "America Picturesque": Ibid.

422. "OLD WESTERNERS": Los Angeles *Evening Herald*, January 16, 1929.

422. "quite my ideal": Clum, "It All Happened," p. 50.

422. "shot [his]": Letter from John Madden to Stuart Lake, November 6, [no year], Lake Collection.

422. "never killed": Letter of October 25, 1928, ibid.

Selected Bibliography

Manuscript and Archival Sources

BOLLER, ROBERT. "Reminiscences of Robert M. Boller as Told to Mrs. Geo. F. Kitt." Typescript in Arizona Historical Society Collection, Tucson.

CLUM, JOHN P. Papers in Special Collections, University of Arizona Library, Tucson.

Cowboy Depredations File. Special Collections, University of Arizona Library, Tucson.

"Earp Brothers Dictations given Bancroft book agents." Bancroft Library Collection, Berkeley, California.

Earp Family Entries, General Cashbooks. Wells Fargo & Company Corporate Archives, Wells Fargo Bank, San Francisco, California.

Earp Family Papers. Arizona Historical Society Collection, Tucson.

GRAY, JOHN PLEASANT. "When All Roads Led to Tombstone." Typescript in Arizona Historical Society Collection, Tucson.

HANCOCK, JAMES C. Papers in Arizona Historical Society Collection, Tucson.

HALLIWELL, HILDRETH [grandniece of Allie Earp]. September 21, 1971, recorded interview, University of Arizona Library.

HAYDEN, Carl. Carl Hayden Biographical Files, Arizona Historical Society, Tucson.

[Hayhurst, Pat]. Summary/Transcript of Documents 45 and 94, District Court of the First Judicial District, Cochise County, in Arizona Department of Library, Archives and Public Records, Phoenix.

JONES, MELVIN W. Typescript Reminiscences in Arizona Historical Society Collection, Tucson.

LAKE, STUART NATHANIEL. Collection in Huntington Library, San Marino, California.

MCLAURY, WILL. Letters, New-York Historical Society, New York City.

Minutes of the Tombstone Common Council, 1880–1882. Special Collections, University of Arizona Library, Tucson.

Miscellaneous files. Arizona Historical Society Collection, Tucson.

Newspaper files of the Arizona Historical Society, Tucson; the Bancroft Library, University of California at Berkeley; the Barker Texas History Center and Perry-Castaneda Library, University of Texas at Austin; and the Colorado Historical Society, Denver.

OAKES, GEORGE WASHINGTON. Oakes File, Arizona Historical Society, Tucson.

RINGO, JOHN. Ringo Ephemera File, Arizona Historical Society, Tucson.

TINKER, FRANK. "Monograph on John Peters Ringo." Typescript in Arizona Historical Society Collection, Tucson.

TRAYWICK, BEN T. Private Collection of Earp-Tombstone Materials, Tombstone, Arizona.

TRITLE, FREDERICK. Scrapbooks in Arizona Historical Society Collection, Tucson.

Published Materials

ADAMS, ANDY. *The Log of a Cowboy: A Narrative of the Old Trail Days.* Lincoln: University of Nebraska Press, 1964.

BARTHOLOMEW, ED. *Wyatt Earp, 1848 to 1880, the Untold Story.* Toyahvale, Texas: Frontier Book Co., 1963.

———. *Wyatt Earp, 1879 to 1882, the Man & the Myth.* Toyahvale, Texas: Frontier Book Co., 1964.

BOWMAN, JOHN S., ed. *The World Almanac of the American West.* New York: Pharos Books, 1986.

BORK, A. W., and GLENN G. BOYER. "The O.K. Corral Fight at Tombstone: A Footnote by Kate Elder," *Arizona and the West,* vol. 19, no. 1 (Spring 1977), pp. 65–84.

BOYER, GLENN G. *An Illustrated Life of Doc Holliday.* Glenwood Springs, Colo.: The Reminder Publishing Co., 1966.

———, compiler and ed. *I Married Wyatt Earp: The Recollections of Josephine Sarah Marcus Earp.* Tucson: University of Arizona Press, 1976.

———. "Morgan Earp—Brother in the Shadow," *Old West* (Winter 1983), pp. 16–20.

———. "Postscripts to Historical Fiction About Wyatt Earp in Tombstone." *Arizona and the West,* vol. 18 (Autumn 1976), pp. 217–36.

———. "The Secret Wife of Wyatt Earp." *True West,* vol. 30, no. 6 (June 1983), pp. 12–17, 62.

———. *The Suppressed Murder of Wyatt Earp.* San Antonio: Naylor Co., 1976.

———. "Those Marryin' Earp Men." *True West,* vol. 23, no. 4 (April 1976), pp. 14–21.

BREAKENRIDGE, WILLIAM. *Helldorado: Bringing the Law to the Mesquite.* Boston and New York: Houghton Mifflin Co., 1928.

BURNS, WALTER N. *Tombstone, an Iliad of the Southwest.* Garden City, N.Y.: Doubleday, Page & Co., 1927.

BURROWS, JACK. *John Ringo: The Gunfighter Who Never Was.* Tucson: University of Arizona Press, 1987.

BUTLER, ANNE M. *Daughters of Joy, Sisters of Misery: Prostitutes in the American West, 1865–90.* Urbana and Chicago: University of Illinois Press, 1987.

CHAMBERLAIN, D. S. "Tombstone in 1879: The Lighter Side." *Journal of Arizona History,* vol. 13, no. 4 (Winter 1972), pp. 229–34.

CLUM, JOHN. "It All Happened in Tombstone." *Arizona Historical Review*, vol. 2, no. 3 (October 1929), pp. 46–72. Also reprinted, with John D. Gilchriese as editor, in *Arizona & the West*, vol. 1, no. 3 (Autumn 1959), pp. 232–47.

CLUM, WOODWORTH. *Apache Agent: The Story of John P. Clum*. Boston: Houghton Mifflin Co., 1936.

COX, WILLIAM R. *Luke Short and His Era*. Garden City: Doubleday & Co., 1961.

CUNNINGHAM, EUGENE. *Triggernometry: A Gallery of Gunfighters*. New York: The Press of the Pioneers, 1934.

DEARMENT, ROBERT K. *Bat Masterson, the Man and the Legend*. Norman: University of Oklahoma Press, 1979.

DEVERE, JEAN. "The Tombstone Bonanza, 1878–1886." *Arizoniana*, vol. 1, no. 3 (Fall 1960), pp. 16–20.

DOYLE, DON HARRISON. "Social Theory and New Communities." *Western Historical Quarterly*, vol. 8, no. 2 (April 1977), pp. 151–65.

DUFFEN, WILLIAM A. "Notes on the Earp-Clanton Feud," *Arizoniana*, vol. I (Fall 1960), pp. 20–22.

EARP, WYATT. *Wyatt Earp: His Autobiography*. Privately printed, 1981.

ERNST, ROBERT R. "Dodge City Sued." *True West*, vol. 33, no. 11 (November 1986), pp. 32–37.

FAULK, ODIE B. *Arizona: A Short History*. University of Oklahoma Press, 1974 ed.

———. *Tombstone: Myth and Reality*. New York: Oxford University Press, 1972.

FULTON, RICHARD W. "Millville-Charleston, Cochise County." *Journal of Arizona History*, vol. 7, no. 1 (Spring 1966), pp. 9–22.

GARD, WAYNE. *Frontier Justice*. Norman: University of Oklahoma Press, 1981 ed.

HALEY, JAMES L. *Apaches: A History and Cultural Portrait*. Garden City, N.Y.: Doubleday & Co., 1981.

HILL, GERTRUDE. "Henry Clay Hooker: King of the Sierra Bonita," *Arizoniana*, vol. 2, no. 4 (Winter 1961), pp. 12–15.

HINKLE, MILT. "The Earp and Masterson I Knew." *True West*, vol. 9, no. 2 (December 1961), pp. 24–27, 53–54.

HINTON, RICHARD J. *The Handbook to Arizona: Its Resources, History, Towns, Mines, Ruins and Scenery.* Tucson: Arizona Silhouettes, 1954 reprint.

JACKSON, W. TURRENTINE. "Wells Fargo: Symbol of the Wild West?" *Western Historical Quarterly*, vol. 3, no. 2 (April 1972), pp. 179–96.

JAHNS, PAT. *The Frontier World of Doc Holliday: Faro Dealer from Dallas to Deadwood.* Lincoln: University of Nebraska Press, 1979 ed.

KELLNER, LARRY. "William Milton Breakenridge: Deadliest Two-Gun Deputy of Arizona," *Arizoniana*, vol. II (Winter 1962), pp. 20–22.

LAKE, CAROLYN, ed. *Under Cover for Wells Fargo: The Unvarnished Recollections of Fred Dodge.* Boston: Houghton Mifflin Co., 1969.

LAKE, STUART N. *Wyatt Earp, Frontier Marshal.* Boston and New York: Houghton Mifflin Co., 1955 ed.

LAMAR, HOWARD R., ed. *The Reader's Encyclopedia of the American West.* New York: Harper & Row, 1977.

LOCKWOOD, FRANK C. *Pioneer Days in Arizona.* New York: Macmillan Co., 1932.

LOOMIS, NOEL. "Early Cattle Trails in Southern Arizona." *Arizoniana*, vol. 3, no. 4 (Winter 1962), pp. 215–17.

LYON, PETER. *The Wild, Wild West.* [New York?: 1960?] Reprinted from *American Heritage* (August 1960).

MCGRATH, ROGER D. *Gunfighters, Highwaymen and Vigilantes: Violence on the Frontier.* Berkeley: University of California Press, 1987.

MARCUS, JACOB R., ed. "An Arizona Pioneer: Memoirs of Sam Aaron." *American Jewish Archives*, vol. 10, no. 1 (October 1958), pp. 95–120.

MARTIN, DOUGLAS D. *Tombstone's Epitaph.* Albuquerque: University of New Mexico Press, 1951.

MASTERSON, WILLIAM BARCLAY. *Famous Gunfighters of the Western Frontier.* Houston: Frontier Press of Texas, 1957.

MYERS, JOHN M. *Doc Holliday.* Boston: Little, Brown and Co., 1955.

———. *The Last Chance: Tombstone's Early Years.* Lincoln: University of Nebraska Press, 1973 ed.

MYRICK, DAVID F. "The Railroads of Southern Arizona: An Approach to Tombstone." *Journal of Arizona History,* vol. 8, no. 3 (Autumn 1967), pp. 155–70.

NIETHAMMER, CAROLYN. "Frontier Restaurants: The West Wasn't Won on Beans Alone." *True West,* vol. 31, no. 5 (May 1984), pp. 44–47.

O'NEAL, BILL. *Encyclopedia of Western Gunfighters.* Norman: University of Oklahoma Press, 1979.

PALMQUIST, BOB. "Tombstone's Dogberry." *True West,* vol. 34, no. 4 (April 1987), pp. 20–24.

PARSONS, GEORGE W. *The Private Journal of George Whitwell Parsons.* Phoenix: Works Project Administration, 1939.

PATTERSON, RICHARD. *Historical Atlas of the Outlaw West.* Boulder: Johnson Books, 1985.

———. "Highway Robbery!" *True West,* vol. 33, no. 12 (December 1986), pp. 20–25.

PENDLETON, ALBERT S., JR., and SUSAN MCKEY THOMAS. *In Search of the Hollidays.* Valdosta, Ga.: Little River Press, 1973.

PRIBILSKI, DAN. "Straight-Shootin' .45s," *The Roundup,* vol. 25, no. 6 (June 1987), pp. 24–25.

PUTNAM, JACKSON K. "The Turner Thesis and the Westward Movement: A Reappraisal." *Western Historical Quarterly,* vol. 7, no. 4 (October 1976), pp. 376–404.

ROBERTS, GARY L. "The Fremont Street Fiasco." *True West,* vol. 35, no. 7 (July 1988), pp. 14–20.

———. "The Wells Spicer Decision: 1881." *Montana, the Magazine of Western History,* vol. 20 (Winter 1970), pp. 63–74.

———. "The West's Gunmen: I, The Historiography of the Frontier Heroes." *American West,* vol. 8 (January 1971), pp. 10–15, 64.

———. "The West's Gunmen: II, Recent Historiography of Those Controversial Heroes." *American West,* vol. 8 (March 1971), pp. 18–23, 61–62.

ROSA, JOSEPH. *The Gunfighter: Man or Myth?* Norman: University of Oklahoma Press, 1969.

RYAN, PAT M. "Trail-Blazer of Civilization: John P. Clum's Tucson and Tombstone Years." *Journal of Arizona History,* vol. 6 (Summer 1965), pp. 53–70.

SELIGMANN, G. L., JR. "Crawley P. Dake." *Arizoniana,* vol. 2, no. 1 (Spring 1961), pp. 13–14.

SHANDORF, PETER. "'Man's Best Friend' Dr. George Goodfellow." *True West,* vol. 34, no. 7 (July 1987), pp. 14–19.

SONNICHSEN, C. L. *Billy King's Tombstone: The Private Life of an Arizona Boom Town.* Tucson: University of Arizona Press, 1972.

STELTER, GILBERT. "The City and Westward Expansion: A Western Case Study." *Western Historical Quarterly,* vol. 4, no. 2 (April 1973), pp. 187–202.

STEVENS, PETER F. "Wyatt Earp's Word Is Good with Me!" *American West,* vol. 35, no. 2 (February 1988), pp. 44–47.

STICKANN, RICHARD. "Virginia City Fire." *True West,* vol. 34, no. 2 (February 1987), pp. 50–55.

STREETER, FLOYD BENJAMIN. *Prairie Trails & Cow Towns: The Opening of the Old West.* New York: Bonanza Books, 1971.

TRACHTMAN, PAUL. *The Gunfighters.* New York: Time-Life Books, 1974.

TRAYWICK, BEN T. *The Chronicles of Tombstone.* Tombstone: Red Marie's Bookstore, 1986.

TURNER, ALFORD E., ed. *The Earps Talk.* College Station, Texas: Creative Publishing Company, 1982 ed.

———. *The O.K. Corral Inquest.* College Station, Texas: Creative Publishing Company, 1981.

UNDERHILL, LONNIE, ed. *Tombstone, Arizona, 1880 Business & Professional Directory.* Tucson: Roan Horse Press, 1982.

United States House of Representatives, Executive Documents 58 and 188, 47th Congress, 1st Session.

WAGONER, JAY J. *Arizona Territory 1863–1912: A Political History.* Tucson: University of Arizona Press, 1970.

WALKER, HENRY P. "Retire Peaceably to Your Homes: Arizona Faces Martial Law, 1882," *Journal of Arizona History,* vol. 10, no. 1 (Spring 1969), pp. 1–18.

WALKER, HENRY P., and DON BUFKIN. *Historical Atlas of Arizona.* Norman: University of Oklahoma Press, 1979.

WALLACE, ROBERT. *The Miners.* New York: Time-Life Books, 1976.

WALTERS, LORENZO. *Tombstone's Yesterday: True Chronicles of Early Arizona.* Glorieta, N.M.: Rio Grande Press, 1968.

WATERS, FRANK. *The Earp Brothers of Tombstone: The Story of Mrs. Virgil Earp.* Lincoln: University of Nebraska Press, 1976 ed.

WATKINS. T. H. "American Characters: The Hard-Rock Miner of the Early West." *American Heritage,* vol. 29, no. 1 (December 1977), p. 92.

———. *Gold and Silver in the West: The Illustrated History of an American Dream.* New York: Bonanza Books, 1971.

WEST, ELLIOTT. "The Saloon in Territorial Arizona." *Journal of the West,* vol. 13, no. 3 (1974), pp. 61–73.

———. "Wicked Dodge City." *American History Illustrated,* vol. 17, no. 4 (June 1982), pp. 22–31.

WHITE, RICHARD. "Outlaw Gangs of the Middle Border: American Social Bandits." *Western Historical Quarterly,* vol. 12, no. 4 (October 1981), pp. 387–408.

WILSON, JAMES A. "West Texas Influence on the Early Cattle Industry of Arizona," *Southwestern Historical Quarterly,* vol. 71, no. 1 (July 1967), pp. 26–36.

WOOSTER, ROBERT. "'A Difficult and Forlorn Country': The Military Looks at the American Southwest, 1850–1890." *Arizona and the West,* vol. 28 (Winter 1986), pp. 339–56.

WRIGHT, BOB. *Dodge City, the Cowboy Capital, and the Great Southwest.* N.p., 1913.

WYMAN, MARK. "Industrial Revolution in the West: Hard-Rock Miners and the New Technology." *Western Historical Quarterly,* vol. 5, no. 1 (January 1974), pp. 39–57.

Index